The Third Republic Defended

The Third Republic Defended

Bourgeois Reform in France, 1880–1914

Sanford Elwitt

Louisiana State University Press
Baton Rouge and London

Copyright © 1986 by Louisiana State University Press
All rights reserved
Manufactured in the United States of America

Designer: Christopher Wilcox
Typeface: Galliard
Typesetter: G & S Typesetters
Printer: Thomson-Shore, Inc.
Binder: John Dekker & Sons, Inc.

Portions of Chapters IV and VI herein appeared previously in "Social Reform and Social Order in Late Nineteenth-Century France: The Musée Social and Its Friends," *French Historical Studies*, XI (Spring, 1980), and
"Education and the Social Question: The *Universités Populaires* in Late
Nineteenth Century France," *History of Education Quarterly*, XXII (Spring,
1982), respectively.

Library of Congress Cataloging-in-Publication Data

Elwitt, Sanford.
  The Third Republic defended.

  Includes bibliographical references and index.
    1. France—Social policy.   2. France—Economic
policy.   3. France—Politics and government—1870–1940.
I. Title.
HN425.E48   1986   361.6'1'0944   86-2914
ISBN 0-8071-1294-1

For Marcia, with whom
I even can be silly

The day of combination is here to stay.
Individualism has gone, never to return.

—John D. Rockefeller

"We *must* have a bit of a fight, but I don't care about going on long," said Tweedledum. "What's the time now?"

Tweedledee looked at his watch and said, "Half-past four."

"Let's fight till six, and then have dinner," said Tweedledum.

—Lewis Carroll, *Through the Looking-Glass
and What Alice Found There*

Contents

Preface and Acknowledgments

This book tells the story of the accumulation and concentration of bourgeois political power in *fin-de-siècle* France. Having written previously about the Third French Republic's formative
years (*The Making of the Third French Republic: Class and Politics in
France, 1868–1884* [Baton Rouge, 1975]), I turn my attention to the
political and ideological forces generated by transformations in production between the mid-1880s and the Great War. Among those
forces I found that the "social question" contributed mightily to the
formation of a distinctive bourgeois political culture and shaped, if it
did not determine, the dimensions of republican politics. To put the
matter starkly but accurately: The awful but inescapable reality of
class—with all its menacing implications for the stability of the
regime—could no longer be ignored, obfuscated, shoved aside,
mocked, or repressed. The social had become the political—and
with a vengeance.

What follows is a history of *politique sociale*. It bears no resemblance to most of the social histories of this or that town or this or
that industry being produced in alarmingly large numbers. Few of
them deal with fundamental issues of political power. They mostly
ignore those who organized and controlled labor, those who commanded the nation's capital resources, those who defined and often
enforced the terms of political combat, and those for whom republican defense was serious business—as if such individuals existed on a
planet different from the one inhabited by the working class.

Dominant and subordinate classes (speaking strictly about the hierarchies that existed in the world of production but which, of course, were reproduced in society at large) not only inhabited the same planet but occupied the same towns and cities. They knew each other very well. Moreover, they shared common citizenship in the French Republic, a republic, notwithstanding its democratic character, that was bourgeois to the extent that it provided the political muscle necessary to sustain capitalist production. As a result, social questions, however localized, became political questions. They struck at the heart of bourgeois political power.

As it turned out, the bourgeois Republic not only survived the shock of the Great Depression of the nineteenth century and the effects of capitalist concentration, but it prospered. That course of events has to be explained more fully than it has been. To do so we have to redraw and extend the boundaries of French political history and to rethink and reconstruct how bourgeois political power was produced and reproduced. I have tried to do that by enlarging on what is conventionally meant by "politics" to include the several and intersecting worlds of business, management, social science, and state officialdom. The leading figures all understood themselves to be engaged in politics and to be concerned with political power. This book recreates their story, their *politique sociale*. The story, alas, lacks heroic proportions because I found no heroes; nor did I find villains, only men of power and their auxiliaries who did their utmost to defend the social order that they had built and, for the time being at least, succeeded in doing so.

My thanks to the American Philosophical Society and to the American Council of Learned Societies for the financial support that allowed me to complete the research for the book.

Several generous colleagues read the entire manuscript and provided me with tough but supportive criticism—no less than I expected. Edward Berenson insisted that I pay attention to the power of ideas. Charles Freedeman put his encyclopedic knowledge of French economic history at my disposal. John Laffey once again proved to be this historian's historian. Bonnie Smith shared with me her penetrating insights into the complexities of French society. They all deserve to partake in whatever notoriety this book may attract. Other colleagues either read parts of the manuscript or talked with me about it: Stanley Engerman, William Hauser, Donald Kelley, Christopher Lasch, Herman Lebovics, Donald Reid, Judith Stone, and Mary Young. They, too, have earned my gratitude. I also am indebted to the Davis Center for Historical Studies at Princeton University and to its director, Lawrence Stone, for providing me with a forum to air my views on *solidarisme*. Likewise, the Center for European Studies at Harvard University and the director of its French section, George Ross, invited me to talk about my interpretation of French social science.

Jean DeGroat and Helen Hull typed and retyped several drafts with characteristic forbearance and good humor. Bless them both. My copyeditor, Trudie Calvert, did wonders for my prose and put up with my irrational hostility toward hyphens. The good folks at the Louisiana State University Press, Catherine Barton, Elizabeth Carpelan, and Margaret Fisher Dalrymple, continue to demonstrate that graciousness and the highest professional standards need not be mutually exclusive.

My wife, Marcia Elwitt, to whom this book is dedicated, is not a professional historian. But as a teller of fables, she is a historian and one who writes well. She resolutely monitored my style and the construction of my argument. Our sons, Jonathan and Samuel, are also historians from whom I have gained boundless pleasure by talking with them and sharing my books.

Finally, I cannot end these acknowledgments without paying homage to those comrades with whom I collaborated in the unforgettable experience of turning out ten issues of *Marxist Perspectives*: Carol Duncan, Michael Greenberg, Ann Lane, Eugene Lieber, Jay Mandle, John Womack, Jr., Harold Woodman, and the dozens of other comrades across North America. We had a good run.

Abbreviations

ACF	*Almanach de la Coopération Française.*
AHS	*Annales d'Hygiène Sociale.*
AMS	Archives du Musée Social
AN	Archives Nationales
BAIP	*Bulletin Administratif de l'Instruction Publique.*
BLFE	*Bulletin de la Ligue Française de l'Enseignement.*
BMAP	*Bulletin Mensuel de l'Association Polytechnique.*
BPB	*Bulletin de la Participation aux Bénéfices.*
BSES	*Bulletin de la Société pour l'Education Sociale.*
Education sociale	France, Ministère du Commerce, de l'Industrie, Postes et Télégraphe, *Congrès international de l'éducation sociale: Procès-verbal sommaire* (Paris, 1902).
EF	*Economiste Français.*
Exposition 1889	France, Ministère du Commerce, de l'Industrie et des Colonies, *Exposition universelle internationale de 1889: Rapports du jury international* (12 vols.; Paris, 1891).
Exposition 1900	France, Ministère du Commerce, de l'Industrie, Postes et Télégraphe, *Exposition universelle internationale de 1900: Rapports du jury international* (46 vols.; Paris, 1901).
HBM	*Bulletin de la Société Française des Habitations à Bon Marché.*
REP	*Revue d'Economie Politique.*

RIE	*Revue Internationale d'Enseignement.*
RIP	*Revue des Institutions de Prévoyance.*
RIS	*Revue Internationale de Sociologie.*
RS	*Réforme Sociale.*
RSS	*Revue de la Solidarité Sociale.*

The Third Republic Defended

Introduction

In 1894, the journal of the Société d'économie sociale, an association of entrepreneurs and industrial managers, affirmed its position that "the best defense against socialism is social reform." Several years later, Léon Bourgeois, who had served as prefect of the coal-mining department of the Tarn in the early 1880s and president of the council of ministers in 1895 and was the chief oracle of solidarism, denounced the politics of class struggle waged by the French bourgeoisie and the working class alike: "Capital," he insisted, "is inevitable. Thus, everything depends upon establishing its limits. Capital itself must not be condemned—only its abuses."[1] Both statements in their different ways reflect the political dimensions of movements for social reform in *fin-de-siècle* France; also, and more broadly, both alert us to what studies of the period often pass over in silence, namely, considerations of the impact of class forces on French politics.[2] This book addresses the largely unexplored question of how the relations between labor and capital at a time of economic transformation shaped political patterns and determined bourgeois ideological perspectives.

Why do I place social reform at the center of this study? There are two reasons—one general, the other specific. First, we know a good deal about working-class politics and ideologies, about socialism,

1. *RS*, XXVII (1894), 725; Léon Bourgeois and Alfred Croiset, *Essai d'une philosophie de la solidarité: Conférences et discussions* (Paris, 1902), 74.
2. For some revealing information on the economic interests and the financial connections of France's governing elite, see Jean Estèbe, *Les Ministres de la République, 1871–1914* (Paris, 1982), Chaps. 6, 7.

syndicalism, strike patterns, and other aspects of the French labor movement. We know much less about parallel political developments within the French bourgeoisie, which is appalling considering that that class commanded the French nation's economic resources. My intention is to contribute toward filling that gap; what follows, therefore, is history "from the top down," the limitations of which I recognize but for which I make no apologies.

Second, the conception of social reform used here extends beyond discrete programs for working-class welfare to systems for social management applied on a nationwide scale—industry's "social machinery," as contemporaries put it. Consequently, although I do not ignore the details of reform, my emphasis falls most heavily on the political and ideological constructions that lay behind them. If, as the statements quoted above suggest, social reform became a vehicle to further the association and collaboration of labor and capital and became a weapon against socialism, then such an emphasis may open up a new perspective on *fin-de-siècle* French politics. By this I do not mean to advance any view that purports to identify a uniform social program hatched in backrooms or boardrooms by a monolithic bourgeoisie. Nor do I intend to argue that a ruling-class conspiracy existed to keep workers in their place. Moreover, the positive, constructive side of social reform, especially as envisioned by those whom I call social liberals, should not be open to doubt. Nevertheless, we will find that a remarkably high degree of consensus on the social question united disparate and otherwise antagonistic fractions of the French bourgeoisie.

The chapters that follow explore the dimensions, the limits, and the political implications of that consensus. For the most part, they steer clear of the relatively well-charted channels of high politics. Rather, they focus on a network of businessmen, managers, engineers, and social scientists whose perspectives on the labor question and whose political connections contributed to defining the contours of republican social politics and ideology. A relatively small group on the face of it, their influence radiated outward and penetrated those areas in which France's political business was transacted.

The themes of social reform, social defense, and the social question itself recur repeatedly in bourgeois political discourse during the

nineteenth century in France. For several decades at least since the
1820s, the "dangerous classes" of urban and industrial centers engendered a mixture of fear, morbid fascination, and occasional bouts of
murderous hostility. Instances of the last are well known: Lyon in
1831 and again in 1834; Paris in 1840; the June Days; and the *semaine
sanglante* of May, 1871. Aside from repression, responses to the social
question remained on the level of unfocused or ill-tempered preoccupations with working-class poverty, degradation, and demoralization. No solutions or even systematic attempts to find solutions to
the upheavals precipitated by the steady advance of capitalist production appeared. Not surprisingly, in a world governed by the assumptions of political economy, capitalism was expected to provide
its own solutions in the form of progress and plenty. Even those
early socialists who harshly condemned exploitation did so within a
framework set by the terms of capitalism itself. Thus, vague notions
having to do with a "social Republic" or such self-advertising slogans as "property is theft" substituted for genuinely serious considerations of capitalism's social consequences.[3]

Only in the final decades of the century did the social question, in
the form of a sharpened focus on the relations between labor and
capital, receive close, systematic, and widespread attention in bourgeois circles. As a result, the outlines of a distinctive corporate perspective appeared in social politics, one based upon perceptions of
unalterable class divisions. This represented a new departure. Previously, France's political classes responded to the social question in
quasi-utopian terms leavened with visions of unimpeded social mobility. The latter, after all, was what constituted the Republic's greatest promise. Thus Jules Ferry (who would later change his mind) in
1870 spoke with undeniable seriousness of "this fusion of classes
which is the goal of democracy."[4] Twenty years later, few echoes of
those words remained in the air. Classes not only existed, but the
lines between them had hardened. There being no question of turning the clock back, the thrust of bourgeois social politics shifted

3. Bernard Moss, *The Origins of the French Labor Movement* (Berkeley, 1976), Chap. 3;
William Colemen, *Death Is a Social Disease: Public Health and Political Economy in Early
Industrial France* (Madison, Wisc., 1982), Chaps. 3, 10.

4. Quoted in Louis Legrand, *L'Influence du positivisme dans l'oeuvre scolaire de Jules
Ferry* (Paris, 1961), 137.

from "fusion" to association, to collaboration, and to cooperation. That shift took concrete form on the programmatic level and in the conflicting as well as converging ideological currents that ran beneath it.

The reasons behind the new departure may be located in the progressive transformations of the French industrial economy, transformations that held great promise and equally great dangers for a society governed by the assumptions of liberal democracy. Although French capitalism did not proceed from competition to concentration at the same pace and with the same rhythm as that of other countries, notably Germany, both the geographic and quantitative expansion of production in the leading manufacturing and mining sectors had become the rule rather than the exception by the 1890s.[5] A brief statistical rundown will help illustrate the point. Although by 1900 the number of firms employing fewer than five workers still accounted for more than 90 percent of the total, those employing more than fifty workers occupied more than 40 percent of the labor force. By 1906, the evolving pattern had become even more apparent: firms employing more than one hundred workers accounted for 40 percent of the labor force; from another perspective, 1 percent of all industrial enterprises employed 50 percent of the labor force and contributed to the national income in similar proportions. This "accelerated concentration" in industry was most evident in the key sectors of mining and metallurgy. For instance, whereas the number of coal-mining companies declined by 12 percent between 1880 and 1906, the number of mineworkers increased by 78 percent in the same period. Manufacturing industries registered a 50 percent increase in their work force between 1886 and 1896, a remarkable jump considering that during most of the time the French economy was mired in depression. Production of coal and ferrous metals had "taken off" as the larger and more efficient firms of the north and the

5. Jean Bouvier, François Furet, and Marcel Gillet, *Le Mouvement du profit en France au xix siècle* (Paris, 1965), appendixes; Maurice Lévy-Leboyer, "La Croissance économique en France au xix siècle: Résultats préliminaires," *Annales, Economies, Sociétés, Civilisations,* XXIII (1968), 788–807; Marcel Gillet, *Les Charbonnages du nord de la France au xix siècle* (Paris, 1974); Georges Villain, *Le Fer, la houille et la métallurgie à la fin du xix siècle* (Paris, 1901); Paul Bairoch, "Le Mythe de la croissance économique rapide au xix siècle," *Revue de l'Institut de Sociologie,* No. 2 (1962), 22–53.

northeast displaced those of the center and the southeast. Furthermore, industrial production, investment, and concentration marked the greatest gains in the modern sectors of metallurgy, machinery construction, electrical equipment, and chemical products. Even in the older sectors such as cotton textiles, concentration proceeded apace: In 1906, nearly 60 percent of the labor force worked in mills employing from one hundred to five hundred operatives; 32 percent worked in those with more than five hundred. Thus it seems reasonable to conclude that private or "individualistic" capital, the ideal model of orthodox political economy, no longer dominated production. It had been displaced by "social capital," organized in corporations *(sociétés anonymes)*. Production became socialized on a scale previously unknown.[6] *By 1906*

Statistical exercises, however, have their limitations; we must turn to less precise indicators that have the virtue of highlighting the political implications of the changing face of the economy. For nowhere is it written that masses of labor and capital when mixed together automatically produce a volatile compound. I do not deal with the internal life of the labor movement, for that is beyond the scope of this study; the substantial literature on the subject suggests a variety of political responses on the part of the working class that defies neat categorization. It does seem clear, however, that labor militancy, especially among the unskilled and semiskilled workers outside the venerable trade *syndicats*, took on proportions not seen since the 1840s and, for a brief moment, in 1869–1870.[7] This devel-

6. *Exposition 1900*, V, 295–96; *La Concentration des entreprises industrielles et commerciales: Conférences faites à l'Ecole des hautes études sociales* (Paris, 1913), 16, 20–21, 226–31; Jean Bouvier *et al.*, *L'Ere industrielle et la société d'aujourd'hui, 1880–1980* (Paris, 1979), 252, 291; Vol. IV, Pt. 1 of Fernand Braudel and Ernest Labrousse (eds.), *Histoire économique et sociale de la France*, 4 vols.; B. R. Mitchell, *European Historical Statistics, 1750–1950* (New York, 1978), 53; France, Direction Générale de la Statistique, *Annuaire Statistique* (1894), 362–67, (1909), 175–77; Jean-Jacques Carré, Pierre Dubois, and Edmond Malinvaud, *La Croissance française: Un Essai d'analyse économique causale de l'après guerre* (Paris, 1972), 31, 526; Léon Vincent, "Evolution de la production intérieure brute en France de 1896 à 1938," *Etudes et Conjonctures*, No. 10 (1962), 929; Karl Marx, *Capital*, ed. Friedrich Engels (3 vols.; New York, 1967), III, 436–37.

7. Rolande Trempé, *Les Mineurs de Carmaux* (2 vols.; Paris, 1970); Michelle Perrot, *Les Ouvriers en grève* (2 vols.; Paris, 1974); Fernand L'Huillier, *La Lutte ouvrière à la fin du Second Empire* (Paris, 1957); Michael Hanagan, *The Logic of Solidarity* (Urbana, Ill., 1980); Madeleine Rebérioux, "Demain: Les Ouvriers et l'avenir au tournant du siècle," *Revue du*

opment reflected changing relationships in the workplace that followed from transformations in production. Labor found itself progressively barred from access to the means of production while simultaneously becoming socialized within the productive process.

As for capital, both objective factors and subjective perceptions contributed to a heightened awareness of the labor question. The vagaries of the balance sheet tell part of the story. During the first phase of the international Great Depression (1873–1896), from 1873 to 1882, French industry fared relatively well. Output rose, as did wages—although unevenly in the latter case. Partly this increase was a result of the Freycinet Plan to build the third railway network, a countercyclical measure that stimulated demand in ferrous metals, coal, and machinery and apparently had a multiplier effect throughout the economy. The good times ended abruptly in 1882, signaled by the collapse of the Union générale bank. Soon after, the minister of finance, Léon Say, scuttled what remained to be completed of the railroad project, which only made matters worse. Wages ceased to increase at the previous rate and in some sectors fell, while industrialists struggled to cut labor costs and to increase efficiency. The relatively high cost of labor inherited from the 1870s had placed French capitalists at a competitive disadvantage vis-à-vis those of other countries on the international market.[8] That situation persisted, prompting one later commentator to characterize competition among nations as "economic warfare."[9] Thus it is no accident that the number of strikes rose by 250 percent between 1880 and 1890, that they broke out over the issue of wages more than any other, and that they increasingly involved organized labor formations—a pattern that held into the first decade of the twentieth century.[10] A new order of social relations took shape toward the end of the century, its dynamic, as perceived at the time, driven by the

Nord, LXIII (1981), 667–74; Michelle Perrot, "Les Ouvriers et les machines en France dans la première moitié du xix siècle," *Recherches*, Nos. 32/33 (1978), 347–74.

8. W. Arthur Lewis, *Growth and Fluctuations, 1870–1913* (London, 1978), 46–47, 50, 107; Bouvier *et al.*, *L'Ere industrielle*, 490–91; Jean Bouvier, *Le Krash de l'Union générale* (Paris, 1960).

9. *BSES*, III (1903), 27.

10. Bouvier *et al.*, *L'Ere industrielle*, 519; *Annuaire statistique* (1909), 157.

"concentration of labor in confrontation with the concentration of capital."[11]

The transformation of social relations resulted in contradictory consequences: "renewed material prosperity" and "reawakened class antagonism." Behind the glitter of the *belle époque* with its huge profits and generous dividends lurked the "stirrings of struggle and revolt" that "swelled in the popular consciousness."[12] Those stirrings already had reached the level of measurable tremors agitating the political terrain by the mid-1880s, and they threatened to widen and deepen during the subsequent two decades—as, in fact, they did.[13] In response, battalions of businessmen, reformers, and politicians, frequently led by the individuals we shall come to know, mobilized behind a concerted effort to forestall a full-scale eruption of labor against capital. Their efforts, which reflected various ideological persuasions and practical considerations, took many forms: social engineering, profit sharing, working-class housing, cooperatives, company unions or union-busting, adult education, and technical training. Such measures, considered as simple exercises in social reform or social control, were not unique to the late nineteenth century; they had been around for a long time. But not before had they appeared within the context of a generalized political strategy aimed at fixing the pattern of labor/capital relations. And not before could it be suggested that, taken together, they represented a powerful current of corporate paternalism in the flow of social politics, a current that ran contrary to the liberal and democratic conventions inherited from a previous age. That contradiction, as manifested in the politics and the ideology of social reform, will constitute one of the central themes of this book.

Having introduced the term "paternalism," I had better explain myself lest its use provoke misunderstanding, not to say hoots of derision in some quarters. Paternalism does not mean patriarchy; nor, as used here, does it bear any resemblance to the social relations

11. G.-L. Duprat, *La Solidarité sociale* (Paris, 1907), 265.

12. *RSS* (1908), 49; Jean Bouvier, *Histoire économique et histoire sociale* (Geneva, 1968), Chap. 1.

13. Michael Rust, "Business and Politics in the Third Republic: The Comité des Forges and the French Steel Industry, 1896–1914" (Ph.D. dissertation, Princeton University, 1973), 345.

characteristic of slave or seigneurial societies or to those supposedly resting on lower-class deference and ruling-class obligation. Moreover, paternalism should not be confused with a system—such as that of Japan—in which the state enforced a strict set of hierarchical relationships while driving forward a revolutionary transformation of the economy. Despite echoes of the precapitalist world, with its orders and its hierarchies, paternalism in France represented neither some "feudal" or "aristocratic" hangover nor did its proliferation signal the "feudalization" of the bourgeoisie.[14] In ideology and in political practice, paternalism addressed not the past but the present—and perhaps even the future. French paternalism, far from disguising or retarding economic and social transformations, reinforced them. What appeared to be merely a set of *ad hoc* responses to the labor question took on the aspect of a comprehensive system for social management and social defense.[15]

Manifestations of paternalism in the form of employer-sponsored programs for working-class welfare may be found scattered about the industrial landscape as far back as the 1820s.[16] But the question remains whether these programs constituted merely an adaptation of patriarchal habits to competitive pressures, that is, attempts to blunt the edge of market relations—what one might call laissez-faire with a human face. In any event, reliance on the automatic mechanisms of the marketplace governed bourgeois social policy during the first three-quarters of the century. The wisdom of political economy for the most part went unchallenged.[17] Thus a manufacturer of chemical products in Paris, one J.-M. Baudouin, could insist even in the late 1860s, in words worthy of the senior professor of the Industrial Revolution, Andrew Ure, on the counterproductivity of moral education for working-class children, an education that might turn their heads

14. For a discussion of the varieties of paternalism, see Eugene D. Genovese, *Roll, Jordan, Roll* (New York, 1974), 661–65. For a view of French paternalism similar to mine, see Michael Miller, *The Bon Marché: Bourgeois Culture and the Department Store, 1869–1920* (Princeton, 1981), 7–10. Arno J. Mayer, *The Persistence of the Old Regime* (New York, 1981), argues that the European bourgeoisie fell under the spell of aristocratic values.

15. Duprat, *La Solidarité sociale*, 264.

16. Peter N. Stearns, *Paths to Authority* (Urbana, Ill., 1978), Pt. 2.

17. A good example of that wisdom may be found in the writings of Henri Baudrillart, *e.g.*, *Salariat et association* (Paris, 1867); "Des Rapports du travail et du capital," *Journal des Economistes*, 1st ser., XXXIV (1853), 375–96; "De la solidarité à propos du reproche d'individualisme, *Journal des Economistes*, 2nd ser., I (1854), 321–39.

from the duties at hand: "In many areas of human labor, children make important contributions to social production."[18]

Such expressions rarely show up in *fin-de-siècle* France, but not because entrepreneurs and managers had become sentimental or suddenly had discovered the virtues of philanthropy.[19] Rather, political as well as economic conditions had changed. As I have written elsewhere, the Third French Republic was constructed on an alliance of industrial capitalists, petty bourgeois, and farmers. Even temporary alliances with some advanced sections of the working class were formed.[20] French capitalists, although they fought with one another, had their political flank covered, and could afford the luxury of operating according to conventional liberal social assumptions. But what was appropriate to the 1870s and to the 1880s did not hold for the subsequent decades. Industrialists and their counterparts in the worlds of politics and social science, faced with a revived working-class movement, found those assumptions wanting, if not downright dangerous. Given the magnitude of the contending forces, however, the other extreme—repression—offered no serious alternative, although it was employed sporadically, at Anzin in 1884 and at Fourmies in 1891. The price of peace is generally less than the price of war; even a ruling class armed with superior firepower may stand to suffer losses that it considers unacceptable.

It was in this context that paternalism appeared to offer a new path to the Promised Land of "social peace" (a phrase in common use at the time but rarely found before 1870).[21] Paternalism meant more than even comprehensive welfare programs, in which respect it supplemented but did not displace laissez-faire practices.[22] Likewise, paternalism encompassed more than mechanisms for social control,

18. Quoted in Claudio Jannet, "L'Etat des familles et l'application des lois de succession dans la Provence," *Enquête sur l'état des familles et l'application des lois de succession,* 1st ser., 1867–68 (Paris, 1892), 442–43.

19. On the various forms of philanthropy, see Jacques Donzelot, *La Police des familles* (Paris, 1977).

20. Sanford Elwitt, *The Making of the Third Republic: Class and Politics in France, 1868–1884* (Baton Rouge, 1975).

21. Jean Dubois, *Le Vocabulaire politique et social en France de 1869 à 1872* (Paris, n.d.), 363.

22. For a comparison with mid-Victorian Britain, see Patrick Joyce, *Work, Society and Politics* (London, 1980), Chap. 4. For a useful overview of paternalism, although marred by sociological jargon, see Nicholas Abercrombie and Steven Hill, "Paternalism and Patronage," *British Journal of Sociology,* XXVII (1976), 413–29.

although it certainly contained abundant quantities of that element. A number of considerations suggest a broader conception of paternalism and its utility in the context of late nineteenth-century social politics and ideology. First, not until that time do we find social reform embedded in a system of social management that extended beyond the point of production. Indeed, what gave this new paternalism particular force was that in design it effectively eliminated the boundary between work and other aspects of social life. Its searchlight left nothing in the shadows; its sweeping surveillance left no place to hide. Second, paternalism was most closely associated with corporate enterprise and viewed by managers as the linchpin of their social machinery. This association reflected the social nature of production itself; hence my insistence on the qualitative differences between paternalistic systems and welfare programs of an earlier age. Third, as the relationship between master and man became one between manager and worker, the impersonal bureaucratic structure of the modern enterprise required rules and norms for it to function efficiently and productively. Reciprocal obligations and duties, formerly a matter of custom, of marketplace transaction, or even of struggle, became transformed into a kind of working-class subordination to managerial decree, but decree routinized into commonsensical experience. Thus paternalism replaced force, or purported to make force unnecessary, and was designed to reinforce the authority of capital; it became synonymous with social engineering. Fourth, paternalism—if, of course, it worked (a big "if")—contributed to the consolidation of bourgeois hegemony by substituting association and collaboration between classes for an autonomous working-class political culture. Fifth, paternalism constituted a key ingredient in the "science" of social reform—what contemporaries revealingly called "social science." Finally, although paternalism characterized the practices of industrial entrepreneurs and managers, it had considerable political resonance. By way of numerous bourgeois parapolitical organizations, among them the Musée social, the Comité de défense et de progrès social, the Société française des habitations à bon marché, and the Société d'économie sociale, paternalism put its stamp on republican social politics. Those politics, so the argument ran, left no place for "enemies to the right or to the left" and entailed the formation of the broadest possible consensus, unencumbered by past political habits and prejudices.[23] A key element in the consensus involved two distinct but interconnected reformist tendencies, represented by conservative social economists and solidarist social liberals.

The label "social economist" applies originally to those individuals associated with the social investigator and mining engineer Frédéric Le Play and with the Société d'économie sociale which he founded in 1856. (The term "social economy" appeared in both France and Britain at least as early as the 1830s. Jean-Baptiste Say used it to identify what he called the "social" dimensions of political economy. John Stuart Mill used it to characterize the "natural history of society.")[24] From its inception through the remainder of the century and into the next, the Société monitored labor/capital relations and kept a close watch on working-class political activity and on strike patterns (Chapter I).[25] Its core membership was heavily weighted toward big business and included industrialists, managers, and engineers. By the last decade of the century they had found collaborators and allies among social scientists and major political figures of diverse persuasions. It was, however, the original cohort—those most directly involved with the machinery of large-scale production—that laid out the dimensions of subsequent bourgeois social politics. Despite their attachments to big business, social economists recognized that the claims of industrialists to run their enterprises in the manner of absolute princes portended serious social consequences. They saw clearly enough that the high ground of capitalist control over production, which they never questioned, could be defended only by adapting the rules of the marketplace to the conditions prevailing in the industrial workplace. In other words, they injected the social component into political economy. This

23. Henri Rovel, *Association du capital et du travail: Suppression des grèves* (Nancy, 1901), 22.

24. Jean-Baptiste Say, *Cours complète d'économie politique* (2 vols.; Paris, 1840), II, 557; John Stuart Mill, "On the Definition of Political Economy; and on the Method of Philosophical Investigation in That Science," *London and Westminster Review,* XXVI (1836), 1–29. I am indebted to John Laffey for providing me with the reference to Mill's article.

25. The reports of the Société's proceedings in the 1860s were published in *EF,* for the 1870s in the *Bulletin de la Société d'Economie Sociale,* and for the 1880s and after in *RS.*

meant abandoning a fatalistic vision of unending class struggle in favor of systems for paternalist reform designed to contain the potentially explosive forces of class antagonism within an unyielding yet flexible corporate shell. In this respect, the social economists were both precocious and toughminded: precocious because they anticipated in the 1860s and 1870s the shape of things to come, toughminded because they faced without the slightest illusions the hard political implications of industrial concentration. Individuals such as Emile Cheysson, pioneer in social engineering (Chapter II), and Charles Robert, chief architect of profit sharing (Chapter III)— both of whose careers spanned the last three decades of the nineteenth century—exemplified the social economists' approach to reform. Eventually, they would find like-minded associates in unlikely places.

Social economists were in bad political odor during the 1870s and 1880s for three reasons. First, they suffered from their previous association with the defunct Second Empire, which several, including Le Play, Cheysson, and Robert, had served. Second, they retained associations with big business at a time when republican politicians were busy making a living by defending small producers against the so-called financial aristocracy. Third, and most important, social economists stubbornly held to "social distinctions incompatible with the stated attitudes of the regime."[26] In other words, they insisted on keeping questions regarding class relations at the head of the political agenda although contemporary political leaders proclaimed their faith in the Republic to dissolve—as it were automatically—class antagonisms. But by the final decade of the century, social economists emerged from the shadows to become respected and respectable members of a conservative republican reform coalition. Ostracized from the 1878 Paris Exposition, they returned in force to those held in 1889 and 1900, both of which featured showcases for French industry's social machinery.

What had changed? For one thing, according to the political economist Emile Levasseur (who was in a position to know), the primary concern of the social economists to devise systems "to regulate the

26. *Exposition 1900*, V, 7.

relations that evolve from the contact between classes, especially those between workers and employers" directly confronted the problems of production, efficiency, and labor discipline. For another, the social economists' perspective embraced nothing less than the totality of social relations, at a time when sweeping systems appeared attractive. Characteristically, Cheysson claimed for social economy "all the sciences that have as their object the study of man in society"; the economist Charles Gide, social liberal and godfather of the French cooperative movement, described it as the "science of social peace and well-being." An alternative view of social economy may repay consideration. Although it would be a mistake to reduce it, in the words of the friendly commentator Dick May, to a "sociology tailored to the interests of the privileged classes and the *patronat*,"[27] the observation should not be dismissed out of hand because social economists concerned themselves primarily with integrating workers into the productive process.

Mademoiselle May's comment points to a related aspect of *fin-de-siècle* social politics—its links to social science. Why did she refer to social economy as a "sociology," meaning a comprehensive design for a hierarchical and conflict-free society? One explanation emerges from the pages of a treatise on the technical education of workers. The author, Paul Melon, wrote:

> Social science studies and explains the nature of human societies; it analyzes social facts, draws parallels among them, and arranges them. . . . In an age in which public attention focuses on the determinants of the modern organization of labor and on the wage system, as well as the various institutions that provide for present well-being and future security, social science's importance increases daily. In France, a number of organizations . . . concern themselves with these questions which, taken together, constitute the heart of social economy and whose solutions rest on the three great principles: the freedom of labor, private property, and association.

Melon went on to list those organizations, and we will have the opportunity to observe them in action (Chapters III and IV): the Ecole libre des sciences politiques, the Société pour la participation

27. Emile Levasseur, *Questions industrielles et ouvrières* (Paris, 1890), 375; Emile Cheysson, "Cours d'économie politique," *Journal des Economistes,* 4th ser., XX (1882), 360; *Exposition 1900,* V, 1–2; Jeanne Weill (Dick May), *L'Enseignement social à Paris* (Paris, 1896), 27.

aux bénéfices, the Société française des habitations à bon marché, the Unions de la paix sociale, and *Réforme sociale*.[28] All of them, like those mentioned above, were instruments of bourgeois reform, had overlapping membership, and reached into high political circles. Melon put social science into a specific historical context and thereby gave it clear political definition as an instrument for managing class relations. Also, perhaps inadvertently, he revealed a dangerous contradiction that social science was expected to resolve: the contradiction between the "wage system," inherited from an earlier age, and the "modern organization of labor," that is, industrial concentration. Two major questions follow: (1) Was the wage system with all the ingrained political and social habits of several generations (on both sides of the barricades) compatible with new patterns of production? and (2) how could the "freedom of labor" be reconciled with "association"? Enter the solidarists (Chapter V), who claimed to have found answers to those questions.

Perspective rather than hardened doctrinaire positions differentiated solidarists from social economists. The former considered themselves the bearers of a "radicalized" liberal tradition and were politically progressive, whereas the latter harbored authoritarian tendencies, were wedded to the interests of big business, and considered any infringement of the rights of capital to be the thin edge of a socialist wedge. Yet no social economist would have disagreed with Léon Bourgeois' defense of the proposition that "individual property constitutes the extension and the foundation of freedom."[29] And for that matter, social economists had described their own projects for the association of capital and labor—the essence of solidarism—as exercises in *solidarité* fully a decade before Bourgeois, Charles Gide, and others had made it a household word.[30] Gide himself, in a historical tableau of successive "schools" of political economy, called social economy the "new school of political econ-

---

28. Paul Melon, *L'Enseignement technique et l'enseignement supérieur en France* (Paris, 1893), 73.

29. Bourgeois and Croiset, *Essai d'une philosophie de la solidarité*, 34.

30. *Exposition 1889*, I and II, *passim*; Léopold Mabilleau, "L'Instruction civique," France, Ministère de l'Instruction Publique et des Beaux-Arts, *Recueil des monographies pédagogiques publiées à l'occasion de l'Exposition universelle de 1889* (4 vols.; Paris, 1890), IV, 203.

omy," the "school of solidarity."[31] Gide was simply indicating how transformations in ideological perspective had accompanied transformations in production. More useful for purposes of looking at the relationship between solidarism, social reform, and social science are the sociologist G.-L. Duprat's comments of 1907. Noting that "collectivism [read: socialism] presents a constant danger," he identified solidarism as both *the condition for the existence and for the scientific understanding of social phenomena.*[32] Translated into plain language, Duprat's statement linked social conservation (his reference to "collectivism" suggests as much) to social science, with solidarist-inspired reform its chief instrument. Moreover, he did so in unmistakenly political terms.

There was, of course, the collectivism of order and unity as well as that of disorder and struggle. For the solidarists, the former represented the first line of defense against the latter. That meant the vigorous pursuit of reform—corporate paternalism on a grand scale. Solidarists greeted reformist trade unions with undisguised enthusiasm, believing that such organizations would counteract the influence of militant syndicalism and provide workers with a corporate structure. Moreover, they recognized that autonomous but non-socialist labor formations afforded workers a sense of their own dignity and solidarity, which then could be extended to broader solidarity and cooperation with their employers. Also, solidarists argued that limited state action on behalf of the acceptable material interests of labor had earned legitimate and serious consideration. In contrast, the more hard-line social economists tended to condemn such action with fighting words, calling it "state socialism." But both agreed on the superiority of private reform initiatives.[33] Solidarists especially welcomed corporate programs for both the welfare and discipline of labor as part of their general concern to limit capital's "abuses" and to provide for workers' "social education." They stocked their own pharmacopoeia of social medicine with such wonder

31. Charles Gide, "L'Idée de solidarité en tant que programme économique," *RIS,* I (1893), 385; Gide, *L'Ecole nouvelle* (Paris, 1890), 154.

32. Duprat, *La Solidarité sociale,* 162, 244.

33. Léon Bourgeois, *L'Education de la démocràtie française* (Paris, 1897), 182–84; *Revue Populaire d'Economie Sociale,* I (1902–1903), 74–75; Emile Cheysson, "La Solidarité sociale," *Economiste Français* (1903), 11.

drugs as cooperatives, *cercles populaires*, and *crédits populaires*, prescribed to alleviate the worst symptoms of exploitation without eroding the integrity of the system. In this way, solidarist reform, with its emphasis on distributive justice and the reciprocal obligations of labor and capital, promised to place capitalist relations on a firmer footing than before, by providing a legitimacy morally superior to that offered by the market.[34]

Having taken the high road, solidarists considered the politics of class struggle to be a moral transgression against society and not merely a conventional weapon of political combat. This view produced some tough talk about socialism. According to Célestin Bouglé, sociologist and solidarist ideologue, the "transformation of the economic system" and the construction of a "workers' state" (*Etat populaire du travail*) deserved only scorn. Gabriel Séailles, a "radical solidarist" whose role in education I will discuss (Chapter VI), went even further. He denounced right-wing, xenophobic nationalism—mostly a headline-grabbing sideshow—not because it was a hotbed of reaction, but because it chased a phantom enemy. The true national enemy, "internationalism, identified with belligerent and brutal proletarian *revendications*," carried on the "real war, silent, subdued, without noisy cannonades and trumpet blasts, the war of classes."[35] Countervailing forces lay at hand. Among them, popular education proved to be the one most systematically employed by those who sought to stave off the war of classes and to buttress the reign of social peace.

I have referred to the "social education" of the working class as a component of social reform. It should be clear from the modifier "social" that more is meant than simply what went on in the primary schoolroom. In fact, I will have very little to say about formal primary education in those chapters (VI and VII) devoted to social education. The social education of workers, as the historian Henri Hauser put it, was concerned with acquainting them with "social facts," which is to say that it contributed to the process of working-class integration.[36] As such, social education provided solidarism

34. *Education sociale, passim.*
35. *RSS* (1906), 471–72; Gabriel Séailles, *Patrie et patriotisme* (Troyes, 1910), 2–5.
36. Henri Hauser, *L'Enseignement des sciences sociales* (Paris, 1903), 327.

and social economy with their cutting edge and, to borrow Antonio Gramsci's formulation, constituted a weapon for French capital in the "war of position on the cultural front." One anonymous commentator, reporting on the Social Economy exhibit at the 1889 Paris Exposition, made explicit social education's contribution to the reproduction of capitalist relations: "Only the social education of the people can lead to practical and peaceful solutions to the social question, persuade workers to deal seriously with serious questions, and shield them from every sort of malicious rabble-rouser."[37]

Programs in social education focused on the years following school-leaving when young men and women either already had entered the labor market or were about to. It was during those years that businessmen especially feared that working-class young adults would lose whatever moral habits and social convictions they had absorbed in the primary classroom. Moreover, it made sense to spread the values of association and collaboration among those elements of the population that had direct and immediate experience with the demands of industrial production. Hence social education was commonly referred to as providing workers with an "apprenticeship in social life."[38] Viewed in these terms, the various vehicles for popular adult education—*universités populaires*, *cours d'adultes*, and *conférences populaires*—take on the aspect of instruments for working-class acculturation. Following that logic, it may be useful to consider social education not so much as a collection of dreary exercises in political indoctrination, "obey and ye shall be rewarded," but as a systematic effort to extend the reach of paternalist reform from the mundane level of the workplace to the realm of consciousness. Thus whatever activities workers engaged in—mutualism, cooperatives, or simply production gangs—advanced their social education to the extent that they reinforced the habits of association, replicated the productive tasks performed in industry, and contributed to the spirit of collaboration.

For those whose destiny prescribed a lifetime of labor—an increasingly larger proportion of the population—education appeared

37. *Exposition 1889*, II, 243.

38. Paul Crouzet, "Etat actuel de l'enseignement populaire social," *Premier congrès de l'enseignement des sciences sociales* (Paris, 1901).

to offer the opportunity for improvement by acquisition of skills in the dozens of technical-training programs and industrial institutes created during this period. At least large claims were made to that effect.[39] It is true that apprentice schools and courses in technical instruction turned out thousands of qualified workers, a small percentage of whom rose to the level of foreman. It is also true that productivity and efficiency, measured in output and profits, increased, and at a rate more rapid than that of wages. But here, too, we must probe beneath the practical designs for industrial education and ask two questions: (1) How did it fit into the broader conception of social education? and (2) What role did it play in the overall political strategy for social reform? In other words, it becomes necessary to explore dimensions of industrial education not usually associated with such an apparently straightforward enterprise. That is the purpose of Chapter VII.

Finally, my conclusion will consider some of the implications for *fin-de-siècle* French politics suggested by the themes that I have outlined.[40] Specifically, I will propose that the politics of bourgeois reform foreshadowed and prepared the ground for the formation of a ruling-class bloc anchored in a conservative consensus on the social question. I will, in other words, put a new construction on the politics of "republican defense."

39. *Exposition 1900*, V, 182.
40. Among the many books written about the period, I have found only two useful for the political story: Pierre Sorlin, *Waldeck-Rousseau* (Paris, 1966); and Madeleine Rebérioux, *La République radicale?* (Paris, 1975).

I
The Counterrevolution
of Social Science

Gaston Richard, Emile Durkheim's successor in the chair of sociology at Bordeaux, announced in 1897 that "social science will play the biggest role in the struggle against socialism." Richard, who became an officer in the antisocialist forces arrayed under the banner of social science, need not have couched his statement in the future tense. His contemporaries, such as Durkheim and the latter's predecessor at Bordeaux, Alfred Espinas, had weighed in heavily in the struggle against socialism with their various intellectual efforts. Moreover, the ground had been prepared in France and considerable spadework done for several preceding decades. Indeed, if we take Friedrich Hayek's argument in *The Counterrevolution of Science* (the title of which this chapter shamelessly borrows) and refract it through the prism provided by Herbert Marcuse in *Reason and Revolution*, we can trace the tradition back to the French Revolution—even before "socialism" entered the political vocabulary. Paul Lazarsfeld added another link to the chain, connecting social investigators working in the 1830s and 1840s, such as Adolphe Quételet, to Frédéric Le Play.[1]

Le Play: Social Science and Bourgeois Reform

We remember Le Play chiefly for his nostalgic appeals for the reconstitution of patriarchal authority, for his idealization of primogeni-

---

1. Gaston Richard, *Socialisme et la science sociale* (Paris, 1897), 193; W. S. F. Pickering, "Gaston Richard," *Revue Française de Sociologie*, XX (1979), 163–82; Emile Durkheim, *De*

ture, for his elaborately structured empirical method, and for his unshakable faith in the regenerative power of religion. It is less often recalled that his investigations and attitudes stemmed from his preoccupation with the social question, initially provoked by the revolution of 1830 and later reinforced during his service to the Russian mining and metallurgical tycoon, Prince Demidov. Those experiences convinced Le Play of the dangers as well as the inevitability of class antagonism, and they account for his obsession to surround bourgeois social relations with a framework of prebourgeois patriarchy. In that effort he failed, as he was destined to do, but left as his legacy the outlines of an ideological system and a conception of social management that deeply influenced the character of late nineteenth-century social reform.

Under Le Play's inspiration, social science for the first time became thoroughly and systematically enmeshed with the social question. From his time forward the social question—specifically the relations between capital and labor—defined social science, at least in its political dimension. Moreover, Le Play's approach and that of his collaborators bequeathed to French social science its unique political cast. His strictures on order and hierarchy, on corporate forms of social organization, on paternalism (what he called *patronage*), on the responsibilities as well as the rights of "social authorities" (business leaders who pursued the path of "social peace"), and on the evils of laissez-faire became the common currency of social politics and reform during the succeeding generation. Notwithstanding Le Play's fascination with religion and tradition, which spiced his writings with a distinctly feudal flavor and occasional tall tales (for instance, ascribing the supposed stability of Chinese society to the introduction there of the Decalogue by a son of Noah), he knew that

---

la Division du travail social (9th ed.; Paris, 1973), Chap. III, Conclusion; Brian Turner, "The Social Origins of Academic Sociology: Durkheim" (Ph.D. dissertation, Columbia University, 1977), Chap. 6; André Lalande, "La Vie et l'oeuvre d'Alfred Espinas," *RIS*, XXXIII (1925), 113–44; Friedrich von Hayek, *The Counterrevolution of Science* (Glencoe, Ill., 1964); Herbert Marcuse, *Reason and Revolution* (New York, 1954). For a view similar to Marcuse's, see Rudolph Heberle, "On Political Ecology," *Social Forces*, XXXI (1952), quoted in Leon Bramson, *The Political Context of Sociology* (Princeton, 1961), 12; Paul Lazarsfeld, *Philosophie des sciences sociales* (Paris, 1970), 102–44.

"instability" and "disorganization" accompanied the expansion of industrial enterprise.[2]

Le Play did not propose to turn back the clock or halt the march of progress, but rather to equip the "ruling classes" with the weapons to combat the forces of disorder, antagonism, and socialism. This was less a scientific exercise than a political program for dealing with the labor question, and one not dissimilar in original inspiration to solidarism. Henri de Tourville, one of Le Play's most faithful disciples, testified that Le Play's obsession with the observation and classification of lower-class populations stemmed from a concern with "the proper organization of the working class," which was "industry's primary problem because wage labor constituted its essential machinery" and determined "its basic costs."[3] As far as it goes, this representation of Le Play's perspective is accurate and has the virtue of calling attention to his preoccupation with the mechanics of capital accumulation and reproduction. But to reduce Le Play to the level of vulgar economic calculation does justice neither to the complexities and contradictions embedded in his antiliberal corporate ideology nor to his considerable, if indirect, influence on *fin-de-siècle* bourgeois social politics.

The author of a book on "the leaders of counterrevolution in the nineteenth century," published in 1907 under the imprint of the right-wing Action française, included Le Play in his Pantheon on the grounds that Le Play had enlisted "social science" in the campaign to reestablish the order subverted by the rampant individualism unleashed in 1789. Le Play, the writer argued, knew that "social peace" could be achieved only through "an understanding of social reality." The essence of that reality, as Le Play himself described it,

2. Michel Dion, "Sociologie et idéologie dominante dans l'oeuvre de F. Le Play et Durkheim," *La Pensée*, No. 158 (1971), 61–68; Robert Nisbet, "Conservatism and Sociology," *American Journal of Sociology*, LVIII (1952), 167–76; Frédéric Le Play, *Les Ouvriers européens: Etudes sur les travaux, la vie domestique et la condition morale des populations ouvrières de l'Europe, et leur relations avec les autres classes, précédé d'un exposé de la méthode d'observation* (6 vols.; Paris, 1877–79), I, 142, 204–205, 448, 472; *La Question sociale et l'Assemblée* (Paris, 1873), 14, 59–62; Edmond Demolins, *Le Play et son oeuvre de réforme sociale* (Paris, 1882), 12.

3. Frédéric Le Play, "La Question sociale en France," *Annuaire des Unions d'amis de la paix sociale*, IV (1879), 6–28; Tourville quoted in Dion, "Sociologie et idéologie dominante," 59.

consisted of a hierarchy of unequal classes that reproduced the industrial division of labor. At the pinnacle of the hierarchy stood a
"genuine superior class formed by talent, wealth, or birth." Inequality, Le Play insisted, far from being an unfortunate and temporary
stage in historical development, was firmly rooted in human nature
and, more important, was essential for the reproduction of wealth.
Thus he drew the distinction between those who lived in the realm
of freedom and those who lived in the realm of necessity; between
those who commanded capital and those who obeyed its com-
mands. This distinction struck at the heart of bourgeois liberalism,
which held that marketplace relations determined social relations
and tended toward equality. In practice, of course, the opposite was
true and never more apparent than at a time of increasing capitalist
concentration, as Le Play recognized. Too many among the superior
classes, however, did not respond to the symptoms of class polarization by exercising their paternal obligations in forging links of corporate solidarity with their workers. All too often they battened on
the "system of uncertain employment and unstable wages, which
stirs up war between the employer and the worker." Stubborn adherence on the part of capitalists to the practices dictated by laissez-
faire promised political disaster for the social system capital had
created. Individual liberty, if taken as a license for social irresponsibility, inevitably produced social warfare and repression. The Paris
Commune of 1871, to which Le Play reacted with near hysteria, only
confirmed his worst fears.[4]

Le Play mounted his counterrevolutionary campaign along two
fronts: against liberalism and against socialism, for in his view the
former lead inexorably to the latter, and both were the bitter fruit of
the French Revolution:

> If the French Revolution genuinely had liberated the lower classes from the
> old regime's alleged oppression, we should be able to establish that mutual
> respect between masters and servants [terms he used to characterize all em-
> ployers and employees] progressively has replaced the old antagonisms. Now,
> it is clear . . . that a transformation has occurred in precisely the opposite
> direction. . . . Under the old regime, each master went into combat sup-

    4. Léon Dimier, Les Maîtres de la contrerévolution au xix siècle (Paris, 1907), 259–60;
Frédéric Le Play, La Paix sociale après le désastre (Paris, 1872), 42–43; La Question sociale,
14–35, 53; Les Ouvriers européens, I, 454; Demolins, Le Play et son oeuvre, 8, 12.

ported by his dependents, his workers, or his servants; henceforth, he confronts them armed against him. Previously, after the battle, one found in the workplace and in the home peace and tranquillity. Today, the battle rages in the home as it does in the workplace.

The means to reverse this tendency lay in the hands of those "social authorities" properly instructed in social science, which explains "how Societies establish for themselves Well-being based upon Peace and Stability." More specifically, Le Play singled out two essential reforms to which social science should address itself: devising "the proper organization of labor" and creating the "bonds of mutual reciprocity between masters and servants." The task of social science, then, involved not only investigating how society with all its conflicts and antagonisms was constituted, but also—and more important—fashioning the social machinery to return society to its natural state of class harmony. Paradoxically, respect for traditional relationships, although assumed to be natural, had to be enforced. Le Play's definition of "social harmony" as a state of "mutual goodwill" between classes argued for the imposition of conditions under which such harmony would emerge.[5]

Whatever Le Play's intentions may have been, this formula well suited the interests of big business, especially its more conservative, not to say reactionary, elements. Corporate managers such as Stéphane Mony, who ruled the Commentry-Fourchambault metallurgical complex with an iron hand in the 1870s and who professed admiration for Le Play, translated these sentiments into practical terms: "Labor and capital are necessarily bound together; one can state that it is a universal, inevitable, and indissoluble association."[6] Mony's self-serving declaration comes as no surprise, given his immediate concerns with the prerogatives of capital and with labor discipline. What may be surprising is the extent to which social liberals recapitulated the identical theme at the end of the century.

As did many self-appointed engineers of wholesale social reconstruction, Le Play veered toward an authoritarian utopianism, perhaps originally derived from his youthful association with the Saint-Simonians, whose counterrevolution against bourgeois liberties

5. Frédéric Le Play, *La Réforme sociale en France* (2 vols.; Paris, 1867), I, 48–49; *Les Ouvriers européens*, I, 475, 564; *Réponse à Lucien Brun* (Paris, 1872), 43.
6. Stéphane Mony, *Etude sur le travail* (Paris, 1877), 394.

Hayek correctly identified.[7] Whatever its source, Le Play's authoritarian utopianism stemmed from his efforts to fit a straitjacket of prebourgeois social stasis to a world moved by dynamic bourgeois social relations and dominated by capitalist production. He drew most of his examples from an eccentric and altogether fantastic conception of medieval society as one suffused with harmony as well as hierarchy. Also, and equally significant, he found much to admire in contemporary Russian society, especially the preservation of the rural community and seigneurial jurisdictions following emancipation. The utopian component in all of this consisted of Le Play's experimenting with the idea of reproducing such social relationships in his own country, which he grudgingly came to recognize was impossible. If that were the end of it, we should dismiss him as a slightly mad dreamer. But—and here the decisive authoritarian element comes into play—he insisted that the relations of labor and capital could be constituted on a structurally analogous basis. Because Le Play disdained routine politics and politicians of any stripe (except Napoleon III, whom he admired and who employed him), he anointed France's big bourgeoisie for leadership in installing a corporate order, initially at the point of production and then, by extension, in society as a whole. This project entailed the construction of a system in which the bourgeoisie undertook social reform as a means of both contributing to working-class welfare and fighting socialism. Therefore, Le Play was preoccupied with and encouraged big business's welfare programs for workers, which he identified in such companies as Creusot, Anzin, the Chemins de fer du Midi, and the Holzer steel works in Unieux (Loire). In addition to providing material benefits, these programs were "powerful instruments for education" and reinforced "feelings of social solidarity." And if the choice were forced between material and moral improvement, Le Play preferred the latter: better "to encourage the habits of work and thrift among the lower classes than to seek to improve their material condition."[8]

Le Play's meanderings among the thickets of rural and urban com-

7. Demolins, *Le Play et son oeuvre*, 6; Georg Iggers, *The Cult of Authority* (New York, 1952), *passim*; Hayek, *Counterrevolution of Science*, Chap. 2.

8. *RS*, I (1882), 40, 50; Le Play, *Les Ouvriers européens*, II, 13; *La Paix sociale*, 44–46;

munities across two continents (he considered French Canada an excellent example of stability and order) left him with two lessons:
first, that the West had suffered a breakdown in authority that could
not be reconstituted on the old basis; and second, that a fundamental conflict existed between bourgeois ideology and capitalist production. On the latter score, the ideology held to a model of individuals operating in an open competitive marketplace, whereas the
tendency toward concentration in the workplace produced a confrontation between organized capital and organized labor. Only the
creation of corporate solidarity between the two antagonistic forces,
Le Play concluded, could avert social catastrophe. He saw clearly
that the collective organization of capitalist production required a
parallel social organization. Socialism offered one answer: the expropriation of the bourgeoisie; social science another: the dictatorship
of the bourgeoisie. Le Play was concerned only with working out
the implications of the latter. To do so he had to expose the Janus-
like features of bourgeois hegemony, which depended as much on
authority and compulsion as on contract and consensus. Le Play did
not concede that bourgeois control of the means of production
should submit to external restraints—especially from the working
class—and that the bourgeoisie should maintain anything less than
vigilant surveillance of its property. Nor did he doubt that entrepreneurial freedom stood any chance of survival should the bourgeoisie
fail to undertake whatever measures were necessary to enforce labor's association with capital. The logic of those propositions forced
Le Play to project a corporate vision of the social organization of
production. Lazarsfeld, contemplating Le Play's "surprising" mar-
riage of a rigorous scientific method with hard-line antilabor politics, concluded that "far from limiting himself to the conservative
tradition of someone like Burke," Le Play "belongs more appropriately in the modern context of 'fascism.'"[9]

Lazarsfeld was a sober and careful scholar as well as a remarkably

---

quotes from Pierre Collignon, *Frédéric Le Play, sa conception de la paix sociale* (Paris, 1932),
90–100; and Le Play, *La Réforme sociale*, I, 11.

9. *Annuaire des Unions d'amis de la paix sociale*, I (1875), 20; Lazarsfeld, *Philosophie des
sciences sociales*, 137.

successful academic entrepreneur, not given to polemics or name-calling. In this case he seems to have identified a tendency implied in Le Play's system rather than a "fascist" political program. Considered on that level, Lazarsfeld's judgment appears less harsh, less historically anachronistic, and more suggestive than at first glance. It is true that Le Play came closer to a fascist (corporate) perspective than did those turn-of-the-century scribblers and *boulevardiers* (Charles Maurras, Maurice Barrès, Edouard Drumont, and Paul Déroulède, among others), none of whom dealt directly with the social question. Unlike them, he was self-consciously elitist, never dreamed of descending to the gutter, and did not indulge in the rabble-rousing anticapitalist rhetoric favored by late nineteenth-century protofascist politicians and echoed—with far more menacing overtones—by the genuine article in the 1920s and 1930s.[10] If the "fascist" label applies to Le Play at all, it is because of the contradictions built into his conception of ideal social relations. He mapped out a one-way street. On the one hand, for all his talk about social peace and the obligations of the ruling class, Le Play did not admit of any conflict between those conservative principles and the absolute authority of capital; nor, as much as he denounced the excesses of laissez-faire, did he admit of any restrictions on the political freedom of capitalists except their own consciences and their paternal responsibilities. On the other hand, Le Play granted none of that freedom to the working class, which, he insisted, should accept capitalist authority or be encouraged, by whatever means, to do so. To that end he organized the Société d'économie sociale in 1856 to propagate his ideological perspective in circles where it counted—the worlds of business, management, and politics.

Political Dimensions of Social Science: The Société d'économie sociale

From its beginnings in 1856 as a small group of like-minded businessmen, managers, and engineers, the Société d'économie sociale had grown by the 1890s into an influential parapolitical organization, well connected to the several precincts where bourgeois social poli-

10. Zeev Sternhell, *La Droite révolutionnaire* (Paris, 1978), Chaps. 1, 6–7, 9.

tics—and therefore those of the Republic—were determined. What began as a narrow sect became a significant force behind conservative social reform and contributed to the identification of social science with social management. Furthermore, despite the Société's uncompromising defense of the political interests of capital, it developed close ties to social liberals and others concerned with order and progress. Three factors account for this transformation. First, Le Play's influence waned following his death in 1882. Second, the social question in its acute phase of sharp tensions between labor and capital became a matter of pressing concern for France's political classes, as testified by the dispatch of troops to the strike-bound coal mines of Anzin in 1884 and the liberalization of the laws on association in the same year. Finally, the Société had gained a well-deserved reputation for exploring ways to reinforce collective production with parallel structures of social organization and discipline. The social rather than the individual character of labor and capital came to be viewed as the determining measure of all things in society and their unification the primary purpose of social politics. Just after the turn of the century, the sociologist G.-L. Duprat drew attention to these changes: "We of the twentieth century owe to the sociologists of the nineteenth a new orientation for our studies and concerns, or at least a new point of view from which to examine the several questions previously posed from an individualist or vaguely collective perspective and which today contribute abundant material for *social* economy, *social* esthetics, *social* machinery, and, finally, *social education*."[11] Duprat outlined ideas that already had become central to much of French social science, a return to variations on Comteian themes and a retreat from the Spencerian jungle.

Operating on a more modest scale, the Société d'économie sociale exemplified the "new orientation." Although best known for its detailed investigations of industrial relations, especially strikes and other manifestations of social conflict, the Société's influence on bourgeois reform derived from the political perspectives that animated and informed those investigations. A highly politicized and ideological conception of social science emerged. It concentrated on institutions to surround the individual worker, his family, neighbor-

11. G.-L. Duprat, "Education sociale et solidarité," *RIS*, XI (1903), 922.

hood, and place in production within an all-encompassing framework: labeled, classified, and engineered.[12]

Earlier forays into social science, with the exception of the Saint-Simonians, who took class questions seriously, dealt mostly with a conception of an undifferentiated mass of poor workers: their real miseries, their supposed dissolute habits, and their supposed moral depravity. Solutions to these social questions, if touched on at all, generally considered only reforms in hygiene, housing, and—rarely—conditions of work. They did not address the issue of the relations of labor and capital with a view to modifying them; political economy's theology placed such considerations under taboo.[13] That changed after midcentury, not least because class questions could no longer be ignored.

Armand Audiganne, one of France's leading experts in industrial and labor relations in the 1860s and an associate of the Société, criticized several of his contemporaries (including Le Play) as well as previous social investigators for slighting the political dimensions of observed phenomena and for paying insufficient attention to the construction of harmonious relations between bosses and workers. In his detailed survey of scores of French industrial communities, Audiganne reversed the previous pattern of social investigation, concentrating not on only one side of the social equation, the material conditions of labor, but on the moral ties that bound labor and capital. Nevertheless, in keeping with the temper of the times, Audiganne held workers primarily responsible for their own self-improvement. Nothing could nor should be done to reverse the tendency toward "large-scale industrial concentration." But workers had the opportunity to benefit from the system by adopting the "principles of mutuality" and by organizing their lives according to the bourgeois values of work and thrift. Audiganne cannot be labeled a corporatist, but his outlook did prefigure that of subsequent

12. Paul de Rousiers, "The French School of Social Science," *Annals of the American Academy of Political and Social Sciences*, IV (1894), 620–46; Robert Pinot, "Le Travail: Les travaux de fabrication," *La Science Sociale*, XI (1891), 402–17.

13. Louis Chevalier, *Laboring Classes and Dangerous Classes,* trans. Frank Jellinek (New York, 1973), appeared to accept both the definition and the implications of the concept of social pathology. See Claude-Lucien Bergery, *La Géométrie de l'école* (Paris, 1833), for a precocious blueprint for human engineering resembling Jeremy Bentham's *Panopticon.*

social scientists and reformers on the matter of social solidarity and working-class cultural integration. None of the latter would have taken exception to his conclusion: "The formation of an appropriate popular consciousness surely promises to become the most formidable fortress of social order."[14]

The deliberations of the Société d'économie sociale during the mid-1860s reflected its bourgeois members' precocious apprehension of the political dimensions of the social question. Steeped in the world view of political economy, they showed no reluctance to recognize and to confront the question of class relations in French society. Ironically, it was precisely the uncompromising principles of political economy that proved to be unsettling. "The laws of liberalism," as Edouard Dolléans and Georges Dehove wrote, met the resistance of "economic reality."[15] Elements of a corporate vision began to appear as the focus shifted from the abstraction of the Unmoved Mover in the marketplace to the harsh reality of the workplace.

Already in the early 1860s members of the Société had begun to hedge their bets on the ultimate rationality of market relations. Business prevailed over theory. The financier and eminent political economist Louis Wolowski, for example, rehearsed his belief in the fundamentals: the laws of supply and demand and of the inevitable opposition between capital and labor. But the latter did not necessarily condemn society to a state of "permanent warfare." The elements of solidarity existed in the productive process itself: "Every advance of capital presents opportunities to labor, and whatever renders labor more intelligent and increases its efficiency contributes to the worker's material improvement and at the same time profits capital." Of course, Wolowski was preaching to the converted. Multitudes, however, remained to be converted: "Nowadays the people have begun to think; we must make sure that they think proper thoughts." Working-class consciousness could be shaped

14. Armand Audiganne, *Populations ouvrières et les industries de la France* (2 vols.; Paris, 1860), I, xx, 219, II, 407, 414; *EF,* June 2, 1864.
15. Edouard Dolléans and Georges Dehove, *Histoire du travail en France* (2 vols.; Paris, 1953), I, 355.

through the industrialists' commitment to paternalist reform: mutual aid funds, social insurance, and the like. Although such measures required "personal sacrifices," Wolowski conceded, they were a small price to pay for "order and discipline on the job" and for "a defense against disastrous temptations and an instrument of moral upliftment."[16]

Not everyone agreed that routine labor practices should depart from the habits consistent with the rules of political economy. An industrialist from the Vosges and an inspector-general of the Corps des Ponts-et-Chaussées—typical in their backgrounds of the Société's membership—argued against the legitimacy of combinations and associations, whether of workers, employers, or both in concert. The first of these drew a special reproach: combinations represented the "violent manifestation" of the social "illness caused by disregarding the basic principles of supply and demand." Because "natural economic forces" determined wage rates (up or down), any attempt to neutralize those forces through political action was socially disruptive and potentially destabilizing.[17] In other words, both labor and capital took their chances in the marketplace, but the latter was in command of the productive process. This model may have worked well enough in a world dominated by small units of production, although even there entrepreneurial authority mocked the supposed equality of boss and worker. With the growth of large-scale industry, however, the model turned into a recipe for the permanent warfare Wolowski feared, unless, of course, countervailing pressures toward collaboration could be generated.

Competition, as Le Play pointed out, tended to benefit larger industries at the expense of the smaller and of the individual. The corporation, he argued, represented the wave of the future and promised to reproduce itself in all "aspects of social activity." Competition progressively produced its opposite—concentration—which exerted a powerful magnetic force on increasingly wider spheres of social relations. Transformations in industrial organization, especially increasing pressures for capital accumulation, would have their greatest impact on working-class life. Large-scale industry, unable to

16. *EF,* January 14, 1864, May 10, 1863.
17. *Ibid.,* January 21, July 14, 1864.

scatter its resources or to decentralize, uprooted the worker from familiar surroundings without replacing them with equally powerful attachments. Those had to be created—in a sense artificially.[18]

Much of the Société's early activity involved exploring and recording just such mechanisms designed to create stable industrial relations. Political considerations received close attention. Léon Donnat, the Société's secretary-general during the 1860s who later turned on Le Play, raised the primary questions from which all else followed: how to hold society together in the face of advancing industrialization and how to "reconstitute collaboration between classes" and "reconcile disparate points of view." To fulfill these conditions required heavy doses of bourgeois paternalism. Among the enterprises in which "respect for social hierarchies" reigned, Donnat singled out a machine tool firm in Hérimoncourt, a small town in the Doubs. The employer reportedly maintained peaceful relations with his workers by providing housing at low rents, running a company store, supervising the establishment of a workers' consumer cooperative, and financing education for both children and adults. Charles Thierry-Mieg, of the Alsatian textile dynasty, reported on a similar but much larger project undertaken in Mulhouse (Haut-Rhin). Its bourgeoisie had sponsored the construction of more than five hundred houses by the early 1860s. Sale terms dictated 300 to 400 francs down with monthly payments ranging from 18 to 25 francs. The installment payments corresponded to the average rental in Mulhouse and represented roughly 25 percent of a skilled worker's wage. Those terms, especially the down payment, restricted buyers to only the best-paid workers, thereby reinforcing the creation of a "labor aristocracy." Furthermore, as Thierry-Mieg pointed out, these obligations left workers with no loose change to squander on drinking and other vices. Finally, the prospect of property ownership encouraged habits of thrift and hard work within a "working class totally bereft of the moral and material resources" it had once possessed when small and scattered industry had dominated the countryside.[19]

18. *Ibid.*, July 21, 1864, January 10, 1863.
19. Léon Donnat, *La Politique expérimentale* (Paris, 1885), 331–43; *EF*, February 4, 1864, May 25, 10, 1863.

Indeed, as a Protestant pastor from the mill town of Sainte-Marie-aux-Mines (Haut-Rhin) remarked, only work and obedience would enable laborers to appreciate the "miracles of industrial progress made possible by machines." This may sound like the routine nostrums of political economy favored by factory masters on two continents, and that it certainly was; but it also calls attention to the authority and force that manufacturers had at their disposal to give substance to the Invisible Hand. As the pastor pointed out, however, employers were responsible for taking initiatives to create a climate of cooperation and association between themselves and their workers.[20] If capital accumulation generated class conflict, as political economy insisted, paternalism could at least smother that conflict or deflect it from the path of confrontation, thereby preserving authority and rendering force unnecessary.

The question of routinizing industrial entrepreneurs' authority became central to the Société's exercises in the promotion of practical social science. In each instance the emphasis fell on the machinery required to maximize not only production but order, discipline, and obedience. One company whose labor policies gained special attention as a supposed model of effective social management was the coal-mining firm of Blanzy in Montceau-les-Mines (Saône-et-Loire). According to Amédée Burat, secretary of the coal producers' association, the Comité des houillères français, the company by 1872 had established "good relations" with its workers, suffered no strikes, and remained impervious to outside agitation. Burat explained that this state of affairs resulted from the company's carrot-and-stick tactics. Blanzy occupied a particularly advantageous position because it was able to construct *ex nihilo* a community for its workers: Montceau-les-Mines, a village at the beginning of the century, had grown to a town of twenty thousand inhabitants by 1890. Blanzy's engineers and managers had designed a total environment, centered on five *cités ouvrières*, including schools, churches, stores, a hospital, and a variety of recreational facilities for every taste. Dispensation of these benefits was closely controlled and could be withdrawn at any moment from those judged "undeserving" of the company's largesse. At the point of production, in the mines and at the

20. *EF,* October 6, 1864.

pitheads, the measures taken to enforce discipline and order were undisguised. The company's "organization of labor" followed the military rule of command and strict hierarchy: The chief engineer supervised several "division" engineers who in turn supervised a dozen "captains" and thirty-five foremen. The foremen, drawn from the workers' ranks, wore uniforms and "were ever mindful of their position—even off the job." [21]

Did this elaborate hierarchical structure create social peace? Burat found mixed results. Many workers remained sullen and selfish, concerned only with "less work and higher wages." Worse, the local shopkeepers exerted some political influence over the miners, distributing "subversive" newspapers, pamphlets, and flyers at election time. (It was not unusual for petty bourgeois radicals to exercise political leadership in working-class communities.) All the more reason, Burat insisted, for the company to monopolize commodity distribution in the town. Far from being a failure, Burat concluded, Blanzy's paternalism simply was incomplete. Many tasks remained "to extend education, honor labor, tighten up command . . . finally, to set against those disruptive elements a union (faisceau) of working people from all classes." [22] Events would prove that time was short: Blanzy experienced its first big strike in 1882, which, as we shall see, had a significant impact on the company's labor policies and its strategies for social management.

In the 1870s and 1880s, as in the 1860s, not everyone connected with the Société d'économie sociale agreed that industry's labor problems demanded heavy infusions of paternalism. Echoes of laissez-faire resonated. One commentator denounced the whole business as an unwarranted infringement on "individual action" and on the "free and productive play of competition," barely distinguishable from socialism. He singled out company-sponsored housing for criticism because it rendered the worker a "prisoner" of debt and prevented him from changing jobs at will. He then gave a somber estimate of paternalism's political implications: it threatened to reduce the worker to "serfdom" or to "slavery." This certainly was special pleading, but also an inadvertently telling insight into the con-

21. *Bulletin de la Société d'Economie Sociale* (1872), 636–43.
22. *Ibid.*, 644, 646.

tradictions of paternalism: that the vision of corporate solidarity was fundamentally incompatible with bourgeois social relations—a system of free labor. Thirty years earlier Pierre Proudhon, from a different perspective, had leveled a similar charge against Le Play, whose system he characterized as "the scientific organization of servitude."[23]

Emile Cheysson, of whom much more in the following chapter, appeared to address just such anxieties a few years later. As an engineer and an industrial manager (Le Creusot), he was well positioned to argue that paternalist reform could strengthen rather than undermine the rule of capital. Sounding like an old-fashioned conservative (which he was not) fulminating against the horrors of dark, satanic mills, Cheysson mocked the pretensions of political economy and its "implacable and brutal law," according to which "labor is a commodity whose cost is regulated by supply and demand." Thus, he remarked ironically, "social science," a system to manage complex class relations, finds itself "substantially simplified." Political economy and employers who operated by its rules spoke of "freedom" and "progress in human dignity." The reality, however, was "unemployment, poverty, and hatred," in other words, political dynamite. All such assumptions that promised "peace, stability, and well-being" delivered only misery. They amounted to nothing more than a "wall of cardboard" set up against an "army that mounts an assault on society." Short-term gains, Cheysson insisted, could be won only at the cost of long-term disaster: "The boss who makes of unemployment a principle or at least his practice not only compromises his enterprise's prosperity and his own peace of mind, but turns his plant into a menace to public order, like a high-pressure boiler lacking a safety valve." Were not the interests of capital better served by factories that "possessed a disciplined labor force, devoted to the firm, . . . skilled in its tasks and content in its work"? Cheysson appealed not to charity, philanthropy, or altruism, all of which he disdained, but to bourgeois self-interest and the larger interests of society. These interests were served best by the systematic development of "permanent ties" of solidarity between labor and capital. By this

23. *Ibid.*, 647; Pierre-Joseph Proudhon, *De la justice dans la révolution et dans l'église* (3 vols.; Paris, 1858), III, 132, quoted in Catherine Bodard Silver (ed.), *Frédéric Le Play on Family, Work, and Social Change* (Chicago, 1982), 10.

formula Cheysson intended neither the abridgment of capital's authority nor the imposition of any economic sacrifices. Just the opposite: paternalist reform, geared toward anchoring the worker to one factory and to its extended environment, made good business sense. It made for a stable work force, at once more efficient and (theoretically) amenable to disciplinary control. Therein, Cheysson concluded, lay the "surest way to solve the labor question and to recover social peace."[24]

During the subsequent two decades the perspective on the labor question that Cheysson and others adopted focused even more sharply on class tensions, strikes, and the menace of socialism. Following the 1884 strike at Anzin, Gabriel Ardant, managing director of the Vieille-Montagne zinc mines and foundries, examined what went wrong at a company noted for its generous paternal benefits. First, "at Anzin, as in all French industry, we find two clearly distinct classes." Their ranks were fixed according to "capabilities and aptitudes." Workers remained workers because of their inability to improve themselves; bosses became bosses because their thrifty habits enabled them to amass capital. Each class served a socially necessary function and needed the other; yet war raged between them. Ardant fixed blame for the strike on the resistance of "inefficient workers" to the introduction of a modified version of the "butty" system (a form of subcontracting long in use at Anzin) in the mines. That is, they resisted a system of production in which work teams, whose members were arranged hierarchically, operated as independent associations of producers, enforcing quotas and discipline. According to Ardant, the system stimulated individual initiative and "raised the worker's moral level." But he passed over quickly the primary calculation behind subcontracting, which was to weaken the miners' union by setting the teams in competition with one another. Not that Ardant left unacknowledged the political purpose behind subcontracting; he linked it specifically to Anzin's paternalist strategy, designed to weld the miners to the company.[25]

24. *Bulletin de la Société d'Economie Sociale* (1876), 170–72, 177–78, 183–84.

25. Gabriel Ardant, "Le Mineur d'Anzin; la famille et le patronage de la compagnie," *RS*, III (1884), 193–96. The miners' union, according to Michelle Perrot, *Les Ouvriers en grève* (2 vols.; Paris, 1974), I, 304–306, was strong and militant. Charles E. Freedeman acquainted me with the "butty" system.

What, then—to return to the original question—went wrong? The problem lay in the increasingly common collective organization of production, the displacement of entrepreneurial control by the impersonal corporation (*société anonyme*). Under these conditions, effective paternalism required a cadre of managerial experts that approached labor questions no less scientifically than they approached the details of technical operations. Apparently, Anzin had not recruited such a cadre. The problem easily could be corrected by a more thorough application of managerial control and surveillance, leavened with a serious program to improve the miners' material and moral welfare. The principles of command and obedience, however, remained paramount: "From the top to the bottom of the hierarchical ladder all should understand the value that the managing director attaches not only to production, but to social peace." (Ironically, the strike at Anzin erupted into violence when the managing director, Guary by name, refused to consider even the miners' minimal demands.) At any rate, Anzin, Ardant observed, appeared to have learned the lesson—albeit the hard way—that "the social and the technical questions are of equal importance." Once that lesson was applied, the "close ties" of solidarity "would suffice to prevent some fanatic from rousing the mass of laborers."[26]

As class conflict heated up in France, beginning with the strike wave in 1889–1890, it became obvious that the laboring masses had not escaped the influence of "fanatics." That, at least, was the conclusion drawn by the social scientists associated with the Société d'économie sociale. They examined a series of strikes, including those in the textile industry of Amiens (Somme) and in the coal fields of Lens (Pas-de-Calais) in 1893 and the Carmaux (Tarn) coal mines in 1892. Even though the issues and the forces arrayed varied greatly from place to place, in each case they wrote off workers' wage demands as irresponsible, unjustified, and destructive of national industry. The report on Lens, written by Albert Maron of Roubaix, purported to demonstrate the mineworkers' privileged wage position. Maron, however, neglected to spell out the implications of his own figures, that wages, based on piece rates, were unstable because they varied as a function of the demand for coal and that the com-

26. Ardant, "Le Mineur d'Anzin," 204–206; Perrot, *Les Ouvriers,* II, 571.

pany had a habit of cutting back on the number of hours miners worked in the pits without providing compensatory wage adjustments. The report on Amiens stressed how the textile firms had gone out of their way to provide their employees with a wide range of welfare benefits. But those benefits applied only to working men, who were losing their jobs to cheaper female and child labor. In Carmaux, according to the industrial manager Alexandre Gibon, similar cradle-to-the-grave paternal programs reaped only a harvest of bitterness and struggle. Gibon, however, did not take into account the long history of conflict between Carmaux's management and the mineworkers. Specific aspects of the disputes that led to the strikes received only marginal attention in these investigations.[27] They were outweighed by political considerations, reflected in a hard line against labor unions. Curiously, Maron, Gibon, and others took a harsher position toward the labor movement than some of the employers in the affected areas a few years later. Whereas the latter appeared willing to tolerate unions (under the law they had no choice) and could even speak positively about them, the former condemned the *syndicats* for betraying the workers' best interests by indulging in politics. Gibon conceded that *syndicats* had a legitimate role to play in "dealing seriously and calmly with working-class concerns," but felt they surrendered all claims to sympathy by refusing to obey the rules. Far from promoting association and solidarity between labor and capital, the *syndicats* had taken the road of "agitation . . . this agitation is political or, to put it bluntly, openly revolutionary."[28]

More often than not the distinction between acceptable economic concerns and unacceptable political agitation became blurred. According to Maron, the Lens branch of the Chambre syndicale des mineurs du Nord invented a bogus economic issue to plant among the miners "the idea of the necessity of class struggle." The local union's campaign to equalize wage rates for the members of work

27. Albert Maron, "L'Histoire et le bilan de la grève du Pas-de-Calais," *RS*, XXVII (1894), 45, 51–52, 191; Paul Hubert-Valleroux, "Les Grèves d'Amiens," *RS*, XXVI (1893), 273–74; Alexandre Gibon, "La Grève de Carmaux: La Conciliation et l'arbitrage dans l'industrie," *RS*, XXV (1893), 260–61; Rolande Trempé, *Les Mineurs de Carmaux* (2 vols.; Paris, 1974), Vol. I, Chaps. 2–4.

28. Jean Huret, *Les Grèves: Enquête* (Paris, 1901), 128–37; Gibon, "La Grève de Carmaux," 262.

teams disguised an attack on "individual initiative" and the principle of "free labor." Economic demands, therefore, concealed the true purpose behind the strike: to install a "collectivist" order in accordance with the program of "revolutionary socialism." Albert Gigot, managing director of the Forges d'Alais (Gard), saw a similarly sinister political conspiracy operating at Carmaux, where he had led the company's arbitration team in 1892. Repression, Gigot suggested, was the only effective way to deal with such a threat. He noted with approval the intervention of police and militia in the Homestead strike of 1892. Much the same estimate of a political showdown emerged from the events in Amiens: "In today's economic order socialism is the real, the implacable enemy, and workers' *syndicats* pursue its goals by provoking laborers against the bosses."[29]

Once again workers pursuing their material improvement were presented as uppity ingrates, mockers of authority, and, worse, dupes of alleged revolutionaries. Ordinarily, such talk could be dismissed as simply a bourgeoisie's routine self-serving habit of escalating the slightest challenge to its authority into a mortal threat to the entire social order. Two considerations, however, argue for a somewhat more nuanced interpretation: first, even those who invoked the specter of revolution did not spare their class brethren criticism for failing to construct social machinery to shelter the workplace from the storms of the marketplace; and second, they consistently saw sweeping paternalist systems as the only resolution of class conflict. Thus the "science" of social reform served the cause of social peace as it struck a counterrevolutionary blow against syndicalism and socialism.

"Fresh Troops" for the Class Struggle

"Fresh troops" for the class struggle is how the *Revue Socialiste* in 1895 characterized the Unions des amis de la paix sociale, a political action group originally spun off from the Société d'économie sociale. Whereas the Société pursued its scrutiny of every aspect of the labor question, the Unions developed a propaganda network that

29. Maron, "L'Histoire et le bilan de la grève," 48, 57, 197; *RS*, XXV (1893), 533; Hubert-Valleroux, "Les Grèves d'Amiens," 303.

penetrated to the deepest recesses of provincial France. They drew their cadres from diverse walks of life, making it initially difficult to establish their precise class composition. In 1885 Léon Donnat estimated the Unions' membership at 3,254, 8 percent of which were men of the cloth, mostly parish priests and a few bishops. The Unions' roster identified a substantial number of members as *châtelein*—a pretentious word denoting either a prosperous farmer, a landlord, or a bourgeois occupying a country house, if only on weekends. This category usually showed up on the Unions' rosters for industrially underdeveloped departments. But this does not necessarily mean that the Unions were bastions of the backwoods, dominated by rustics ideologically mired in the old regime.[30] Two factors suggest otherwise.

First, a rural bourgeoisie may be assumed, in the France of the 1890s, to harbor concerns about production, the market, and especially labor similar to those of its industrial counterparts. Moreover, in a number of overwhelmingly rural departments large holdings dominated (in many cases accounting for upward of 50 percent of the arable land) and included substantial populations of wage laborers.[31] Finally, a number of the Unions' members were officers of departmental *sociétés des agriculteurs*, traditional strongholds of commercial farmers. Thus it seems reasonable to conclude that the so-called *châteleins* did not necessarily lead lives of bucolic isolation or of rural idiocy.

Second, and more directly indicative of the Unions' political complexion, a disproportionally large number associated with business enterprise were industrial bosses: engineers, managers, and directors of big companies. Companies represented included the Société des mines et fonderies de zinc de la Vieille-Montagne, Le Creusot (its chairman, Henri Schneider), the metallurgical complex of Terrenoire, the Société des mines de la Loire, the Société des mines de Carmaux, the Compagnie des Messageries maritimes, the Saint-Gobain chemical and glass works, the Compagnie parisienne du gaz, the Chemins de fer du Midi, the Chemins de fer de l'Est, the biggest

---

30. Donnat, *La Politique expérimentale*, 346; *RS*, XXVIII (1895), 10–40.
31. Michel Augé-Laribé, *La Politique agricole de la France de 1880 à 1940* (Paris, 1950), 36; France, Ministère de l'Agriculture, *Statistique agricole de France* (Nancy, 1887), 324.

insurance companies, and several of the big textile firms of the Lille-Tourcoing-Roubaix (Nord) complex. Adding to this list the dozens of civil and mining engineers—the core of middle management—associated with the Unions reveals an organization thickly populated by individuals deeply involved in command of production.[32]

Alexis Delaire, secretary-general of the Société d'économie sociale during the 1890s and a tireless booster of paternalist management, drew specific attention to the Unions' political function. He linked their propaganda and educational work to the objectives of social science, namely, to put an "end to the era of revolutions" and to discover the "key to permanent stability" in the workplace and in society at large. The Unions' activist mission, according to Delaire, consisted of several tasks: to provide a clearinghouse for observations and facts about social reality, especially industrial relations throughout France and in other parts of the world; to refute "reigning misconceptions" about contemporary society, such as the belief that social and political antagonisms were unavoidable and the notion that individuals possessed the right to revolt against authority (which Delaire, following Le Play, ascribed to the poisonous influence of Jean-Jacques Rousseau); to encourage "industrial bosses" to take upon themselves the "essential obligations of paternalism"; to recognize publicly those employers who "protect their workers against unemployment and maintain harmony in the plants"; and to join in creating opportunities for workers to save and invest in industry.[33]

Nothing in this agenda necessarily qualifies as counterrevolutionary; it could be viewed as a perfectly straightforward claim to validate capitalist control of production. But the context in which the strategy evolved as well as the targets it sighted suggests a broader purpose. If the twin purposes of reform were to forge social solidarity and to beat back socialism, then the agenda may be taken as counterrevolutionary but not necessarily reactionary. Bourgeois constructions of the social question, whether of the conservative variety presented here or in the garb of social liberalism, easily could accommodate both counterrevolution against socialism and pro-

32. *RS*, XXVIII (1895), 10–40; *Annuaire des Unions d'amis de la paix sociale*, II (1876), 214–15.
33. Alexis Delaire, *Les Unions de la paix sociale* (Paris, 1882), 11–23.

gressive reform. This is what Le Play appeared to have in mind when he first proposed the creation of the Unions back in the mid-1870s. Perhaps somewhat prematurely, he considered the Unions to be one of several battalions mobilized for a political and cultural offensive against militant labor and socialism. Recognizing that bourgeois paternalism could not rest comfortably on good works alone, to say nothing of repression, Le Play envisioned a value structure that could compete with and ultimately prevail over socialism, while forming an ideological base for the corporate solidarity of capital and labor. His problem, and why he quickly passed into obsolescence, was his insistence on a cultural alternative based upon religious values, specifically the strictures of the Decalogue.[34]

There was, however, only a slim chance that the employment of religious indoctrination as an instrument of labor discipline would produce less conflict than it generated. Company bosses such as the Marquis de Solages of Carmaux and the Chagots of Blanzy had adopted such tactics in the 1880s, only to suffer grief.[35] Because the Unions held on to a religion-tinted ideology in the 1870s and 1880s, they earned a richly deserved reputation for reaction and remained on the fringes of French social politics. By the 1890s, the Unions appeared to have gotten the message and muted their religious tones. Not coincidentally, respectable political and business leaders such as Jules Siegfried, Paul Leroy-Beaulieu, Joseph Chailley-Bert, Edouard Aynard, and Auguste Isaac joined their ranks, symbolizing the ascendancy of broad class interest over narrow sectarianism (Siegfried, Leroy-Beaulieu, and Chailley-Bert were Protestants; Aynard and Isaac Catholics). For some socialists the Unions' new look made them a serious threat to labor for it signaled an alliance of the republican party with "all sorts of reactionaries." A popular newsletter devoted to social questions, written from a perspective sympathetic to the Unions and to which such dissimilar spirits as Charles Gide and Georges Sorel contributed, disputed the charge of reaction. What were the Unions but "patriotic" formations dedicated to combating class antagonism and to promoting national solidarity? They prac-

---

34. *Annuaire des Unions d'amis de la paix sociale,* I (1875), 13.

35. Trempé, *Les Mineurs de Carmaux,* Vol. I, Chap. 5; Perrot, *Les Ouvriers,* II, 673; Robert Beaubernard, *Montceau-les-Mines: Un "laboratoire social" au xix siècle* (Avallon, 1981), Chap. 4.

ticed a "moral science" devoted to affirming the values of property, hierarchy, and class collaboration. So, too, had been Le Play's original vision twenty-five years earlier: the Unions were a "scientific enterprise," concerned only with advancing the "science of social peace."[36] That conception of the political mission of social science found echoes in the new sociology.

Sociology and the Social Question

Similar political perspectives linked the engineering and managerial cadres of late nineteenth-century France to the sociologists, most of whom would identify themselves as radicals. The former, practical men, and the latter, professional intellectuals, shared an outlook on social science that assigned to it a leading role in the campaign against socialism and other sources of disorder. As Leon Bramson and others have pointed out, French sociology evolved within a distinct political context. Edmond Demolins, who had close ties to both the social economy group and big business, stated in 1892—a year marked by extensive domestic unrest—that the chief business of social science was to provide employers with the tools to manage the social environment within which production took place. The application of social science to industrial relations, he argued, would enable French capital to avoid the "communitarian" traps of "state socialism," on the one hand, and "revolutionary socialism," on the other. Scientific management left capital's authority intact and encouraged labor's "self-help." An admirer of British trade unions because of their allegedly conservative pragmatism, Demolins suggested that such formations could strengthen the solidarity between classes. Nonpolitical trade unions, as corporate organizations of labor, would promote working-class discipline and routinize peaceful relations between labor and management. Everything, of course, hinged on the domestication of the labor movement and its isolation from socialist infection.[37]

36. *Revue Socialiste*, No. 128 (1895), 223–27; *Revue Populaire d'Economie Sociale*, I (1902–1903), 21–24; *Annuaire des Unions d'amis de la paix sociale*, I (1875), 19.

37. Bramson, *Political Context of Sociology*, Chap. 1; Frank Hartung, "The Social Function of Positivism," *Philosophy of Science*, IV (1945), 120–33; Nisbet, "Conservatism and Sociology"; Edmond Demolins, *Conférence à la Sorbonne sur l'avenir de l'éducation nouvelle*

Gaston Richard took an equally frank stand on the political tasks of social science. His capsule version of socialist doctrine is less interesting than are his conclusions:

> Socialism presents us with two cleverly intertwined but distinct notions: the end of competition and the atrophy of capitalist property. Social science must commit itself to eliminating this crude and dangerous evasion. The destruction of capitalist property, whether violent or gradual, because it tends to condemn society to total immediate consumption, would amount to the sharpest imaginable thrust against healthy competition. One cannot mitigate the effects of competition except by respecting the natural laws of social evolution, laws that have made capitalist enterprise the most powerful instrument for the human transformation of nature.

Because sociological knowledge was based on "positive science," Richard claimed, it was ideally suited to devise the systems necessary to contain the violence built into economic competition. In a revealing analogy, he compared the efforts to shield the proletariat from the worst blows of competition with advances in criminology, a field in which it had become obvious that repression and punishment had no rehabilitative effect. Workers and criminals alike needed education in the habits of "mutuality, solidarity, and social consciousness."[38]

The sociologist Alfred Espinas, who lectured on social economy at the Sorbonne in 1894, shared similar interests in the working class and similar political perspectives. While at Bordeaux, where he preceded Emile Durkheim in the chair of pedagogy and sociology, Espinas became actively involved in the promotion of physical education, gymnastics, and sports. Such exertions, if mistakenly advertised as "opium for the masses," were widely held to constitute healthy outlets for popular energies and had become integral to the educational system, to which Espinas made substantial contributions. He believed it equally important that French youth engage in the mental calisthenics to prepare their minds for the reception of acceptable political doctrine. Espinas made his position clear; his lectures, titled "Social Philosophy of the Eighteenth Century and

---

(Paris, 1899), 1–24; Henri Gaillard de Champris, *La Réforme de l'éducation nationale et l'Ecole des Roches* (Verneuil, 1917), 9–14; Edmond Demolins, *Le Socialisme devant la science sociale* (Paris, 1892), 11–13, 37, 65–69. Italics and English rendering in the original.

38. Richard, *Socialisme et la science sociale,* 190, 164, 187, 197, 199.

the Revolution," argued the superiority of private property over so-cialism. The latter, in its Marxist revolutionary and international form, he condemned as a "dangerous utopia, contrary to nature, irreconcilable with economic laws and the hierarchy of social organisms."[39]

Although Espinas characterized socialism as unnatural and paid his respects to economic laws, he was hardly a narrow-minded ide-ologue. He used his lectern as a platform from which to argue for a social system flexible enough to provide for the reconciliation of classes through reform. Socialists, Espinas claimed, intended just the opposite; hence the importance of social scientists taking an activist part in the "elimination of social evil," especially widespread pov-erty, which required only instrumental measures to protect workers against the "arbitrary actions of their employers" and against the "cruel hardships" that afflicted them. In that connection, Espinas noted with approval the trend among employers toward setting aside "increasingly large portions of their revenues for various wel-fare programs." But however encouraging those trends might be, they only skirted the social question and did not touch on the fun-damentals of social organization. It was in these areas, according to Espinas, that social science—and especially social economy—would find its true vocation.[40]

The business of social science, according to Espinas, consisted of validating a "higher form of socialism" based on "sentiments of har-mony" and collaboration, in other words, a nonsocialist collec-tivism. He took as his model the "organic" conception of society, to which he gave explicit political content. The "salvation of the coun-try" depended upon the subordination of the individual to the group. Moral as well as political imperatives followed; for "the real-ity of nations as moral personalities and the belief in their superior dignity is the dominant fact of contemporary history." Partisan poli-tics, the radicalism and "dogmatic intransigence" for which Espinas confessed a youthful enthusiasm, had become a dangerous diver-sion. In the face of growing social antagonism his generation had

39. Lalande, "La Vie et l'oeuvre," 131–40.
40. Alfred Espinas, "Leçon d'ouverture d'un cours d'histoire de l'économie sociale," *RIS,* II (1894), 322, 343–46.

learned in the "school of politics" the lessons of "political utility." This education in realism produced respect for the "organic solidarity" of the nation and for such republican monuments as obligatory military service and the subjugation of colonial populations. Espinas took military service very seriously, and not merely as a patriotic exercise. Echoing a common view in those years, by no means the exclusive property of professional patriots, he characterized the army as "the great school of social discipline: there, those bereft of wealth and education have learned to accept hierarchies, to bear necessary inequalities as the natural order of things, to depend upon an elite for safety under fire; and, once returned to civilian life, they carry with them that respect for order without which no society can endure."[41]

Espinas' preoccupation with working-class "civilian life" accounted for his interest in the military. The values of order and discipline assimilated in the barracks served equally well in the factory, where an analogous system prevailed. Dedication to work and to corporate solidarity prepared workers to take their predetermined subordinate place in the hierarchy of production. There, as in all "social entities, organization rests on subordination and subordination requires inequalities that cannot be maintained without some compulsion." Compulsion, however, need not be exercised exclusively through the imposition of external authority. Precisely those "sentiments of deference," the process of "collective labor," and the apprehension of "collective solidarity" reinforced "obedience." As a result, even the "humblest callings" and the "meanest tasks" could lose their pall of drudgery and be accomplished with "cheerfulness and *joie de vivre*."[42]

Far from rehearsing bourgeois homilies for the edification of workers (the only *blouses* to be found in the Sorbonne dressed janitors, not students), Espinas was instructing a future elite in its duties, while explaining both the techniques and the rewards of scientifically grounded social management. His vision of happy factory hands whistling while they worked may have bordered on the ludicrous, not to say the insulting, but his conception of social science

41. *Ibid.*, 344, 337, 342–43.
42. *Ibid.*, 336.

as an ideological instrument to fashion the tools for collective solidarity and class collaboration was no joke.

Espinas did not stand alone. Other social scientists working in the 1890s, not coincidentally at the peak of industrial struggle, focused on the labor question. René Worms, in his outline of the method and purpose of social economy, claimed for it the status of a "concrete science" applied to the totality of social relations. Although he insisted that social economy's territory extended beyond the social question, that is, the relations of labor and capital, he acknowledged that the condition of the industrial worker occupied an important area for its explorations. Moreover, as a science social economy only made manifest the material and moral ties that bound—or should bind—distinct classes. Its mission firmly excluded "drawing up an indictment against contemporary society." Worms's essay appeared in the *Revue Internationale de Sociologie*, the pages of which were well stocked with similar studies on the social question, not unlike those in *Réforme Sociale*, although from a different perspective. Most of them had a practical rather than a theoretical purpose and included essays on "social pathology," social reform, crime and criminality, education, and at least one attack on Marxism, written by Thomas Garrigue Masaryk. Also, each issue included a chronicle of "social movements" (labor questions, strikes, and social reform) in several European countries and in the United States.[43]

Finally, we cannot ignore the towering figure of Emile Durkheim. His conception of "organic solidarity," although derived in a different manner from that of Espinas, owed something to the latter's work and held similar sociopolitical implications. If anything, Durkheim's system was more self-consciously political, as well as subtler, than was Espinas'. Shocked and disturbed by what he perceived to be the climate of disorder in France, Durkheim set about to make social science an instrument for the reconstitution of order, as had other social scientists before him. "It is necessary," he said, "that our

43. René Worms, "L'Economie sociale," *RIS*, VI (1898), 461, 528; Paul de Lilienfeld, "La Pathologie sociale," *RIS*, II (1894), 825–61; Albert Jaffé, "La Question des logements ouvriers en Allemagne," *RIS*, IV (1896), 734–40; Paul Sollier, "La Médecine sociale," *RIS*, I (1893), 506–16; E. de Roberty, "Le Crime individuel et le crime collectif," *RIS*, VI (1898), 743–63; Thomas Masaryk, "La Crise scientifique et philosophique du marxisme contemporaine," *RIS*, VI (1898), 511–28.

society regain its sense of organic cohesion; that the individual feel the social mass that surrounds and absorbs him . . . and that this feeling rules his behavior."[44]

In *De la division du travail social* and various lesser writings Durkheim gave these general principles concrete form. He was most concerned with the behavior and the moral discipline of the contemporary worker. Durkheim not only insisted that the division of labor constituted the essence of industrial organization, he also represented it—in good materialist fashion—as the realization of society's highest moral values and the mainspring of social cohesion. This strictly normative argument hinged on the assertions that a finely tuned division of labor necessarily contributed to the formation of social solidarity, that society as a web of interconnected relations embodied the soul of order, and that therefore capitalist production, far from being the source of class antagonisms, actually dissolved them. Thus class categories made no sense in a horizontally organized world in which all individuals performed mutually interdependent functions. On the basis of this analysis, Durkheim could then easily proceed to the paradoxical conclusion that those functions were undifferentiated in the sphere of society as a whole (solidarity) yet highly differentiated in the sphere of production (division of labor). Durkheim thereby reduced capitalism to a more or less efficient and complex organization for production that, *mutatis mutandis*, best suited his normative goals of social cohesion, personal liberty, and a bountiful industrial harvest.[45]

The political implications of Durkheim's treatment of capitalism became readily apparent when, on one hand, he dismissed it as a socially irrelevant construct and, on the other, denounced Marxist socialists for fomenting disorder by falsely characterizing it as an exploitive labor system. Moreover, he took particular umbrage at Marxists for claiming a monopoly on socialism. Durkheim, too, thought himself a socialist, by which he meant the rational organization of industrial relations. Any other conception of socialism, espe-

44. Emile Durkheim, "Cours de science sociale: Leçon d'ouverture," *RIE*, XV (1888), 38; *Socialisme et Saint-Simon* (Paris, 1917), Chaps. 6–7; Alfred Espinas, *La Société animale* (Paris, 1978).

45. Durkheim, *De la division du travail social*, xxxviii, xliii–xliv, 362.

cially one that projected a vision beyond economic planning and other forms of structural reorganization, he considered unscientific and unacceptable. Another normative conclusion followed: just as the orderly division of labor was the normal state and disorder the anomic, so solidarity between capital and labor was normal and conflict a "pathological form." As Philip Abrams pointed out, this conception of solidarity assumed the "interdependence of specialized occupations," which, although true enough in a mechanical sense, allowed Durkheim to deny the social reality of class distinctions. Sustaining the organic metaphor that runs through *De la Division du travail social,* Durkheim likened antisocial behavior (criminality and other "pernicious occupations") to a cancer that invaded the body and disrupted the operation of its vital forces.[46]

Durkheim harbored no illusions about production following a predetermined course toward some utopia where the "peaceful and regular cooperation of divided functions" reigned. But he rejected the accusation (source unidentified) that the division of labor in modern industry inevitably relegated the worker to the level of a "machine." On the contrary, "The division of labor presupposed that the worker, far from remaining bent to his task, maintains contact with his collaborators and constantly interacts with them. Thus he is not a machine repeating motions of whose purpose he is ignorant, but he knows that they lead in some direction toward an end that he perceives more or less clearly." Under such conditions the worker acted like a "living cell in a living organism, one that vibrates unceasingly in resonance with neighboring cells." Three comments may be made here. First, little distinguishes Durkheim's idealized state of organic harmony at the point of production from Espinas' cohort of whistling workers. Second, workers may not have been turned into machines, but, as Marx pointed out, machines forced the "separation of the intellectual faculties of the production process from manual labor."[47] Third, after taking great pains to demonstrate

46. Turner, "Social Origins of Academic Sociology," 283–84; Philip Abrams, *Historical Sociology* (Ithaca, N.Y., 1982), 27–29; Durkheim, *De la division du travail social,* 343–44; Steven Lukes, *Emile Durkheim: His Life and Work* (New York, 1972), 173.

47. Emile Durkheim, "Deux lois de l'évolution pénale," *Anneé Sociologique,* IV (1901), 403, quoted in Lukes, *Emile Durkheim,* 167; Durkheim, *De la division du travail social,* 363, 365; Karl Marx, *Capital,* ed. Friedrich Engels (3 vols.; New York, 1967), Vol. I, Chap. 15, quote on p. 423.

the natural solidarity between workers and capitalists, separated only by function, Durkheim wound up his study of the division of labor with an exclusive concentration on the mechanical and moral organization of workers; the capitalist as actor disappears.

Yet despite his emphasis on the centripetal forces generated by the division of labor, Durkheim did not believe that it contained any inherent mechanism to produce the highest stage of solidarity. No laissez-faire liberal, he supported social reform from a perspective that resembled that of the social economists, but he went beyond. He considered social reform to be a positive step in and of itself and not an instrument of social control in the crude sense, but he consistently linked it to the development of moral solidarity within the working class. Durkheim's dissatisfaction with the inadequacies of social organization did not extend to capitalist relations as such, only to their dysfunctions, which fueled disorder. The expectation that contractual relations in industry would suffice to support order was an especially dangerous illusion: "The contract is only a truce and a precarious one at that; it merely suspends hostilities for a time." Class distinctions, under such arrangements, remained intact. For reinforcement Durkheim proposed regimentation flexible enough to leave "some room for discord." A practical man unattracted to utopian sirens, he considered it "neither necessary nor even possible that social life be free of struggles." But unlike his socialist enemies, Durkheim located struggle in human nature and not in society, which, by definition, formed a harmonious organism. Hence the political function of solidarity was "not to suppress competition" but to empty it of its class dimension.[48]

It is not clear precisely what sort of regimentation Durkheim had in mind. Early in his career he commented favorably on the schemes of the German social economist Albert Schäffle, who advocated the reconstitution of guilds uniting employers and employees. And in his Sorbonne lectures Durkheim made reference to "moral discipline to provide the necessary regulating influence." According to Steven Lukes, Durkheim considered other modes of discipline as well. He "stressed the need to *introduce* new norms of behavior, above all in the industrial sphere, in the context of occupation associations, and

---

48. Durkheim, *De la division du travail social,* 357.

as part of an extensive reconstruction of the economy." No great imaginative leap is required to follow Durkheim from that position to what Brian Turner called a "corporate vision of social peace," one outlined in the well-known epilogue to *Suicide*.[49]

None of the individuals mentioned above nor those discussed in succeeding chapters attempted an ambitious system on the scale of Durkheim's. Nevertheless, they shared a similar corporate vision and, on the decisive political level, invested social science with the specific mission of designing systems for social management. Because their focus concentrated on the labor question and because they sought to reestablish the reign of order, they necessarily embraced counterrevolutionary strategies—including far-reaching programs for social reform. Paul de Rousiers and Edmond Demolins in 1895 outlined what had to be done. In their manifesto for the creation of the International Society of Social Science, they called for a new method for the study of society. Their sober estimate of the dimensions of the crisis led to plans for an attack across a broad front. They proposed total mobilization: studies of education, agricultural modernization, industrial concentration and mechanization, the productivity of labor, the eclipse of ecclesiastical moral hegemony, and the potential of French colonies to absorb immigrants. These were not designed as mere academic exercises; behind them lay a sense of urgency triggered by social crises, specifically, the "working-class question."[50] By 1895 neither the method nor the purpose was new. The politics of social management was already well established and fundamental to the republican consensus.

49. Emile Durkheim, "Le Programme économique de M. Schaeffle," *REP*, II (1888), 3–7; *Moral Education*, trans. Everett Wilson and Herman Schnurrer (Glencoe, Ill., 1961), 49; *Le Suicide: Etude de sociologie* (Paris, 1897), 378–84; Turner, "Social Origins of Academic Sociology," 344; Lukes, *Emile Durkheim*, 167.

50. Paul de Rousiers and Edmond Demolins, *Société internationale de science sociale: L'Origine, le but et l'organisation* (Paris, 1895), 3–9.

II
Emile Cheysson and the Ideology of Social Engineering

According to the socialist Gustave Rouanet, Emile Cheysson's principal political contribution to social economy was "to rid the doctrine of reactionary extremism, thereby rendering it respectable among bureaucrats and establishment intellectuals."[1] That was no small achievement, considering the murky vapors of right-wing Catholic ideology that surrounded social economy during the years of Le Play's domination of the movement. Cheysson built a bridge between reformers of the original LePlayist dispensation and the social liberalism of republican, solidarist reform. His "great cause," to which he devoted most of his adult life, was the establishment of "harmonious relations between labor and capital, the prevention of class struggle."[2] The success of his efforts depended upon a favorable ideological climate within ruling republican circles, which, in turn, depended upon the urgency with which those circles regarded the social question. The progressive infiltration of social economy into mainstream reform during the last two decades of the century resulted from the impact of increasingly collective and concentrated production on French social relations.

Born and raised in Nîmes, Cheysson moved to Paris, where he attended the Ecole polytechnique, which by that time (the mid-1850s) had become the choice *grande école* for bright and ambitious youths of modest circumstances who aimed toward high positions in business, the state bureaucracy, or both. Cheysson followed that course.

1. *Revue Socialiste,* No. 128 (1895), 223.
2. *Rentier,* February 17, 1910, quoted in Musée social, *Mémoires et documents* (1910), 153.

After advanced civil engineering studies in the Ecole des ponts-et-chaussées he became, in 1859, the chief engineer for the Chemin de fer de l'Est, stationed in Reims. He came to the attention of Le Play, joined his group in the mid-1860s, and worked on the design of the 1867 Paris Exposition under his direction. From that position Cheysson launched a forty-year career as a tireless propagandist for the program of social economy. His connections extended to the worlds of business and politics. Cheysson lectured at the Ecole libre des sciences politiques, at the Ecole des mines, the Ecole des ponts-et-chaussées, and to various engineering societies. He was a key figure in organizing the social economy exhibit at the 1889 Paris Exposition, held high office in the Société de statistique de Paris, and participated in the founding of the Musée social. He was active in dozens of reform associations (108 by one reckoning), including the Ligue nationale de la prévoyance et de la mutualité, the Alliance d'hygiène sociale, the Société française des habitations a bon marché, the Ligue antialcoolique and the Société générale des prisons. Cheysson's entire career, in which he worked over the problems of industrial relations, paternalism, public health, prison reform, family structure, and alcoholism, testified to his preoccupation with the problems of class relations in general and the labor question in particular. He also made substantial contributions to economic theory (Joseph Schumpeter ranked him among the "economists of eminence"), especially in the areas of wage-price calculations and the fiscal consequences of public welfare programs.[3]

Throughout his working life Cheysson remained outwardly faithful to his earliest associations. He regularly invoked the teachings of

3. Ibid., 85–86; Alfred de Foville, "Emile Cheysson," Journal of the Royal Statistical Society (1910), 22–23, Léopold Mabilleau, Opinion, February 12, 1910, both quoted in ibid., 133, 168; Joseph A. Schumpeter, History of Economic Analysis, ed. Elizabeth B. Schumpeter (New York, 1968), 841–42; R. F. Hébert, "The Theory of Input Selection and Supply Areas in 1887: Emile Cheysson," History of Political Economy, VI (1974), 109–31; R. F. Hébert and R. B. Ekelund, Jr., "French Engineers, Welfare Economics, and Public Finance in the Nineteenth Century," ibid., X (1978), 636–68. I am indebted to Lamar Jones for calling my attention to the two articles cited immediately above. On the role of graduates of the Ecole Polytechnique and the Ecole des Mines in the French mining and metallurgical industries, see André Thépot, "Les Ingénieurs du corps des Mines, le patronat et la seconde industrialisation," in Maurice Lévy-Leboyer (ed.), Le Patronat de la seconde industrialisation (Paris, 1979).

the "master" (as Le Play was known to the faithful) much in the manner of the disciple who legitimizes his deviation from the path of the sage by invoking the latter's authority. Cheysson's deviation amounted to the separation of social economy from routine partisan politics, thereby clearing the way for it to realize its higher political mission in the pursuit of order, labor discipline, and "the practices essential to harmonious relations between labor and capital."[4]

Apprenticeship: Manager of Men

For Cheysson, theory began with empirical observation at the point of production. The ideas that later emerged as full-blown prescriptions for paternalism, association, and corporate community first appeared in 1869, modestly but significantly, in a study of *institutions patronales* at Le Creusot as an outgrowth of his work on the Exposition. By an ironic twist, his pamphlet appeared scarcely a year before a wave of strikes rocked that giant metallurgical complex. As we shall see, Cheysson turned this coincidence to personal and professional advantage.

Creusot posed a particular challenge to the social engineer. Big business, as Cheysson observed frequently, changed the terms of the relations between labor and capital and raised the stakes in the maintenance of a loyal and productive work force. "Authoritarian patronage" worked only in small enterprises in which workers and the boss had daily, intimate contact. Large corporations offered neither such opportunity nor such reinforcement; they therefore required institutional solutions. His approach was eminently practical, befitting a graduate of the Ecole polytechnique and the Ecole des ponts-et-chaussées. He made it clear at the outset that the company's efforts to elevate its labor force's "material and moral level" made good

---

4. Emile Cheysson, "Cours d'économie politique," *Journal des Economistes,* 4th ser., XX (1882), 360. A full bibliography of Cheysson's 546 books, articles, speeches, statistical compilations, and reports can be found in Alfred de Foville (ed.), *Emile Cheysson: Oeuvres choisies* (2 vols.; Paris, 1911). Cheysson has received almost no attention from historians of French social reform and social science. Terry N. Clark, *Prophets and Patrons* (Cambridge, Mass., 1973), mentions him only briefly; Jacques Duroselle, *Les Débuts du catholicisme social en France, 1822–1870* (Paris, 1951), not at all; and Georges Weill, *Histoire du mouvement social en France* (Paris, 1911), cites him only in two footnotes.

business sense. Improvements in working conditions produced "social harmony," which paid handsome dividends in the "prosperity of the factory." The successes of social engineering showed a return on the balance sheet. As he repeated nearly forty years later, demonstrating rigid consistency as well as unswerving ideological commitment: "Moral forces, including harmonious relations and the well-being and proper organization of the family of workers, are powerful economic weapons; leaving aside sentiment and philanthropy, they go to the heart of basic interests, and their effective manipulation will spell the difference between life or death for an industry. Industrialists have no choice but to harness these moral forces, if they do not want to risk destruction under the blows of foreign competition or paralysis by internal disorder."[5]

Creusot paid higher wages than the average for the French metallurgical industry. That system contained certain manipulative opportunities to the extent that wages were linked to the quality of work, individual output, and the consumption of raw materials. Presumably, healthy competition among workers distracted them from less productive pursuits. During periods of low demand the company maintained normal levels of employment. Whatever losses it may have incurred (and these were bound to be minimal because workers went on short time during slack periods) were more than compensated for by the "services rendered by a disciplined and devoted laboring population" that displayed "touching solidarity."[6]

The Schneiders' good works did not end at the factory gates but extended to provision of low-rent housing, cheap and wholesome food supplied at the company store, and durable clothing available at the same place. Creusot ran schools for workers' children and for workers themselves, although contrary to the impression Cheysson gives, only a small number (230 out of a labor force of 15,000) regularly attended industrial training sessions. Nevertheless, industrial courses provided a mechanism whereby the company recruited

5. Emile Cheysson, *La Prévention des accidents* (Paris, 1893), 9; Cheysson, *Le Creusot: Condition matérielle, intellectuelle et morale de la population; institutions et relations sociales* (Paris, 1869), 1–2, 14; Cheysson, *Le Devoir social et la formation sociale du patron* (Paris, 1905), 8; *Exposition 1889*, II, 427–36.

6. Cheysson, *Le Creusot*, 22–29; Karl Marx, *Capital*, ed. Friedrich Engels (3 vols.; New York, 1967), I, 241.

workers into higher job grades on the basis of classroom performance. Those rewards depended on acceptable behavior as well as
successful examinations. This remarkable system, Cheysson thought,
"contributes enormously to . . . respect for authority." Totaling up
the moral score, he found the results commensurate with Creusot's
efforts. Workers displayed a pattern of high fertility, and the crime
rate, especially "outrages against modesty, adultery, and other of-
fenses against public morals," stood at a gratifyingly low level.[7]

Yet it appears that Cheysson had been whistling in the dark. Two
massive strikes closed down the blast furnaces in 1870. Specific workers' demands quickly escalated into a full range of grievances and
developed a pronounced political tone. Its authority challenged,
Creusot's management did not back down. Police and troops helped
break the second strike (the first had ended in a standoff) and delivered its leaders to the courts for judgment.[8]

No record exists of Cheysson's reaction to the violent disruption
of the Schneiders' paternal paradise, although his subsequent work
indicates that he did not settle for easy answers, such as blaming socialist agitators—as was the habit of others. Moreover, he soon found
himself in a position to apply principles to practice. Opportunity
frequently springs from adversity. So it was for Emile Cheysson,
whom Creusot's boss, Eugène Schneider, hired as managing director
in 1871 to "restore order and discipline in the factories." According to
Alfred de Foville, Cheysson found in Schneider a kindred spirit
whose dedication to the well-being of his workers provided the "best
foundation for industrial prosperity." Cheysson, for his part, considered Creusot a "great laboratory" in which to conduct his social experiments. There he learned "to manage the world of work" and to
promote the "solidarity of capital and labor."[9]

Cheysson moved along several fronts simultaneously, expanding

7. France, Ministère du commerce et de l'industrie, Conseil supérieur de l'enseignement technique, *Rapport sur l'enseignement technique* (Paris, 1885), 13; Cheysson, *Le
Creusot*, 8–17.

8. Fernand L'Huillier, *La Lutte ouvrière en France à la fin du Second Empire* (Paris, 1957),
37–55.

9. Alexandre Gibon, "La Grève de Carmaux: La Conciliation et l'arbitrage dans l'industrie," *RS*, XXV (1893), 260–80, 340–56, 515–33; Foville (ed.), *Emile Cheysson*, I, 23–24;
Paul Delombre, in *Temps*, February 9, 1910, quoted in Musée social, *Mémoires et documents*
(1910), 123–26.

tenfold the company's primary and technical school network, developing a company-run pension fund, and taking a direct role in the adjudication of workers' grievances. During his three years at Creusot, Cheysson played to the hilt the role of the benevolent manager, adopting the standard paternal psychology that perceived workers as "credulous and guileless," unselfish and unstinting in their comradeship, and thus prey to the "insidious sophisms of agitators."[10] Like children, workers required both constant attention and encouragement in the management of their affairs to turn them from the paths of mischief. Creusot remained for Cheysson a model of the terrain on which the battles for association, social peace, and corporate community would be won or lost. To that end he shaped the theoretical concerns of social science to support the tactics of social engineering within a political strategy for the containment of class antagonism.

The experience at Le Creusot taught Cheysson some important lessons about class relations and class struggle that he would not forget. Unlike his contemporaries in the liberal republican establishment of the 1870s and early 1880s, he did not attempt to bury the social question beneath a heap of rhetoric. Nor did he hide behind ritualistic pronouncements denying the existence of classes. To the contrary, Cheysson's entire theoretical output as well as his political action for social reform rested on a conception of social relations that fixed both labor and capital in their respective places. Classes surely existed, but their relationship was one of an interdependent hierarchical order rather than a state of perpetual struggle. That order did not emerge automatically. It had to be defined and imposed—an essentially political task. Once order had been established, workers and employers could join together in solidarity under the banner of national unity rather than confront each other under the clouds of class antagonism.[11]

Back in Paris and comfortably situated in a well-paid high bureaucratic position (engineer in chief of Ponts-et-Chaussées), Cheysson turned his attention to the elaboration and propagation of "all the

---

10. The school network apparently included those set up at the Schneiders' coal mines in La Machine (Nièvre) in 1871 (Ecoles industrielles privées, F^{12} 4766, AN); quote in Foville (ed.), *Emile Cheysson*, I, 29.

11. Foville (ed.), *Emile Cheysson*, II, 95.

sciences that have as their object the study of man in society." Social economy formed the foundation of all those sciences, including sociology, because it provided both the ideological and the instrumental apparatus for the management of social relations. Social economy, as Cheysson and others argued, represented a new stage—beyond political economy—brought about by the changing character of social relations. Unlike political economy, it held fast to no rigid principles except, of course, the natural primacy of capital; and, again unlike political economy, it more or less openly confronted the political implications of social questions stemming from the collective organization of production. That was why social economy's prescriptions, despite their corporatist and antiliberal ideological shell, found an increasingly receptive audience among social liberals. And why not? As Cheysson said in 1889, careful social management paid off in society's ability to navigate successfully between the Scylla of "revolutionary socialism" and the Charybdis of "state socialism."[12]

From Marketplace to Workplace

For Cheysson, the lessons of Creusot were reinforced by the proceedings of the first post-Commune Congrès ouvrier held in Paris in 1876. The congress was a tame affair even when viewed from the perspective of those who regarded the resurrection of the workers' movement with near hysteria. Not until the congress of 1879 did the stalwarts of class struggle, led by Jules Guesde, lay claim to working-class leadership—and then only at the cost of splitting the movement. Nevertheless, the congress provided Cheysson with the opportunity to introduce several themes on social reform, variations of which he and other social economists and their collaborators in business and politics would develop for the next thirty years.[13]

12. Cheysson, "Cours d'économie politique," 360; Cheysson, *La Lutte des classes* (Paris, 1893), 26; *Exposition 1889*, II, 357.

13. Daniel Ligou, *Histoire du socialisme en France* (Paris, 1962); Georges Lefranc, *Histoire du mouvement ouvrier français* (Paris, 1963). The ideological roles of French businessmen were probably greater than those of their counterparts in Britain, Germany, and the United States. This observation raises doubts about Theodore Zeldin, *France, 1848–1945* (2 vols.; Oxford, 1973–77), I, 1–8, 427–33, who argues that intellectuals defined the terms of political discourse.

In a report on the congress delivered to the Société d'économie sociale, Cheysson drew the line between the politics of social science and the politics of socialism. The movement for social peace took its inspiration and its program, he argued, from the dispassionate investigations of social science and thereby found the way between bourgeois complacency and perpetual class antagonism. He contrasted the agitation of working-class leaders with the work of the social economists and their bourgeois collaborators within and without the Société. Whereas the former fed on class antagonism and aimed only at intensifying class struggle, the latter sought "to bridge the gap that separates [workers] from the ruling classes *[classes dirigeantes]*" in the spirit of "the law of harmony and of solidarity" according to which "are united the various members of a single great family."[14]

Here Cheysson struck a note that appears to suggest the effects of a LePlayist hangover (the "master," no doubt, was in the audience). Le Play considered the extended family the bedrock of society; but he also used the familial image to describe an essentially corporate, hierarchical organization of industry. He regularly held up as examples of responsible patriarchy those industrialists who exercised tight control over their workers, provided them with cradle-to-grave benefits, and fought unions. It is to this image, with its clear political complexion, that Cheysson referred and to which he held. In his report on patronage at the social economy display at the 1889 Paris Exposition, Cheysson characterized the world of bosses and workers as the "industrial family." Far from signaling an attempt to revive prebourgeois or preindustrial conceptions of patriarchy, the invocation of "family" was a rhetorical device to provide a familiar metaphor for the formulation of a thoroughly modern model of paternalism in the workplace to replace the dog-eat-dog model of political economy's marketplace.[15] "Solidarity," a term not usually associated with the right-wing social economists, easily fit this ideological framework, hence the congruence between them and social liberals at the end of the century.

14. Emile Cheysson, *Les Ouvriers et les réformes nécessaires* (Paris, 1877), 6, 44–45.
15. *Exposition 1889,* II, 368; Emile Cheysson, "La Monographie d'atelier," *RS,* XXXII (1896), 780.

Political economy, Cheysson agreed, had explained and legitimized with particular cogency and force the competitive struggles in the marketplace, and it validated a liberalism that reproduced those struggles in the political arena. For those very reasons, however, political economy was ideologically ill-suited to provide for the politics of social peace in a world increasingly dominated by collective production. Moreover, the impact of the Great Depression on the French economy during the 1880s and early 1890s—falling prices and shrinking profits—raised questions about the validity of orthodox political economy's "laws." The crisis produced not only the inevitable shakedown of weak enterprises—an outcome fully consistent with political economy's commandments—but generated pressures for combination, concentration, and tighter control over production. These developments, whether inevitable or not, had the effect of breaking down barriers to capital accumulation by channeling unprecedented power into the hands of the industrial bourgeoisie. That was the good news; the bad news was that they also threatened unremitting social warfare. That is where corporate social reform with its vision of harmony and class collaboration came in. It appeared to offer an ideology upon which peace in the workplace could be maintained. But the failure to transform that vision into reality threatened to open the door to political reaction in two sequential steps: first, by encouraging employers to resort to authoritarian rule thinly disguised as instrumental social management; and second, by setting up a confrontation between militant labor and militant capital. Although social economists maintained a deep distrust of state intervention in industrial relations, they would, under such conditions, be forced to call upon it to join the battle. Cheysson's associate Georges Picot, a historian turned social reformer, put the matter bluntly: "Neither constitutional forms nor politics as usual" had much impact on vital social questions. "The law should facilitate the creation of collective entities that promise to bring classes together."[16]

Cheysson distinguished between the laws of political economy, which remained unchallenged, and the consequences of their opera-

16. Cheysson, *La Lutte des classes*, 27; *Les Ouvriers*, 9; Georges Picot, *La Lutte contre le socialisme révolutionnaire* (Paris, 1895), 9–13, 47–57.

tion within the industrial community. Political economists surrendered too quickly before the forward march of economic laws and
considered the rights of employers—which he did not dispute—
apart from their implication for social relations. They "accept with
easy resignation the miseries which they do not suffer . . . and neglect the moral forces and the human element that operate behind
pure economic factors." Social economy, with its concern for
producers rather than production, did not so much offer an alternative to political economy as provide a system of social management for a world governed by the laws of capitalist production. It
was on this basis that, later on, the sociologist René Worms characterized social economy as "political economy infused with the principles of sociology." Worms, like Cheysson, carefully separated the
social question from the fundamentals of social relations.[17]

In a lecture on political economy at his friend Emile Boutmy's
Ecole libre des sciences politiques in 1882, Cheysson continued to
keep his distance from the classical mode: "Each century makes its
mark on history through its dominant characteristic. As for our
own, which soon will run its course, and which, from the perspective of material progress, may be labeled the age of steam and electricity, it is characterized, on the moral level, by a preoccupation
with the internal organization of societies. It is the century of social
questions." Cheysson was no historian. But that did not prevent him
from understanding, on the basis of experience, that the great "science of wealth," which had appeared—not accidentally—simultaneously with the appearance of "labor as a factor in social relations,"
provided dangerously thin ideological ice for a world in which "the
division of labor demanded social cooperation." Political economy,
in other words, offered no effective political weapons with which to
enforce "peace in social relations." To the contrary, in "complex societies," whose normal condition was "instability," the attainment of
class harmony could not be left to the operation of "automatic and
spontaneous principles."[18] In essence, his argument reduced to a
recognition that the ideology spawned in the marketplace could not,

17. Cheysson, *Les Ouvriers,* 57–58; René Worms, "L'Economie sociale," *RIS,* VI (1898),
461, 463.
18. Cheysson, "Cours d'économie politique," 351, 353, 356–57, 374.

in and of itself, act as an effective instrument of hegemony in the modern workplace. Social economy, ideologically adapted to collective production and big business, provided just such an instrument.

The social responsibilities of employers figured prominently in the social economists' prescriptions for reform. Unlike their British and American counterparts—Fabians and Progressives—they were suspicious of state intervention and accepted it only as a last resort or as an instrument to facilitate corporate industrial organization. That meant the injection of large doses of paternalism into the industrial community, particularly as impersonal corporations were displacing single-owner enterprises in which "authoritarian *patronage*" had enforced social peace. Cheysson worried mightily about what he called the "moral" implications of industrial concentration. In 1884, at one of the fortnightly sessions of the Société d'économie politique (the French equivalent of the Cobden Club), he expressed deep concern over the decline of small industry, which, despite its stone-age technology, had the virtue of "stability born of mediocrity"; it suffered neither "booms nor crises, neither strikes nor unemployment." Big industry, admittedly, played a socially essential role in the expansion and modernization of production. But society paid a heavy price for its products, because labor was reduced to the "endless repetition of identical tasks" and the capitalist elevated to unchallenged command of the process of production. Instead of social peace, society found itself confronted by class antagonism. Yet, as the doyen of political economists Emile Levasseur sardonically pointed out at the same session, the economist's business was to observe the facts, not to deplore or to celebrate their consequences. Cheysson agreed, but insisted on the higher claims of "social health." The question remained as to what variety of social politics was suited to meet those claims, or, put another way, how to manage the social dimensions of a necessary transformation so that the entire system did not self-destruct.[19]

Only paternalistic management in large companies could "avert the dangers of legal [state] intervention." The "wind that blows in from Germany" (state-regulated welfare programs), Cheysson argued, "carries with it socialism." As an example of the coming storm

19. *Exposition 1889,* II, 427–36; *Journal des Economistes,* 4th ser., XXVIII (1884), 308–23.

he pointed to a law of 1889 making workmen's compensation obligatory. Such measures simply reinforced the reflexive selfishness of employers, which Cheysson acknowledged despite his professed confidence in their qualifications to act as "social authorities." Employers, he argued, who fixed their gaze exclusively on the bottom line of the balance sheet and who mocked "humanitarian gestures"—restrictions on female and child labor, limitations on the hours of work, measures taken to improve working conditions—because they allegedly did nothing but increase costs, confused their short-term interest in profits with their long-term interest in a well-ordered and harmonious enterprise. Paradoxically, these same "egoistic employers" called for obligatory reform, "that is, state socialism," the consequences of which would be to submit everyone to the same tyranny and eliminate the essential ingredient in the recipe for industrial peace: a loyal and deferential work force.[20]

Despite the difficulties posed by the proliferation of big companies, Cheysson insisted that the *patron* or the manager retain the closest possible ties with his labor force. He conceded no contradiction between efficient management and the personal touch: the *patron* "has close knowledge of his workers. He interests himself in their affairs, without excessive familiarity, but with goodwill; he knows them personally and addresses them by name; he provides them with personal services and they seek his advice when in difficulty; he shares their joys and their sorrows; he looks them in the eye in a demonstration of respect without seeking popularity and without in the least weakening discipline; he is repaid by their goodwill. When he leaves [the shop] he receives respectful and friendly goodbyes; he lives in an atmosphere of confidence and peace." Ideally, this paternal relationship would be routinized from the top to the bottom of the industrial hierarchy.[21] But that required jettisoning certain ideological baggage.

Cheysson's perspective on, and contribution to, an ideology of paternalism grew out of his criticism of market relations. Those relations had produced an unhealthy moral climate for workers and *patrons* alike. The former fell prey to socialist agitators; the latter risked becoming callous and corrupt, a condition that would render them

---

20. *Exposition 1889*, II, 446–50.
21. *Ibid.*, 446.

unable and unfit to exert authority within the industrial family. As an example, Cheysson pointed to the cavalier attitude taken by many employers toward the problem of cyclical unemployment. Perhaps with Creusot's policy in mind, he denounced blind adherence to what he called the "English theory," which accepted unemployment as an inevitable consequence of market forces and "which concerns itself exclusively with raw materials and machinery while regarding as a total abstraction human tools." Moreover, employers who regarded with suspicion scientific determinations of working-class attitudes—a necessary precondition of effective reform—took a dangerously shortsighted view of their basic interests: "These measures [of reform] are designed to enlist the collaboration of workers" with their bosses "without prejudicing the interests of other classes."[22]

Class Struggle and Social Reform

No decisive break with political economy was required to pursue the politics of class collaboration through social reform. The habits of laissez-faire, however, did stand in the way of such politics and had to be discarded, as did the tendency of workers to deal with employers on the basis of mutual antagonism—that is, class struggle. Reform in the workplace required cooperation and association without challenging the fundamentals of property relations. Capital lay "at the foundation of civilization." The "real friends of the people should welcome its increase" both because "it liberates us from the threat of constant need" and promotes the upward mobility of talented children from "the most humble families." Thus it followed that "labor has the most immediate interest in the development of capital. Capital and labor are bound together in solidarity." Likewise, employers who encouraged associations "do not do so strictly from philanthropic motives; rather they respond to calculated interest. They know that, if the needs of the worker and his family are not met, he becomes embittered, unstable, and that these discontents . . . translate into friction, upheaval, and blows that bring the industrial machinery to a standstill."[23]

The extent to which Cheysson's strictures found a favorable recep-

22. Cheysson, *Les Ouvriers*, 7–8, 35.
23. Cheysson, *La Lutte des classes*, 10; Foville (ed.), *Emile Cheysson*, II, 110–13.

tion in the boardrooms of big business will be examined in detail in Chapter IV. But clearly his message was reaching France's corporate leaders. The chairman of the department of the Nord's delegation to the social economy section of the 1889 Paris Exposition reported that "the heads of our industries [textiles, mining, metallurgy], those that have become so extensive as to depend on the science of political and social economy, must control their masses of workers and . . . create benevolent associations which assure cooperation and the smooth functioning of production." At the 1894 Lyon Exposition, the jury reporting on the social economy section noted local employers' efforts to divert workers from the paths of socialism and communism. Those efforts included company-sponsored associations and the payment of premiums for extraordinary productive efforts. These measures were applied mostly to large enterprises whose workers tended to be "lost in the crowd." Employers benefited directly by claiming a "moral right to control the amounts disbursed and to supervise the pace of work." The jury included the banker Edouard Aynard, the president of the Lyon chamber of commerce and of the Société d'économie politique et sociale de Lyon, the industrialist Auguste Isaac, and Cheysson himself.[24]

Despite this good news and Cheysson's exhortations to employers to "double as social engineers," he did not believe the tasks of paternal organization could be left exclusively in their hands. The job might better be shared with experts schooled in "social science" and in "the organization and direction of social mechanisms," who were prepared to install those "institutions designed to harmonize the interests of workers with those of the factory." In an article entitled "Engineers and Workers," a civil engineer named Polenceau made an exceptionally clear case for social engineering: "The engineer has charge of souls . . . we stand between capital and labor; our job is to teach capital the hard truths of labor's struggle for existence, to demonstrate where its true interests lie. The devotion of our personnel

24. Léon Say, *Exposition universelle internationale de 1889. Groupe d'économie sociale: Rapport général* (Paris, 1891), 55; Auguste Isaac, "Le Patronage à l'exposition de Lyon," *RS*, XXXIII (1897), 158–61, 170. For more on Isaac, see Annie Kriegel, *Aux Origines du communisme français* (2 vols.; Paris, 1964), I, 459, and M. Moissonnier and A. Boulmier, "La Bourgeoisie lyonnaise aux origines de l'Union civique de 1920?" *Cahiers d'histoire de l'Institut de recherches marxistes*, XXXVIII (1981), 124–31.

will be greater, its zeal for work will be stimulated; it will want to perform well so as to win our approval because it will sense in us a *patron* who loves, esteems, and cares for his workers; and [in the end] capital will profit enormously."[25]

Social engineering, as Hayek has reminded us, followed in the footsteps of the oldest tradition of social science. An enduring faith in the objective quality of facts, their accumulation, and their application to moral and social improvement—all characteristics of the Enlightenment—could be turned from revolutionary to counter-revolutionary purposes. An agent of bourgeois political liberation from a feudal straitjacket could become an agent of bourgeois social defense against potential disorder. For Cheysson the threat of disorder stemmed from two sources: the concentration of factory production and the political emancipation of the working class. Neither could be reversed. The worker, cut off from the attachments formed in the family workshop or "uprooted from the land," found himself locked into "enormous agglomerations" in which he functioned "only partially as a man" whose "tasks are precisely regulated by the machine that he operates and by the technical demands on labor."[26] (Cheysson understood his world far better than his younger contemporary Emile Durkheim.) Political emancipation—universal suffrage and the right of workers to associate in *syndicats*—posed a serious danger to the social order because workers were only imperfectly integrated into the processes of social production and therefore did not identify their own interests and well-being with those of capital.

According to his closest associates, Cheysson invented the term and the function of "social engineer" in response to a pressing need to work out the complicated mechanisms essential to the "solidarity of capital and labor." The social engineer acted as a "manager of men," whose primary task was to forge the tools of industrial integration and to provide for the management of "daily life in the shop,

25. Emile Cheysson, "Le Rôle social de l'ingénieur," *RS*, XXXIV (1898), 522; *Les Assurances ouvrières: Leçon d'ouverture à l'Ecole libre des sciences politiques, le 15 novembre 1892* (Paris, 1894), 14–15; *RS*, XXXVII (1899), 715–16.

26. Friedrich von Hayek, *The Counterrevolution of Science* (Glencoe, Ill., 1964), Chap. 2; Emile Cheysson, *Discours prononcé à l'assemblée générale de la société amicale des anciens élèves de l'Ecole polytechnique, le 24 janvier 1904* (Paris, 1904), 3, 7.

the details of the organization of labor, instead of limiting himself to an exclusive preoccupation with costs and returns."[27]

Cheysson first had noticed the employment of social engineers to monitor the labor force in a steel plant in Delft (the Netherlands). By the early twentieth century the practice had been adopted in France, primarily in several eastern and central metallurgical complexes whose management hired young engineers to amass social facts such as the circumstances surrounding strikes. They also gathered intelligence on the shop floor, mixing with workers and, in one case, joining the production line for a year. Occasionally, even the wives of industrialists acted as social engineers. Madame Léon Lévy, wife of the managing director of Commentry-Châtillon, organized commissaries, laundries, and vocational training for workers' wives. Cheysson's favorite social engineer was Georges Benoît-Lévy, a consultant to several companies on working-class housing. Benoît-Lévy assigned to the social engineer the primary task of "suppressing strikes. He creates workers who are more intelligent, physically fit, and content with their lot"—in other words, an aristocracy of labor. From this point of view, which was becoming increasingly common among businessmen and politicians—social reform reduced to the manipulation of social mechanisms. The task took on particular urgency because of the tendency of big industries to attract "peasants," to turn them into workers overnight, and, in the process, to create an "overheated mass" of men that constituted a "powerful thrust toward collective action." Industrial prosperity, therefore, depended in large measure on the manager's ability to seal off unskilled workers from unacceptable political influences.[28]

The invisible hand of laissez-faire gave way to the velvet glove of social science. Cheysson underlined the decisive importance of direct observation and the accumulation of social facts in the proper approach to social questions. As long as political economy dealt in abstractions such as the "exclusive study of wealth," it could not cope with those questions. But, transformed and committed to the

27. Musée social, *Mémoires et documents* (1910), 93, 126; Cheysson, *Discours prononcé*, 8; Cheysson, "Le Rôle social de l'ingénieur," 524.

28. Musée social, *Annales* (1907), 109–12; Cheysson, *Le Devoir social*, 3–5, 14–15; Cheysson, *Les Questions ouvrières* (Paris, 1892), 5–6.

"study of conditions that produce the well-being, the peace and the life of the greatest number," political economy turned itself into "social economy."[29] Serious and durable reform, the first line of social defense, rested on the discovery of "social laws" derived from elaborate statistical studies and regularly published in the journal of the Société de statistique de Paris, in which Cheysson was a leading figure. These studies focused on unemployment, wages, poverty (which Cheysson called a "pathological state"), housing, and alcoholism. The proliferation of such investigations during the last two decades of the century did not happen by accident. One encounters in them an obsessive concern for the sources of disorder and for the reforms necessary to establish social peace.[30] Pure statistical studies, which Cheysson considered to be the business of the state, did not in themselves yield a social benefit. At best they provided raw materials for the monograph—a detailed, almost anthropological, examination of families. Monographs were not the product of bureaucrats "who saw more but not better"; rather, they were produced by dedicated "savants" such as Le Play and himself, whose concerns focused on social questions and on the "moral and economic life of the people."[31]

These somewhat intrusive investigations into private realms were sharp "instruments of social peace" and formed part of the overall strategy of social economy to provide the "general patterns to be followed by industrialists" within the framework of the "freedom of labor and association." The purpose of scientific inquiries into the conditions of working-class life and labor—the "social machinery," in Cheysson's words—was to "understand how to manage workers and to satisfy their needs in order to obtain from them a happy and devoted collaboration, instead of facing discontented and bitter collaborators" who always "stood ready to deliver some hard blows to the employer." Cheysson did not shrink from delivering this mes-

29. Cheysson, *Les Questions ouvrières*, 12–16; Cheysson, "La Monographie," 635.

30. See, for instance, Octave Dumesnil and Edouard Mangenot, *Etude d'hygiène et d'économie sociale: Enquête sur les logements, professions, salaires et budgets* (Paris, 1899); Adolphe Coste, *Hygiène sociale contre le pauperisme* (Paris, 1882); Emile Chevallier, *Les Salaires au xix siècle* (Paris, 1887).

31. *RS*, XXX (1895), 640–44. Cheysson borrowed the last quotation from the director-general of statistics of the Kingdom of Italy.

sage directly to workers, albeit in somewhat different terms. To employees of the Piat machinery works in Paris he preached order and collaboration: "In order to be viable and healthy, industry needs peace in the workplace. Today this peace has become an essential condition for industrial success as well as for the well-being of working-class families. The day when this truth is accepted will mark the end of internal struggles, which are disastrous for workers, employers, the country, and only play into the hands of foreigners."[32] Not for the first time, nor the last, national solidarity was invoked against internal class antagonism and in support of the corporate association that lay at the heart of paternalism.

Home and Hearth

Cheysson's departure from the conventional wisdom of midcentury social economy emerged less sharply in his comments on the family and on women. In his frequent references to domestic life and work Cheysson took as his starting point the fixed division of labor characteristic of modern industrial economies. He situated the family and the *foyer domestique* within that system. Far from conceiving of the family as a refuge from the brutal world of the factory and the market, Cheysson placed it squarely at the center of that world. The family was the key to the social question, and on its "proper constitution" depended "peace in the workplace." In Cheysson's view the working-class family had fallen on hard times. It had suffered a "growing disorganization" through the century. State intervention had only compounded old errors with new ones as it created "all kinds of costly, burdensome, and encumbering organisms."[33] In the presence of that failure, the family, like all other collective institutions, required the expertise of the social engineer.

As the "true social molecule" and the "primordial association" validated by "natural law," the family supposedly constituted the foundation of the social hierarchy. Cheysson recognized no contradiction

32. Cheysson, *Les Assurances ouvrières*, 5; Cheysson, *Les Questions ouvrières*, 7–17; Cheysson, "La Monographie," 791; Cheysson, *Le Capital et le travail* (Paris, 1885), 27.

33. *Exposition 1889*, II, 370; Foville (ed.), *Emile Cheysson*, II, 9.

between a variety of prebourgeois relationships and the quintessential bourgeois relationship of the cash nexus. Nor, given his manipulative and instrumental approach to all forms of social life, should he have. In a capitalist economy, the family provided a core of moral reinforcement for the worker, who spent most of his waking hours in the corrupting atmosphere of the factory, the mill, or the mine. Morality, however, had a higher purpose that transcended its own rewards: "Public prosperity or decadence hangs on the solidity of the family or its weakness." Idealization of family life combined with hard-headed pragmatism: "The family owns its home; it cultivates its fields; it has no debts; it is sober; it saves; it has an abundance of legitimate offspring and nearly no bastards; it does not go out on strike." Thus Cheysson supported a combination of employers' funds and mutual aid societies designed to alleviate workers' anxiety by providing retirement benefits. Because only family men qualified for such programs the incentive to marry and settle down was powerful.[34]

However well constituted, the working-class family had little chance of fulfilling its social mission unless properly housed. This problem impelled business leaders and conservative reformers such as Jules Siegfried and Georges Picot—collaborators with Cheysson in the Musée social (see Chapter IV)—to promote the construction of cheap and salubrious workers' housing. Their purpose, in Siegfried's words, was "to combat misery and socialism." First publicized in a Congrès international des habitations ouvrières in the 1889 Paris Exposition, the movement blossomed soon after into the Société française des habitations à bon marché.[35]

Cheysson took a keen interest in workers' housing and collaborated with Picot in a survey of the subject sponsored by the Société d'économie sociale in 1887. Referring to the home as the working-class family's "shell or its nest," he argued that its quality decisively

---

34. Emile Cheysson, *L'Homme social et la colonisation* (Paris, 1897), 7–9; *Exposition 1889*, II, 362–67; Emile Cheysson, *La Division du travail entre les divers facteurs sociaux* (Paris, 1904), 15–17.

35. Jules Siegfried, *La Misère, son histoire, ses causes, ses remèdes* (Paris, 1879), 195–99; *Exposition 1889*, II, 181–228; R.-H. Guerrand, *Les Origines du logement social en France* (Paris, 1967), 271–306.

influenced family, and, by extension, social stability. "If one considers [the house] from the social point of view, it ceases to appear as a simple material construction of bricks, stones, and framework and becomes a kind of extension of the family's personality." With his characteristic passion for collecting data on many subjects, Cheysson ranged far afield—indeed, across the ocean. In Dayton, Ohio, he found in the National Cash Register Company (NCR) the ideal "industrial home" run by "social engineers." Information on NCR's housing and other good works came from William Howe Tolman, the American self-styled social engineer, with whose writings Cheysson was familiar and who had addressed several meetings of the Société d'économie sociale. Cheysson quoted Tolman with approval more than once and was particularly attracted by his hard-headed approach to social reform, expressed as follows: "Industrialists have begun to understand that everything that promotes the worker's happiness, contentment, and skills provides a definite boost to business and adds a powerful element to industrial stability."[36]

The existence of slums posed the greatest danger for family stability and public security. Not only did they engender corrupting moral habits—Jules Simon called them the "anterooms of the cabaret"—but they were the breeding ground for an "epidemic of social hatred no less dangerous than tuberculosis or typhoid." Despite his harsh criticism of state intervention, Cheysson recognized its unique ability to provide the empirical foundations for reform. Facts had to be gathered on the current state of housing, and only the government commanded the resources to conduct a survey. Moreover, only the state, in its traditional (for France) role as chief contractor for public works was in a position to "organize efficient and economical transportation" to enable workers, "at the end of the working day, to return to a pleasant home in the suburbs." Finally, the law providing for the compensated expropriation of substandard housing had been subject to abuses, notably in excessive payments to property owners. Cheysson recommended that additional legislation make mandatory deductions from assessed value in the amount necessary to modify

36. *Exposition 1889,* II, 224; Cheysson, *La Division du travail,* 18; Cheysson, *Les Cités-Jardins* (Paris, 1905), 21; William Howe Tolman, *Social Engineering* (New York, 1909), iii.

the dwellings, thereby reconciling "the two fundamental principles of human society: public health and property."[37]

Employers had more stake in property than anyone else, and to them Cheysson assigned the leading role in the construction of working-class housing. He appealed to common sense as well as to self-interest. No employer should expect the "devoted collaboration" of any worker who, "subject to the tortures of miserable housing," fell prey to the "sentiments of hatred against society in general and against the factory in particular." Left to fester, that hatred "will surely manifest itself in 'sabotage' or in strikes." Thus industrialists "must solve this problem to defend their obvious interests as well as to fulfill their social duties." Several courses were open: employers could build houses for workers; supply mortgages to individuals or to cooperative ventures; or form associations of their own to build large projects—*cités ouvrières*. By the time Cheysson had made this pitch for low-cost housing (1906) most working-class housing had been built by individual companies or by associations of employers. The latter defined the pattern among the pioneering reformers of the Mulhouse textile and chemical industries.[38]

Cheysson had very specific views regarding the internal design of houses, which he expounded at great length, even including details about the water closet. He also had strong opinions about external design and setting. Massive tenement blocks such as those built by the London County Council under the inspiration of the social economists' ideological kin, Sidney and Beatrice Webb, were not what Cheysson had in mind. He described a conception of "garden cities" in which each dwelling would be surrounded by a bit of lawn and each cluster of houses by a greensward (*parc*). Such an arrangement purported to reproduce the rural world workers had lost. This modernized version of a bucolic paradise promised to replant the worker's roots in the land, the loss of which "is the principal source of all social ills." To seek prescriptions he, Picot, Siegfried, the politi-

---

37. Foville (ed.), *Emile Cheysson,* II, 338–39, 346–47; *Annales de l'Alliance d'hygiène sociale,* No. 4 (1906), 362–66.

38. Foville (ed.), *Emile Cheysson,* II, 348–49; *Annales de l'Alliance d'hygiène sociale,* No. 4 *bis* (1906), 375; *Exposition 1889,* II, 179–81; Jules Siegfried, *Les Habitations à bon marché* (Paris, 1898).

cal economists Charles Gide and Paul Cauwès, and the director of
the Musée social, Léopold Mabilleau, formed the Association des
cités-jardins de France. According to Benoît-Lévy, France's leading
technical expert on garden cities, they aimed at nothing less than a
wholesale reengineering of urban life: "to change cities as we change
habits."[39]

"What should the new city be?" Benoît-Lévy asked. "It should be
the city of industry." This definition suggests a functional model of
the industrial city based upon that of the factory, or—more perti-
nent to the plans of social engineers—a community that existed as
an extension of the factory and whose inhabitants lived the portion
of their lives apart from the workplace according to the rhythm of
production set by entrepreneurs and managers. New installations
outside established industrial centers best served these purposes.
Cheysson noted that a number of firms had built factories in the
countryside. His old employer, Creusot, constructed an electrical
works in the tiny village (five hundred inhabitants) of Champagne-
sur-Seine. The company projected a population of thousands. The
industrial village was not designed to provide a rural refuge from
industrial work so much as to reinforce the mechanism of labor discipline. Two factors operated. First, rural industrial implantations
isolated workers from their fellows elsewhere and enabled employers
to develop strategies for social domination both on and off the job.
Second, agricultural labor, if only on a small scale, provided a diversion and consumed energy, practices, Cheysson wrote, quoting Le
Play, "essential to peace in the workshop." Cheysson also quoted
Jules Méline's celebrated *Retour à la terre*, signaling a certain meeting of the minds: "When the worker has a small parcel of land close
to the factory which his family can help cultivate, it will be possible
and simple to arrange periods of unemployment to coincide with
those requiring agricultural labor; we may discover that the worker
has more interest in tilling the soil than in working at the factory and
that unemployment will prove to be a positive benefit. Unemployment, under those conditions, can be regulated precisely and will be-

---

39. Foville (ed.), *Emile Cheysson*, II, 361–79; Georges Benoît-Lévy, *La Cité-Jardin*
(Paris, 1904), 249.

come a safety-valve for industry." Méline, of course, neglected to account for market forces in determining employment patterns, but his meaning was clear.[40]

Following a similar path, Cheysson became involved in a campaign to revive rural-based industry. In 1910 (the year of his death) he chaired the Ligue nationale pour le relèvement des industries rurales et agricoles. That organization's purpose was to "reverse the flight from the countryside" and to "strengthen familial ties by refurbishing rural industries." The league, which—in keeping with the spirit of bourgeois solidarity—maintained "absolute political and religious neutrality," distributed small electric motors to power mechanical operations in rural homes. Supplied with these motors, a family was expected to preserve its "solidarity" by working together, wife and daughter alongside the husband.[41] Thus would the contented farmer have the opportunity to escape becoming a discontented worker.

Working-class women usually were found tending gardens and vegetable plots, keeping them at home, where Cheysson insisted they belonged. He sketched the stereotypical portrait of the women: soft, nurturing, and, above all, modest. These qualities were to be admired for themselves and for their social utility, especially because they dissolved male passions and male tendencies toward precipitous action such as strikes. But women were more than merely decorative tamers of the male animal. They played active social roles. As the "keystone of the family" the woman held the responsibility for ordering domestic life. Under her care "the healthy, clean, and cheerful domicile becomes a *home* embellished by female charm and it confines her husband, firmly protected against corrupting influences beyond its portals." Above all, she provides stability in place of disorder and, because sex knows no class, the uniformity of female social obligations "brings together all the women of the world, those of the bourgeoisie and those of the people."[42]

In one of his discussions on "home economics and the social ques-

40. Benoît-Lévy, *La Cité-Jardin,* 250; Cheysson, *Les Cités-Jardins,* 5–13.
41. *RSS* (1910), 12.
42. Cheysson, *Les Ouvriers,* 12–14, 27–33; *RSS* (1906), 433–34. Italicized English word in the original.

tions," Cheysson made his purpose plain. Preceding a detailed outline of the methods for instructing women in household management, he rehearsed a review of the great social dislocations of the time. He regretted the "abyss" that had formed between workers and bosses, the overblown pretensions of workers and their political leaders (socialists), the dangers of strikes, and other assorted social pathogens. Women in this threatening situation were required to take on the responsibility for "social action to contribute to the amelioration of the material and moral condition of workers." Women "held the secret of the alleviation of misery, of the well-being of the worker, of the reconciliation of classes, of social peace, and of the moral unity and greatness of the nation."[43]

None of this happened automatically; proper instruction was required. Prescriptions for household management took predictable form: lessons in child-rearing, budgeting, mending, laundering, hygiene, and care for the sick. These tasks, completed efficiently and lovingly, promised to transform the cold and uninviting *foyer domestique* into a warm center for family sobriety.[44]

Household tasks for working-class women replaced work for wages, whose debilitating consequences for families Cheysson deplored. He attacked particularly the sweating system, which existed everywhere despite government regulation and surveillance, and argued that such regulation contributed to the problem because employers set up small domestic shops to evade the intrusions of government factory inspectors. (Here the particular bent of Cheysson's reformist zeal is exposed; as much as he sounded the alarm about the unregulated marketplace, he did not appear to be troubled by the unregulated workplace.) So he made a virtue of a vice, concluding that only private initiatives could put an end to sweating by promoting good works for male workers so that they did not force their women to work by getting sick, incapacitated, or drunk, and by contributing to the education of working-class women in the routines of their domestic responsibilities. In the end, Cheysson announced, the

43. Foville (ed.), *Emile Cheysson*, II, 313–30; *RSS* (1906), 452.
44. *RSS* (1906), 452; Emile Cheysson, "Discours," *Congrès d'hygiène sociale* (Paris, 1904), 9.

issue was a moral problem, and solutions must be sought at that level. Curiously, the existence of widespread sweating contradicted the LePlayist idealization of small industry for its moral benefits. As Emile Chevalier pointed out at the 1889 Exposition, small industry bred the most unhealthy conditions and thrived on the worst possible exploitation of labor. Economies of scale and other factors enabled big business to afford the good works necessary to keep workers content, productive, and out of trouble. The logic of this argument, of course, led to the cannibalization of small business by large. Cheysson, as we have seen, reluctantly agreed.[45]

Cheysson assigned to women of the upper classes and especially the wives of the industrial bourgeoisie similar roles—albeit from a reverse perspective. Too many women of that class had no sense of their duties as *patronnes* or of the social importance of domestic management. They tended, he alleged, to be frivolous and uncomfortable in an industrial setting and ignorant of the "poetic and lyrical" quality of the domestic occupation and its genuine "moral beauty." Elsewhere, institutions existed to train such women. Cheysson mentioned Simmons College in Boston, the School of Sociology and Social Economy in London, and the School for Social Education in Amsterdam. French women needed similar training as part of their "professional instruction, moral education, and social formation." Thus Cheysson remained rigidly consistent within his general scheme as he conceived of the social role of the bourgeois woman in terms analogous to that of her industrialist husband. He did not give a thought to the possibility that bourgeois women inhabited different psychological universes than their menfolk while sharing the same social universe. He did not expect bourgeois women to play active public roles in social reform—he looked for no French Jane Addams—but he did expect them to acquit their social responsibilities as members of a ruling class.[46]

45. Emile Cheysson, "Le Travail des femmes à domicile," in Foville (ed.), *Emile Cheysson*, II, 383—409; *Exposition 1889*, II, 521—23.
46. Cheysson, *Le Devoir social*, 17—20. For a thorough discussion of the social roles played by upper-class French women in one part of the country, see Bonnie G. Smith, *Ladies of the Leisure Class: The Bourgeoises of the Nord* (Princeton, 1981).

The Politics of Social Economy

Emile Cheysson never entered politics, at least not in the narrow sense of running for office or holding ministerial position. But he was intensely political, consistently approached the problems of social relations from a political perspective, and moved in political circles. Toward the end of his career, in what he called his "social testament," Cheysson explained that the campaign for class collaboration and national corporate unity constituted a politics that necessarily superseded a more traditional sort: "Social action . . . provides us with an oasis, where divisive winds do not blow; a neutral terrain where one can work regardless of one's starting point, free of political and religious differences, in the great patriotic and humanitarian effort." Rather than removing social reform from politics, Cheysson suggested that it become the principal focus of politics in a statement in 1909, when, after several years of ritualized combat pitting church against state, politics took up the more serious business of controlling socialism, labor unrest, and strikes.[47]

In response to the wave of strikes that battered France in the late 1880s and early 1890s, Cheysson saw political opportunities where some of his associates in the Société d'économie sociale reached for their revolvers. Ever vigilant, the Société had monitored the course of the miners' strike at Carmaux in 1892 and produced a report on the events. One commentator clearly saw the strike as a political action. The workers "seem to have no other purpose but to subvert patronal authority and liberty. . . . It is not a question of wages, nor of the length of the working day, but only of an effort to achieve a moral victory over capital." Another, Albert Gigot, formerly prefect of police in Paris and director of the Forges d'Alais, saw in this episode the failure of paternalism and a renewal of irrepressible class warfare. He urged employers and the state to take the harshest measures. The *rapporteur*, Alexandre Gibon, former manager of the Commentry steel works, laid blame for a festering situation on the state and politicians, especially Jean Jaurès, socialist deputy for the Tarn.

47. Foville (ed.), *Emile Cheysson*, II, 7.

Gibon suggested that outside arbitration, as had been tried at Car-maux, was at a dead end and that employers everywhere should pro-mote committees of conciliation at the factory level, which, he said, would have the effect of sealing off workers "from leaders, agitators, politicians, and revolutionary socialists." Cheysson drew the politi-cal conclusions. He claimed that the impulse for such troubles came from the national, indeed international, organization of workers. He proposed to divide and conquer: "Split up the masses, organize them in each factory, and work out arrangements with them to create conciliation boards. These then can be used as one of the means . . . to bridge the gap of social antagonism by [demon-strating] the devotion of employers to their workers."[48]

The political tactics that Cheysson prescribed relied on units already in existence: the dozens of mutual aid societies, savings asso-ciations, and consumer cooperatives, among others, sponsored by several big companies. Although none of them were formally consti-tuted to deal directly with labor/capital relations nor did they or-dinarily operate under overt company control, they did exhibit the quality of corporate association that he believed held out the best hope for social peace. More than sentimental attachments were in-volved, despite Cheysson's repeated invocation of "mutual respect" and "devotion." Referring to the report prepared for the 1889 Paris Exposition by the Compagnie des Mines de Blanzy, which employed nearly six thousand workers, he drew attention to three benefits of association claimed by the company's management: first, workers who engaged in associations were not "ripe for socialism" because they learned self-reliance and the habits of cooperation among them-selves and with management; second, the company could separate the "stalwart types" who worked within the various associations from "agitators and noisy loafers" who did not; and third, premiums paid to senior miners as a reward for high levels of production reached by their crews combined with free rent to those same cadres tended to form an aristocracy of labor within the work-force. In

48. Musée social, *Archives*, 1202 (1), iv; *RS*, XXIV (1892), 466; *RS*, XXV (1893), 534; Alexandre Gibon, "Des Conditions de l'harmonie dans l'industrie," *RS*, XXV (1893), 775–76.

Cheysson's words, such "properly directed associations are the best safety-valve against popular passions" and contribute to the "consolidation of social peace."[49]

Blanzy's system earned Cheysson's approval because the company had departed from traditional patriarchal forms of labor management while maintaining entrepreneurial authority. Subsequent events, however, proved even enlightened paternalism insufficient and showed how paternalism mutated into repression. Jules Chagot, grandson of the company's founder, had exercised absolute authority according to the canon of Catholic patriarchy. The strike of 1882 exposed the bankruptcy of that regime. Control of the company passed first to Chagot's nephew, Léonce, who instituted reforms in the late 1880s, and then in 1893 to Chagot's grand-nephew, Lionel de Gournay, who promised even more paternalist benefits. But Gournay remained in the same familial mold, albeit somewhat modernized. He had studied at a Jesuit *collège* and then traveled to England to learn business. Gournay's efforts were not sufficient to insulate Blanzy from the great strike wave that crested in 1899. Although the strike ended without a clear-cut victory for either labor or management, Gournay was forced to resign by a board of directors that had become impatient with paternalist reform carried out at the expense of stockholders' dividends. He was replaced by Emile Coste, a Protestant *polytechnicien* who appeared to bear all the marks of Cheysson's ideal social engineer. Coste, however, quickly became impatient with a system that required a combination of effective profit-maximizing management and paternalist reform. He was not prepared to buy social peace at the price of compromising the company's profit potential or its absolute authority over its workers. Dedicating himself to productivity in place of paternalism, Coste attempted to make use of Gournay's most important innovation—the installation in 1899 of a yellow union at Montceau-les-Mines to combat the independent miners' *syndicat*.[50]

Yellow unions quickly became commonplace in French industry. A

49. *Exposition 1889*, II, 442–43, 471–75.
50. Léon de Seilhac, *Les Grèves* (Paris, 1903), 193–201; Robert Beaubernard, *Montceau-les-Mines: Un "laboratoire social" au xix siècle* (Avallon, 1981), 103–297.

national network existed by the early 1900s composed of 852 *syndicats* of workers, employers, and farmers. Although not passive tools of capital and capable of displaying great militance on economic issues, yellow unions did not translate those efforts into political struggles against capital. Rolande Trempé notes that workers in the yellow union sponsored by the Société des Mines de Carmaux routinely battled the company over wages and then supported its candidate for the Chamber of Deputies against Jaurès.[51]

Blanzy's yellow union drew on workers who claimed to have gone on strike against their will in 1899 to provide the shock troops to break up any subsequent strike—which they tried and failed to do in 1900. In an effort to expand the yellow union's effectives, the company awarded all workers a 5 percent wage increase at the end of 1899, with the promise of more for those who joined its union. Many took the bait. The union counted fifteen hundred members (roughly 25 percent of the work force) by the end of 1900. Its avowed purpose was to purge "collectivist" or any other politics from the factory and the streets and to "establish with the bosses relations of dignity, discipline and respect." Although the union did not rule out defense of workers' interests, it "encouraged . . . only those demands" judged "serious and grounded in real concerns." The union's manifesto also struck a strong nationalist note. Calling the "reds, men without a country," it proclaimed itself made up of "free laborers organized to defend our national industry against those who play into the hands of England and Germany."[52]

On the national level the program of the Jaunes (as they were called after the yellow placards put up by the union in Montceau) replicated that of Blanzy. It condemned the Revolution of 1789 as "essentially bourgeois," paving the way for the "oppression of the poorest classes," and sought a realignment of class forces through collaboration. Thus socialists, because they preached class struggle and inter-

51. Seilhac, *Les Grèves,* 201; Rolande Trempé, *Les Mineurs de Carmaux* (2 vols.; Paris, 1971), Vol. II, Chap. 5.

52. Marcel Lefranc, *Les Syndicats indépendents du Creusot et de Montceau-les-Mines* (Paris, 1902), 15–26. That the Jaunes would act as instruments of class collaboration was made explicit by a spokesman for the Lille *patronat,* Delcourt-Haillot, "Rouges et jaunes dans la dernière grève," *Action populaire,* No. 7 (1903), 269–300.

nationalism, were the archenemies. Whereas the "reds" were led by "lawyers and teachers, that is, theoreticians and dreamers, the Jaunes' leaders were workers and bosses, that is, professional men." Yellow unions supported "collaboration with employers in order to get rid of the politicians and the agitators who exploit labor by sabotaging factories." Class struggle subverted national production and the "economic organization of our people" necessary to sustain France's competitive position in world markets. The Jaunes called for an *entente cordiale* between workers and employers, which, they claimed, reflected the organic relationship between "manual labor, intellectual labor [management], and capital." Their stated goal was nothing less than *"absolute national harmony."* [53]

Cheysson did not comment directly on yellow unions although he must have been aware of their existence. Perhaps he found the noisy, right-wing, anti-Dreyfusard, and anti-Semitic supporters of yellow unions, such as Pierre Biétry, distasteful to associate with. Cheysson, after all, was no hoodlum. Nevertheless, yellow unions certainly corresponded to his model of a working-class formation well-equipped for the business of class collaboration and corporate solidarity. The Fédération des Jaunes' strident nationalism, militant antisocialism, and appeal to class collaboration paralleled his own political perspective and that of others with whom he was associated, such as Paul Leroy-Beaulieu, a member of the federation's national council.[54] But here again the ideal of class collaboration harbored sinister political implications. Yellow unions, employed by the likes of Emile Coste, who engaged in unremitting warfare against the independent union, only sharpened the class struggle. The handshake of association could easily turn into the fist of reaction.

If Cheysson believed paternalism as it was practiced to be inadequate and to harbor reactionary tendencies, he did not say so. His report on *institutions patronales* displayed in the social economy group at the Paris Exposition of 1889 was filled with boundless opti-

---

53. Pierre Biétry, *Les Jaunes de France et les questions ouvrières* (Paris, 1906), 23, 33–35, 46, 88.

54. Zeev Sternhell, *La Droite révolutionnaire, 1885–1914: Les Origines françaises du fascisme* (Paris, 1978), 285, 313; Seilhac, *Les Grèves*, 202; Charles Gide, *Les Institutions de progrès social* (Paris, 1905), 146n.

mism. Times, however, change. Cheysson's intense involvement in the varieties of social management during the 1890s and early 1900s suggests that, by then, he believed paternalism to be insufficient. Many roads led to the establishment of social authority and social peace. Therefore, it was no accident that he became interested in the cooperative movement.

Cheysson, as well as its other partisans, found producers' and consumers' cooperatives ideal instruments for the association of classes that they all sought. For him, cooperative association promised to liberate the working class and, ultimately, to liquidate classes through the "elimination of the proletariat and the wage system" and the "resolution of the antagonism between capital and labor by means of their mutual interpenetration and mutual identity." Cooperatives captured the imagination not only of social economists such as Cheysson and Charles Gide (who will be discussed in Chapter V), but of solidarist social liberals such as Henry Buisson and Léon Bourgeois. The pages of their organ, the *Revue de la Solidarité Sociale*, regularly featured articles on various aspects of the cooperative movement.[55]

Cheysson appeared at the 1896 congress of the Alliance coopérative internationale held in Paris at the Musée social, of which he was an architect and vice-president. That meeting provided one of the many forums in which men from the worlds of business, politics, and social science shared their common ideological perspective on social reform. Jules Siegfried, pillar of the big bourgeoisie of Le Havre and its political boss, president of the Musée social, philanthropist, social reformer, and conservative republican, presided over the congress. Henry Buisson, another participant, was soon to become secretary-general of the French section of the Alliance, replacing the social economist and proponent of profit sharing, Charles Robert. Joining Buisson and Robert were several individuals who had experimented with the latter's system in their own businesses: the publisher Albert Chaix, the machinery manufacturer Ernest Piat, and the wallpaper manufacturer Laroche-Joubert. Robert Pinot and Paul de Rousiers, both social scientists, big business lob-

---

55. *Exposition 1889*, II, 243; Cheysson, *La Lutte des classes*, 20; Jean Gaumont, *Histoire générale de la coopération en France* (2 vols.; Paris, 1923), II, 549–50; *RSS* (1904–1907).

byists, and directors of the Musée social, also took part in the congress, as did Eugène Rostand (the poet's father) and Charles Rayneri, leading promoters of peoples' savings banks (*crédits populaires*). René Waldeck-Rousseau, future head of the "Government of Republican Defense" and a leading exponent of class collaboration among France's political nobility, participated. The congress received the highest possible benediction in a reception tendered by the president of the Republic, Félix Faure—formerly Siegfried's political lieutenant in Le Havre—at the Elysée Palace. Three years previously, in an attack on the politics of class struggle, which appeared—significantly—in the *Revue Internationale de Sociologie*, Cheysson had referred approvingly to Faure's call for class collaboration delivered at a *banquet populaire* in Le Havre.[56]

Cheysson's connections extended further. His interests in forging a union of classes through association and in the future of French industrial power turned his attention to imperial and colonial ventures. In the early 1890s Cheysson served as chairman of the central committee of the Société de géographie de Paris, one of several French geographic societies whose academic interest in far-off lands provided a useful cover for the promotion of colonial and imperial ventures. He also took part in the Congrès international de sociologie coloniale held in conjunction with the 1900 Paris Exposition and devoted to the examination of the relationships of domination and dependency between the metropolis and the colonies. His collaborators included the Prince d'Arenberg, president of the Comité de l'Afrique française; the colonial publicists Joseph Chailley-Bert and Eugène Etienne; Auguste Isaac; Ernest Lavisse; Pierre Brazza, the explorer; Georges Picot; Jules Siegfried; and Gustave Le Bon.[57] Those social scientists, who like Cheysson were associated with the *Réforme Sociale* and Société d'économie sociale groups, only recently had begun to add their voices to the chorus chanting the *mission civilisatrice*. Earlier, Le Play had objected to colonial ex-

---

56. André Siegfried, *Mon père et son temps* (Paris, 1952), 43–59; Gaumont, *Histoire générale*, II, 648–49; Cheysson, *La Lutte des classes*, 11on.

57. John Laffey, "Les Racines de l'impérialisme français en Extrême-Orient," in Jean Bouvier and René Girault (eds.), *L'Impérialisme français d'avant 1914* (Paris, 1976), 15–37; *Exposition 1900*, Congrès international de sociologie coloniale.

pansion on the grounds that France could not afford to deplete her population. The next generation of social economists argued that colonies needed not manual labor, of which places such as Indochina, the Sudan, and the Congo had an abundant supply, but "businessmen, managers, and overseers of native labor." More fundamentally, they dealt in the social Darwinian "struggle for existence" currency common to imperialist propagandists of the time. Nor did they neglect to emphasize the worldwide competition among European powers, about which they drew freely on the contemporary oracle of political economy, Paul Leroy-Beaulieu's *Economiste Français.*[58]

No stranger to such sentiments, Cheysson routinely referred to the struggle for existence as a fact of human life. Those who sustained that struggle contributed to the "triumph of individualism." This was true among nations as among classes. Although he paid lip service to the constants of human nature and the similarities of diverse peoples, Cheysson focused on the evolutionary process by which different societies reached different levels of "civilization." Rather than eventual equality, this process produced "a growing inequality among the races." From that position it took Cheysson only a short step to argue for a hierarchy of peoples that precisely paralleled the hierarchy of classes. He saw in religion the fundamental test of levels of civilization. Animism, totemism, and fetishism corresponded to the most primitive; monotheism to the most advanced. Among the former, he singled out Islam in sub-Saharan Africa as particularly fanatical and hostile to "our" missionaries.[59]

To buttress his arguments for the importance of empire to internal social cohesion, Cheysson appealed to the authority of Gustave Le Bon, the racist, nationalist, and bitterly antisocialist polemicist. Le Bon, in his enormously popular *Lois psychologiques de l'évolution des peuples,* purported to demonstrate the racial superiority of Europeans and from that proposition derived what he considered to be an ethical justification for imperialism. He was, however, more interested in combating socialism at home, in the service of which he "presumed to use social science to manipulate society" and to forge

58. *RS,* XXXVIII (1899), 338–50; *Le Mouvement social,* I (1892–93), 92, 160.
59. Cheysson, *La Lutte des classes,* 19–20; Cheysson, *L'Homme social,* 3–6.

national solidarity. Le Bon influenced a number of social scientists, including Emile Boutmy, who designed his Ecole libre des sciences politiques to train colonial administrators and political engineers in "conservative, positive, enlightened, and serious" politics.[60] Cheysson did not need Le Bon to instruct him in the politics of social science. But he did borrow Le Bon's historicist justification for the existing order: "The political institutions of a nation reflect both its civilization and the consequences of its history." For that reason Cheysson, like Le Bon, was an opponent of colonial assimilation to the metropolis. Opponents of assimilation, as John Laffey has pointed out, did not necessarily oppose economic exploitation of the colonies, but they did oppose the introduction of French labor law (such as the 1884 law on associations, expanded in 1901) into those colonies where metropolitans managed native labor. What is significant is that Cheysson's view that colonizers should steep themselves in "comparative sociology" and act as "scientific missionaries" replicated his prescriptions for social engineering in domestic industry. The *mission civilisatrice* demanded that colonizers deal with natives in a peaceful manner and "show the flag of France as a symbol, not of oppression or of cruelty, but of freedom, protection, and justice."[61] He had made similar demands on French industrialists.

We turn now to the several manifestations of paternalism as they appeared in response to the collectivization of production, capitalist concentration, and accentuated class antagonism. We will meet Cheysson again, along with other social economists and reformers, social liberals, and solidarist ideologues. What Anatole Leroy-Beaulieu said of Cheysson applied with equal force to the others: "For [him] social science had for its principal goal: social peace! It must work for the reconciliation of men, of classes."[62]

60. Robert A. Nye, *The Origins of Crowd Psychology* (London, 1975), 51–53; Emile Boutmy, *Projet d'une Faculté libre des sciences politiques* (Paris, 1871), 11; Boutmy, *Le Recruitment des administrateurs coloniaux* (Paris, 1895).

61. Cheysson, *L'Homme social*, 12, 14–19.

62. Musée social, *Mémoires et documents* (1910), 99.

III
Profit Sharing, or the Wages of Virtue

During the last decade of the nineteenth century the intensity of confrontation between labor and capital increased sharply. Social peace seemed beyond the calculations of the most earnest reformers, beyond the ability of the most single-minded social scientists, and beyond the grasp of the most resourceful businessmen. France was not alone in undergoing the stresses of class struggle. The United States, in 1894 alone, registered 1,394 strikes, of which the Pullman strike remains the most famous. For businessmen and their collaborators, the search for the principles and elements of social order became a matter of urgent concern. One businessman believed that he had found at least part of the answer. In 1902, Elbert H. Gary, chairman of the United States Steel Corporation, pronounced the following benediction on profit sharing and employee stock ownership plans: "They make the wage earner an actual partner . . . a real capitalist . . . [who will] have as keen a desire to see the institutions of this country protected as those who have greater riches, and [who] may be relied upon to lend their influence and their votes in favor of the protection of property and person." Gary was referring to a system of industrial relations that had begun to attract the attention of American businessmen during the latter part of the nineteenth century.[1] His remarks indicate that he recognized

1. Stuart Brandes, *American Welfare Capitalism, 1880–1940* (Chicago, 1976), 86–87; Daniel Rodgers, *The Work Ethic in Industrial America, 1850–1920* (Chicago, 1978), 46–50. Many other studies deal with this theme. Among the ones I found most useful were Robert Wiebe, *The Search for Order* (New York, 1967); Samuel Haber, *Efficiency and Up-*

that profit sharing had more to do with politics than with productivity. French businessmen and their collaborators had made a similar discovery earlier.

In France, where profit sharing first received systematic ideological elaboration and practical application, its exponents knew very well what political dividends it might generate. The French bourgeoisie, after all, had considerable experience with class conflict and therefore could appreciate the benefits to be derived from all forms of association between capital and labor. The political economist Emile Levasseur, noting that þrofit sharing "is usually adopted with the object of stimulating the productivity of the employees," emphasized that it is "recommended as the most equitable form of remuneration and as the surest remedy for the antagonism between labor and capital. . . . It creates in the employee a pecuniary and moral interest in the success of the business while it leaves the management and the authority undivided in the hands of the employer." By "reinforcing harmony in the workplace," profit sharing provides an "effective stimulant to the development of social peace."[2]

In France profit sharing formed part of a comprehensive system of paternalist reform, management of labor, and social engineering. It engaged the efforts not only of industrialists but of politicians and, most visibly, such social scientists as Levasseur, Emile Cheysson, and others. Social scientists long had been in the business of analyzing social relations and producing prescriptions for their smooth operation. As they sought solidarity and community to match the increasingly corporate and collective character of social production, many turned to paternalist reform. As we have seen, this was especially true of adherents of Frédéric Le Play's social economy movement— itself the lineal descendant of the "social arithmetic" and "moral statistics" of the first half of the century. But whereas the latter on the whole stuck to laissez-faire economics ("political economy"), the former appeared willing to countenance alterations in the free mar-

---

lift: *Scientific Management in the Progressive Era, 1890–1920* (Chicago, 1964); and James Gilbert, *Designing the Industrial State: The Intellectual Pursuit of Collectivism in America, 1880–1940* (Chicago, 1972).

2. Emile Levasseur, *The American Workman* (Baltimore, 1900), 468; BPB, XXIV (1902), 35.

ket for labor power to the extent necessary to promote the association of labor and capital. One of them, the economist Charles Gide, went so far as to place profit sharing on a hierarchy of stages that would ultimately lead to the cooperative association of production in which the capitalist—but not capitalism—would disappear. None of these developments would have occurred had not the French economy moved from competition toward concentration, rendering obsolete the old-fashioned patriarchy, with its direct if not intimate contact between employers and workers, as a means of control. As Emile Cheysson observed, in an age of "progress, democracy, universal suffrage, coalitions, *syndicats*, and the regimentation of labor," neither unreconstructed patriarchy in the workplace nor undiluted liberalism in the marketplace were luxuries the French bourgeoisie could afford.[3] That is why the spirit of corporate association materialized during the second half of the century and not before. Nevertheless, competition and its attendant threat to social stability inspired some entrepreneurs to explore modes of association before midcentury.

Edme-Jacques Leclaire: Utopian Capitalist

Charles Robert, who did more than anyone else to promote profit sharing, described the career of Edme-Jacques Leclaire, whom Robert called a "conservative in the true sense of the word." Leclaire, the son of a poor shoemaker in Tonnerre (Yonne), left school at the age of ten and apprenticed himself to a painting contractor. At the age of twenty-six in the early 1830s he went into business for himself in Paris with the help of the banker Adolphe d'Eichthal, who apparently recognized in Leclaire the makings of that rare combination of socially responsible businessman and profit maximizer. Leclaire also attracted the attention of H.-A. Frégier, a senior official in the prefecture of the Seine and the author, in 1838, of *Les Classes dangereuses de la population dans les grandes villes*. Frégier contrasted the "gross" nature of most painters with those who worked for Leclaire, for he trained his foreman carefully, treated his workers fairly, kept them

---

3. Charles Gide, *Les Institutions de progrès social* (Paris, 1912), 499–501; *Exposition 1889*, II, 385.

out of the wine shops, and thereby created a stable hierarchy on the job.[4]

In 1842 Leclaire launched a profit-sharing plan for his workers. Political as well as profit considerations lay behind his project: "I am a calculating man, a businessman; I would rather earn 100,000 francs and dispense half of it, than earn 25,000 and keep it all for myself. In the former case, my profit is greater than in the latter and, moreover, I have the satisfaction of living in peace with my employees and of knowing that my orders will be obeyed." Robert drew further implications from Leclair's plan. He announced that Leclaire had acted "in the spirit of social science," meaning that he had conducted an experiment in social relations. According to Robert, the experiment was immensely successful: "In that small corner of Paris poverty had disappeared, strikes are unknown, the proletariat itself no longer exists."[5] Perhaps because of the implications of those claims Leclaire immediately came under attack from both the left and the right. The working-class newspaper L'Atelier denounced him as a fraud and his plan as a device to keep wages down. The police denied him permission to hold a meeting with his workers to discuss the plan. They considered it a political matter, for it involved "a question of the regulation of wages which ought not to be encouraged and which, in fact, is prohibited by law; the worker must be entirely free to fix his own wage."[6] Thus Leclaire found himself condemned, on one hand, for behaving like a self-aggrandizing entrepreneur and, on the other, for meddling in the free market for labor power. Both charges were true, creating an apparent contradiction.

Leclaire partook of that peculiar pre-1848 socialist ideology that envisioned the elimination of predatory and exploitive capitalist property not by destroying it but by enlarging the opportunities for workers to collaborate in capitalist enterprise.[7] He intended to lay the foundations for a producers' cooperative in which selected work-

---

4. Charles Robert, *Biographie d'un homme utile* (Paris, 1878), 9–22, 49.

5. Charles Robert, *La Suppression des grèves par l'association aux bénéfices* (Paris, 1870), 81; Bernard Mottez, *Systèmes des salaires et politiques patronales* (Paris, 1966), 79.

6. Robert, *Biographie*, 23–35; *Exposition 1889*, I, 104; Léon Poinsard, *La Guerre des classes peut-elle être évitée?* (Paris, 1898), 25.

7. Bernard Moss, *The Origins of the French Labor Movement* (Berkeley, 1976), 38.

ers would form a "management council" in association with the company's management but under its ultimate control. Leclaire took his inspiration from such socially conscious republicans as François Arago, who believed that the way to achieve working-class well-being lay "not in impoverishing the rich, but in enriching the poor." He thus won the approval of the Saint-Simonians Eichthal, Olinde Rodrigues, and Michel Chevalier and favorable notices from Louis Blanc in his *Organisation du travail,* although Leclaire made a point of registering his disapproval of Blanc's politics. The point was, of course, that profit-sharing plans, faithfully carried out, eliminated the need to seek political solutions to the social question. In this way profit sharing itself became a form of politics. François Arlès-Dufour, a Lyonese banker and silk broker, understood the point perfectly. "I believe," he wrote, "that profit sharing, as practiced in this model company, holds the key to the great problem of the proletariat. The worker's shirt and jacket will be replaced by a suit as he is transformed into an associate" of capital. Leclaire's system quickly found imitators, including the Laroche-Joubert paper mills in Angoulême, the Compagnie des Chemins de fer Paris-Orléans, and the Compagnie d'assurances générales.[8]

Leclaire's experiment reflected the pre-1848 progressive bourgeoisie's genuine concern to eliminate an exploitive wage system while leaving intact the economic structure of which that system was an expression. It did not intend the demise of capitalism but its reinvigoration. As industrialization proceeded and social struggles sharpened, association for social peace became all the more vital. A system that was progressive could also be conservative. These lessons Leclaire absorbed, as is clear from his words, written under conditions radically different from those before 1848.

Toward the end of his life (he died in 1872) Leclaire turned from practical concerns to modest philosophizing. He wrote a pamphlet in 1871, in the form of an imaginary dialogue between an old worker and a bourgeois during the last, bloody days of the Paris Commune.

---

8. *Exposition 1900,* Vol. XVI, Pt. 1, p. 349; Robert, *Biographie,* 22, 40, 48; Paul Bureau, *L'Association de l'ouvrier aux profits du patron et la participation aux bénéfices* (Paris, 1898), 108.

The document recapitulated in a didactic mode Leclaire's life's work: advancing the cause of social peace through association between enlightened capital and responsible labor.[9]

To gain maximum polemical effect and to remain true to his own origins, Leclaire cast the bourgeois as narrow-minded, cliché-ridden, and just plain thick, whereas the worker was full of wisdom, thoughtful, and realistic. The bourgeois ritually condemned the Commune, holding it up as a negative example to demonstrate that "well-being comes only from work" and not from utopian paroxysms. But, replied the worker, sensible workers neither expect charity nor intend to menace property. They do insist on their legitimate demands, whose satisfaction, as the bourgeois agreed, forms the basis of "public safety." All classes, the worker went on, must collaborate in reform. "Classes?" the bourgeois exclaimed in astonishment. "But since 1789 there are no longer classes in France; there are only citizens."[10]

The foregoing provided the overture to Leclaire's two-pronged argument: (1) not only did classes exist, but social stability rested upon their collaboration; and (2) the best defense of property lay in the recognition and amelioration of injustices generated by unequal property relations. So the bourgeois, Leclaire's straight man, quoted Adolphe Thiers at tiresome length on the inviolability of property, and the worker responded: "There remains the central question which M. Thiers ignored, which is that you can do nothing of significance without the help of those less fortunate than yourselves. It remains, then, to explain if the great architect of the universe determined that your collaborators compound their misery while by their work you amass millions."[11]

Despite the evangelical tone of that statement, the worker had, in fact, a modest proposal in mind—profit sharing. He reminded the bourgeois that physical and intellectual properties belonged as much to workers as did capital to capitalists. Certainly, his opposite number agreed, the wage paid by the employer belongs to you; no one contests that principle. That, the worker countered, missed the

9. Edme-Jacques Leclaire, *Dialogue entre en vieil ouvrier et un bourgeois sur l'association de l'ouvrier aux bénéfices du patron* (Paris, 1871).

10. *Ibid.*, 5–12.

11. *Ibid.*, 33–34.

point. Worker/employer relations turned on the latter's ability to compel the former to sell his "two properties" at whatever price the employer chose to pay. This system perpetuated mutual antagonism between two classes that ultimately depended on each other. Profit sharing made that mutual dependency concrete. It provided the worker with a fair return for his labor, gave the worker a stake in the enterprise—which would also benefit the employer—and, above all, contributed to "social peace." In the end, the bourgeois embraced the worker's argument and both agreed that profit sharing could not be enforced through law—that would violate the freedom of labor and of property—but only through moral pressure. This truly, they further agreed, was a revolutionary adventure, the best kind of revolution, "a peaceful transformation of the conditions of labor."[12]

At about the same time that Leclaire launched his social experiment, the textile entrepreneurs of Upper Alsace introduced similar systems. For the Alsatians profit sharing was only one of many projects carried on in the spirit of paternalist reform. As owners of the most advanced and concentrated sector of the French textile industry in the mid-nineteenth century, they had an immediate concern with the social dimensions of labor/capital relations, which they approached in their characteristically hard-headed fashion, refusing to flirt with even the tepid "socialism" of the young Leclaire.[13]

Gustave Steinheil may be taken as a representative example. He owned the Steinheil-Dieterlen mill in Rothau, which produced finished cotton cloth and employed seven hundred workers. As early as 1847, he had introduced several programs for his employees, including a pension fund, company housing, a fund for the widows and orphans of workers, nurseries, kindergartens, and an old-age home. Profit sharing was the centerpiece of the system, to which Steinheil pointed with satisfaction as a key to stability and low turnover.[14]

Steinheil did not conceal the essential purpose of his company's

12. *Ibid.*, 15–32.
13. *Bulletin de la Société industrielle de Mulhouse*, XXXII–XL (1862–70); Eugène Veron, *Les Institutions ouvrières de Mulhouse et ses environs* (Paris, 1866), 333–51.
14. Robert, *La Suppression des grèves*, 191–92; *Exposition 1889: Congrès internationale de la participation aux bénéfices, compte-rendu in extenso* (Paris, 1890), 182–84 (hereinafter cited as *Congrès de la participation*).

system. In an address to the Société industrielle de Mulhouse in 1867 he drew the distinction between productive and nonproductive associations: "The bad association is one in which workers join together to press for higher wages from the owners, themselves organized to resist workers' demands. *The good and true association is that which, through the agreement between the owner and his workers, establishes the industrial family.*" In the aftermath of the Paris Commune Steinheil raised the alarm. Apparently, association had not progressed far enough to do the job. Workers and employers had formed into two "hostile camps." Dire consequences threatened: "If the abyss that separates workers from employers continues to grow and to deepen, our civilization will end up in ruins." He did not expect, nor did he desire, the disappearance of the wage system, for wages did not depend on the greed of employers, but varied according to the law of supply and demand. Nor was work for a wage slavery, undignified, or incompatible with republican liberties. Yet the market could not be left to work its will independently of all human intervention. Association, especially profit sharing, provided just the right balance between market forces and voluntary constraints necessary for the "solidarity" of capital and labor. Jean-Jacques Bourcart of Guebwiller had a similar experience. He had been a pioneer in the establishment of *bibliothèques populaires* and *cours populaires* and had helped the founder of the Ligue française de l'enseignement, Jean Macé, get his start. Bourcart organized a profit-sharing plan in his spinning mills for selected "literate" workers. He personally presided over the committee that ran the program. But problems arose, stemming, Bourcart claimed, from the infiltration of "the theories and the intrigues of increasingly menacing groups of workers."[15] Both Bourcart's and Steinheil's experiences seemed to suggest that no single element of paternalist reform, operating in isolation, had much chance of success. The lesson was not lost on Charles Robert.

Charles Robert: Apostle of Profit Sharing

The models of paternalism—and their limitations—provided by the Alsatian entrepreneurs influenced Charles Robert, who grew up

15. *Exposition 1889*, I, 177; Gustave Steinheil, *La République et la question ouvrière* (Paris, 1873), *passim*; Robert, *La Suppression des grèves*, 114.

amid the tightly woven extended textile families of the region. He knew firsthand of Steinheil's efforts and those of Frédéric Engel-Dollfus, another paternalist pioneer. Those initial experiences colored his approach to the labor question, in general, and to profit sharing, in particular. No one worked more diligently to spread the gospel of profit sharing than did Robert in his positions as high state functionary in the 1860s, insurance executive, and social scientist. No one more directly placed the question of profit sharing within the broad context of the relations of labor and capital. Finally, no one did more to make the essential connection between systems of profit sharing and social science's concerns for the principles of order. As Robert's collaborator and biographer, Albert Trombert, put it, Robert's work was truly "sociological."[16]

Robert began his public career in the Ministry of Education, where he served as secretary-general to the minister, Victor Duruy, during the last seven years of the Second French Empire (1863–1870). In that capacity he seconded his superior's efforts to make instruction available to the working classes. Duruy lobbied long and hard at the imperial court for state subsidies to groups involved in organizing popular libraries and adult education courses for workers. He considered every such establishment a blow struck for "imperial democracy." Workers' education, according to Duruy, enhanced the goal of "labor freely associated with capital, and harmony between the three principal agents of production: intelligence, capital, and the wage system." Duruy, following the logic of his position, publicly proclaimed his enthusiasm for profit sharing. In an address to Leclaire and his workers, Duruy projected great possibilities: "I hope that soon your flag will be raised over all our industries, because it carries within its folds the idea of justice and of social harmony." No narrow educator, Duruy, like Robert, understood how education and industrial association promised to provide twin supports for an economic system undergoing the stresses of concentration. So did their employer, Napoléon III: "The Second Empire, concerned to maximize its popularity, publicly expressed its interest in projects beneficial to the interests of the working classes."[17]

16. Albert Trombert, *L'Oeuvre sociale de Charles Robert* (Paris, 1909), 10–11, 14–32.

17. Jean Rohr, *Victor Duruy, Ministre de Napoléon III: Essai sur la politique de l'instruction publique au temps de l'Empire libéral* (Paris, 1967), 148; Charles Robert, *Discours prononcé à*

Perhaps Duruy chose Robert to be his second-in-command because of the identity of their views. At any rate, as early as 1861 Robert had already expressed himself on education, the social question, and the association of labor and capital in terms strikingly similar to those he would use to promote profit sharing. Arguing for the establishment of a system of obligatory primary education—not coincidentally, Duruy's highest priority—Robert linked the "prosperity of industry" with the "intellectual and moral development" of the working class. He invoked the authority of the liberal philosopher Victor Cousin, who placed education in the same category as the military and public works: "It is one of society's armaments." All of France's industrial regions, Robert noted, placed obligatory primary education at the head of their agenda for social reform: "Manufacturers . . . understand that only a few years devoted to primary education would produce for their factories a breeding ground of good workers." He did not expect those manufacturers to embrace popular education for philanthropic motives. Those who put schools in their factories did so in the name of "personal interest" not because of "generous sentiments." Insufficient attention to education, Robert warned, would prove "detrimental to public safety, to the smooth administration of the nation, and to the prosperity of the worker and his family."[18]

Robert frequently appeared in Duruy's stead at prize ceremonies mounted by sponsors of adult education. On one such occasion, in Lyon, he addressed the Société d'enseignement professionnel du Rhône, an organization financed by the Lyonese big bourgeoisie to offer workers and commercial employees courses in political economy and social science. They included lessons on cooperatives, business enterprise, "economic crises," colonization, labor questions, and "progress." In his speech, Robert exhorted the audience of businessmen and workers to support the campaign for obligatory education. It promised great social benefits; in its absence great social dangers threatened. Education, "the fundamental foundation

---

la distribution des prix de la Société d'enseignement professionnel du Rhône, le 12 juin 1870 (Lyon, 1870), 4; Congrès de la participation, 285; Bureau, L'Association de l'ouvrier, 108.

18. Charles Robert, De la nécessité de rendre l'instruction primaire obligatoire en France et des moyens pratiques à employer dans ce but (Montbéliard, 1861), 7–9, 18–22, 37, 43.

for public security," provided for the worker "the basis of morality and order, . . . permits him to make rational decisions, and insulates him against false systems." Education also reinforced the spirit of solidarity and association and thereby contributed to the "domestic tranquillity" necessary to the conduct of social transactions. The alternative was dreadful to contemplate: "Ignorant persons resemble a gigantic mute, strong enough to shake mountains and to make the earth tremble." Robert warned of "demagogic delerium" that "envisions only bloody ruins, upheaval, and armed insurrection." Finally, he urged that popular education be approached as a "science," and that it teach the lesson that "economic science demonstrates [to workers] what benefits flow from truth, liberty, and justice."[19]

Imperial social policy, not only in education but in public welfare and industrial relations, received Robert's extended praise. (As a servant of the regime he could hardly afford to be critical of its policies, but he did not have to go out of his way to publicize its achievements.) Robert drew particular attention to the associationist, corporatist, and paternalist character of that policy—themes to which he would return in his campaign for profit sharing. He did not, for instance, find the liberalized law on workers' associations (1864) a threat to social peace. To those who predicted that the law would lead to violence, he responded that "far from unleashing a plague of strikes, the law will open the door to fruitful transactions" and encourage workers to hew to the path of legality rather than the path of "disorder and utopias." Additionally, the principle of association could operate vertically as well as horizontally so that "each industrial group, composed of an owner and his workers, would form a cluster (*faisceau*) of associated interests." Of such stuff, if prematurely in 1869, was the ideology of the corporate commonwealth made.[20]

As an occasional participant in Frédéric Le Play's Société d'études d'économie sociale in the 1860s, Robert pushed employers' paternalism to match, and eventually replace, that of the state. Commenting on a report on the condition of workers in the Alsatian textile town of Sainte-Marie-aux-Mines, he deplored "the demoralization

19. Rohr, *Victor Duruy*, 148; Robert, *Discours prononcé*, 6–8, 16, 23.
20. Charles Robert, *Les Améliorations sociales du Second Empire* (2 vols.; Paris, 1868), I, 10, 41–43; Robert, *La Suppression des grèves*, 21.

of the laboring classes . . . their excessive taste for pleasure, and their distrust of the upper classes." But on the bright side, the Alsatian tradition of popular education was having a "good influence."[21]

Profit sharing received extensive public recognition during the Paris International Exposition of 1867, mounted to advertise the social and industrial achievements of the Second Empire. In the course of preparations for the exposition, Robert had occasion to work with Emile Cheysson, inaugurating a collaboration across a broad spectrum of reform projects that endured until Robert's death in 1899. The publicity brochures for the exposition and for a projected Société d'études pratiques pour la suppression des grèves announced rather extravagantly that "profit sharing . . . appears to many industrial leaders as a way to end for all time the era of strikes and, in all cases, to attenuate the consequences of unemployment. . . . Wherever profit sharing has been tried, production increases and the conditions of work improve."[22]

In fact, the era of strikes had just begun, and with a bang, not a whimper. In 1869 workers in the mining and metallurgical complex of the upper Loire basin (the departments of the Loire and the Haute-Loire) struck the principal forges and mining companies in the region. The following year striking workers closed down the gigantic blast furnaces of the Schneider company at Le Creusot, France's largest iron and steel manufacturer. Confrontations between strikers and management edged toward violence, and troops appeared to maintain order. Most menacing, from the point of view of those concerned with order, was the political complexion of the workers' demands concerning wages and working conditions. Socialist slogans emanated from the ranks of the strikers.[23]

According to Albert Trombert, Robert's close associate, those strikes inspired his first tract on profit sharing. Certainly the title Robert chose suggests as much: *La Suppression des grèves par l'association aux bénéfices* (The elimination of strikes through profit sharing).

21. *EF*, February 10, 1863.
22. *Notice préliminaire de l'enquête du dixième groupe à l'Exposition universelle de 1867* (Paris, 1867), 34, quoted in Trombert, *L'Oeuvre sociale*, 11; Bureau, *L'Association de l'ouvrier*, 108.
23. Fernand L'Huillier, *La Lutte ouvrière en France à la fin du Second Empire* (Paris, 1957); Yves Lequin, *Les Ouvriers de la région lyonnaise* (2 vols.; Lyon, 1978), Vol. II, Chap. 3.

Although he recognized that employers could be narrow-minded, shortsighted, and lacking a sense of paternal responsibility, Robert insisted that the strikes were organized by the International Workingman's Association (the First International), which he labeled an "international ministry of industrial warfare." He maintained that workers indeed had the right to strike to "protect their wages and their families from gross abuses." Yet the strike itself only exposed the "profound ignorance in which the masses wallow" and which allowed outside agitators to capture their allegiance. But if he could be condescending toward workers, Robert did not spare employers the lash of his harsh moralizing. Twenty years later, in the presentation of profit sharing at the 1889 Paris Exposition, he lamented that capitalists could sometimes be the worst advertisement for capitalism: "The *patronat* has revealed itself to be an admirable instrument of social progress; but . . . it is easy to trace the somber picture of the bad *patron*, driven to amass a fortune at full steam and at any cost, pitiless and hard, without heart or feelings, treating his workers with less consideration than horses in the stables, provoking hatred and thereby fomenting revolution, a real threat to the state." Robert did not suffer from that liberal even-handedness that calls down a plague on both houses. He simply did not believe that every capitalist could be trusted to operate according to the long-term interests of capitalism. That is why they needed experts, ideologues, and social engineers—social scientists—like himself.[24]

Workers remained distinctly the junior partners in Robert's various associationist schemes. That idea, too, followed in the tradition of corporatist social science represented by Le Play's social economy group. Whatever lip service was paid to the "organic community" or the "industrial family," the boss remained the boss. Robert insisted that the "dictatorship of the *patron*" was fundamental to profit sharing. Any worker involvement in the operation of an enterprise would be "deplorable," resulting in "disorder, anarchy, ruin." The great advantage of profit sharing lay in its attraction to workers' venal interests. "When that interest flags, depression and social peril follow; when it grows, productivity and public safety benefit."[25]

---

24. Trombert, *L'Oeuvre sociale*, 2–3, 6–19; *Exposition 1889*, I, 74.
25. Robert, *La Suppression des grèves*, 20, 64–65.

On balance, public safety and material interest remained the chief justifications for profit sharing. A silk thread manufacturer named Bonnet employing four hundred workers in Jujurieux (Ain) and another fourteen hundred in Lyon claimed that he put aside 20 percent of his profits for the distribution of bonuses in 1867. Robert noted approvingly that "this scheme to involve the worker in the productive process produces the most admirable results." An optical instruments manufacturer, Baille-Lemaire, whose profit-sharing plan drew the attention of the social scientist organizers of the 1889 exposition (and to whom we will return), drew the distinction between doing well and doing good: "Let us have no talk of philanthropy. We badly deceive ourselves if we allow sentiments of goodwill to intrude where only pure considerations of interest should prevail." The risks of relying on charitable sentiments rather than on the "principles of social economy" would be "serious, from the point of view of the general interest, private interests, or even the interests of workers."[26]

Yet not everyone agreed that a contradiction existed between doing well and doing good. The economist Paul Bureau noted that "any institution that contributes to the maintenance and to the advancement of harmony between bosses and workers . . . genuinely profits patronal interests, even those of a purely pecuniary nature." Albert Piche, the president of the Société d'éducation populaire des Basses-Pyrénées, pointed out that, for a "philanthropic boss who wants to improve the material conditions of his workers without it costing him anything," profit sharing presented a unique opportunity. Not only did it promise "economies in raw material and in labor-time," but it provided the entrepreneur with the means to organize social relations in his plant on a corporate basis, to be the "maestro of a social concert" (*chef d'orchestre d'un concert social*).[27]

No less a figure than the German corporatist social scientist Gustave Schmoller agreed that those who did good also could do well. Schmoller, Otto von Bismarck's favorite political economist and the dominant figure in the "socialism of the chair" (*kathedersozialismus*) school, admired the French experiments in profit sharing, and he

26. *Ibid.*, 45; *Exposition 1889*, I, 225; Poinsard, *La Guerre des classes*, 7.
27. Bureau, *L'Association de l'ouvrier*, 126; *Congrès de la participation*, 240–42.

possessed an unerring eye for the economic and the political bottom line: "All the entrepreneurs [who engage in profit sharing] agree that all their people, their zeal, their determination to economize on raw materials and on the use of machinery, more than makes up for their losses in profit; that, as a result [of their workers' efforts] *they have done good business,* and that these portions of the profit have not come out of their pockets." Schmoller went on to pronounce profit sharing a "powerful force for the education" and discipline of workers. "The enemy who previously hated and distrusted the employer can now become his close associate." [28]

The Ideology of Profit Sharing

The social economy group of the Paris Exposition of 1889 included a section on profit sharing, organized as an "international congress" with Italian, German, and English participants as well as French. The International Congress on Profit Sharing featured Emile Levasseur as honorary president (Robert was president) and included among its sponsors the leader of Le Havre's bourgeoisie, Jules Siegfried, Charles Gide, the radical Alsatian textile entrepreneur Auguste Lalance, the conservative syndicalist Joseph Barbaret; and two former political associates of Léon Gambetta: Auguste Scheurer-Kestner of the Alsatian textile and chemical family and René Waldeck-Rousseau, future leader, in 1899, of the "Government of Republican Defense." The same year the Exposition took place, Siegfried chaired a committee of the Chamber of Deputies that reported out a bill validating profit sharing as a form of wage. The committee's *rapporteur,* Paul Doumer, said that profit sharing was to be considered neither a "handout nor a real stake in the property of the firm." Waldeck, who learned about social reform in Nantes from the tradition of the physician-reformer Ange Guépin, had sought a reconciliation between labor and capital for many years. Between 1883 and 1885, when he was minister of the interior in Jules Ferry's second government, Waldeck sponsored a ministerial inquiry, written by Barbaret, on profit sharing. He saw it both as an "important

28. *REP,* V (1891), 192–93.

moral influence" on workers and a way of facilitating "the easy recruitment of capable employees."[29]

During the decade beginning with the 1889 exposition, numerous
experiments in profit sharing and other forms of paternalism were
recorded, their ideology made explicit, and their function in the mobilization of management and the discipline of labor made manifest.

New forms of social production, engendered by industrial concentration, demanded new relationships between labor and capital.
The "dissociation of the interests of workers and bosses" had become the most visible manifestation of the contemporary organization of production. Traditional modes of patriarchal control, therefore, had outlived their usefulness and had to give way to some form
of enlightened paternalism. To take that step required a realistic
understanding of the market in labor power, an appreciation of the
political dangers inherent in the exercise of repressive authority, and
a recognition of the potential power of independent workers' associations. The problem reduced to three elements: to generate a consensus on the universality and inevitability of the wage system as
well as recognition of its equally inevitable tendency toward class antagonism; to design systems of welfare and remuneration that would
supplement the wage and neutralize antagonism without encroach-
ing on entrepreneurial profits; and, finally, to create on this basis
new forms of association regularly constituted and not subject to arbitrary paternal authority. Profit sharing, as one among many paternalistic experiments, was promoted as a solution that would secure
the "patron's preeminence," promise "security" to the "ruling industrial class," and provide "a measure of discipline, economies of production, and a bulwark against strikes."[30]

The failure of patriarchal authority to stem the tide of strikes was
most glaring in the coal-mining industry. The disruptions in the Loire
coal fields began a series of actions that in the following two decades
spread to Carmaux, the Grand'Combe, Anzin, and Montceau-les-
Mines. Mineowners attempted to rule their workers with notori-
ously heavy hands. Mostly Catholic, they behaved as if imbued with

29. BPB, XI (1889), 104; Congrès de la participation, 32, 288; Pierre Sorlin, Waldeck-
Rousseau (Paris, 1966), Chap. 5.
30. Bureau, L'Association de l'ouvrier, 101; Exposition 1889, I, 68, 70–72.

"a divine right," as if "heaven itself had entrusted to their care a population to be indoctrinated and regimented."[31] They thus compounded the exploitation intrinsic to the labor/capital relationship with senseless bouts of reaction. In the end they risked the integrity of their enterprises by employing means purportedly geared to preserving that integrity. When government officials, such as the future solidarist reformer Léon Bourgeois, refused to supply troops to break a strike, the owners erupted in indignation.[32] Robert, no enemy of the mining magnates, nevertheless insisted that they shared responsibility for impending disaster: "An international miners' strike would lead to the suspension of all mining operations, bring to a standstill the social and economic life of the entire world, force work stoppages in countless factories, drive hysterical crowds into the streets, immobilize rail traffic, and, thus, in one blow, compromise domestic tranquillity and national defense."[33]

At Carmaux, the problem of harnessing workers' associations took on a special urgency. Miners and the Société des Mines de Carmaux had been involved in struggle on and off for thirty years. The Marquis de Solages, head of the company, supported right-wing political causes and played the stern patriarch. But despite his aristocratic escutcheon he was above all a profit-maximizing, ruthless, and resourceful capitalist. In March, 1892, a major strike broke out over disputes about wages and working conditions. The strike lasted two weeks and ended inconclusively. The struggle subsequently took on a political cast. The leader of the miners' union, Jean Calvignac, was elected mayor of Carmaux on a socialist ticket. The company fired him and some of his collaborators. The miners struck again and held on for several months. All arbitration attempts failed.[34]

The situation in the mining industry and elsewhere reflected what the social scientist Léon Poinsard in 1898 pointed to as a contradiction in the position of those owners who clung to their traditional patriarchal habits. On one hand, they attempted to maximize the benefits of the free market in labor power, viewing the wage as "the

---

31. *Exposition 1889*, I, 75–76.
32. Michelle Perrot, *Les Ouvriers en grève* (2 vols.; Paris, 1974), II, 700–702.
33. *Exposition 1889*, I, 70.
34. Rolande Trempé, *Les Mineurs de Carmaux* (2 vols.; Paris, 1971), Vol. II, Chap. 3.

price of an ordinary commodity for which one pays as little as possible." Those conditions made workers seek to "raise the wage above its natural limits set by competitive factors and the needs of consumption." On the other hand, these same owners insisted that their authority derived from a purported premarket condition of the solidarity between the "patronal family" and the "working-class family." They could not have it both ways.[35]

One escape from the contradiction that did not compromise paternal authority involved the establishment of company-sponsored workers' associations on the model recommended by Cheysson and Robert, or yellow unions. As we have seen, the Blanzy Company at Montceau-les-Mines took that course in 1900. The union's program announced its "aim to modify and transform the wage system not in the spirit of collectivism but in the spirit of individual property." To that end it called for profit sharing. Paul Delombre, onetime minister of commerce and a good republican, made the same claim for profit sharing, which, he said, gave every worker the opportunity to become a "little capitalist" and thus contribute to the solidarity of capital and labor.[36]

Such sentiments neatly dovetailed with the social reformers' conception of the constructive *syndicat,* one that devoted its attention to the welfare and the "social education" of workers. Poinsard counseled employers to act according to the principle of utility, that is, to seek "profitable ways of using the organization to smooth their relations with labor, to avoid misunderstandings and conflicts, in a word to reduce the difficulties of *patronage.*" Profit sharing furthered this process of class collaboration in two ways: first, as a wage supplement, it avoided the "economically advantageous" but "socially dangerous" condition of low wages, which otherwise "corrupts the population" and foreshadows a "future of bitter struggles and immense ruin"; second, it "stimulated the worker's zeal on the job and increased his productivity." In the end, profit-sharing systems were, from the owner's point of view, "sound social and industrial economics."[37]

35. Poinsard, *La Guerre des classes,* II, 44.
36. Charles Gide, *L'Economie sociale* (Paris, 1905), 143–48; Gide, *Les Institutions,* 146n; *BPB,* XXIV (1902), 95.
37. Poinsard, *La Guerre des classes,* 35–36, 127, 172.

At the end of the century—a time of widespread social upheaval—others echoed Poinsard. Political considerations, as always, commanded their attention. Paul Delombre noted that profit sharing tended to create built-in wage increases but did so "in the most equitable manner" imaginable by linking the benefits accrued to the "prosperity of the firm," which in turn "depended directly on the solidarity between workers and employers." Emile Cheysson, on the occasion of his reception of the first Charles Robert medal for valorous service to the cause, invoked what had become for him the standard familial metaphor. To the extent that profit sharing joined together (*solidariser*) workers' and employers' interests, it transformed the workplace into "one big family." Wherever the experiment had been undertaken seriously, Cheysson claimed, "peace has been secured, strikes averted." (One wonders whether he had forgotten Blanzy, where profit sharing had been introduced in 1854.) [38]

As Robert had insisted many times, the chief purpose of profit sharing was neither philanthropic nor economic; it was political—as a defense against strikes and against socialist and syndicalist "agitators." Laroche-Joubert boasted, "Never, in sixty years, never did the thought of a strike take shape in the minds of our workers; and if occasional misunderstandings occurred, they quickly disappeared thanks to cooperation." Indeed, in some circles profit sharing was considered a magic formula for the "exorcism of strikes," if only workers understood that it constituted the "best solution to the difficulties that separated them from their employers." Workers, however, could not be reasonably counted on to share those sentiments. Baille-Lemaire, speaking frankly as usual, warned that profit sharing was no "universal panacea." No one should expect it to "heal all social wounds and inaugurate the reign of justice and goodwill on earth." After all, "the first concern of the employer is to reduce his costs in order to maximize his income and gain the upper hand over his competitors." Only then did the workers' share enter into the calculation, and only at the end of the year. In the meantime they had to live from day to day without regard for the uncertain prize that awaited them. But despite his pessimism—or realism—Baille-Lemaire had to admit that profit sharing offered "great moral ad-

38. *BPB*, XXIV (1902), 36, 85–88.

vantages" to businessmen to the extent that it engaged the workers' interest in the success of the enterprise—if only indirectly and at a distance. A manufacturer of plumbing supplies in Rouen agreed: profit sharing "has the great advantage of acquainting employees with the innumerable concerns and difficulties with which the boss must constantly contend. Most important, workers will come to understand that without thrift and planning no business can survive."[39]

How Profit Sharing Worked

By 1891 80 companies engaged in some form of profit sharing, and that number was to increase to 120 in the subsequent decade. The enterprises, their products, their size, and their relative proportion of highly skilled artisanal labor to factory-based unskilled or semi-skilled labor varied considerably. But there was a pattern that corresponded to changes taking place within French industry as a whole. Whereas in the 1870s most firms that had profit-sharing plans produced services—such as insurance companies—or commodities that required the application of intensive skilled labor—such as publishers and jewelry manufacturers—those that inaugurated plans in the 1880s and beyond included a much greater percentage of large industrial establishments manufacturing such items as textiles, steam engines, heavy machinery, electrical equipment, and cars for urban tramways.[40]

Profit-sharing plans varied from industry to industry and from firm to firm, but some common features can be distinguished. Distributions generally were a percentage of the annual net profit and ranged from 3 to 10 percent of the workers' average annual wage. In a survey of thirty-nine companies conducted in 1901, the secretary of the Société des participations aux bénéfices, Albert Trombert, found that the average of all distributions came to 9 percent of the total annual wage bill. The actual amount of the net profit remained hid-

39. *Exposition 1900,* Vol. XVI, Pt. 1, p. 346; *Almanach de la coopération française,* 9th year (1901), 79–81; Albert Trombert, *La Participation aux bénéfices en France, d'après une enquête récente* (Paris, 1902), 12; *Exposition 1889,* I, 154, 158; *Exposition 1900,* Vol. XVI, Pt. 1, p. 413.

40. *Exposition 1889,* I, 94–96; *Exposition 1900,* Vol. XVI, Pt. 1, pp. 295–99; *Almanach de la coopération française,* 8th year (1900), 159–62.

den in company books, to which only owners and managers had access. The Masson publishing company, for instance, organized a council of workers and managers—a *conseil de famille*—to handle profit-sharing policy. But management reserved the right to establish the annual percentage of distributions on the grounds that it alone possessed knowledge of all aspects of the company's operations. The leverage that such arrangements afforded is obvious. Occasionally, shares varied according to the ratio of labor to capital in an enterprise. Companies that operated with a high proportion of labor to capital could afford to pay out larger amounts than those in the reverse situation. The less capital invested the less the costs of capital and, thus, the higher the rate of exploitation. It was, as always, a matter of calculation and not of generosity. Baille-Lemaire, the jewelry manufacturer who believed that generous sentiments had no place in business, reserved 75 percent of his profits for capital amortization. Once the costs of capital had been met, he divided the revenues equally between his workers and himself.[41]

In other instances profit sharing became a mechanism for cost cutting and rewarding good behavior. The Compagnie Générale Transatlantique distributed to its ships' crews 90 percent of the revenues generated by shipboard economies, as calculated by the company, and to dock workers 95 percent of the "benefits resulting from the proper handling of cargo." Ferdinand de Lesseps' Suez Canal Company, which paid high wages (nine to twelve francs per day for skilled workers and foremen), carefully monitored its workers' output and quality of work, rewarding and punishing accordingly. The company had a "generous pension plan" that amounted to 60 percent of the last three years' wages after thirty years of employment. The money came from accrued shares in the company's profits. Lesseps claimed that the system "guarantees complete solidarity between the firm and its employees. . . . We are a family."[42]

Good behavior, translated as the willingness to collaborate rather than the determination to struggle, was the political goal of profit

---

41. *Exposition 1900,* Vol. XVI, Pt. 1, p. 295; *BPB,* XXIV (1902), 56, 61–62; Albert Trombert, *Guide pratique pour l'application de la participation aux bénéfices* (Paris, 1892), 81–85; *Exposition 1889,* I, 153–54.

42. Trombert, *Guide pratique,* 88; *Exposition 1900,* Vol. XVI, Pt. 1, pp. 368–75.

sharing. Leclaire's old company had a council composed of 120 workers who had demonstrated "irreproachable conduct and morality." They, in collaboration with the *patron*, administered the company's profit-sharing apparatus, which included a mutual aid society. Before 1871, only the members of the council shared in the profits. But morale problems among other workers (and perhaps fresh memories of the Commune) forced the company to extend benefits to everyone. Nevertheless, the system remained geared to the formation and replenishment of a labor aristocracy. Membership in the council and in the administration of the mutual aid society were privileges "eagerly sought after by deserving workers" and could lead to a foreman's job.[43]

The furnace and stove factory of J.-B. Godin, like Leclaire a self-made man and sometime utopian socialist, demanded of workers admitted to association a veritable loyalty oath: "I recognize that the purpose of this association is to reward those who collaborate in the common effort and that, conceived in the spirit of solidarity and justice, its purpose is to realize peace among men; that each member of this association must behave according to the principles of equity . . . and refrain from any activity that may foment trouble or discord." Members of the association and all other workers who benefited from the distribution of Godin's profits stood to lose their rights for any one of six infractions: drunkenness; sloppy family habits or failure to maintain tidy quarters; "dishonest behavior"; poor work performance; "lack of discipline, disorder or acts of violence"; and failure to provide proper education for their children. Not only were these categories subject to arbitrary interpretation, but, for the most part, senior workers policed the behavior of their fellows.[44]

Closely related to acceptable political behavior was turnover, which profit sharing was intended to minimize. Every plan recorded at the end of the century demanded a minimum length of service, ranging from two to seven years, as a precondition for receiving benefits. Amounts distributed in the paper factory of Larouche-Joubert in Angoulême varied according to seniority. The Companie de Fives-

43. *Exposition 1900*, Vol. XVI, Pt. 1, pp. 335–40.
44. Trombert, *Guide pratique*, 207; *Exposition 1889*, I, 116–18.

Lille, a diversified producer of rolling stock, machinery, and refined beet sugar, admitted workers into its plan after three years of continuous service, but they could not claim title to their accounts until the end of a further twelve years with the company. Moreover, each year's share was not distributed but was deposited in a retirement account. Workers who left their jobs voluntarily or who were fired "through their own fault" before the fifteen years expired received nothing. "This final condition," the company reported, "obviously is designed to attach the workers to the firm." The House of Boivin, lacemakers in Paris, set aside 21 percent of its profits in good years and deposited the money in the bank. Workers had the right to draw on their accounts when they had reached the age of fifty but lost everything if they left the company and went to work for a competitor within two years. At the Baccarat crystal works turnover was especially low. Of the twenty-two hundred workers employed there at the end of the century, sixteen hundred had put in at least five years on the job and a substantial percentage had been with the company for twenty-five years or more.[45]

In the chemical dye plant in upper Alsace owned by Auguste Scheurer-Kestner and his family, profit sharing had been instituted in the 1850s. Shares for workers who had put in less than five years on the job were deliberately maintained at the lowest possible level, averaging a mere twenty-two francs annually over the period 1877 to 1884. Not coincidentally, nearly 60 percent of the workers in the Kestner factory had been employed more than five years. The American Nicholas Gilman commented that the company "has attained the chief end it had in view in instituting profit sharing." The Imprimerie nationale boasted that its plan had succeeded admirably in creating a cadre of workers "fervently loyal to the establishment." Because of its reputation the company was deluged with employment applicants. Elsewhere, only foremen and workers of the "first class" had access to employer/employee councils, resulting in a structure resembling the Prussian Diet. Auguste Lalance went so far as to suggest that large industries such as weaving, spinning, and ma-

45. *Exposition 1889*, I, 85, 201; *Congrès de la participation*, 323–24; Alfred Renouard and Léon Moy, *Les Institutions ouvrières et sociales du département du Nord* (Lille, 1889), 68–70; *RIP*, IV (1890), 546; *Exposition 1900*, Vol. XVI, Pt. 1, p. 320.

chinery production limit the number of workers admitted to profit-sharing plans, in effect dividing workers against one another. Failing that, he urged companies to create savings banks in which they would deposit at interest the total amount of the workers' share. Otherwise, Lalance argued, such companies would be forced to bear insupportable burdens, or, conversely, the individual shares would be so minute as to render the system useless.[46]

The Société Anonyme de Tissus de Laine des Vosges, which manufactured muslins and employed 727 workers in 1889, devised a unique profit-sharing plan. The company set aside up to 15 percent of its profits annually, which it wrote off under general expenses, thereby reducing its net paper profit. Individual shares were allotted on the basis of a point system. Of one hundred possible points, forty were allocated for productivity, thirty-six for seniority, and twenty-four for "steadiness, that is, sobriety." Shares, however, were not distributed as a simple function of each individual's total points. Rather, a single worker's points were multiplied by all the points gained in the factory and divided by the maximum attainable (72,700). Thus every worker stood to benefit not only from his own productivity, longevity in the firm, and sober conduct, but from those of his fellows as well. Hence a system was created with built-in mutual surveillance and moral pressure on the shop floor. After the amount of the shares was determined, each worker received only a small percentage in cash. The balance was deposited in a savings account at 5 percent interest and could be withdrawn only after a worker reached the age of sixty or had put in twenty years of service. Those who left the company, voluntarily or involuntarily, surrendered all claims to benefits. Mining companies used similar techniques to reward the leaders of work gangs for high levels of productivity and a stable, sober work force.[47]

Rewards for exemplary behavior and inducements to enter the ranks of privileged workers represented the carrot. There was also a

46. Nicholas Gilman, *Profit Sharing between Employer and Employee* (Boston, 1889), 200–202; *Exposition 1889*, I, 149; Trombert, *Guide pratique*, 96, 204; *Exposition 1900: Congrès international de participation aux bénéfices, procès-verbal sommaire* (Paris, 1901), 20.

47. *RIP*, IV (1890), 337–48; François Husson, *La Seconde révolution française: Solution et dénouement pacifique de la question sociale ouvrière* (Paris, 1892), 115.

stick. Moral tests such as those administered by a plumbing-supply manufacturer in Paris easily turned into political surveillance. Since the employer set the standard of a worker's "moral value," the worker found himself subjected to an arbitrary process that threatened as much to punish as to reward. Assuming that most workers lacked the moral character to save, a manufacturer of electrical equipment in Paris distributed only a small portion of the annual benefits, reserving the rest for the national retirement fund; however, "that precautionary measure did not apply to those workers who had demonstrated thrifty habits by holding an account in a savings institution."[48]

Once enrolled in a profit-sharing plan, workers developed a stake in maintaining their association and employment, thus making the system an arm of labor discipline. The experience of the Piat iron foundry of Paris and Soissons (Aisne) illustrates this point particularly well. Piat had been a model *patron* who had sponsored a mutual aid society in 1856 and a pension fund, a library, schools, and a choral society in 1876. He began a profit-sharing plan in 1881, but it took some time to get going. In 1882, foundry workers struck and his employees joined in the strike—reluctantly, according to him. The following year Piat had the plan in operation. He noticed the difference: "Last year none of [the workers] troubled himself or appeared to think about participation. Today it occupies them much more and preoccupies them. The workman who is ready to leave the shop, for one reason or another, thinks of it twice. Two years more of this regime, and these sentiments will certainly increase in intensity."[49]

Not infrequently, workers never realized their shares directly. Rather, the amounts allocated went to finance the various savings banks, pension funds, schools, housing, and accident insurance that were the pride of paternalism. Nearly all of the companies that adopted profit-sharing plans reserved at least part of the distributions for workers' welfare programs. This meant that to the extent that shares were a supplement to wages, workers paid for their

48. Auguste Isaac, "Le Patronage à l'exposition de Lyon," *RS*, XXXIII (1897), 238; *Exposition 1889*, I, 208.
49. Gilman, *Profit Sharing*, 183–84.

fringe benefits out of their own pockets. Sometimes workers were forced to invest their shares in the company. Dividends materialized, if at all, only after a certain number of years of steady and loyal service.[50] One variation on the system was adopted by Harmel Frères, a textile mill in the Marne. The company's owners, who considered themselves followers of Le Play, divided wages into two parts: the regular weekly wage and what they called the *salaire de famille*, that is, the weekly cost of maintaining a family. Thus if a worker earned 30 francs per week and sustenance for his family cost 33.60 francs, he would be paid an additional 3.60 as his "share" of the company's profits. In this manner the company disguised the payment of a subsistence wage as profit sharing.[51]

Finally, this effort to circumvent the worst ravages of the market in labor power depended on the market for manufactured commodities. That was why proponents of profit sharing resisted state intervention to make it compulsory. Determined to maintain his own profits, the employer, under poor market conditions, would be forced to exert downward pressure on wages to maintain his margin, thereby producing a "social dislocation." But nothing prevented entrepreneurs from reducing or even eliminating their workers' share during hard times without any compensatory increase in wages.[52]

The membership roster of the Société des participations aux bénéfices may be taken as a useful litmus test of the extent to which a cross-section of the French big bourgeoisie, politicians, and reformers supported this variant of the corporate form of social relations. It included two directors of the Compagnie des Mines du Nord at Lens; two of Lille's largest textile manufacturers; the managing director of the Imprimeries Chaix, one of France's largest publishing houses; a director of the Saint-Gobain company, the nation's leading producer of glass; several representatives of substantial wool-producing enterprises in Elbeuf, Reims, and Oissel (Seine-Inférieure); the managing director of one of Paris' largest department stores, the Grands Magasins au Louvre; the Armand Colin publishing house; Peugeot

---

50. Isaac, "Le Patronage," 240; Trombert, *Guide pratique*, 25; *Exposition 1889*, I, 94–96; Gide, *Les Institutions*, 141–42.
51. *Exposition 1900*, Vol. XVI, Pt. 1, pp. 404–405.
52. *Congrès de la participation*, 255–56.

Frères, manufacturers of iron and steel implements; Caillard et Compagnie, machinery producers; Dollfus-Mieg, textile entrepreneurs in Alsace; the Compagnie universelle du canal maritime de Suez; Arlès-Dufour et Compagnie, silk merchants and brokers in Lyon; and a host of businessmen from the mining, metallurgical, textile, and machine industries throughout France. Among the politicians and reformers, the Société included on its roster Paul Delombre, the Comte de Chambrun, Emile Cheysson, Jules Siegfried, and Auguste Scheurer-Kestner.[53]

In its survey of the progress made toward extending profit sharing throughout French industry, the Société's bulletin for 1898 gave equal measure to economics and politics. Profit sharing was preferred to piece work because it encouraged the worker to look forward to a "fruitful future" instead of "squandering his wages." High wages, which "each employer theoretically could pay out, would spell the ruin of his plant" because his labor costs would bear "no relationship to the state of the market." Profit sharing corrected this imbalance in favor of the employer and "welded the worker to his factory in the spirit of solidarity." Down the road lay the corporate utopia, "no wages, no premiums; all are equal." The vision ended in a "community of workers. Profit sharing will replace the wage system."[54]

No such prospects were in the offing, nor did profit sharing necessarily lead to the replacement of the boss by cooperative management, as Charles Gide had suggested. Capital remained, and with it the capitalist; labor remained, and with it the worker. The wage system would also endure. In the final analysis, political considerations indicated the superiority of profit sharing over premiums and bonuses added to the basic wage. The latter system left the worker isolated, working only for himself, and caring nothing for the health of the company. The former operated only through association and locked the worker in a collective effort that had the appearance of collaboration among equals but that, in fact, was ultimately controlled by management. Even though routine invocations to the for-

---

53. *BPB*, XX (1898), i–ii; *BPB*, XXIV (1902), 203–207.
54. *BPB*, XX (1898), 47–49, 231.

mation of an industrial family continued to be pronounced, this system should not be mistaken for refurbished patriarchy.[55] It aimed at circumventing class antagonism when possible and smothering it when necessary, and it had a very modern ring to it.

Stanley Jevons, the English neoclassical political economist, did not directly comment on profit sharing when he wrote the following, but his words may be taken as a succinct statement of its political dimension: "Industrial divisions should be perpendicular, not horizontal. The workman's interests should be bound up with those of his employer, and should be pitted in fair competition against those of other workmen and employers."[56] We do not know whether any of those who appear here had read Jevons, but similar circumstances produced similar responses. Jevons' words could easily have come from Charles Robert, Emile Cheysson, Charles Gide, Léon Poinsard, or any of the businessmen and politicians who promoted profit sharing. They all agreed that the collective character of production (the "vertical") and militant labor rendered both dog-eat-dog competition (the "horizontal") and patriarchy obsolete. Corporate enterprise required corporate social policies.

Not everyone, however, agreed that enforced class collaboration held the solution to the problem of antagonistic class relations. Paul Bureau thought that big business, with its multilayered organizational structure and complex division of labor, engendered separation rather than solidarity, a political abyss between labor and management that profit sharing could not bridge. Another commentator labeled profit sharing a blatant fraud, which "hypocritically promotes capital at the expense of labor, is a trap for workers, and can only undermine their basic interests." Those were the words not of a socialist or a syndicalist militant, but of Maurice Zablet, a contributor to the *Journal des Economistes,* which stubbornly held to the principles of political economy while so many others abjured that faith.[57] Nevertheless, these voices were increasingly isolated, drowned

55. Charles Robert, *La Participation aux bénéfices au point de vue du maintien de l'autorité dirigeante* (Paris, 1893), 3; Trombert, *Guide pratique,* 5–7.
56. Quoted in Gilman, *Profit Sharing,* title page.
57. Bureau, *L'Association de l'ouvrier,* 222; *Journal des Economistes,* 5th ser., XXXVI (1898), 269–71.

out by the louder and more numerous voices of corporate associationism. The French bourgeoisie, itself a creature of the market, could no longer afford to allow the market to regulate social relations. Nor, conversely, could it abandon the market. So those bourgeois called for association and cooperation fully realizing that, in doing so, they had abandoned the way of the marketplace for the uncertain political path of corporate solidarity.

IV
Doing Well by Doing Good
The Politics of Paternalism

In his introduction to the section on apprentice education for the 1889 Exposition, Charles Lucas noted the growing involvement of businessmen in social reform: "During the last ten
years boards of directors of big industrial companies as well as a host
of employers, under the influence of increasingly pressing social preoccupations, have begun, at considerable cost which does them
honor, to undertake the recruitment and training of their personnel
while attempting, through a variety of benefits accruing from profit
sharing, welfare and retirement funds, consumers' cooperatives, and
cheap housing, to forge links with their employees and to encourage
the latter's commitment to the prosperity of their enterprises."
Whatever the validity of Lucas' claims for paternal generosity, we
should not only recall the political dimensions of profit sharing but
also recognize that the cost of benefits figured in investment strategy
just like any other costs. As Gaston Rimlinger pointed out: "Social
insurance became one of the means of investing in human capital."
Paternalism ensured employers against disorder as much as it ensured workers against the worst miseries of their existence. No contradiction existed between efforts to increase productivity and improve efficiency, on the one hand, and broader political calculations,
on the other. The textile manufacturers of Saint-Quentin, who understood their priorities very well, dismissed any suggestion that welfare programs reflected philanthropic considerations. Paternalism
paid: "Every effort that industry devotes to improving its workers'
material and moral conditions returns profits." Baille-Lemaire placed

"social machinery" on the same level of importance as plant machinery. Both "have the same function, which is to generate more productive activity and to increase output." The social economist Georges Picot (of whom more below) took a broader view. He advised the businessmen assembled in the Union de la paix sociale of the Nord to consider themselves not a "ruling class" but a "responsible class" and to assert their authority while "multiplying at whatever cost" their efforts to promote class harmony.[1]

Picot's injunction suggests that paternalism, viewed as a broadly ideological managerial strategy rather than simply as a welfare system, had as much to do with politics as with profits—if, indeed, its twin dimensions can be separated at all. Moreover, he and others across the spectrum of the conservative coalition considered paternalism an institutional alternative to state intervention in labor/ capital relations. Although they did not oppose all forms of state intervention and readily accepted it under certain conditions, they much preferred that paternalist institutions rest in the hands of corporate managers and associated politicians and social scientists.

Corporate Production and Social Machinery

Both the Paris expositions of 1889 and 1900 took place just before or during years of sharply increased strike action.[2] This may have been accidental, but the inclusion in both expositions of impressive displays of social machinery was not. Each exposition had its distinctive character, reflecting the intensification and expansion of production, the rhythm of class conflict, and the level of alert adopted by the industrial bourgeoisie. Political and ideological responses followed, recorded in the proceedings of the expositions and put into action in various systems for paternalist reform, which underwent significant transformations in design and scope. The career of Alexandre Gibon

1. *Exposition 1889*, I, 225, 297; Gaston Rimlinger, *Welfare Policy and Industrialization in Europe, America, and Russia* (New York, 1971), 10; Société industrielle de Saint-Quentin et de l'Aisne, *Statutes* (Saint-Quentin, 1885), 20, in F[17] 11706, AN; Eugène Turgan, *Les Grandes usines* (10 vols.; Paris, 1866–70), IV, 240, V, 127–28, VII, 317–20; Unions de la paix sociale, *Unions du Nord: Compte-rendu général* (Paris, 1893), 14–16.

2. Michelle Perrot, *Les Ouvriers en grève* (2 vols.; Paris, 1974), I, 66.

shows how the trappings of patriarchy disguised paternalist politics in a corporate setting.

In 1867 the Commentry foundry and blast-furnace division of the Châtillon-Commentry coal and metallurgical company received honorable mention at the Paris Exposition for its schools and orphanages, *ouvroirs* (workshops for young girls), medical services, and workers' housing. The man responsibile, Alexandre Gibon, ran Commentry from 1863 until 1890. Emile Cheysson, always on the lookout for the exemplary corporate manager, singled out Gibon for his achievements as an "engineer and *patron*." Gibon's experience with "industrial and social realities" provided him with a perspective that predisposed him to concentrate on direct worker/employer collaboration at the factory level. But, as Cheysson pointed out, such collaboration bore no resemblance to relations on the basis of mutual equality. Gibon considered his plant an "enlarged family" and played the role of "father" to his workers, although his paternal solicitude did not lack for discipline.[3]

Gibon worked for several companies in the late 1840s and 1850s before he arrived at Commentry. During that time he became acquainted with the work of Le Play, which set him on the path to his vocation as a "knowledgeable and skillful plant manager, devoted to his workers." When Gibon took charge of Commentry the factory employed a thousand workers; by 1889 that number had risen to fourteen hundred, reflecting increased pig iron production and the use of the area's high-quality coking coal for the manufacture of steel.[4]

Having proved his mettle as a progressive manager of production, Gibon turned his attention to the management of labor. He displayed an obsession with constant personal intervention and surveillance and paid meticulous attention to every detail of his workers' lives on and off the job (he made a point of arriving at work at 4:45 every morning so that he could personally greet the first shift as it came on at 5:00). In 1869, Gibon organized a consumers' cooperative, which replaced the monopoly of local merchants to whom Commentry's workers had been heavily in debt. By 1887, 50 percent

3. Alexis Delaire, *Alexandre Gibon* (Paris, 1898), 120–24.
4. *Ibid.,* 14–51.

of the work force had enrolled in the cooperative and owned three-quarters of its shares. Gibon must have achieved some success because he was attacked by the left-wing republican deputy for the arrondissement of Commentry, Pierre Aujame, for ruining the local merchants and "exploiting" the workers.[5]

What Aujame termed exploitation Gibon considered the acquittal of his social responsibilities and his contribution to social peace. He pointed to the benefits of cooperatives, schools, and housing as proof of the superiority of collaboration over confrontation. Cooperatives in particular provided workers with valuable "economic instruction," that is, an acquaintance with the advantages to be gained from loyalty to the company. Nevertheless, when circumstances dictated, Gibon did not hesitate to resort to manipulation or threats, as when he headed off several strikes by persuading a few favored senior workers to rein in their brethren. In return, he attempted to minimize structural unemployment by refusing to invest heavily in new capital equipment so as to avoid massive layoffs should the market for enlarged capacity suddenly collapse. Gibon calculated correctly that investment in social peace would pay dividends at least as substantial as investment in plant and machinery.[6]

When he retired from Commentry in 1890, Gibon moved to Paris, where he occupied a sinecure as general consultant to the parent corporation and had the leisure and income to indulge in full-time propagandizing for social engineering and paternalism. (He had done some of that while at Commentry for the Unions de la paix sociale.) Gibon wrote frequently for *La Réforme Sociale*, mostly about the threat of socialism and the menace of strikes. His interventions in the meetings of the Société d'économie sociale invariably focused on labor relations in heavy industry (see Chapter II). As did other businessmen of similar experience and ideological bent, Gibon took an active part in several organizations that dealt with the social question: the Comité de défense et de progrès social, the Musée social, the Société anonyme des habitations à bon marché de St. Denis, the Ligue nationale de la prévoyance et de la mutualité, and one of France's principal big business lobbies, the Société d'encouragement

5. *Ibid.*, 52–55, 71–72.
6. *Ibid.*, 56–70.

pour l'industrie nationale, in which Cheysson held a prominent place.[7]

In his commentaries on labor/capital relations Gibon was driven to several contradictory positions, not an unusual occupational hazard encountered by the peddlers of paternalism. He stood foursquare for laissez-faire, whose nostrums he repeated with mind-numbing regularity. But for him, political economy stopped at the factory gates. Equality could not be tolerated in business; social peace could not be left to chance. Absolute authority, Gibon insisted, was "indispensable to management; without authority an industrial regiment quickly ends up in disarray, as an army in battle without leadership and hierarchical command from the general down to the corporal." This hard-nosed, top-sergeant approach to social relations was not a rhetorical pose. As enterprises became larger, massed concentrations of workers more numerous, and social tensions heightened, bourgeois self-righteousness could not conceal a mood of embattlement and fear. Despite his self-assurance, Gibon appeared defensive and nervous: "No one can deny that the current financial scandals [the reference is to Panama] have produced rumblings of discontent, and this discontent mobilizes troops ready to march against capital; capital is the enemy against which some would arouse the masses. . . . We must treat the evil men responsible for these scandals as criminals; but these corrupt men, adventurers, pirates, are a disgrace to the country and should suffer the full weight of the law; however, capital accumulated by labor and serving labor . . . demands respect as much for its source as its achievement." Martial metaphors, although softened by appeals to reasonableness, ill-fitted conceptions of solidarity based upon common interest or even enlightened paternalism. Yet it was just such paternalism that Gibon apparently preached when he encouraged industrialists to build workers' housing, institute profit sharing, and perform other good deeds. The contradiction may be resolved by noting that each paternal prescription addressed the same maladies: strikes, disorder, and upheaval. Doing good meant, above all, defending order.[8]

7. RS, XXVII (1894), 273; Delaire, Alexandre Gibon, 77–96; Folio 1202, p. ix, AMS.

8. Alexandre Gibon, "Des divers modes de rémunération du travail," Mémoires et comptes-rendus de la Société des Ingénieurs civils, No. 2 (1890), 238, quoted in Alberto

Social prescriptions, like medical ones, must be dispensed by experts. Gibon had concluded on the basis of his own experience that the emerging cadres of industrial engineers and corporate managers required training in "economic and social science" so they could manage their labor forces more effectively. The engineer's vocation demanded that he penetrate the worker's home and encourage him to save ("without thrift there is no freedom") and to appreciate the pleasures of family life. Rather than remaining aloof from the social mechanisms of the factory, the engineer had to get down on the shop floor, "enlighten the worker" on all these matters, and engage in "friendly discussions, first with foremen, then with production-team leaders, and finally with the masses themselves." The result of these efforts would be the routinization of surveillance, the reinforcement of hierarchical relationships within the plant, and the insulation of workers from disruptive political influences. Nothing less should be expected from the tough industrial manager, who brandished the iron fist of control encased in the velvet glove of reform. But Henri Hauser, from an altogether different background as a scholar and educator ideologically inclined to social liberalism, made much the same point. He did not speak of profits and losses or productivity and efficiency, but he understood the political bottom line. As committed to the containment of class struggle as Gibon, Hauser deplored the lack of training in "social economy" among "those personnel from which we recruit our social general staff. Not only do future state engineers require a thorough knowledge of working-class needs, but the same goes for employers, landowners, civil engineers, all the bosses in positions to command men." [9]

Léon Say, chairman of the 1889 Exposition's social economy group, did not see any contradiction between free-market relations and various strategies for the command of men. On one hand, Say barely concealed his disdain for those who appeared to depart from the

---

Melucci, "Action patronale, pouvoir, organisation: Règlements d'usine et contrôle de la main-d'oeuvre au xix siècle," *Mouvement Social,* No. 97 (1976), 140; Alexandre Gibon, "Des conditions de l'harmonie dans l'industrie," *RS,* XXV (1893), 695, 765–66, 779.

9. Alexandre Gibon, "L'Enseignement des sciences sociales dans nos grandes écoles industrielles," *RIP,* IV (1890), 259–64; Henri Hauser, *L'Enseignement des sciences sociales* (Paris, 1903), 194.

path of laissez-faire orthodoxy, specifically singling out proposals for state intervention in production relations. According to Charles Gide, who had a different view, Say took "malicious" pleasure in underscoring the "irony" of awarding the Grand Prize in the section dealing with state intervention to the Liberty and Property Defense League of England, an organization devoted exclusively to combating any abridgment of entrepreneurial freedom. On the other hand, Say did not object to paternalism, understanding that it reinforced rather than subverted the employer's authority and, as Cheysson pointed out, made good business sense.[10] Yet, in taking that stance, Say inadvertently skirted the path of reaction. A doctrine that claimed for capital the prerogative to set the terms of production in the workplace risked compromising its only morally defensible principle: the freedom of the individual in the marketplace. If, in other words, what Karl Marx called the "silent compulsion of economic relations" characteristic of capitalist production proved insufficient, then the extraeconomic compulsion implicit in paternalism—always the mailed fist in the velvet glove—mocked the bourgeoisie's expressed faith in the evenhanded operations of the laws of political economy.[11] Thus a politics of paternalism, to the extent that it was anchored in social defense, could, *force majeur*, shade into a politics of repression.

A similar contemporary projection came from an unexpected quarter, Paul Leroy-Beaulieu's *Economiste français*. Leroy-Beaulieu had little regard for paternalism in any form because of its corporate antiliberal implications. He believed in the Invisible Hand, which, of course, meant a tough stand against working-class combinations. Moreover, he argued that far from promoting social peace in the workplace, paternalism had the opposite effect. Paternalism invited socialism and produced unpleasant counterrevolutionary strategies because an emphasis on fringe benefits called attention to inadequate wages. Welfare programs, then, would be perceived as a swindle and provide grist for the busy mills of left-wing agitators. Leroy-

10. Léon Say, *Economie sociale. Exposition universelle internationale de 1889. Groupe d'Economie sociale: Rapport général* (Paris, 1891), vi–ix; *Exposition 1900,* V, 48; *Exposition 1889,* II, 371–76.

11. Karl Marx, *Capital,* ed. Friedrich Engels (3 vols.; New York, 1967), Vol. I, Chap. 28.

Beaulieu thus turned the argument for paternalism's political rationale on its head and exposed the paternalists' belief that the relative level of wages was irrelevant and exclusive reliance on market forces dangerous for capital. As the Lyonese industrialist Auguste Isaac pointed out, large enterprises, on several of whose boards he sat, could not afford to ignore paternalist strategies. Where they operated, "stability prevailed," "conflicts" were "less acute," and socialists and "communists" were absent. Premiums or other payoffs for loyal and diligent work took on the "character of a reward, that is to say a kind of generosity that reserves for the [employer] the moral right to direct and to control the employee."[12]

Cheysson's commentaries on *institutions patronales* for the 1889 Exposition were full of the law-and-order notions prevalent in Isaac's remarks a few years later. Hardly a dimension of working-class life escaped control and surveillance in the companies whose paternal programs Cheysson described. In each case efforts to import or to sustain the political mastery of capital over labor received heavy emphasis. Thus the zinc processor Vieille-Montagne's antialcoholism campaign included equal parts of prevention and repression. The sale of alcoholic beverages was barred from company housing, and strict rules against drinking were enforced in the factories. The company ascribed its low turnover in part to its tough policy on alcoholism, which meant that offenders quickly got the gate *pour encourager les autres*. At Anzin, after the great strike of 1884, the company's managers combined a hard line against organized workers with a multitude of welfare programs ranging from expanded housing, free education, and workmen's compensation to sport and recreation societies. Philanthropy was not involved. The company's paternalism gave it the leverage to enforce its rules of behavior on and off the job. Anyone who did not toe the line was swiftly deprived of benefits. Similar installations existed elsewhere, for instance at Baccarat and at Blanzy, but with contrary results. Baccarat recorded no strikes—although surely its failure to mechanize had something to do with that—whereas Blanzy experienced several. Excessive controls could backfire, as Jules Chagot discovered. Although the com-

12. *L'Economiste français*, May 20, 1893; Auguste Isaac, "Le Patronage à l'exposition de Lyon," *RS*, XXXIII (1897), 162, 170.

pany's mutual aid societies purportedly were run by workers' representatives, "employer's collaborators" always seemed to have the last word.[13] No one likes playing with a stacked deck.

The textile manufacturers of Roubaix attempted a variation on direct control that despite its brief and unsuccessful existence reproduced several of the elements of corporate paternalist politics. I refer to the *syndicat mixte*. After passage of the 1884 law removing most legal fetters on associations, the mill owners grasped the opportunity to create an association based on the principle of "*the union of capital and labor*." This corporate structure, in their view, held the advantage over separate workers' and employers' associations because it elevated "industrial interests" over particular interests (Jevons' "vertical" associations), thereby neutralizing class struggle. Although neither yellow union nor company union, the *syndicat mixte* worked to similar purposes. It brought together employers and workers in a tight formation within each factory and each factory within an industrywide cluster. Superficially, labor and capital enjoyed equal representation in each mill and in the industry's *conseil syndical*. But some were more equal than others. Six workers sat on each factory council, presided over by the boss or a "reliable employee" appointed by him. The council and an exclusively workers' committee on "social studies" took up all questions relating to industrial relations and acted as a propaganda mechanism to recruit unaffiliated workers. Their discussions, in theory, could take up any issue, but in actuality they were restricted by the authority of the employers' council to act on or dismiss any initiative emanating from the workers' groups.[14]

The *syndicat mixte* existed primarily to supervise the multitude of good works, welfare projects, philanthropies, and cooperatives organized by the Roubaix bourgeoisie. In this respect it resembled company-sponsored associations elsewhere. But the rigid hierarchical form of the *syndicat* made the difference. By associating workers and

13. *Exposition 1889*, II, 458–65, 482, 513; Georges Michel, *Histoire d'un centre ouvrier: Les Concessions d'Anzin* (Paris, 1891), 229–57.
14. *RS*, LIV (1907), 444–47; Alfred Renouard and Léon Moy, *Les Institutions ouvrières et sociales du département du Nord* (Lille, 1889), 83–85; *Exposition 1900*, Vol. XVI, Pt. 1, pp. 554–55.

management at every point, the textile entrepreneurs hoped to instill the collective, corporate spirit on which the efficient functioning of the industry depended. Moreover, by involving workers or their representatives in the details of running the various associations, the employers expected to relieve the pressure for higher wages. Employers opposed wage increases on purely competitive grounds, arguing that the industry could not afford higher labor costs. But their argument concealed the operations of a cutthroat market for labor power within the industry—in which they held the upper hand—behind appeals to "familial" solidarity. Paternalism as practiced in Roubaix was less an attempt to maintain obsolete conceptions of patriarchal authority and responsibility than a weapon wielded by capital in its ongoing struggle with labor.[15]

The Catholic orientation of the Roubaix bourgeoisie, reflected in the hagiolatrous nomenclature attached to several mutual aid societies (Saint-Joseph, Notre-Dame, Saint-Henri), suggests an ideological cast not typical of French industry as a whole. But we should not leap to the conclusion that the *syndicat mixte*'s confessional garb disqualifies it from being classified as a variant of bourgeois paternalism. Although the Roubaix bourgeoisie brought to its businesslike and practical efforts its own unique ideological and cultural baggage, its associations, designed to foster class collaboration, operated for the same political purpose as those elsewhere. At another time, when religious questions were taken seriously as political issues, liberal reformers, social scientists, and establishment politicians would have ignored the *syndicat mixte* or greeted it with hostility. That they did not and that the likes of Charles Gide and Léon Say joined with the stalwarts of the Société d'économie sociale to give the *syndicat mixte* favorable notice testifies to the primacy of class interest over ideological hangovers from another age.[16] Confessional discord had become too expensive.

Nevertheless, *syndicats mixtes* did not prosper. Their number throughout the Nord fell consistently during the waning years of the

15. *RS*, LIV (1907), 451; Henri Rollet, *L'Action sociale des catholiques en France, 1871–1910* (2 vols.; Paris, 1948), I, 309–11.

16. Charles Gide, *Les Institutions de progrès social* (4th ed.; Paris, 1912), 184; Say, *Economie sociale*, 117.

nineteenth century as the number of employer and working-class organizations (mostly the latter) increased.[17] In Roubaix the local
bourgeoisie tried to interest white-collar employees and shopkeepers
after failing to recruit workers in any great quantity.[18]

The decade and a half following the 1889 Exposition witnessed an
accelerated and widespread installation of social machinery, perhaps
spurred by the near collapse of the international economy in 1893
and the rapid growth in the number of *syndicats ouvriers*. Not only
did this happen industry by industry but the accent shifted quantitatively and qualitatively to comprehensive systems of direct and
indirect control, in which politicians, businessmen, and managers of
both social economy and social liberal persuasions played leading
practical and ideological roles. The former had been active for a long
time and their influence still counted heavily; the latter, among them
Gide, Jules Siegfried, and Léon Bourgeois, although hardly appear-
ing from nowhere, surfaced in force. With the influx of individuals
less obsessed with narrow conceptions of paternalism and more
committed to the long-term interests of capital as opposed to quick
victories at any cost, social reform took on the aspect of a complete
political strategy. Association, cooperation, and class collaboration
received more attention than previously. But nothing fundamental
had changed. Social liberals only extended the original perceptions
of the social economists as to which way the political winds were
blowing. Ironically, the former developed the corporate implications
latent in the latter's ambiguous criticisms of political economy,
thereby providing a veil of respectability—and impeccable republican credentials—for the French bourgeoisie's contribution to the
ongoing class struggle.[19]

Approaches to the labor question became politically more sophisticated and far-reaching. Bourgeois paternalism prefigured a sce-

17. Charles Gide, *Economie sociale* (Paris, 1905), 143–48; Adolphe Créhange, *La Solidarité dans les associations professionnelles* (Bordeaux, 1907), 3–20; Léon de Seilhac, "L'Association nécessaire," *Action Populaire*, Nos. 9–10 (1902), 347.

18. This information courtesy of Bonnie G. Smith.

19. Seilhac, "L'Association nécessaire," 337; Gide, *Les Institutions, passim*. I use the term
"class struggle" broadly to incorporate political, ideological, and other forms of social relations and antagonisms. It need not, and usually does not, take on the form of open
combat.

nario developed by Karl Mannheim in a radically different context forty years later. Mannheim observed that "the problem of social control" could not be resolved if "the workings of society as a whole" were "artificially divided into water-tight compartments such as economics, political science, administration, and education. We do not realize," he went on, "that all these seemingly separate sciences are in fact interrelated, that they refer to social techniques whose ultimate aim is to secure the functioning of the social order by bringing an appropriate influence to bear on the behaviour and attitudes of men." Mannheim, of course, was talking about social democratic planning and not about bourgeois social management. Nor did he intend to make an explicit case for the rationalization of corporate forms of social organization.[20] Nevertheless, reformist perspectives in France during the 1890s and early 1900s, especially among social liberals, bear a striking and, for social democrats I suppose, a disconcerting similarity to Mannheim's outlook.

Capital, Labor, and the State

In contradiction to paternalist reform, social democratic planning began and ended with the state. Yet changing attitudes toward the role of the state in social relations became evident in the 1890s. Hard-liners such as Alexandre Gibon considered outside intervention in class confrontations—particularly during strikes—at best a nuisance and at worst encouragement for workers to press their demands on management. The banker Edouard Aynard, with Auguste Isaac a leader of the Lyonese big bourgeoisie and active in housing and educational projects for Lyon's working class, supported legislative action in the Chamber of Deputies that restricted child and female labor and promoted mutual aid societies while opposing the establishment of an eight-hour day for miners. Aynard clearly drew the line between state support of the young and the purportedly weak and interference in market relations. By favoring mutual aid societies, in which capital and labor theoretically collaborated on equal terms, he came down on the side of association. In 1889

20. Karl Mannheim, *Man and Society in an Age of Reconstruction* (London, 1940), 270.

Cheysson had only harsh words for the state, which he accused of imposing on society a "suffocating monotony." Yet by 1893, he had changed his tune. Unmediated class collaboration remained the preferred route to social peace, but the State and its multiple instruments could not be ignored, if only in the interests of political calculation: "Better that it is with us than against us."[21]

Charles Gide showed a deeper appreciation of the role of the state in bourgeois society. In his survey of the social economy group at the 1900 Exposition, Gide noted with satisfaction the attention paid to state institutions for "social betterment" (he used the English). Confounding the Cassandras of political economy, the state turned out to be not the enemy of entrepreneurial freedom but its ally. The establishment of mediation boards to settle industrial disputes, a nationwide pension fund, measures to promote working-class housing, and various extensions of the educational system, to mention but a few, complemented and paralleled rather than usurped paternalist programs. Furthermore, Gide saw nothing intrinsically distasteful in "municipal socialism" of the sort practiced in places such as Birmingham, Brussels, and Turin. The republican state, in Gide's view and those of other social liberals such as Waldeck-Rousseau, fulfilled its *raison d'être* by defending capitalist production and its reproduction in both the ideological and material spheres. This approval did not translate into consistent knee-jerk support of capital against all of labor's demands, for the interests of individual capitalists did not correspond necessarily to the interests of capital as a whole. It was the business of the state to find political ways to accommodate the acceptable demands of the working class—acceptable in the sense of not subverting the fundamental relationships that made the system work. Léon Bourgeois understood this back in 1882 (and he never forgot it), when, as prefect of the Tarn, he scolded the Marquis de Solages, owner of the Société des Mines de Carmaux, for his repressive labor policy—much to the latter's indignation. Bourgeois' strategy was simple: the workers so far "had escaped the influence of revolutionary collectivism"; should the state

21. *RS,* XXV (1893), 260–80, 340–56, 515–33; Jean Jolly (ed.), *Dictionnaire des parlementaires français* (10 vols.; Paris, 1960–70), I, 428–29; *Exposition 1900,* V, 50–51; *HBM,* V (1893), 24.

opt for "an untimely deployment of force," socialist "agitators would have a field day denouncing the republican government as no more favorable to workers than other regimes and we will have opened the door to revolutionary doctrines."[22] Sometimes the bourgeoisie had to be protected from itself.

State action did not poach on employers' territory. Quite the contrary, it gave the industrial bourgeoisie and social managers the opportunity to concentrate on the social and mechanical machinery at the point of production and provided an umbrella for the work of parapolitical organizations such as the Société française des habitations à bon marché, the Musée social, and the Société d'éducation sociale. These groups, all of which appeared after the mid-1890s, institutionalized previously *ad hoc* arrangements on the factory level and concerned themselves with workers as a class. The social machinery became more intensively directed toward maximizing efficiency and productivity, while retaining earlier forms of surveillance and control. According to Michelle Perrot, Charles Schneider of Creusot rejected LePlayist "paternalism" (what I call patriarchy) in favor of a policy of "material profit and security." The Paris-Orléans railroad company proudly advertised an accelerated program of technical education for its workers—not an isolated case (see Chapter VII).[23] Gide foresaw a profitable future for corporate paternalism, "institutions for moral health," which he considered "the quintessentially twentieth-century form of employer intervention." He noted, however, that new forms of paternalism would require a "working-class population that has benefited from an advanced economic, social, and moral education," in other words, an ideologically integrated working class. Given these conditions, the contemporary enterprise would become a paradigm for the corporate social organization of labor. Even intensified work had its bright side. It

22. Gide, *Les Institutions*, 19; *Exposition 1900*, V, 48; Gide, *Economie sociale*, 239–40; Marx, *Capital*, III, 791; Gareth S. Jones, "Society and Politics at the Beginning of the World Economy," *Cambridge Journal of Economics*, I (1977), 85; Rolande Trempé, *Les Mineurs de Carmaux* (2 vols.; Paris, 1971), II, 645–46; Perrot, *Les Ouvriers en grève*, II, 705.

23. *Exposition 1900*, V, 54; Michelle Perrot, "The Three Ages of Industrial Discipline in Nineteenth-Century France," in John Merriman (ed.), *Consciousness and Class Experience in Nineteenth-Century Europe* (New York, 1979), 160; Compagnie du Chemin de fer d'Orléans, *Notice sur les institutions fondées par la compagnie* (Paris, 1900), 18–19.

provided increased free time "for the recreation necessary to recuperate from the wounds caused by intensive labor—thus concentrated efforts constitute genuine moral progress. . . . These days we hear a great deal of talk about building a 'People's Palace'; let us rather make the factory itself into a genuine people's palace."[24]

Gide's metaphor may have been overdrawn, but there was nothing fanciful about the political conception behind it. He only spun out the implications of concentrated production for labor/capital relations and perhaps for society as a whole. As an ideologist that was his business. One crucial question remained: Where did labor formations fit into the picture? Failing the *syndicat mixte* and the noxious odors of the *jaunes*, the best prospects lay with nonmilitant *syndicats ouvriers*. To the extent that labor unions defended the legitimate economic interests of workers, that is, avoided politics, they were welcomed by paternalist reformers. Gibon and Cheysson worried about strikes incessantly, but Gide pointed out that not all *syndicats* favored strikes as a defensive weapon and that strikes did not necessarily constitute the best test of militancy.[25]

Léon de Seilhac, the Musée social's expert on trade unions, claimed to have found elements of calm and reason in workers' strike actions by the turn of the century. Other sources prove that the new tactics reflected better working-class organization rather than a uniform shift away from militancy. Nevertheless, Seilhac drew the important distinction between economic and political strikes. The former could have the paradoxical effect of strengthening ties between classes. They "highlight the legitimacy of certain demands and the ridiculousness of others. The strike exposes the areas of working-class discontent and allows employers to consider them seriously." Seilhac could not condemn political strikes harshly enough. Paul de Rousiers, whose conception of social science included cheerfully knocking troublemaking workers on the head, insisted that carefully selected workers, encouraged to assert their solidarity, constituted a potentially conservative force to further class collaboration: "Social

24. Gide, *Les Institutions*, 158, 169–70; *Exposition 1900*, V, 192–93.
25. *Questions Pratiques de Législation Ouvrière et d'Economie Sociale*, III (1902), 23; Gide, *Economie sociale*, 97–98.

peace, if it is to rest on solid foundations, requires a working-class elite capable of organizing itself." [26]

Conservative trade-union leaders echoed these positions. Auguste Besse, president of the Union fraternelle des employés du commerce et de l'industrie, deplored that "workers up until now [1901] have used the *syndicat* only as an aggressive weapon . . . to struggle against their bosses." That narrow conception of the function of the *syndicat* "has become a stumbling block on the path to social progress." For conservative bourgeois reformers and social liberals alike, Besse's union provided an admirable model for all working-class formations, blue-collar as well as white. The Union's 1903 general congress proved its loyalty to social peace by elaborating a program of "exclusively *trade* and *corporative* demands" and steered clear of the "theory of class struggle as a basis for its principles." [27] Nevertheless, the "theory of class struggle" was abroad in the land, and even the most progressive reformers seized every instrument of political leverage they could. Experience had taught that the power of capital to impose its will on labor depended upon time, place, and circumstances. Direct control, especially if patently repressive, had severe limitations, especially in the absence of mechanisms for force. Only the state possessed such weapons, and it could not be counted on to defend employers' interests at every turn. But the limited role played by the state in social relations created opportunities for the French bourgeoisie to broaden its conception and implementation of paternalist systems.

Real Estate and the Social Question: Working-class Housing

Building societies organized by industrialists to finance the construction of working-class housing had become common in France, as in other capitalist countries, by the end of the nineteenth century.

26. Edward Shorter and Charles Tilly, *Strikes in France, 1830–1968* (Cambridge, 1974), Chap. 13; Léon de Seilhac, *Les Grèves* (Paris, 1903), 21–22, 193–201; Paul de Rousiers, "Le Paternalisme allemand," *La Science Sociale*, XXXI (1901), 408.

27. *BSES*, I (1901), 15; *Revue Populaire d'Economie Sociale*, II (1903), 111–14.

Sixty-five were in place by 1903 with sixteen more under way. They can be traced back at least to the 1860s, when industrialists such as Jean Dollfus of Mulhouse (cotton textiles, machinery, and chemical dyes), Jules Chagot of Blanzy (coal mining), and Richard Waddington of Rouen (cotton textiles) put up housing blocks, which they then rented to favored workers, charging off the rents against the ultimate purchase price. No less an authority than Henri Baudrillart, who, befitting his stature as one of France's leading economists, kept his eye on the political bottom line, pronounced these projects and others like them essential to the moral health and stability of the working-class family. Efforts to expand working-class housing command attention for other reasons, however. First, whatever initiatives appeared at midcentury, the movement neither gathered strength nor received concentrated attention among the French bourgeoisie until the last decade of the century. Second, it occupied a central place in the politics of social reform. As one of the leading advocates of working-class housing, Georges Picot, put it: "The only [social question] currently subject to a definite solution, without any risk of socialism, is that of improving housing. . . . Does this not constitute an obligation for the owners of capital?" Third, the leading figures in the movement were also active in other areas of paternalist reform, social economy, and social science. Finally, the campaign for low-cost housing, although thoroughly treated by Roger Guerrand in isolation, has not been linked to the broad areas of social management and labor discipline.[28] Consequently, I will have less to say about blueprints and bricks than about politics and ideology.

Workers' housing first gained general recognition and attention at the exposition of 1889, where a Congrès international des habitations ouvrières convened under the aegis of the social economy section. Jules Siegfried (to whom we shall return shortly) presided. He "exalted the worker-owner become 'thrifty, prudent, insulated against

28. Léon de Seilhac, *Manuel pratique d'économie sociale* (Paris, 1904), 109; *Questions Pratiques*, III (1902), 48; *Exposition 1889*, II, 193–94; Eugène Véron, *Les Institutions ouvrières de Mulhouse et ses environs* (Paris, 1866), 300; *Bulletin de la Société Industrielle de Mulhouse* (1864–69); Henri Baudrillart, *L'Amélioration des logements d'ouvriers dans ses rapports avec l'esprit de famille* (Paris, 1889); *HBM*, I (1890), 21; R.-H. Guerrand, *Les Origines du logement social en France* (Paris, 1967).

revolutionary and socialist utopias, finally wrested from the clutches of the cabaret.'" Picot, a distinguished historian (he wrote a multi-volume study of the Estates General) and well-connected in big business circles (he sat on the board of the Paris-Lyon-Méditerranée railroad), delivered the report for the congress. In it and elsewhere he developed three intertwined themes: that environment uniquely determined working-class behavior; that social reform was the first line of defense in "the battle against revolutionary socialism"; and that the bourgeoisie reinforced its dominant position in society through coordinated acts of paternalism. Displaying a shrewd appreciation of hegemonic strategies, Picot noted that "the influence of a class . . . depends exclusively on the services it provides." Thus paternalist reform was "good politics."[29]

Picot did not conceal his disdain for conventional politics. He denounced socialist politics and that of the Chamber of Deputies in equally harsh terms. The former looked to the state to solve social problems; the latter proved incapable of any consistent action. Picot even went so far as to question the legitimacy of parliamentary politics in any important sphere and advocated delivering increased authority into the hands of the Conseil d'Etat—a curious position for one who wrote off the experiments of the Second Empire as futile exercises in "state socialism." Instruments of social reform, he insisted, belonged in the hands of employers, their organizations, and experts—like himself—who understood their interests. As did the social liberals and solidarists, Picot chose association, but for somewhat different reasons. Association constituted a "unique counterweight to democracy," which produced a leveling effect on society. Moreover, association—and here we glimpse the corporate vision—arranged individuals according to their "social functions" as well as promoting the collaboration of capital and labor. In the last analysis Picot was driven to a contradictory ideological position, in which a stubborn adherence to laissez-faire confronted the realities of capitalist concentration. His attempted synthesis harbored deeply reactionary tendencies to the extent that it cast doubt on the effective-

29. *Exposition 1889,* II, 181–228; Guerrand, *Les Origines du logement social,* 284; Georges Picot, *La Lutte contre le socialisme révolutionnaire* (Paris, 1895); Picot, *Un Devoir social et les logements d'ouvriers* (Paris, 1885), 92, 94.

ness of liberal government at a time of class polarization. Several alternatives were available: stiffened reliance on the social dictatorship of capital; state intervention in productive relations; or some combination of the two in the form of state-sponsored corporate organization for labor discipline. In general, Picot held to the first position, one that tallied closely with those of his fellow social economists and won him enough respect in those circles to get him elected president of the Société d'économie sociale for 1892.[30]

Recounting the horrors of the slums in Paris and Lille in gruesome detail, Picot compared those conditions with the tidy dwellings provided workers by the bourgeoisie of Mulhouse, Le Havre, and a score of industrial towns. Contrasting social behavior and political values followed inexorably: in the former case, corruption and degradation; in the latter, "morality and family solidarity. . . . That is a universal law." Proper housing not only encouraged attachments to property, "everyone's passion," but renewed those community bonds characteristic of the *ancien régime* and broken by the Revolution. In an uncertain world of rampant individualism and the threat of "social warfare" entrepreneurial sponsorship and control of *cités ouvrières* promised to create "social hierarchy" on a new basis. Alexis Delaire, editor of *La Réforme Sociale*, to which Picot occasionally contributed, described such projects as manifestations of "social paternalism" *(patronage social)* carried on by the "true social authorities"—LePlayist code for big businessmen.[31]

The Congrès international des habitations ouvrières generated the momentum for the formation, in 1890, of the Société française des habitations à bon marché. Siegfried served as president, Picot and Cheysson as vice-presidents, and Charles Robert as treasurer. Members of the society's board included Edouard Aynard, a major figure in the Société d'économie politique et d'économie sociale of Lyon (see Chapter VI); Charles Blech, textile entrepreneur in Sainte-Marie-aux-Mines (Haut-Rhin) and a longtime proponent of popular education; Dr. Octave du Mesnil, one of France's "social doc-

---

30. Picot, *Un Devoir social*, 25, 60–61, 67–68; Picot, *La Lutte*, 58–77; *RS*, XXIII (1892), 40.

31. *Exposition 1889*, II, 184; Picot, *Un Devoir social*, 9–14, 47; Picot, *La Lutte*, 9–13; Alexis Delaire, *Les Logements d'ouvriers et le devoir des classes dirigeantes* (Lyon, 1886), 4–6.

tors," who wrote one book on housing conditions and coauthored another; and Eugène Rostand, patriarch of savings banks and mutual credit societies. Among other active members of the society— all from the big bourgeoisie or associated with it—were Jacques Siegfried, who ran the family textile business in Le Havre; J.-J. Bourcart, a pioneering paternalist in upper Alsace; Delaire; Jean Dollfus, president of the Société industrielle of Mulhouse; Gibon; Albert Gigot, former prefect of police in Paris and managing director of the Forges d'Alais; Emile Menier, chocolate tycoon and one of Nicaragua's largest landowners; Eugène Schneider of Le Creusot; Armand Peugeot, manufacturer of corset frames, hardware, bicycles, and—shortly—automobiles; Albert Trombert; Léon Say; and Joseph Barberet, the conservative labor leader expelled from the 1879 Congrès ouvrier by Jules Guesde.[32]

Jules Siegfried's leading role in promoting low-cost housing and his wide-ranging activities in other areas of paternalist reform and politics merit him special attention. Elsewhere, I have sketched his earlier career: his upbringing in the tightly knit community of Protestant textile manufacturers of Mulhouse, where his relatives had been active for decades in the mutually reinforcing businesses of making money and sponsoring good works for the local labor force; his sharp business sense as a cotton broker in Le Havre, where he amassed a fortune by cornering a sizable portion of the Bombay cotton market during the American Civil War; his retirement from business (left to his brother Jacques' management) and plunge into politics and philanthropy, resulting in his election as mayor of Le Havre, in effect making him political boss of that city throughout the remainder of the century; and his leadership in the formation of the Le Havre circle of the Ligue de l'enseignement.[33]

Siegfried showed an early interest in paternalist reform, which became a consuming passion. He considered such ventures necessary "for the preservation of order in society" and "the best weapon

32. *HBM*, I (1890), 76–87; Octave Du Mesnil, *L'Hygiène à Paris: L'Habitation du pauvre* (Paris, 1890); Octave Du Mesnil and Charles Mangenot, *Etude d'hygiène et d'économie sociale* (Paris, 1899); *RIP*, IV (1890), 121.

33. Sanford Elwitt, *The Making of the Third Republic: Class and Politics in France, 1868–1884* (Baton Rouge, 1975), 208–15.

against revolution." According to his son André's admiring testimony, Siegfried led an exemplary personal life, every waking moment of which, it seemed, was devoted to transforming the French worker into a "content and calm citizen." He led an ascetic existence and was obsessed with the nutritional value of food, to the extent of weighing each portion on a balance at every meal and not even sparing invited guests. Nor did he spare anyone else, having published several brochures aimed at a working-class audience on how to eat sensibly on a modest budget.[34]

The paternalist was also, and above all else, an ideologue, although by no means rigid. Siegfried accepted the basic tenets of political economy without following its precepts blindly. In an essay on the causes of working-class poverty, he recited the conventional litany, arguing that hard times for workers resulted from such "accidental" economic conjunctures as shrunken markets, mechanization, and excessive competition for employment. The poor contributed to their own misery by drinking excessively, observing "Holy Monday," and generally lacking in prudence and thrift. Siegfried did not rule out state action to provide for the poor but preferred private charity. He cited as worthy examples *comités de patronage* in various industrial centers that organized employment bureaus and scouted opportunities for emigration. Siegfried expected emigration to play a key role in reducing the pressure on the domestic labor market and in ridding society of misfits. He looked to Algeria and other French colonies to absorb excess population—a solution that would have warmed the heart of his political lieutenant, colonial lobbyist, and future president of the Republic, Félix Faure.[35]

In 1875, Siegfried and other members of the Le Havre business community organized the Cercle Franklin to provide a setting in which workers would find enlightenment, diversion, and recreation. The Cercle prefigured the foundations that the Musée social would promote on a national scale twenty years later. It combined the functions of a YMCA, a company social club, and an adult education

34. Jules Siegfried, *Le Cercle Franklin du Havre* (Le Havre, 1877), 20–22; André Siegfried, *Mes souvenirs de la troisième république. Mon père et son temps: Jules Siegfried, 1836–1922* (Paris, 1952), 41, 55; Roger Merlin, *Jules Siegfried, sa vie, son oeuvre* (Paris, n.d.), 40.

35. Jules Siegfried, *La Misère, son histoire, ses causes, ses remèdes* (Paris, 1879), 44–54, 58–63, 115–23.

center—a controlled off-the-job environment. Its original inspiration came from a similar institution in Mulhouse and from England,
where such institutions as the Workingman's Club of Manchester
had become famous for promoting the "intellectual and moral well-
being of the working class" and for providing alternatives to smoking, drinking, and congregating in pubs and on the streets. Among
its activities the Le Havre Cercle sponsored a choral society, which
on one occasion performed a "Cantata for the Republic" that "celebrated, in robust tones, fraternity, labor, and peace." It encouraged
family solidarity by organizing Sunday concerts, outings, and informal discussions on all subjects except religion and politics. Siegfried
insisted that religion had no place in the Cercle because "the workers
will suspect that religion serves only as a cover for political indoctrination." Indeed, as his involvement in reform movements expanded, Siegfried found that the religious conflicts that had
obstructed the formation of a solid bourgeois political front became
increasingly inconvenient. Despite his Calvinism (which he took
very seriously) and his association with such anticlerical militants as
Jules Steeg and Auguste Scheurer-Kestner, Siegfried had no difficulty collaborating with the fervently Catholic Comte de Chambrun
in the foundation of the Musée social, nor did he hesitate to add his
name to the roster of the Unions des amis de la paix sociale in 1891.[36]

Work on the Cercle Franklin led Siegfried to working-class housing, first in Le Havre and then on a nationwide scale. This became
his favorite project among many, including profit sharing, and it
provided maximum scope for his paternalist zeal. In his home town
Siegfried helped organize a building society that constructed 120
"small, clean, and charming" houses. Thirty years later he noted a
substantial drop in mortality rates among dwellers in the model
community compared to those prevailing in "rotten tenements." In
addition to their contribution to working-class health and well-
being, low-cost housing represented an investment in order: "Do we
want to combat both misery and socialism; do we want to erect fortresses of order, morality, political and social moderation? Then let
us build *cités ouvrières!*" Jules Simon, one of Siegfried's heroes, un-

---

36. Siegfried, *Le Cercle Franklin,* 5–6, 10, 18; Merlin, *Jules Siegfried,* 29; *RS, XXII
(1892), 17.

derscored the point that business could only profit from such enterprises: "Messieurs the capitalists. . . . Put your money in a public assistance fund, such as the Société française des habitations à bon marché. The only money that you are certain not to lose, the money that will remain in your hands until the hour of your death, is the money that you will have invested [in public housing]."[37]

With the collaboration of other members of the society, Siegfried, a member of the Chamber of Deputies, wrote a bill in 1892 on working-class housing that became law in November, 1894. The law authorized state savings institutions to underwrite loans to building societies and exempted all such constructions from taxes on doors, windows, and land for an initial period of five years. It also put a ceiling of 4 percent on the interest subscribers to the societies could earn (still above the prevailing rate, which hovered at 3 percent in those years of deflation), limited annual rent to a maximum of 323 francs and the purchase price to a maximum of 5,700 francs. These measures had the effect of lowering both building costs and rents while assuring builders an ample rate of return on their investments. They also brought the state into the business of working-class housing, but only marginally and in a limited way. As Picòt had argued in 1889, state involvement in construction or in actual ownership constituted unacceptable competition with private enterprise. Siegfried, no enemy of private enterprise, did not disagree, but he noted the experience of the building societies sponsored by the London County Council (the Webbs' bailiwick). Its experiments in what he called "a little state socialism" proved that "England, the homeland of individual initiative . . . did not hesitate to abandon abstract principles as it proceeded resolutely down the path toward necessary reforms."[38]

In arguing for his bill, Siegfried mixed business, politics, and bourgeois paternalist imperatives. Real estate speculation histori-

37. Merlin, *Jules Siegfried*, 33–36; *Exposition 1889: Congrès international de la participation aux bénéfices* (Paris, 1890); Jules Siegfried, "Les Habitations à bon marché," in Jules Siegfried *et al.*, *Les Applications sociales de la solidarité* (Paris, 1904), 215–17; *HBM*, I (1890), 36–39, IV (1893), 50–51; Siegfried, *La Misère*, 195–99.

38. Gide, *Les Institutions*, 252; Siegfried, "Les Habitations," 221, 225; Siegfried, *Les Habitations à bon marché* (Paris, 1898); Seilhac, *Manuel pratique*, 231–45; *Exposition 1889*, II, 222–24.

cally had favored "luxurious buildings habituated by the bourgeoisie." But "capitalists looking for profitable investments" had ignored opportunities in workers' housing. There, he pointed out,
they will discover "the double advantage of doing good deeds and
gaining a greater return on their capital—not to be disdained under
current conditions of a depressed rate of interest." Echoing Picot,
Cheysson, Delaire, and others, Siegfried pronounced the question
of housing the preeminent social question, without whose resolution all other reforms would prove barren. That this was the case
followed from big industry's steady encroachment into rural regions
or from the expansion of existing industries, like Anzin and Creusot,
into new areas. Almost overnight previously placid villages became
swollen centers of production. Housing had not kept up, and workers were forced to occupy makeshift dwellings. Trouble quickly ensued, in the form of "accumulated discontent with our economic
system," disruption of family life, alcoholism, and "mute anger
against society." Proper housing promised an end to such social dangers and, in addition, produced a stable work force attached to industry and to employers "by a material bond."[39]

Those material bonds might unravel should the worker have no
stake in his property. Industrialists who provided free housing either
by necessity—to encourage "nomadic workers" to settle down—or
by choice—as a wage supplement to selected workers—considered
their largesse to be both a "benefit for the worker" and a "chain to
anchor him." But the worker quickly forgot the benefit and remained conscious only of the chain. Hence it was necessary to impose rents if not to guarantee purchase after years of loyal service.
Only in factories where "peace reigns between employers and workers" did free housing make sense. Elsewhere, among laborers exhibiting tendencies toward "distrustful independence," employers
who indulged in such "paternal hospitality" stood to receive not the
slightest gratitude in return. A stake in property did not guarantee
social peace, however, as the experiences of Blanzy and Creusot
demonstrated. Both had elaborate networks of *cités ouvrières*, and
both witnessed massive strikes at the end of the century.[40]

39. *HBM*, III (1892), 48–49.
40. *Exposition 1889*, II, 191; *HBM*, V (1894), 117.

Nevertheless, the movement to promote working-class housing gathered considerable momentum during the 1890s. Constructions took many forms, both in material aspects and in expressions of social purpose. Armand Peugeot organized the Société coopérative immobilière to build houses in Valentigney (Doubs; population 2,014 in 1881). The society purchased land and advanced workers money to build their own houses, with a twenty-year mortgage payable in annual installments of 4.5 percent interest. Peugeot preferred this arrangement because the land was cheap; his workers had the opportunity to build according to their own tastes rather than to a standardized model; and they tended to stay put. Emile Menier's chocolate factory in Noisel (Seine-et-Marne) employed 1,500 workers (of which 600 were women) and produced 50,000 kilograms of chocolate per day. He began construction of his *cité ouvrière* in 1874 and by 1889 had built 200 dwellings housing 1,000 persons. Each was "exceptionally light and airy" and included a kitchen, three bedrooms, and an attic. A garden surrounded each house, isolating it from its neighbor. Apparently the ideal of association did not extend to sociability among workers. Menier retained title to the houses for which he charged 150 francs annual rent, calculated to coincide with average rents in neighboring towns so that the renter was not "humiliated by what would appear as charity." The company selected its tenants from among favored workers and progressively reduced rents for those with ten, fifteen, and twenty years on the job. "This system was designed to perpetuate a stable labor force; in effect, it offered rewards for seniority." Menier also installed a company store, commissaries for bachelors, a school, a library, and, the most visible symbol of bourgeois pride, a savings bank.[41] Curiously, in both the United States and Britain, large chocolate companies, Hershey and Cadbury, built similar total environments for their workers.

One-industry towns specialized in these constructions. In the village of Rosières (Cher), where a single metallurgical firm employed most of the able-bodied male population, the company had constructed more than two hundred houses for its employees by 1906. The standard architectural pattern for such projects was two attached

---

41. HBM, V (1894), 115–16; Adolphe Joanne, *Géographie du Doubs* (Paris, 1881), 67; *HBM*, III (1892), 450–53; *Exposition 1889*, II, 192.

units of two stories each surrounded by a small garden. The dwellings were distinguished by their uniformity and symmetry, reproducing the "homogeneity" and denying the "individuality" of the company's workers. This pattern was part of a plan deliberately "conceived according to the designs and logic of bourgeois order." Along with the company's other paternalist enterprises, such as its mutual aid society and its pension fund—both controlled by management, working-class housing enlisted "spatial order in the service of social order." The strategy worked through the turbulent years of the 1890s when the company defeated a major strike, but the company could not maintain its labor force in isolation indefinitely or suppress its collective solidarity. By 1906, when outside influences had penetrated Rosières, the company's hegemony suffered irreparable damage.[42]

Entrepreneurs who financed housing construction out of their own pockets generally did not earn a return on their investment much above 3 percent. Picot, noting that situation in the cases of Creusot, Anzin, Blanzy, Thaon (Vosges), Flixecourt (Somme), Honfleur (Calvados), and elsewhere, considered it evidence of an employer's sacrifice on behalf of working-class welfare. Sacrifice it may have been and in some cases undoubtedly was. But that is not the point. For huge companies like several of the above and for the Paris-Orléans railroad, which subsidized construction companies in several towns, the costs of housing must have appeared as mere motes in their accountants' eyes. Moreover, French industrialists, trapped between high labor mobility and depressed prices, were engaged in cutthroat competition to attract and hold workers. Housing costs may have seemed like a sensible long-term investment, especially if they could use low rentals to reduce upward pressures on wages. Finally, as Picot himself admitted, political considerations entered into the employer's calculations, as he "gathered around his talented and loyal workers," enabling him to "imbue them with his own values."[43] Clearly, some sacrifices weighed more heavily than others.

42. Michel Pigenet, "L'Usine et le village: Rosières (1869–1914)," *Mouvement Social,* No. 119 (1982), 33–39, 41, 58–61.
43. *Exposition 1889,* II, 193–94; Compagnie des Chemins de fer d'Orléans, *Notice,* 28–30; *Revue Populaire d'Economie Sociale,* II (1903), 164–68; *HBM,* IV (1893), 282.

How many working-class housing projects operated on a strictly rental basis and how many charged off accumulated rent against final purchase cannot be established. The choices made seem to have varied according to social considerations and ideological inclinations. In the northern coal-mining town of Lens (Pas-de-Calais), for instance, more than eighteen thousand workers rented quarters in dwellings owned by the coal companies. "The companies feared losing their freedom of action vis-à-vis the workers should they sign over the properties." Did that mean the risk of surrendering opportunities for layoffs? It appears likely. Entrepreneurs in more settled communities took the opposite tack. The Société des habitations ouvrières d'Epinal (Vosges) tied rentals into eventual purchase, so as to afford workers the chance to own property. As an added inducement, it built two-family houses so that the future proprietor could supplement his income by renting the other unit.[44]

In Lyon, Edouard Aynard and several other local bankers organized the Société des logements économiques de Lyon. It claimed a capitalization of 4 million francs (a comparatively large sum) devoted to the building of tenements in silk workers' neighborhoods. These structures attracted special attention because of their exceptionally low unit costs, made possible by the use of a form of reinforced concrete (*mâchefer*). Each building represented solidarity incarnate: the ground floor was occupied by an Association alimentaire that served two thousand meals per day; the first floor by a *cercle d'étudiants*, installed to encourage bourgeois youth to mix with their working-class brethren; and the three other floors by apartments. The society did not throw open its doors to just anyone. According to Aynard, it closely inspected potential renters and admitted only those who passed moral muster. In Marseille, where Eugène Rostand headed a group that built low-cost housing, a similar system and outlook prevailed. Rostand and his group "wrested the construction of working-class houses from the hands of speculators and placed it in the hands of honest capitalists." The result, he claimed as he conducted Siegfried, Charles Gide, and Charles Robert on a guided tour of a newly developed neighborhood, "instilled in the

44. Seilhac, *Manuel pratique*, 105; *HBM*, IV (1893), 119–20.

inhabitants a fondness for the hearth." Here, he announced, lay the best prospects for social peace, analogous to the achievements of profit sharing in the world of production.[45]

Working-class housing may not have incarnated broad visions of social reform, but their practical effect contributed to the expansion of bourgeois paternalism. Neither philanthropic impulses nor charitable motives entered into the picture. Any hint of charity in these projects, as Siegfried pointed out, could only be counterproductive: "The serious worker has no interest in handouts; but he is always grateful to whomever helps him get on in the world."[46] Jules Simon contributed a healthily candid perspective on the question of philanthropy: "If we are shrewd, we ought to concern ourselves with the [working class's] well-being for our own sakes. On the one hand, we provide workers with wholesome housing and, on the other, we eliminate dwellings where the epidemics that are sure to wipe us out grow and develop. Thus, let us not put on airs about being humanity's benefactors when we talk about cheap housing; we also are working on behalf of our personal interest."[47]

Order, discipline, efficiency, and the search for social equilibrium were the concerns of those who promoted and built low-cost housing. The campaign for "garden cities" involved the same people, took its inspiration from the same concerns, and translated them into plans for a totally engineered physical environment. I already have noted Emile Cheysson's interest in this project and his collaboration with Picot, Siegfried, and Charles Gide in the Association des cités jardins. More a propaganda vehicle than anything else, the association, as far as can be determined, produced few immediate concrete results. Businessmen did not rush to build model communities, preferring practical developments of the sort described above (although perhaps Menier's town belongs in the former category). But it is the ideological vision and the political purpose that count; for these reasons the social design of garden cities deserves brief comment.

45. *Exposition 1889*, II, 212–13; *HBM*, V (1894), 329–30, I (1890), 169, 325.

46. *HBM*, I (1899), 200.

47. Meeting of the Société française des habitations à bon marché, February 2, 1890, quoted in *RIP*, IV (1890), 122.

Georges Benoît-Lévy, whom Cheysson admired, brought the perspective of the social engineer to the problem of working-class housing. In a preface to one of Benoît-Lévy's tracts, Gide waxed lyrical over the former's conceptions, conjuring up visions of idyllic communities surrounded by flower gardens and orchards, where birds sang and children romped. Workers required such surroundings to nurture their moral health, "to learn to abandon the degenerate habits of the cities, the mob, the tavern, and the *café-concert*." Benoît-Lévy envisioned the garden city not as a refuge from the rigors of industrial production but as an accommodation to, and a reinforcement of, those rigors. Industrial requirements and the integration of workers into industrial culture remained paramount. "Powerfully organized" production led to sound "social and moral conditions." Garden cities, therefore, in Benoît-Lévy's design, followed that of modern industrial installations: they were rationally organized, totally planned, and inhabited by a mathematically determined number of people. Not for nothing did he liken his scheme to a Fourierist *phalanstérie*. In contrast to the original inspiration, however, the garden city neither posed an alternative to capitalist production nor represented a vain effort to recapture a simpler world. Rather, it created an environment appropriate to an "integrated existence" uniting social labor and social life, where "well-being can be organized." Finally, there were echoes of the social engineer's distrust of conventional politics: "The Garden City will be a town from which politicians are excluded. Management will replicate that of a large commercial establishment, that is, it will be entrusted to a committee of experts."[48]

Nothing in the record suggests that Benoît-Lévy considered politics and politicians redundant. But if the labor question and its management occupied first place on the national agenda, as he and others contended, then it followed that social reform, prescribed and administered by "experts" and the businessmen behind them, was too important to be left to the politicians. This meant, of course, not the eclipse of politics but its reconstitution and redirection. Social reform remained a political matter and in fact formed politics' highest calling. As in the case of profit sharing and other

48. Georges Benoît-Lévy, *La Cité-Jardin* (Paris, 1904), v, 5–30.

forms of paternalism, the removal of reform from the realm of politics constituted a significant political act.[49]

Social Health: The Alliance d'hygiène sociale

Closely related in function, purpose, and personnel to the Société française des habitations à bon marché, the Alliance d'hygiène sociale made its appearance in 1904, bringing together and coordinating the work of regional groups of entrepreneurs concerned with the material conditions of working-class life. Among its leading figures we once again encounter familiar names and that curious collection of ideological bedfellows brought together by the immediacy of the social question: Picot, Siegfried, Cheysson, Gide, Gigot, Barberet, Bourcart, Léon Bourgeois, Léopold Mabilleau (director of the Musée social), Jean Casimir-Périer, and no less than four Rothschilds. Inadequately rendered as "public health," *hygiène sociale* encompassed social projects correlative to the "overall task of moralizing and socializing the popular classes."[50] These enterprises originally were limited to public health measures—sanitation, antialcoholism, the war on slums, containment of disease, and the like—and had been carried on for several decades in numerous regions of France. But not until the expositions of 1889 and 1900 and the subsequent organization of the Alliance did *hygiène sociale* take its place within the system of paternalist reform. Typically, previously scattered philanthropies became visible components of social politics and ingredients in ideological consensus only when the social question displaced other political considerations.

Hygiène sociale emerged as a matter of political concern precisely at the point when industrial transformation, concentration, and expanded urban agglomerations became commonplace across the French landscape, where the locus of production came to resemble a "veritable battlefield." Those circumstances only reinforced the convictions of social economists such as Léopold Mabilleau to make re-

49. "The reduction of the political element is essential for any form of planning" (Mannheim, *Man and Society*, 360).
50. Gide, *Les Institutions*, 267–68; *Bulletin de l'Alliance d'Hygiène Sociale*, No. 1 (1904), 1–4; *AHS*, No. 4 *bis* (1906), 448–51; Luc Boltanski, "Les Usages sociaux des corps," *Annales ESC*, XXVI (1971), 207.

form the first line of social defense against the "ills consequent upon capitalist production." Social liberals differed only in emphasis. Alexandre Millerand, in transit from socialism to nationalism, defined the mission of *hygiène sociale* in terms that neither surrendered order to progress nor vice versa: "Vigilant defense of essential national interests and stewardship of the public wealth" could not be separated from "unceasing improvement of workers' [conditions] and the progressive realization of social reforms." The Alliance itself represented "collaboration in an effort of solidarity and of social protection."[51]

Hygiène sociale was conceived in the broadest terms, incorporating the management of the body as well as the mind. The Société industrielle of Reims sponsored the Société de logement de bon marché to encourage the evacuation of run-down dwellings and set up associations for collective sports and recreation: eight gymnastic societies, ten for music and singing, ten for organized sports, and five shooting clubs. The Alliance concerned itself with physical education, both in the primary school and in informal organizations of teenagers and young adults. It enthusiastically endorsed a ministerial decree of 1902 requiring students to record their hygienic and physical habits on a *fiche sanitaire*, which presumably would be checked periodically by teachers and school inspectors. Long and detailed discussions took place on the physiological effects of various forms of exercise. The psychologist Alfred Binet testified to the benefit of exercising the thoracic musculature. Although deploring "less-than-perfect" ventilation in factories and shops, however, members of the Alliance evaded the root problem. Instead, they recommended exercises "in the fresh air" to flush out bronchial passages. As for work that "frequently produced physical deformities as a result of repetitive motion and unnatural body position," they suggested not a redesign of production but corrective gymnastics.[52]

Of the associations whose activities first came to public attention in the expositions and were later incorporated into the Alliance, several addressed directly the problems of working-class health and environment at the point of production and beyond. The Société pro-

---

51. Emile Cheysson, *L'Economie sociale et la hygiène* (Paris, 1895), 6; *AHS,* No. 4 *bis* (1906), 437–38, No. 4 (1906), 74; Alliance d'hygiène sociale, *Congrès* (Lyon, 1907), 329.
52. Say, *Economie sociale,* 128–29; *AHS,* No. 4 *bis* (1906), 319–32.

tectrice de l'enfance de Reims, founded in 1877, provided assistance to poor mothers and instructed them in the benefits of breastfeeding. By caring for unwed mothers, the Société filled a gap in Reims left by the Catholic Société de charité maternelle, which served only married mothers who had borne more than two children. No mere act of charity or philanthropy, this venture responded to the general preoccupation with France's low birth rate, high infant mortality, and rampant infectious disease—all of which conspired to deplete her physical resources at a time when labor supply was a pressing problem, not to mention the presence of a vigorous, expanding German nation to the immediate east. Another constituent of the Alliance, the Bureau d'hygiène d'Amiens, organized in 1884, published a weekly statistical bulletin on births, stillbirths, marriages, incidence of disease (especially tuberculosis), and deaths; it also supervised public charities, market and slaughterhouse inspections, and health inspections of primary schools. The Alliance's Comité de la Loire in Saint-Etienne financed *cantines scolaires* to provide hot lunches for an estimated 25 percent of primary school students who otherwise would have had to make do with "a chunk of bread and a bit of lard." A similar group in Arras (Pas-de-Calais) controlled the quality and sale of milk as part of its campaign against tuberculosis.[53]

Saving the children required saving the women from their ignorance, their unhealthiness, and their improvidence. Amiens' Bureau d'hygiène organized regular inspection of wetnurses, monitored the relative incidence of breastfeeding and bottle feeding, and dispatched doctors and midwives among working-class mothers to encourage breastfeeding. The Bureau's mania for compilation of statistics, characteristic of and necessary for public intervention to make those lives healthier, had produced the information that 83 percent of infants dead by age two during one year had been bottle-fed. In Paris, the Société philanthropique "rigorously enforced" proper hygienic behavior, employed doctors to visit working-class homes, and set up shelters for new mothers and indigent young women. Those shelters functioned not simply as refuges. They enabled close surveillance of postnatal progress to prevent "poor women" from re-

53. *Exposition 1889*, II, 287, 311–12; *AHS*, No. 4 (1906), 18–33, 79–82, 84–96; Alliance d'hygiène sociale, *Congrès*, 330.

turning to work before their "organs had returned to normal," and they served to prepare morally and physically those without work to earn a living in pursuits other than prostitution.[54]

Edouard Petit, director-general of primary education, like all high officials in the educational bureaucracy, regularly was seized with reformist spasms. In a report to the Alliance on the "role of *institutrices* in *hygiène sociale*," he noted with vigorous approval the extension of schoolteachers' responsibilities in social management beyond the classroom into the home and the family. With the disappearance of the teaching orders, secular teachers adopted the habit of "sisters to the poor." In that capacity, they dispensed charity, organized mutualist societies for young women, and visited homes to check on their charges. Petit envisioned expanded horizons for the teachers' maternalist pursuits, especially in placing women in socially productive employment. Associations of *anciennes normaliennes* (graduates of women's teachers colleges) "can enlist experienced workers, female supervisors, intelligent laborers . . . to enlighten and guide . . . young girls newly emerged from primary school who, in their search for a living, all too often take whatever comes along."[55]

Prevention of accidents in the workplace was another important aspect of *hygiène sociale*. Here again private initiatives were prominent, both as an expression of serious concern for the problem as it impinged on working-class well-being and productivity and as a substitute for state action (perhaps with the idea of rendering factory inspectors redundant). A bill on accident prevention and compensation had been debated in the Chamber of Deputies in the late 1880s. But because of its scope, at once broad and superficial, entrepreneurs argued that it accommodated neither their interests nor those of their workers. Serious regulation and control under state auspices risked "undermining the basic principles of industrial freedom" and, by extension, erected "an obstacle to progress." The deputies preferred that industrialists "close ranks" and form their own associations to monitor the application of factory rules. Aside from being more efficient, this arrangement furthered the collabora-

---

54. *Exposition 1889*, II, 312, 315–17.
55. *AHS*, No. 4 (1906), 58–72.

tion of employers and workers and directly subordinated the latter to the former's paternalist guidance.[56]

Numerous companies, including gas works, textile mills, coal mines, chemical plants, and glass manufactures, installed accident-prevention equipment and other health safeguards. In Amiens, Mulhouse, and Rouen, the local *sociétés industrielles* encouraged dissemination of such equipment throughout their respective regions, publicized new approaches to accident prevention, and brought friendly pressure to bear on their members to give health controls high priority among their paternal responsibilities. A nationwide closing of the ranks was consummated in the late 1880s with the formation of the Association des industriels pour la protection des ouvriers contre les accidents du travail. That group and others like it, such as the Ligue populaire pour le repose du dimanche (created to oppose factory work on Sundays), took as their mission the general moralization of the working class as well as agitation for specific reforms. Whenever and wherever possible, workers were recruited to the cause of *hygiène sociale*. The extent of their involvement depended upon businessmen's measurement of the prevailing political winds. As the Saint-Etienne group of the Alliance concluded, the "syndicalist movement, which has the capacity to conceive and execute excellent plans for safety [in the workplace] when it assumes a reformist posture, produces only disastrous consequences when it takes on a 'liberating' aspect."[57]

The prevailing view held that workers could not be trusted to shape their own lives without the supervision and guidance of bourgeois political leadership incorporated in the Alliance d'hygiène sociale, the Société française des habitations à bon marché, and other paternalist associations, each of which represented a branch of social science. Their cadres were filled, as Jean Casimir-Périer put it, with "men of goodwill" acting as "men of science" mobilized in a united front for "social education and action." They stood for "science and humanity," according to Millerand, and, in Bourgeois' words, constituted "centers for the development of social ideas" put into effect

56. *Exposition 1889*, II, 324.
57. *Ibid.*, 326–34; *AHS*, No. 4 (1906), 177.

under "scientific control." Chief among the scientific controls that Bourgeois had in mind were those directed at moralizing and educating the working-class family, that is, extending the surveillance of labor to its most private sphere, which had the not incidental effect of inhibiting its collective solidarity.[58] Other associations, more openly parapolitical and drawing from the same pool of businessmen, politicians, and reformers, developed ideological and instrumental tools designed to tighten those controls.

Low Road and High Road: The Comité de défense et de progrès social and the Musée social

Organized in 1895 under the banner of "Country, Duty, and Liberty," the Comité de défense et de progrès social sponsored biweekly lectures for working-class audiences in Paris. Its purpose, according to Albert Gigot, one of its directors, was to mount a campaign for liberty against "the horrors of socialism from above and from below." Anatole Leroy-Beaulieu, colonial lobbyist and younger brother of the political economist, served as the Comité's president. Aside from Gigot, Leroy-Beaulieu's fellow directors included Gibon, Delaire (then secretary-general of the Société d'économie sociale), Mabilleau, Cheysson, and Picot. Many of its support cadres came from the Unions de la paix sociale, especially from those in the Nord, which represented protectionist Catholic industrial and agrarian interests. They had no difficulty collaborating with the Protestant free-trader Leroy-Beaulieu, who lent his name to the Unions at about the same time Siegfried did and went on record as considering "religious sentiments *in whatever form* the best foundation for social education."[59]

"Socialism from below" was the Comité's principal target, and in that enterprise it had a model from across the Channel—the Liberty and Property Defense League, which had been founded in 1882 by representatives of British agrarian and industrial interests to defend

58. *Exposition 1889*, II, 283; *AHS*, No. 4 (1906), 18–21, No. 9 *bis* (1907), 27–30; Alliance d'hygiène sociale, *Congrès*, 335.

59. Albert Gigot, "Préface," in Emile Cheysson, *Le Rôle et le devoir du capital* (Paris, 1895), 3–4; *RS*, XXIX (1895), 7; Leroy-Beaulieu quoted in *Revue Socialiste*, No. 128 (1895), 227.

classical liberal principles against socialism and state intervention in the British economy. It won a grand prize in the social economy group of the 1889 Exposition for its resolute opposition to state socialism and, for that matter, any organized efforts at social reform. Its members adhered to Malthusian and Ricardian principles of population and the wage fund, respectively, and situated social problems in the economic, not the moral, sphere. Behind this ideologically pure position lay a firm identity between the League's militants— mostly younger sons of titled landlords with time on their hands and money in their pockets—and big business. For instance, it worked very hard in the early 1890s to forestall the advance of "municipal socialism"—public ownership of utilities and urban transport. Despite their doctrinaire individualism appropriated directly from Herbert Spencer, some of the League's leaders by the end of the century veered toward social reform in pursuit of class collaboration. One of them, Thomas Mackay, though holding to an idealized conception of market relations, devoted some attention to working-class improvement. He was particularly interested in "people's banks" as devices to break down "imaginary barriers" between capital and labor. (Why such barriers needed breaking down remained unexplained.) Another, W. H. Mallock, supported more comprehensive reform projects, earning him the sobriquet, in the words of one historian, of "Fabian of the Right." But a handful of enlightened individualists do not make a reform movement. The Liberty and Property Defense League disappeared from the political landscape, to be replaced by organizations such as the Anti-Socialist Union, which "based its appeal on social reform."[60]

In 1892 the League invited Georges Picot to address its annual meeting (the bourgeoisie, like the socialists, also had their "international"). He returned to Paris with the idea of organizing a similar political action group;[61] the result was the Comité de défense et de

60. Say, *Economie sociale*, 424–37; D. J. Ford, "W. H. Mallock and Socialism in England, 1880–1918," in K. D. Brown (ed.), *Essays in Anti-Labour History* (Hamden, Conn., 1974), 317–42; N. Soldon, "Laissez-Faire as Dogma: The Liberty and Property Defense League, 1882–1914," *ibid.*, 208–33; E. Bristow, "Profit-Sharing, Socialism and Labour Unrest," *ibid.*, 262–89; J. W. Mason, "Political Economy and the Response to Socialism in Britain, 1870–1914," *Historical Journal*, XXIII (1980), 565–89; E. Bristow, "The Liberty and Property Defense League and Individualism," *ibid.*, XVIII (1975), 761–89.

61. *RS*, XXIII (1892), 40; Picot, *La Lutte*, 77.

progrès social. Unlike the League, the Comité did not engage in lobbying; it concentrated on public propaganda. Nevertheless, as part of a powerful network of parapolitical organizations and as one center of conservative reform with big business connections, the Comité served as a link in the chain uniting France's political classes. Thus it cannot, like the League, be consigned to the lunatic fringe.

In the typically moralistic terms favored by bourgeois reformers, the Comité's organizers defined their mission as combating decadence, degeneration, materialism, and atheism. They proposed "moral reconstitution through reform of the individual." Such characterizations of class relations, expressed as "moral crisis," the decline of public morality and patriotism, and the rejection of "eternal moral values," easily can be interpreted as reflecting that "spiritual crisis" of the *fin de siècle* about which historians, following contemporary seekers of "spiritual renovation," have written innumerable volumes. To do so would be a mistake. Two related points are worth making: first, those who spoke that language situated decadence and degeneration only within the working class; and second, "reform of the individual" and moralization meant in practice the ideological discipline of labor. No sentimental handwringing or apocalyptic visions of cultural crisis can be found here, only hard-headed political responses to "agitators who delight in fomenting hatred between classes . . . at the expense of national unity." To counter socialism required first, a "scientific calculation of social ills" and, second, a campaign "to direct social aspirations into practical channels" by distinguishing "realizable reforms and sensible solutions from fruitless utopias and dangerous fantasies." In place of socialism the Comité offered "human solidarity" and the "love of country."[62]

But offerings, like sacrifices to gods, run the risk of being rejected. The self-appointed missionaries to workers did not have an easy time getting across their message. Introducing Cheysson to one of the Comité's audiences, Gigot read a letter from the mayor of Montceau-les-Mines thanking the Comité for a 217-franc contribution to the Blanzy company's welfare fund. The audience of workers,

---

62. *RS*, XXVIII (1894), 561–66, XXIX (1895), 46–48; Eugène Rostand, "Morale nouvelle et progrès social," *Publications du Comité de défense et de progrès social* (Besançon, 1905), 1–7.

who obviously knew of Blanzy's efforts at union-busting and knew the mayor to be a company stooge, greeted Gigot's announcement with hoots of derision and peals of laughter. On another occasion, Leroy-Beaulieu had become sufficiently fed up with disturbances—mostly in the form of anti-Semitic slogans shouted from the gallery ("Vive Drumont," "A bas les Juifs")—that he threatened to summon the police to clear the house. Order was restored only after several more bouts of heckling, which, one member of the Comité claimed, originated not in the working-class sections of the audience but among "bourgeois loafers" and "riffraff." The slogans they shouted ("Spit on Doumer! He's a filthy radical! Down with the radicals! Down with the deputies! Down with the Palais Bourbon! Throw them out!") tend to confirm that estimate. In his inaugural speech, Leroy-Beaulieu defended himself and his colleagues against charges of reaction hurled from raucous audiences. Somewhat lamely but stubbornly, he elevated individualism over socialism, insisting that the latter stood convicted of denying the rights of the individual. Yet he condemned irresponsible individualism and defended the rights of "social authorities," which in the language of paternalism meant the authority of capital over labor.[63]

In a similar vein, Daniel Zolla took to the stump for the Comité and delivered a brutal Spencerian defense of individualism only slightly softened by a summons to the bourgeoisie to perform its "social duty" in helping the unfortunate. "Human existence itself," he announced, assumes "the necessary struggle that exposes the inferiority of those who fall by the wayside but at the same time validates the superiority of those who rise to the top." Zolla defended his position on the grounds that "privilege of birth has been abolished; castes have disappeared; classes are only a memory." Equality of opportunity reigned: "Today there exist only men who are unequal in talent and ability . . . no insurmountable obstacle [remains] to prevent one from rising above one's station, increasing one's station, increasing one's well-being, and accumulating wealth." *Enrichissez-vous*! But if classes no longer existed, capital did, and its pro-

---

63. Gigot, "Préface," 5; Joseph Chailley-Bert, "Le Rôle social de la colonisation," *Publications du Comité* (Paris, 1897), 185, 191; Anatole Leroy-Beaulieu, "Individualisme et socialisme," *ibid*. (Paris, 1896), 2–9.

gressive diffusion and rationalization could profit everyone. Zolla denied that capital had become concentrated, employing a statistical dodge. He quoted the latest national figures showing that the ratio of employers to employees was nearly one to one. Those figures, however, masked the relative distribution of workers and capital across industries. Workers, he then concluded, would find expanded fields for employment, and "all the modest capitalists would find their savings bearing abundant fruit." Zolla certainly stood at the right wing of the solidarist/paternalist network. Yet he shared with social liberals such as Léon Bourgeois an insistence that capital benefited everyone and not only capitalists, a fundamental anti-socialist perspective, and that staple of the ruling-class program to raise workers to a level where they could gain "access to property."[64]

None among the Comité's cadres had much use for state intervention in social relations; this set them apart from social liberals. But their alternative, which equally set them apart from their English counterparts, was association, especially across class lines. Association involved no question of ideological principle, only straight-forward counterrevolutionary politics. Hence the Comité paid considerable attention to employer-dominated groups such as yellow unions. However much its rhetoric may have sounded like *ancien régime* nostalgia, with invocations to "mediating bodies" between the state and the individual and a Tocquevillian hostility to central authority, association in the contemporary context resonated deeply with corporate overtones. As in the case of Cheysson, Robert, Picot, and others, those who embraced association while holding fast to the principles of political economy expected to strengthen capital against its challengers in the labor movement by subordinating them behind a smokescreen of voluntary collaboration. Reluctant as they were to render unto the state what properly belonged to the market, they nevertheless accepted the intervention of the state, if only on the instrumental level, to provide associations with the necessary legal status of "moral personalities" to function effectively as agents of class collaboration. The purpose of association, then, was to occupy territory that otherwise would be occupied by the state as ar-

---

64. Daniel Zolla, "Salariés et capitalistes," *Publications du Comité* (Paris, 1897), 149, 152–57.

biter of conflicting class interests. It also purported to preempt the field against "collectivists" or "anarchists."[65]

Léopold Mabilleau, who had taught philosophy at Caen, where he headed a mutualist group called Solidarité Sociale, raised some of the political implications of association and cooperation. In a lecture for the Comité on the benefits and limits of cooperation, he advanced a narrow perspective on reform and made more of limits than of benefits. By implication, he avoided the aggressive corporatism displayed by some of his collaborators. Mabilleau argued that producers' and consumers' cooperatives were a mixed blessing and that their effects could prove contradictory. Producers' cooperatives constituted a means "to revive petty production, which is the base of the wealth of all nations." Consumers' cooperatives, however, would likely "lead to the displacement of the individual enterprise, to the disappearance of retail trade, replaced by the mechanical and impersonal operations of huge commercial factories staffed by former small businessmen become clerks—in sum, to the elimination of an entire class." Thus he concluded that those who favored cooperation as a solution to the labor problem faced something of a Hobson's choice and must proceed carefully. Yet French capital had an interest in supporting cooperatives. They carried the promise of reconciling workers to the capitalist order, of demonstrating the benefits of association, and of proving that capitalism did, after all, have a human face. Although Mabilleau ridiculed the notion that cooperatives originated as "a kind of bourgeois swindle invented to combat socialism," he did approve of English experiments in the area and noted that they had been encouraged by the "ruling classes," which "found in them leverage for the guidance and the control of the people."[66] Further consideration of the politics of association and cooperation and the roles played by social economists and social liberals will be discussed in the following chapter. The Comité's search for the ideological mechanisms for guidance and control extended to the realm of propaganda for empire.

65. Georges Alix, "La Liberté d'association," *Publications du Comité* (Paris, 1896), 10–26; Etienne Delcourt-Haillot, *Les Avantages accordés aux ouvriers mineurs par les compagnies* (Paris, 1897).

66. Léopold Mabilleau, "La Coopération: Ses bienfaits et ses limites," *Publications du Comité* (Paris, 1897), 76–79, 82, 87.

Joseph Chailley-Bert, son-in-law of Léon Gambetta's political ally and late proconsul in Hanoi, Paul Bert, was an indefatigable agitator on behalf of French colonial interests. He let no opportunity pass to rehearse his views; the Comité provided him with a forum. The setting was congenial: Cheysson, Picot, and Leroy-Beaulieu all took an avid interest in empire, as did their partner in paternalist reform, Jules Siegfried. Elsewhere and often Chailley had made the case for colonies chiefly on the basis of establishing French capital on firm ground to sustain its position in "global economic competition" and to secure its "place in the sun." His arguments recapitulated standard colonialist themes: colonies provided fields for capitalist investment, enabled aggressive entrepreneurs to find outlets for their energies, and promised windfall returns for the "modest capital" held by ordinary citizens. The last, he claimed, was a "social task awaiting action." Chailley couched the settler/native relationship in much the same terms as did Cheysson, that is, in the image of the employer/employee relationship: "The role of the settler is . . . to tutor the native classes [who perform labor] in a way similar to that by which an entrepreneur or a boss deals with his workers to get them to work on his behalf and to teach them new techniques."[67]

In his pitch for popular support of colonial enterprise before one of the Comité's gatherings, Chailley did not mention the analogy between non-Western peoples and French workers. But he made the same point in other ways. He specified three social justifications for the acquisition and development of colonies. First, successful colonization required the domestic cooperation of capital and labor, "which some call solidarity." Second, colonies acted as a social "safety valve" to draw off an excess, underemployed, overeducated, and potentially antisocial population, thereby supplying a field for mobility. Third, colonies could become "laboratories for social experiments" of an unspecified nature. But before the great migration could begin to places like Tunisia, Madagascar, Indochina, and New Caledonia (Chailley estimated an absurd fifteen to twenty million people available as potential colonizers), the ground had to be pre-

67. *Exposition 1900: Congrès international de sociologie coloniale* (Paris, 1900); Joseph Chailley-Bert, "Ou'en est la colonisation française? Notre oeuvre au Tonkin et à Madagascar," *RS*, XXX (1895), 159–63, 176–81.

pared, thus requiring capital. Frenchmen and others already had made deep impressions in Algeria, Indochina, and New Caledonia, where settlers had descended upon native populations. In New Caledonia, their heavy-handed zeal to implant European civilization (read: transforming communal lands into parcels of private property) had resulted in the 1878 insurrection of the *canaques*, a rising "of a people determined to defend the highest values of its civilization." That native uprising, Chailley implied, resulted from the failure of French capital to effect the initial transformations, mainly investments in social overhead (canals, bridges, harbors, railroads, and the like) and in social order. Not only the ground but the people had to be prepared. Then followed the takeoff into self-sustaining progress: "It is masses of capital that first will descend to occupy newly opened territories and which, through the natural workings of solidarity between classes, prepare for the future of the less fortunate, right down to the bottom rung on the social ladder."[68]

It is impossible to determine whether Chailley's vision of limitless employment and stratospheric profits awaiting "hardy spirits" from among the "sons of the people" provoked anything other than skepticism or rude interruptions from his audience.[69] They probably did not. Nor does it matter. Chailley actually was addressing two audiences: the one before him and another of men, like himself, either in power or close to those who were. To the former he offered pie in the sky. To the latter he suggested that many roads led to the formation of a solid phalanx of capital obediently followed by labor and that the promotion of empire was among the most promising and least explored. Chailley did not explain how clouds of words could become a material force for class collaboration. But his efforts constitute another link in the bourgeois ideological chain. The organizers of the Musée social, among those who formed Chailley's second audience, took an alternate route in the same direction, avoiding the bare-knuckle confrontations that punctuated the meetings of the Comité de défense et de progrès social.

The physical settings of the Musée social and the Comité could

---

68. Chailley-Bert, "Le Rôle social," 185, 197–202; Roselène Dousset-Leenhardt, *Colonialisme et contradictions: Nouvelle-Calédonie, 1878–1978* (Paris, 1978), 112.

69. Chailley-Bert, "Le Rôle social," 186–89.

not have been more different. Whereas the latter held its meetings in dingy halls in Paris' popular neighborhoods, the former occupied a handsome townhouse in the Faubourg Saint-Germain—number 5, rue Las Cases—hard by the houses inhabited by the creatures of Marcel Proust's imagination, a few short blocks from Emile Cheysson's apartment on the boulevard Saint-Germain and barely a brisk twenty-minute walk across the Seine from the Rond-Point des Champs-Elysées, where Jules Siegfried and his family resided. Even today one can sit at the Café des Ministres, just around the corner on the boulevard from the rue Las Cases, and watch the elegantly turned-out matrons carrying their Fauchon shopping bags, walking their aristocratic poodles or their meticulously coiffed lhasas, or wheeling formidable prams whose undercarriages remind one of the chassis of Formula One racing cars. There also one can follow the steady lunch-hour parade of businessmen in finely tailored suits and of military officers posted to the Ministry of War on the nearby rue Saint-Dominique decked out in smartly pressed uniforms and boots polished to within an inch of their lives.

The Musée was founded in 1894 as a "center for studies, data collection, and inquiries" relating to "social questions." A corporate headquarters within which captains of industry periodically gathered to discuss the progress made toward social peace, the Musée extended its inquiries to all aspects of working-class life and labor. It also served as a display center for the social wares of big business and as a clearinghouse for various reform and paternalist organizations. But the Musée was primarily a political establishment that stood at the center of an intelligence/propaganda/agitation apparatus that monitored developments in the realm of social relations. It collected vast and rich documentation on socialism and syndicalism. Its archives remain the delight of historians of those movements, although the uses to which the collection has been put do not always correspond to the intentions of the founders, who professed deep anxiety over "disorder in the social economy," provoked, they said, by socialist hotheads.[70]

The Musée social's origins, associations, and connections illumi-

---

70. Hauser, *L'Enseignement des sciences sociales,* 217–18; *Monde illustré,* March 19, 1898.

nate the contours of bourgeois social reform in France at the end of the nineteenth century. It engaged the collaboration of entrepreneurs, politicians, and social scientists of diverse political and religious persuasions in a common effort to promote enlightened capitalism and class harmony.[71] The Musée represented in microcosm both the possibilities and the limits of social reform as well as symbolizing the growing conservative consensus that ran as a constant theme beneath the discordant voices of French politics.

Following the exposition of 1889, the organizers of the social economy section planned to capitalize on their success by pressing forward to build a permanent monument to the ideology of social economy. They drew up plans for a Musée d'économie sociale to be located in the Conservatoire des Arts et Métiers in Paris. The Musée, Emile Cheysson testified, "would conform to the democratic spirit that dominates our country, by exhibiting what we would call the 'social machinery' of the workshop, that is, measures taken to improve workers' conditions and to ensure their cooperation with the boss." To that end a bill to finance the Musée was introduced in 1893 by Jules Siegfried, then minister of commerce, industry, and colonies. It passed the Chamber of Deputies but disappeared in the Senate, a victim, apparently, of procedural snarls rather than of political assassination.[72]

Failing state financial backing, Siegfried, Léon Say, Cheysson, and others sought private financing (Siegfried and Say, of course, had considerable personal fortunes). They found their man (or he found them; it is not clear which) in the Comte de Chambrun, heir to the Lafayette fortune, unrepentant monarchist, pious Catholic, and admirer of Le Play. Chambrun also had been trained in the law and served the Second Empire as prefect, member of the Corps législatif, and senator. Elected to the Senate of the Republic in 1876, he resigned in a huff in 1879 when that year's elections returned a republican majority. Chambrun became active in financing the public presentation of social economy, of which he was a genuine booster. He endowed three courses of lectures in social economy and social edu-

---

71. Emile Cheysson, *Discours prononcé à l'assemblée générale de la société amicale des anciens élèves de l'Ecole polytechnique, le 24 janvier 1904* (Paris, 1904), 1–5.

72. *Exposition 1889*, II, 452–53; Emile Cheysson, *La Lutte des classes* (Paris, 1893), 26.

cation during the 1880s and 1890s: one in the Ecole libre des sciences politiques delivered by Cheysson; a second in the Law Faculty delivered by Charles Gide; and a third in the Sorbonne delivered by the sociologist Alfred Espinas. More than a rich man's patronage of worthy causes was involved. Chambrun had had a long-standing preoccupation with the labor question on a practical level. His Baccarat crystal works allegedly was a model of the paternalist enterprise. It boasted a host of good works for its employees, including a day-care center, a medical and pension fund, funds for the support of orphans and workmen's compensation, free baths and showers, a dispensary, a music society and a library, regular religious services in the plant, and a free school of industrial design that registered one hundred students in 1885. Baccarat remained free of worker-employer antagonisms or, at least, any visible signs of conflict.[73]

Chambrun developed an interest in social economy, originally sparked by contact with Jules Simon and his writings on the social question. Chambrun then took as his personal mission the promotion of "sociology" against "social revolution" and its establishment as a science "above parties" and "particular opinions." To that end he purchased the building in the rue Las Cases at a cost of one and a half million francs for the Musée social and established a capital fund of two million francs, which was to yield an annual revenue of 120,000.[74]

The two other financial angels for the Musée, according to the plaque labeled "*fondateurs principaux*" on the ground floor, were Siegfried and Paul Delombre. The latter was a man of many connections—all of them excellent. A major *progressiste* politician and an organizer with Siegfried of the Association nationale républicaine, a right-center caucus, Delombre held ministerial office during two successive governments in 1898 and 1899 and edited the social and economic sections of France's leading establishment newspaper, *Le Temps*. Delombre also interested himself in numerous reform projects,

73. *Famille,* March 27, 1898; Folio 1202, AMS; Alfred Espinas, "Leçon d'ouverture d'un cours d'histoire de l'économie sociale," *RIS,* V (1894), 321; André Lalande, "La Vie et l'oeuvre d'Alfred Espinas," *RIS,* XXXIII (1925), 137; Gide, *Les Institutions,* 152; France, Ministère du commerce et de l'industrie, Conseil supérieur de l'enseignement technique, *Rapport sur l'organisation de l'enseignement technique par M. Tresca* (Paris, 1885), 15.

74. *Journal d'Argenteuil,* September 26, 1897; Merlin, *Jules Siegfried,* 44–47.

working on the Ligue nationale de la mutualité et de la prévoyance and serving a term as president of the Société de participation aux bénéfices. His concern, he said, was to provide for working people "an easier life . . . less uncertain and less harsh" and "all the opportunities of the sort to anchor the laborer to his household and to his family." Delombre waxed enthusiastically over the full range of paternalist projects: working-class housing, public health codes, clean drinking water, sewers, indoor plumbing, *cités jardins*, sport and recreation societies, social insurance, and pension funds.[75]

The Musée social's organizers were primarily interested in the labor question. Emile Cheysson, who lectured there frequently, testified to the strong influence of LePlayist doctrine on the Musée, and, by clear implication, to the warm welcome given that cranky ideologue's doctrines in circles that previously would have slammed the door on such an association. Cheysson drew attention to the problem of labor posed by industrial concentration first recognized, he said, in the exposition of 1867 and then highlighted in 1889 and in the foundation of the Musée itself. Those several steps marked a "great advance in the history of social science" because they focused directly on "the practices essential to peace in the workplace."[76] Cheysson did not make the connection between social science and social management casually. Everyone associated with the Musée took the same view, that social science realized its highest mission in the world of production where it enforced the rules governing social harmony.

The notion that those who owned or served capital were uniquely qualified to dictate the construction of "machinery for social peace" permeated the ideological atmosphere of the Musée from its inception.[77] Its directing personnel, who nearly replicated that of the Comité de défense et de progrès social, moved among the worlds of business, government, social economy, and social liberalism. Albert Gigot, a member of the Musée's original *comité de direction*, had been prefect of police in Paris before taking over the management of the

---

75. Jolly (ed.), *Dictionnaire*, IV, 1346–47; *Revue Populaire d'Economie Sociale*, III (1904), 330–31.
76. Emile Cheysson, *Le Musée social* (Paris, 1905), 3–4.
77. *Ibid.*, 11.

Forges d'Alais. Paul de Rousiers, who brought his big business connections to the Musée (and vice versa), worked closely with Edmond
Demolins on *La Science Sociale*, whence he progressed to chief lobbyist for the French shipping industry. Robert Pinot, who briefly
directed the Musée's day-to-day operations before Léopold Mabilleau
took over, parlayed his big business connections into the job of secretary-general of the Comité des forges, the iron and steel producers'
organization. Alexandre Gibon capped his career as a militant for
corporate interests with a seat on the Musée's board. And Léon
Bourgeois was designated honorary president of the Musée in
1899.[78] He was in his element. "Solidarity," although not engraved
on the cornice of the house on the rue Las Cases, might well have
been. "Nothing threatens the greatness and the future of France
more than class antagonism," Siegfried announced. "The Musée social brings men together in the spirit of solidarity." Bourgeois heart-
ily agreed. Unavoidably absent from the Musée's inaugural ceremonies on March 25, 1895, he sent a message praising the "noble
effort of Monsieur de Chambrun" whose initiative, "by excluding
partisan passions from the observation of social facts, will contribute
to the injection of equanimity and fairness into politics—both essential preconditions for any scientific task—and will give a powerful boost to the establishment of social peace."[79]

   With Gigot presiding, the ceremonies proceeded, and an impressive occasion it was, attended by a full complement of reformers,
businessmen, and politicians. Many already have appeared in these
pages and will again; others we will meet in subsequent chapters:
Alexandre Ribot, Jacques Bardoux, Henry Buisson, Charles Robert,
Edouard Aynard, Armand Peugeot, Emile Boutmy, Eugène Rostand, Georges Picot, Emile Levasseur, Alfred Espinas, Albert Trombert, Félix Piat, Jules Steeg, and the managing directors (unnamed

---

78. Terry Clark, *Prophets and Patrons* (Cambridge, Mass., 1973), 109. Clark mistakenly
identifies Rousiers as a lobbyist for the munitions industry; he actually was secretary-
general of the Comité des armateurs. See Michael Rust, "Business and Politics in the
Third Republic: The Comité des forges and the French Steel Industry" (Ph.D. dissertation, Princeton University, 1973), 474; Musée social, *Mémoires et documents*, ser. A, circular
No. 1; *RS*, XXIX (1895), 7; Folio 1202, AMS.
   79. Musée social, *Mémoires et documents*, ser. A, circular No. 5; Folio 1202, p. ix, AMS.

in the record) of the Paris-Orléans and the Paris-Lyon-Méditerranée railroads. Following the ritual banquet came a round of speeches. They revealed the manner in which the Musée organizers and supporters conceived of its political mission. Ribot, who once had operated as the conservative republicans' hit man against Gambetta in 1882, went on to serve big business in the Chamber of Deputies (Aynard, Say, Siegfried, and Delombre numbered among his close political cronies) and five times was president of the council of ministers between 1892 and 1917, expressed the general consensus: "Clearly, if property in our society requires defending," the Musée social would do the job by encouraging collaboration, "which eliminates strife, violence, and hatreds." After paying tribute to Chambrun's good deeds, Siegfried got down to serious business. The Musée as a center of "information and surveillance" on all social questions "fills a gap in our social machinery." For the bourgeoisie its activities "will dissolve prejudices and demonstrate the futility of struggles between capital and labor." For workers it would point the way toward "social improvement" through the "closest collaboration between capital and labor." Peugeot was more explicit: "Today we are witnessing a bitter struggle of labor against capital, deplorable strikes, that harm workers as much as industrialists." The need for an institution like the Musée to display industry's paternal regard for labor was urgent. The remarks of others followed the same line.[80]

But what form did this social machinery take? The Musée did not take overtly political action; it had not been designed for that purpose. Its activities involved detailed studies of social questions and intelligence-gathering on the politics of the labor movement. Mabilleau and his staff amassed a huge documentary collection covering every conceivable aspect of social relations at the point of production and beyond: population, mortality, and accident statistics; technical education, family conditions, and the "role of women"; property, inheritance, and "collectivist systems"; the organization of labor, working conditions, *syndicats*, mechanisms for arbitration and conciliation, employer-employee factory committees, paternal institu-

80. Folio 1202, pp. vi−ix, 8−11, 13−15, 30−31, AMS; Emmanuel Beau de Loménie, *Les Responsabilités des dynasties bourgeoises* (4 vols.; Paris, 1943−63), II, 107−13.

tions, and strikes; savings and credit, housing, recreation, nourishment, clothing, heating, and lighting; unemployment, illness, superannuation, and "premature death" among workers.[81]

The Musée's work had been broken down into seven subdivisions, bearing witness to its broad yet intense engagement with social reform and management: urban and rural public health; agriculture; associations (trade unions and cooperatives); mutualism; paternal institutions; law; and surveys and inquiries, domestic and foreign. Each group had dozens of participants, whose diversity is striking. Jules Siegfried headed the section on public health, joined by Charles Gide, Paul Brousse, and Paul Strauss, a leading figure in the Société française des habitations à bon marché. The author of what remains the standard work on French agricultural policy, Michel Augé-Laribé, chaired the section on agriculture. He had the collaboration of the sociologist René Worms and the presidents of a score of France's departmental agricultural societies, which were associations of big farmers. Only one labor leader, the conservative August Keüfer, president of the Fédération du livre, worked on the association section. He found congenial company in the banker Eugène d'Eichthal, the political economist Paul Cauwès, and Gide. They were joined by Auguste Isaac, president of the Lyon chamber of commerce and the author of reports documenting the good works produced by that city's bourgeoisie. The mutualism group included numerous representatives of business as well as Joseph Barberet, Waldeck-Rousseau's favorite syndicalist. Paternal institutions also drew on the business community, men such as Eugène Motte, the Roubaix textile tycoon, and Albert Trombert, Charles Robert's successor as chief promoter of profit sharing. Professors of law and judges staffed the legal section under the direction of Albert Gigot, whose credentials have been noted above. Finally, the group responsible for surveys and inquiries was headed by Cheysson's old collaborator, Alfred de Foville, and included a stellar cast: André Lichtenberger, Alfred Espinas, Anatole Leroy-Beaulieu, Louis Liard, Rousiers, and André Siegfried.[82]

81. Folio 1202, pp. 57–60, AMS.
82. Musée social, *Statutes, personnel, conférences* (Paris, 1911), 17–21; Isaac, "Le Patronage," 158–77, 233–40, 309–23.

The catalog of conferences, lectures, pamphlets, books, and investigative missions produced within the Musée testifies to its single-minded concern with labor: its organization, its politics, its discipline, and its welfare within a paternalist framework. Those who wrote and lectured under the Musée's aegis cast a global net to seek clues to the resolution of the social question. Claudio Jannet produced a study of the Knights of Labor. His collaborators, Octave Festy and Edouard Fuster, studied English dock workers and Westphalian coal miners, respectively. William Howe Tolman traveled from the United States to lecture on paternalism in his country. Léopold Mabilleau examined socialism in the United States and concluded that its weakness resulted from the good works described by Tolman. André Siegfried, who later gained a reputation as an expert on the political culture of several countries, originally studied those territories in the service of the Musée. Among other writings, he produced pamphlets on the Japanese economy and on the labor question in New Zealand.[83]

Naturally, the bulk of the Musée social's output concerned France. Political questions dominated. All of the major strikes in mining, textiles, metallurgy, and the southern vineyards were carefully documented and analyzed. Syndicalism received close attention, as did the activities of the Second International and the several parties, sects, and factions that occupied the socialist landscape in France. Specific questions relating to the details of the labor and production process also came in for examination. These included a survey of the conditions of working-class life and work followed by the treatment of such subjects as unemployment insurance, female labor, public housing, and disease.[84] For the modern researcher the Musée's out-

83. Octave Festy, "Les Ouvriers des docks et entrepôts en Angleterre; le métier, les hommes et les syndicats," Musée social, *Mémoires et documents,* ser. A, circular No. 9; Edouard Fuster, "Les Mineurs de Westphalie, les essais d'organisation ouvrières et l'intervention de l'Etat," ser. A, circular No. 17; Claudio Jannet, "Les 'Knights of Labor' aux Etats-Unis," ser. A, circular 1899; William Tolman, "Plus que le salaire," ser. A, circular 1901; Léopold Mabilleau, "Les Etats-Unis et le socialisme," *Annales du Musée social* (1902); André Siegfried, "Le Développement économique et social du Japon" (1901); "Les Questions ouvrières en Nouvelle-Zélande" (1902).

84. André Souchon, "La Situation des ouvriers en France à la fin du xix siècle," Musée social, *Mémoires et documents,* ser. A, circular 1899; "Le Quatrième congrès de l'Internationale ouvrière," ser. B, circular No. 3; Michel Augé-Laribé, "Les Grèves agricoles du

put provides a rich source of data on the world of the French worker. For contemporaries, the obsessive concentration on amassing social facts was only a prelude to the framing of solutions designed to engineer progress as well as preserve order. The question remained whether the circle could be squared, under what conditions, and at what price.

One study conducted for the Musée illustrates the contradiction and pointed toward its ultimate resolution. Léon de Seilhac, the Musée's chief expert on the labor movement and a friend of the syndicalist leader Edouard Vaillant, wrote a report about a strike in a hardware-manufacturing plant in Fressenville (Somme).[85] The factory employed 200 to 250 workers in 1907, the year of the strike. Two brothers named Riquier had taken over the company in 1870 and ran it as a model paternal enterprise. They also ran the town. Two events then disrupted the climate of employer obligation and employee deference. First, the brothers retired in 1890, leaving operation of the business to their respective sons, who not only introduced managerial efficiency with a vengeance, but worse, lived extravagantly and ostentatiously. Second, the hardware industry became heavily mechanized by the end of the century; to keep afloat in an intensely competitive market the younger Riquiers deemed it necessary to reduce their skilled workers to machine operatives with commensurate downward pressure on wages. The atmosphere in the town became ripe for a blowup, and it occurred when management fired two workers. The first earned too much and was slated to be replaced by a woman and a youngster; the second was alleged to be an active syndicalist. At the first sign of trouble one of the Riquiers panicked and called for troops. Few of the northern contingent were available, being occupied with putting down a strike in the Lens coal field. Riquier then tried to restore calm, but in *tutoyant* the workers (ad-

---

Languedoc," *Annales du Musée social* (1904); Maurice Vanlaer, "L'Industrie textile et les grèves du Nord" (1905); Léon de Seilhac, "Le Monde socialiste. Groupes et personnages" (1903); Edouard Fuster, "La Tuberculose, une maladie sociale" (1905); Emile Cheysson, "La Travail des femmes," Musée social, *Conférences* (1908); Louis Varlez, *Les Formes nouvelles de l'assurance contre le chômage* (Paris, 1903).

85. Jolyon Howorth told me about Seilhac's friendship with Vaillant.

dressing them in the second-person familiar reserved for children, family, and servants) only made things worse.[86]

Up to this point Seilhac did not betray any partisanship or spare the bosses criticism. But once he got into the details of the strike his attitude changed. He claimed that instead of sticking to the economic issues of wages, recruitment, and redundancy, the workers crossed the line and fell into step with radical hotheads from the Fédération du cuivre, who had arrived to spread the word about socialism and capitalist exploitation. The strike swiftly became political, complete with the red flag. Violence ensued, in the course of which the Riquiers fled to Abbeville with the help of a faithful chauffeur in what must have been the town's only automobile. In Seilhac's view, the workers, by abandoning a moderate course, surrendered all claim to sympathy. Troops finally arrived, arrests were made, loyal foremen were rewarded, and the factory reopened. Seilhac drew several lessons, none of which would have displeased his employers. Arrogant bosses could shatter peaceful social relations, but workers become political could not be tolerated. Fortunately in this case the latter were split between militants and company men. Workers had a legitimate claim to the adjudication of their grievances, but once embarked upon the path of disorder they invited repression and deserved it. The Riquiers' failure to maintain a policy of enlightened paternalism did not excuse the workers' action. After all, the former had production factors to consider, which, in the long run, stood to promote the general welfare.[87] The first priority was order, then progress.

In what could have been a commentary on Seilhac's study, Emile Cheysson alleged that the scientific work of the Musée "carried no doctrinal preconceptions, but was only technical; it rested, not on preconceived theories, but on facts, on observation, on precise calculation." Perhaps, but one such "technical" study, that of Paul de Rousiers on English trade unions, carried an unambiguous political message. Rousiers approved of those unions, but not the "new unions," which he found dangerous. He admired the strength of the

86. Léon de Seilhac, *La Grève de Fressenville* (Paris, 1907), 182, 185–87.
87. *Ibid.*, 188–212..

older unions because, he observed, they introduced discipline into the working-class community, and for that reason he saw no need for the bourgeoisie to fear them. He urged his compatriots to support comparable organizations in France: company unions, conservative independent unions, or *syndicats jaunes*. Such support would express the "spirit of justice that inspires the nonworking class" and would have the added, decisive benefit of propelling "the worker down the high road of social progress, whose destination must be social peace."[88] The politics of paternalism admitted of several approaches. French capital could afford to ignore none of them, and in the Musée they all received due recognition.

To commemorate paternal good works the Musée social sponsored a variety of contests, awards, and prize competitions for workers and bourgeois youth. An essay competition focused on the relationship of profit sharing to economic freedom. Charles Robert and Emile Levasseur headed the jury. One worker, who proclaimed his dislike of labor unions and his veneration of his boss, wrote in praise of Jesus, "who died at age 33 for the salvation and the well-being of humanity." Another worker announced that "poverty is a product of social error" and that competition is "the mother of progress." They both received prizes—unspecified. On May Day, 1896, Charles Robert welcomed workers and bourgeois assembled in a spirit of solidarity. They all spontaneously agreed to deplore "supposed contemporary conflicts," after which a "humble worker" toasted Comte de Chambrun.[89]

On the same occasion Cheysson distributed medals to old and faithful workers, who represented "unsung, heroic, loyal labor." Gigot followed with a distribution of prizes to workers who, having reached the age of sixty, had worked in one factory for at least thirty years and had demonstrated "irreproachable conduct." Among those recognized were a sixty-two-year-old employed at Baccarat for fifty years; a mineworker from Saint-Gobain who had spent sixty-one years in the pits (he started at age twelve); a sixty-six-year-old

88. Cheysson, *Le Musée social*, 11; Musée social, *Mémoires et documents*, ser. A., circular No. 2.

89. Musée social, *Mémoires et documents*, ser. B, circular No. 9; *ibid.*, ser. A., circular No. 5.

molder at Creusot who never deviated from "perfect conduct" in fifty-six years on the job; a steelworker at Peugeot who had put in fifty-three years, trained his sons to follow in his footsteps, and managed to purchase a house. At yet another ceremony, thirty-five peasants received life annuities and silver medals as a reward for "courage and honesty" in a lifetime of toil on the soil. So that we should not mistake the magnitude of the Musée's munificence, let it be noted that none of the annuities were to exceed 200 francs and that the recipients ranged in age from sixty-five to ninety-nine. This particular event endorsed a common concern to encourage peasant families to stay on the farm.[90] Moreover, it reinforced a recognition of the value of sober and solid citizens and the rewards awaiting them. The cynical outsider can only marvel at these pathetic if not bathetic scenes: a parade of aged, stooped workers and peasants, no doubt dressed in their Sunday best, receiving the moral equivalent of the gold watch from their bourgeois benefactors. But for the insiders at the Musée these workers represented a validation and sanctification of their work and absolute confidence in the correctness of their path to social peace.

By the end of the twentieth century's first decade the Musée could claim preeminence among the various foundations for paternalist reform. Its patrons occupied the highest levels of politics, the state bureaucracy, and business. The three honorary presidents were the president of the Republic, Armand Fallières, his predecessor, Emile Loubet, and Bourgeois. On the *grand conseil* of the Musée sat business leaders such as Robert Carmichaël, president of the textile industry employers' association; Gaston Griolet, vice-chairman of the board of the Compagnie des Chemins de fer du Nord; Edouard Aynard, regent of the Bank of France; Richard Waddington of the Norman textile family; Eugène Rostand; politicians of stature and reputation such as Jules Méline, Alexandre Millerand, Raymond Poincaré, Charles Dupuy, and Ribot; the vice-rector of the Academy of Paris, Louis Liard; the onetime colonial proconsul, Paul Doumer; Arthur Fontaine, director of the labor office in the Ministry of Labor; and Anatole Leroy-Beaulieu and Emile Levasseur.[91]

90. Folio 1202, pp. 13–27, AMS; *BPB*, XX (1898), 167–68.
91. Musée social, *Statutes*, 21–38.

By the time the Musée commemorated its first ten years of existence, however, the prospects for social peace seemed as distant as
ever. The class struggle that its founders had sought to avoid was
upon them. The next several years witnessed a labor-capital confrontation on an unprecedented scale, culminating in the general
strike of railroad workers in October, 1910. We may wonder, then, at
the optimism expressed by Jules Siegfried on the occasion of the
Musée's tenth anniversary: "Does not our republican democracy do
itself honor by providing a setting in which all nations of the world
may display what they have accomplished toward the moral, material, and social betterment of workers? Would this not be the appropriate time to demonstrate how France, so often falsely characterized
as a nation lacking in seriousness and stability, is rich in generous
initiatives, in hidden resources of self-sacrifice, and in tender sentiments, all expressed in our philanthropic and social projects for welfare, charity and solidarity?" Others expressed less elevated sentiments and perhaps came closer to the truth. Hippolyte Maze, a
founder of the bourgeois Ligue nationale de la prévoyance et de la
mutualité (which had Musée connections), stated the case with exceptional clarity as early as 1890: "Social action is not a function of
pure sentimentality; it must follow from scientific principles. If we
ignore or evade these truths, then we invite disaster."[92]

The contrast only highlights the contradictions embedded in the
ideology of social reform expressed by the Musée social and its
friends. Siegfried projected a genuine and accurate self-image of the
French reforming bourgeoisie, whereas Maze called attention to the
tough calculations that went into reform. In the former, we hear
the familiar refrain of the marketplace; in the latter, the harsh tones
of social management. Yet those who would consider themselves liberals—Siegfried, Bourgeois, Gide, and others—did not seem to be
the least bit uneasy in the company of corporatists, authoritarian paternalists, and social engineers. They clung to their liberal values in
the face of a complex of social relations that had rendered those values inoperative and thereby exposed themselves to the worst alternatives of open reaction in flagrant violation of their principles.

92. Cheysson, *Le Musée social*, 7, 11.

Events were to prove that rhetorical incantations to progressive values and expressions of generous impulses, unless firmly backed up
by a politics of social defense, would not deflect the consequences of
the new reality. Not yet willing to resort to the mailed fist, they were
equally unwilling to leave the labor question to the Invisible Hand.

V
Solidarism
In Search of the Middle Road

In a review of Léon Bourgeois' influential tract on solidarism, Edmond Demolins, the editor of *La Science Sociale*, denied Bourgeois' central proposition that capital and labor were naturally and historically united in the pursuit of social progress and social peace. Demolins dismissed solidarism as an "illusion" and accused Bourgeois of peddling platitudes: "Solidarism is a vague and agreeable formula, which no one has any trouble accepting, which neither bothers nor inconveniences anyone and, moreover, which has no effect on the course of events."[1] Demolins' trivialization of solidarism was to some extent justified. Solidarists, preaching justice and unity rather than exploitation and struggle, did not appear to threaten any fundamental interests, least of all those of the big bourgeoisie, in whose name Demolins spoke. They remained firmly rooted in the liberal tradition and had no intention of challenging established social relations. They insisted, however, that uncontrolled capitalism would produce increased social strife, upheaval, and, eventually, socialism. To the extent that they singled out socialism as the main enemy, the solidarists belong in the camp of counterrevolution. Nevertheless, they frankly confronted the new shape of France's political economy with few if any illusions about traditional liberal approaches to the social question. The solidarists' response took the form of an antimarketplace ideological system, enlisting social reform in the first line of social defense. For that reason

---

1. Léon Bourgeois, *De la solidarité* (Paris, 1896); Edmond Demolins, "L'Illusion de la solidarité," *La Science Sociale,* XXIII (1897), 6–11.

I use the term "social liberalism" to characterize solidarist social politics and ideology.

Solidarists set themselves the task of addressing the competing claims of capital, private property, and individual labor. They had no quarrel with the tendencies toward concentrated production as such—a process that Bourgeois pronounced "inevitable." But they warned that, in his words, "class divisions will only get worse" unless counterbalanced by the "forces of association . . . which will protect [what should be a] naturally integrated existence against the disintegrative effects of economic struggle." Nowhere did Bourgeois suggest that capitalist social relations were anything but the natural order of things. Thus in a single breath he could deplore their consequences and counsel accommodation. Despite the solidarists' claims to offer a viable alternative to both socialism and individualism, their efforts to navigate a middle course floundered on a reef of contradictions built into their own system. For, given their concerns about socialism, solidarists found themselves driven to a position in which protection "against the disintegrative effects of economic struggle" meant subordinating the claims of both capital and labor to the public good while leaving command of the economy in the hands of capital.[2]

One historian recently characterized solidarism as an "organic social philosophy." Such a definition misses the point. There was nothing philosophical about solidarism; it was purely political. Certainly no end of metaphorical references to the "social organism," the *corps social*, and "altruism" punctuate solidarist texts. But the contexts in which such language appears invariably involve transformations in production, concrete relations between labor and capital, and, in general, class struggle. Thus the corporal terminology, which likened society to a harmonious organic structure, turned into a conception of social production as an integrated mechanism, in other words, smoothly functioning social machinery. The solidarist political economist Laurent Dechesne, one of Charles Gide's

2. *AHS*, No. 9 *bis* (1907), 30–31; Célestin Bouglé, quoted in *RSS* (1906), 342. "One form of wage labor may correct the abuses of another, but no form of wage labor can correct the abuse of wage labor itself" (Karl Marx, *Grundrisse: Foundations of the Critique of Political Economy*, trans. Martin Nicolaus [New York, 1973], 123).

collaborators on the *Revue d'Economie Politique* (set up to combat laissez-faire doctrines), identified *solidarité* as a *"fact that results from specialization in production."* Dechesne translated the organic metaphor into "economic solidarity," in which all who contribute to the productive process exist in a state of mutual interdependence. From this followed "moral solidarity," the negation of class struggle.[3]

The Prehistory of Solidarism

Solidarité first shows up in political discourse during the 1840s in the propaganda tracts of utopian socialists and Christian millenarians such as Pierre Leroux and Philippe Buchez. In the case of Leroux, solidarity stood for a divinely sanctioned "social unity." One of Leroux's followers, Grégoire Champseix, in a more ecstatic tone, identified solidarity with the "breath of God that will renew all things." For them solidarism symbolized an eschatological vision of a community of producers engaged in cooperative association—the "social Republic" or the Christian commonwealth. They looked back to a simpler world than theirs, which was in the process of creation by the engines of industrial capitalism; a world in which the pitiless laws of the marketplace had not yet been invented to rule the lives of men and women of all classes.[4]

Others, contemporaries of the utopians and millenarians, took a hard look at the consequences of capitalist production and the threat of undisciplined labor. The 1830s and 1840s witnessed a tremendous outpouring of investigations and inquiries into the moral and material condition of the French working class. René Villermé, Eugène Buret, Charles Dupin, Ange Guépin, and Honoré Frégier, among

3. Michelle Perrot, "The Three Ages of Industrial Discipline in Nineteenth-Century France," in John Merriman (ed.), *Consciousness and Class Experience in Nineteenth-Century Europe* (New York, 1979), 163; Pierre Pécaut, *Petit traité de morale sociale* (Paris, 1907), 9–12; *RSS* (1906), 291; Ferdinand Buisson, quoted in *RIS*, XVI (1908), 199; *Premier congrès d'éducation sociale: Rapports* (Paris, 1901), 471–76; G.-L. Duprat, *La Solidarité sociale* (Paris, 1907), 264; René Maunier, "Sociologues et solidarité," *REP*, XXIII (1909), 705–706; Laurent Dechesne, "La Solidarité," *REP*, XXII (1908), 111–12.

4. Jean DuBois, *Le Vocabulaire politique et social en France, 1869 à 1872* (Paris, n.d.), 424–25; David Owen Evans, *Le Socialisme romantique* (Paris, 1948), 69; Bernard Moss, *The Origins of the French Labor Movement* (Berkeley, 1976), Chap. 2; William H. Sewell, Jr., *Work and Revolution in France* (Cambridge, 1980), 201–206.

others, filled hundreds of pages with lurid descriptions of life in the proletarian quarters of France's industrial centers. Uniformly they painted dark and brooding portraits of material deprivation and moral degradation. They entertained little hope of rehabilitation while conjuring up portents of great danger. Their political perspective did not differ substantially from that of Saint-Marc Girardin, a journalist-oracle of the Parisian bourgeoisie, who likened the insurgent silk workers of Lyon in 1831 to "barbarian hordes" pouring out of the "Caucusus and the steppes of Tartary." What distinguished Villermé and the rest from Girardin and his kind was the formers' effort to subsume exercises in observation, judgment, and manipulation beneath something called "social science." They did not speak of solidarity because it held no meaning for them. But it is no accident that solidarity, understood as class collaboration, emerged as a weapon in the ideological arsenal of their successors—political economists, social economists, and social liberals.[5]

The defeat of the movement for a "social and democratic Republic" during 1848–1850 and the subsequent reaction coincided with the triumph of political economy as an ideological system and a fairly accurate theoretical representation of the realities of competitive capitalism. Although the economy of the Second Empire showed some tendencies toward concentration—notably in banking, ferrous metals production, and mining—big business did not yet dominate the industrial and commercial landscape.[6] It was in this context that political economists placed their own version of solidarity, which, not surprisingly, they viewed as an automatic response to the convergence of interests in the marketplace. They thus translated solidarity from utopian sentiment into bourgeois ide-

5. Louis-René Villermé, *Tableau de l'état physique et moral des ouvriers employés dans les manufactures du coton, du laine et de la soie* (2 vols.; Paris, 1840); Edmond Buret, *De la misère des classes laborieuses en Angleterre et en France* (2 vols.; Paris, 1840); Charles Dupin, *Des forces productives et commerciales en France* (2 vols.; Paris, 1827); Ange Guépin, *Nantes au xix siècle: Statistiques topographiques, industrielles et morales* (Nantes, 1835); Honoré Frégier, *Des classes dangereuses dans la population des grandes villes et des moyens de les rendre meilleures* (2 vols.; Paris, 1840); *Journal des Débats*, December 8, 1831, quoted in Jean Bruhat, *Histoire du mouvement ouvrier français* (2 vols.; Paris, 1952), I, 243. Sewell, *Work and Revolution*, 223–32, provides an excellent analysis of Villermé's work.

6. Jean Bouvier, François Furet, and Marcel Gillet, *Le Mouvement du profit en France au xix siècle* (Paris, 1961).

ology and prefigured the class character of late nineteenth-century solidarism.

Henri Baudrillart addressed himself to the question of marketplace and social relations. An orthodox classical economist in the tradition of Jean-Baptiste Say and Frédéric Bastiat, Baudrillart held the chair of political economy in the Collège de France during the 1850s and 1860s. He then devoted himself to educational reform into which he had made an initial foray in 1867. In doing so, he followed a standard progression among French political economists and their counterparts in Britain and the United States during the last decades of the nineteenth century. Baudrillart's primary school reader, a standard exercise in political indoctrination, went through seven printings between 1885 and 1895. Its emphasis on association and collaboration rather than submission to inexorable market forces suggests that by 1885 his faith in the socially integrative power of automatic mechanisms had eroded.[7]

In a lecture at the Collège de France in 1854, Baudrillart attacked the utopian conception of solidarity, which he characterized as a social vision that took into account neither the division of labor nor the competitive dynamics of the marketplace. That conception, he argued, denied human diversity and, because it pretended "to suppress all inequalities," "led straight to tyranny." But who threatened to tyrannize whom? The answer emerges from Baudrillart's comments on the Le Chapelier law of 1791, which formally prohibited all forms of association but aimed directly at those organized by workers. He insisted that the law, although basically sound, was too rigid. "Industrial freedom," the fountainhead of political economy, was ill-served by the regime of absolute prohibition. Some forms of association "deserved approval" if consistent with freedom. The untrammeled proliferation of workers' associations, which struck at the heart of freedom, did not fit into that category.[8]

Nor did Baudrillart consider them necessary. Market relations, in his view, led necessarily to the solidarity of labor and capital without the application of force—especially at the hands of the state. The

7. Henri Baudrillart, *Les Bibliothèques et les cours populaires* (Paris, 1867); Baudrillart, *Manuel d'éducation morale et d'instruction civique* (1st ed.; Paris, 1885).

8. Henri Baudrillart, "De la solidarité à propos du reproche d'individualisme," *Journal des Economistes*, 1st ser. (1854), 325, 329.

market sufficed: "Exchange is . . . sociability in action. . . . Freedom of exchange is the economic expression of solidarity." Capital, because it created the wealth that ultimately reached the lowest ranks of society, "constituted the final guarantee of sociability" because "it was composed of past labor." Thus, "in the form of raw materials and articles of consumption, capital contributes to society as a whole; especially to those who depend on it for work and wages." Since capital provided for the general welfare by enlarging the social product, it could not feed on the exploitation of labor as its enemies alleged—or so Baudrillart argued. (If he noticed the non sequitur he did not comment on it.) Thus the "antagonism imagined in some quarters between profits and wages" was "chimerical. If it appears for a moment, it quickly vanishes, to be replaced by the harmony of interests." Elsewhere Baudrillart argued that capital and labor were bound by a system of unbreakable mutual relations: labor gives value to capital; capital provides sustenance for labor. Hence a moral as well as an economic relationship linked the two. Hence, also, he concluded that "the improvement of the condition of workers obviously depends on the accumulation of capital." He heaped scorn on those who proposed the regulation of wage levels, for they did not understand that the "reconciliation of labor and capital" and the ability of each to pursue its own interests depended upon the free market in labor power. Within the framework of such a world view, political economists did not need to consider forms of social politics should the mechanism that produced solidarity break down.[9]

The Contradictions of Social Liberalism

The late nineteenth century presented a very different world from the one in which Baudrillart operated. Working-class organizations proliferated, strikes multiplied, and socialism won the allegiance of increasing numbers. Union membership in concentrated industries, such as metallurgy and chemicals, increased dramatically. It was against this background that the solidarists tackled the social question, seeking new ways to effect class collaboration without disturb-

9. *Ibid.*, 333–34, 336; "Des rapports du travail et du capital," *Journal des Economistes,* 1st ser. (1853), 375–96.

ing the basic structure of production. Whereas they did not deny that "the improvement of the conditions of workers" hinged on "the accumulation of capital," they endorsed labor's claim to a stake in the national patrimony and to associations for the protection of working-class interests. Edmond Villey argued that the "working-class organization" is "the only way to guarantee the worker's freedom and to arm the *labor component*. Working-class organizations involve force, but not necessarily struggle." The use of the word "component" *(élément)* suggests a common solidarist assumption: labor and capital form two interdependent parts of a single whole, thereby rendering struggle unnatural. Solidarists saw no necessary contradiction between the social rights of labor and capital, as long as the former remained on the path of legality and the latter open to reform. But their emphasis lay heavily on labor's responsibilities and its self-management. The Republic, as René Waldeck-Rousseau put it, had nothing to fear from workers' associations that had transformed themselves from "centers for propaganda or political agitation" into vehicles for "the investigation of labor's interests."[10] Labor's solidarity constituted one of the building blocks of national solidarity.

Nonrevolutionary and noncollectivist elements in the trade-union movement had followed a similar logic for some time. Louis Pauliat, a politically moderate leader of skilled workers in the 1870s and 1880s, prefigured the attitudes of the next generation of conservative trade unionists and their bourgeois associates. Pauliat insisted that workers must defend their economic interests, especially against "excessive industrialism" (although he did not make the connection between the degradation of skill and the deliberate dismantling of barriers to accumulation), and also do their part to promote good relations between classes: "Workers as well as bosses have a direct interest in increasing production rather than in slowing it down or stopping it altogether." A member of the next generation of conservative trade unionists, Auguste Besse, in 1908 defended the autonomy of working-class formations while insisting on their responsi-

10. Edmond Villey, "La Désagrégation sociale et la lutte des classes," *REP,* XVIII (1904), 438; Waldeck-Rousseau, speech to the Société pour la participation aux bénéfices, quoted in *Exposition 1889,* I, 273.

bility to the Republic. Within the labor movement he distinguished between good and bad *syndicats*: the former took the road of reform, respected the rights of capital, and contemplated striking only as a last, desperate resort; the latter fought the "social transformations" signaled by the progressive advance of solidarity, took a militant anticapitalist stance, and used the strike as its first, rather than its last, weapon. There were, in Besse's view (and he was not alone) solid material reasons to justify interclass solidarity and for the *syndicat* to act as an instrument of peace, not of war. They had to do with a particular conception of productive relations, not unlike that held by social economists: "Can the boss get along without the worker? Can the worker get along without the boss? Can either get along without capital? Is not capital the mechanism, the powerful and indispensable force behind all industrial and commercial enterprise?"[11]

Besse attempted to bridge the contradiction between short-term economic interest and long-term class interest that plagued all social liberals. Short-term alliances between labor and capital occur frequently and can be justified on the grounds of mutual interest: greater profits and consequent incentives for investment may lead to higher wages and expanded opportunities for employment. This situation, however—the excessive industrialism that Pauliat feared— easily could turn to capital's advantage as the "ruin of small independent industry" swelled the ranks of the work force and produced a downward pressure on wages. Over the long haul, therefore, the class interests of labor and of capital would come into opposition as the concentration in production tended to strengthen capital at the expense of labor and provide it with increased political muscle. Open combat followed, as in 1899 when the number of strikes suddenly jumped at the precise moment when French industrial production reached its decennial peak. This state of affairs made a mockery of social peace. Charles Gide, among others, worried about this situation even though he welcomed concentration. In the

11. Louis Pauliat, *Les Associations et chambres syndicales ouvrières* (Paris, 1873), 57, 65; Jean Maitron (ed.), *Dictionnaire biographique du mouvement ouvrier français* (21 vols.; Paris, 1964–84), XIV, 218; Auguste Besse, *L'Education sociale par les syndicats professionnels* (Paris, 1908), 4–24.

absence of countervailing forces, the modern corporation contained no built-in mechanisms for solidarity between workers and managers. No community of interests prevailed, only "unnamed hatred." Concentration without collaboration threatened the social equilibrium. Gide found no panacea in the revival of competitive enterprise. History was moving in the other direction, from individual to collective production.[12]

These estimates of economic realities led solidarists to engage in some tortuous logic and to take internally contradictory positions. The sociologist G.-L. Duprat argued that large-scale enterprise produced "industrial solidarity" because of the "complete division of labor" that characterized such operations. But that only described material conditions for which the political framework remained lacking. The "laborer engaged in the specialized task" could not, on his own, stand up against the power embodied in "the concentration of capital in big business" and in factories equipped with powerful machines driving intensive production. This apparatus armed "entrepreneurs, the 'rulers' of the economy, with an irresistible force." Potential dangers lay in this situation, notably in an opportunity afforded to "organizers of the proletariat" to launch "their struggle against 'bourgeois' or 'capitalist' society." Yet Duprat expressed skepticism about what some called the potential "tyranny of the masses." He claimed that "however indispensable workers may be in an integrated and disciplined modern factory . . . it did not follow that the economic function exercises some sort of hegemony over all other social functions." The organization of production itself determined and justified the continued unchallenged leadership of capital: "Without engineers to manage labor, without entrepreneurs . . . without teachers . . . the 'proletariat' would know only misery and impotence." Revealingly, Duprat linked domestic social progress to France's position in the world economy, for without a "body of technicians" backed up by efficient and satisfied workers "an industrial nation is entirely at the mercy" of foreigners. But individuals frequently followed the path of unenlightened self-interest. It was the

12. Duprat, *La Solidarité sociale*, 135; Edward Shorter and Charles Tilly, *Strikes in France, 1830–1968* (Cambridge, 1974), 361; W. Arthur Lewis, *Growth and Fluctuations, 1870–1913* (London, 1978), 269; Charles Gide, "L'Idée de solidarité en tant que programme économique," *RIS*, I (1893), 394–95; Gide, "Le Néocollectivisme," *REP*, VIII (1894), 426.

business of sociologists steeped in social science to spread the word among capitalists and workers alike that solidarity was "fundamental social fact" derived from the "collective character of society." Therefore, Duprat did not support delivering the management of social relations into the hands of "social authorities," who often were hopelessly reactionary, but he did not explain how, given the organization of production, that could be avoided. Duprat fell back somewhat lamely on the conclusion that the "thousands who sell their labor" should form associations to match those of "concentrated capital." Such associations, he hastened to add, contributed to the consolidation of national solidarity only if they did not come under the influence of leaders who promoted class struggle and strikes. In the end the "organizers of the proletariat" were to be feared after all.[13]

Labor's militancy as well as capital's stubbornness repeatedly confounded the best intentions of solidarists and other social liberals, leaving them trapped between backing workers' rights and a commitment to preserving and legitimizing established social relations— the reason they had taken up the cause of reform in the first place. They engaged in a constant search for political solutions to reproduce their ideological vision of incorporating labor into the national society. Edmond Villey, for example, another of Gide's collaborators on the *Revue d'Economie Politique*, who, like Duprat, supported independent working-class associations, recorded with dismay the wave of strikes that broke over northern France in 1904. He described it as "premeditated social warfare" and accused "instigators among the workers" of violating the "spirit of conciliation and concord" expressed in the bosses' undertaking to maintain current wage levels while acquiescing in the ten-hour day as prescribed by the law of 1900. These events brought to the surface the "mute hostility that frequently arouses the worker against the boss." In the enlightened tones of social liberalism, Villey conceded that "it [hostility] to some degree emerges naturally from the conditions of modern industry." If left unchecked, big business tended toward a wider separation between workers and employers: "Two distinct social classes . . . cannot exist side by side, indifferent to one another;

13. Duprat, *La Solidarité sociale*, 134–36, 157–62, 264–72.

either they collaborate or they come to blows." He feared the worst: "The abyss between the classes deepens, antagonisms sharpen, the struggle broadens and becomes inflamed; it seems that we are driven by overwhelming forces toward a social cataclysm." Having condemned instigators but not, significantly, workers themselves (apparently only victims of circumstances), Villey laid the responsibility for constructing the foundations of social solidarity squarely on the shoulders of the ruling class. He put little stock in state-operated systems of social insurance, not out of any laissez-faire prejudice but because state intervention left the bourgeoisie free to indulge in "ferocious egotism," in hypocritical "pandering to popular passions," and in peddling "that absurd and leveling notion of equality which is contrary to the nature of things." Thus Villey performed a neat ideological pirouette. He simultaneously championed working-class independence—if expressed in peaceful and accommodating forms— and surrounded that independence with a hierarchical structure that reflected actual industrial conditions. The entrepreneur's authority remained unchallenged and deserved to be, as long as he met his social responsibilities. Associations of workers smoothed the path to social peace in the workplace to the extent that they institutionalized collaboration, thereby making coercion (always a risky business) unnecessary. "How much better would the French bourgeoisie, by adopting that course, serve both the people's interests and its own!"[14]

The problem remained of reconciling once and for all the "peoples' interests" with those of capital. Here the social liberals' deep commitment to liberal institutions betrayed them, for to advocate radically abridging the rights of capital undermined the social foundations of the liberal state. Thus they were impaled on the horns of a dilemma. On the one hand, solidarists dedicated themselves to reducing the social costs of production, condemning capitalism's "exploitation of the labor of others" that caused "misery and ruin among workers." On the other, they applauded capital's achievements, pronouncing it the wave of the future against which no political barriers must be erected. "Capitalist solidarity," that is, concentration, dominated production. The handwriting on the wall was clear: "Small business, small industry, indeed small savings disap-

14. Villey, "La Désagrégation sociale," 437–52.

pear, crushed or absorbed by powerful organizations." Workers and other victims of industrial concentration could gain little comfort from the proposition that individual labor was "sacrosanct," as Gide insisted. But he also made the same claim for property and on that basis the solidarists constructed a complete but contradictory ideological system.[15]

The campaign to create opportunities for workers to gain individual property became solidarism's main political weapon. Despite their liberal inclinations, they did not value property for its own sake so much as for its purported effectiveness in blunting the edge of class struggle. Property in the hands of workers would counterbalance the unequal distribution of power between capital and labor. Once raised to the dignity of property owners, workers became full members of the national community. Meanwhile, the power to appropriate the product of labor—another form of property—remained in the hands of capital. In this manner, the struggle for social justice shifted to terrain external to the arena in which production took place, leaving capitalist relations untouched. Property ownership and other forms of social amelioration brought independence and tightened "moral bonds" between classes without changing the relations of dependence that reigned in the workplace. Thus the solidarists' program for property simultaneously promised equality of rights and values and reinforced bourgeois superiority and leadership. In that respect, at least, social liberalism converged with conservative social reform.[16]

Having exalted property for its liberating qualities, solidarists gave it a peculiar twist that seemed to turn it into its opposite. Rights to property, whether in one's capacity to labor or in one's ownership of capital, carried responsibilities. These were mediated by contractual obligations on the moral level—quite unlike those of the marketplace—that required individuals "to pledge themselves to respect each other's rights and liberties." The moral imperative followed from the proposition that "property is so fundamentally one of the attributes of existence that it is the indispensable condition for independence." Yet a formula for independence could serve equally

---

15. *RSS* (1909), 6, 39; Gide, "Le Néocollectivisme," 437.
16. Léon Bourgeois, *L'Education de la démocratie française* (Paris, 1897), 272–73; *REP*, VIII (1894), 37; Charles Gide, *Les Institutions de progrès social* (Paris, 1912), 499.

well for accommodation. Material inequality, or what I call the social costs of production, did not shake the solidarist ideological
structure. It was considered morally defensible because it stemmed
from unavoidably unequal exchange relations ("some profit to the
detriment of others") and it drove individuals to "raise themselves
by dint of hard work, skill, and thrift." Contrariwise, "economic
solidarity" based upon the division of labor legitimized dominant
and subordinate places in society. The sin of "egoism"—usually applied to workers unwilling to accept the counsels of solidarism—
undermined the "social interest," according to which "we must re-
strain our desires, save, and dispose of our wealth carefully."[17]

Persistent references to moral reform and the elevation of human
consciousness within the working class and on mutual obligations
between classes suggest that social liberals subordinated social reform to transformations in attitudes. If that were the case, we should
then write them off as hopeless dreamers. Moral and social reform
operated reciprocally, however, each reinforcing the other. Social
reform, raised as a bulwark against the "complete, global transformation of the economic system," faced limits imposed by fixed productive relations, which, being inherently unequal, harbored the potential for conflict. Neither good works delivered from above nor the
coercion built into the productive process sufficed to consolidate
bourgeois hegemony or to promote social peace. They paid off only
if accompanied by instruments of cultural and ideological integration. Material improvements had a decisive moral dimension in that
they were designed to further genuine class collaboration on the
level of conscious choice—to contribute, in other words, to the
working class's "social education."[18] Hence it was of vital importance for capital that the solidarists' message of unity rather than
struggle find favor in the eyes of labor and that laborers accept dependence on capital in the workplace as bound up with their independence as equal citizens in the national community.

In self-consciously and consistently opposing their systems to that

17. André Malapert, quoted in Léon Bourgeois and Alfred Croiset, *Essai d'une
philosophie de la solidarité: Conférences et discussions* (Paris, 1902), 105–109; Pécaut, *Petit
traité*, 20–27, 64–65, 74.

18. *RSS* (1906), 340–42, 471–72; *ibid.*, (1908), 49.

of their socialist contemporaries, solidarists leaned sharply toward an idealized version of bourgeois ideology that seemed to contradict their realistic appraisal of the tendencies inherent in French economic development. Léon Bourgeois may be taken as typical:

> My socialism tends toward the realization of the conditions within which the individual, any individual, will develop himself fully, will reach the total potential of all his energies and all his faculties, will possess true freedom. I am, for that reason, absolutely opposed to collectivism, to communism, which invokes the power of the state and which tends inevitably to the destruction of freedom. Individual property appears to me to constitute the extension and the foundation of freedom. . . . The development of individual property, not its suppression, is my goal, and my conception of a social ideal is that in which each person would obtain private property in just measure.

Others denounced socialists for devising "social systems contrary to our very nature" and for seeking political solutions to the social question. Yet the solidarists' program for what they called a "rational" approach to social reform based on "observation, experience, and psychology" and on "social realism" also had a political dimension.[19]

Political considerations become manifest when we probe beneath idealized visions of a community of property owners. The steady growth in wage labor remained the principal fact of economic and social life. Consequently, interclass solidarity based on a common stake in property receded in importance before pragmatic mechanisms for working-class integration into industrial society. Social reform, though not to be disdained on strictly humanitarian grounds and the object of close attention, invariably was treated primarily as a political instrument. It contributed to the moral reform of the working class and pointed toward a noncollectivist solution to the problem of class antagonism. Indeed, "rational" systems derived from the "social facts" observed in the world of production—division of labor and differentiation of tasks—tended to reinforce the bonds of authority in the workplace by providing efficient forms of labor organization appropriate to large and complex enterprises. Moreover, they rendered unnecessary the coercion implicit in direct

19. Gide, "Le Néocollectivisme," 423; Bourgeois and Croiset, *Essai d'une philosophie,* 34; Emile Durkheim, "Gaston Richard, *Le Socialisme et la science sociale,*" *Revue Philosophique,* XLIV (1897), 200–205, cited in Brian Turner, "The Social Origins of Academic Sociology: Durkheim" (Ph.D. dissertation, Columbia University, 1977), 284.

paternalist intervention. But solidarists did not mean to pronounce a death sentence on paternalism, only to urge its transformation into a progressive design for social management. In this respect their views extended those of conservative reformers such as Auguste Fougerousse, big-business lobbyist and a leading member of the Société d'économie sociale, who took a similar position during the economic doldrums of the mid-1880s. "Well-organized paternalism," he wrote, "produces solidarity."[20]

Such instances of ideological consensus found concrete expression in numerous parapolitical reform organizations. I have already discussed several in Chapters III and IV. Another was the Ligue nationale de la prévoyance et de la mutualité, a broad bourgeois front formed to promote cooperation, association, and class collaboration. Founded in the late 1880s through the efforts of Hippolyte Maze, a centrist republican senator from the Seine-et-Oise, the Ligue counted among its charter members leading political and business figures: Sadi Carnot, president of the Republic; Jean Constans, lately the gravedigger of the Boulangist movement; Agénor Bardoux, banker and railroad magnate; and Jean Auddifret, textile entrepreneur, deputy from Roanne (Loire), and an advocate of workers' retirement benefits and of the extension of French economic influence in southern China. Maze's conception of the Ligue's role closely paralleled that of the Musée social. He intended to make it a permanent center for the promotion of all institutions—public and private—that fostered foresight (*prévoyance*) among workers, in particular, and the implantation of "social economy," in general. These included cooperatives, savings associations, and pension funds. In keeping with the new spirit of bourgeois class solidarity, according to which the social question overrode considerations of partisan politics, Maze permitted no discussions of politics and religion in the Ligue's meetings or in its bulletin. The recognition that intraclass conflict exacted insupportable social costs had become fixed solidarist doctrine by the last decade of the century. Quarrels between parties ceased to have meaning at a time when the resolution of the social question hinged on cooperation among all political ten-

20. *RIP,* IV (1890), 155; *RSS* (1904–1905), 1; Auguste Fougerousse, "La Crise industrielle en France," *RS,* XVI (1884), 293.

dencies. Patriotism emerged as the highest expression of solidarity, "a solidarity of common defense." Accordingly, the Ligue nationale de la prévoyance et de la mutualité, in company with similar organizations, recruited Catholics and Protestants, conservative reformers and social liberals alike: Cheysson, Fougerousse, Gibon, Charles Robert, Jules Siegfried, Paul Delombre, Jean Casimir-Périer, Emile Levasseur, and the colonial lobbyists and onetime protégés of Gambetta, Eugène Etienne and Maurice Rouvier. Among the projects the Ligue supported and monitored, it singled out cooperative association as "the most necessary for social peace."[21]

Every Man a Capitalist: Cooperation and Association

During most of the nineteenth century, producers' and consumers' cooperatives were constructed for working-class self-defense against the progressive encroachment of capital. Frequently they exhibited a distinct anticapitalism, especially before 1848, as in the case of the Association coopérative de production organized by Philippe Buchez in Paris in 1831 and Louis Blanc's plan for the radical reorganization of production. By the century's last decade, working-class cooperatives continued to attract the attention of syndicalist and other non-Marxist fractions of the French labor movement, but the cooperative movement took a contrary direction and an altogether different political aspect. Capitalists adopted the principles of cooperative association as part of their social machinery.[22] My principal emphasis in the pages that follow will be less on the machinery itself than on its place in the politics and ideology of solidarism.

The bourgeois cooperative movement drew its supporters, propagandists, and theoreticians from the same constellation of reformers that we repeatedly have encountered. Their purpose was neither to abolish the *salariat* (wage labor) nor to displace the *patronat*, but to effect class collaboration by providing labor with the means to

21. *RIP,* IV (1890), 349, 389–403; Jean Jolly (ed.), *Dictionnaire des parlementaires français* (10 vols.; Paris, 1960–67), I, 411; *RSS* (1906), 290–91; Pécaut, *Petit traité,* 141; *RIP,* IV (1890), 390, 417–32.

22. *Exposition 1900,* V, 36; Louis Blanc, *L'Organisation du travail* (Paris, 1841); *EF,* September 21, 1865.

gain a stake in production in association with, or parallel to, capitalist enterprise. Bourgeois reformers became interested in cooperatives—whether of consumers, producers, or farmers—as a logical outgrowth of their sense of which way the wind was blowing. They based their calculations on straightforward material and political terms. The future lay with association, which had come to dominate production, in the shape of large family firms as well as *sociétés anonymes* (joint-stock companies). Associations generated the "collective production of wealth," mobilizing capital and all other "individual forces and energies" on behalf of national production. Thus all forms of association contributed to material progress and social cohesion. Some made even more ambitious claims. Cooperatives were prescribed as the ultimate panacea for France's social ills. "Can one imagine," asked one solidarist, "an organization in which bosses and workers, capital and labor, do not confront each other as antagonists and where there is no fear of strikes or violence?" Jules Siegfried made more specific the political motives that lay behind bourgeois patronage of cooperative associations: "As one appreciates their advantages, socialist and revolutionary doctrines lose their pernicious influence."[23]

As Siegfried's comment suggests, those reformers who promoted the formation of cooperatives did so with a view to undermining socialist influence in the working class or, more precisely, to rendering socialism unnecessary. Collective organization need not be a socialist monopoly. To the contrary, voluntary associations for the "solidarity of individuals" provided shelters from the storms of the marketplace at least as secure as those that emerged from the "meddling of the state," and with the added advantage of not having the "slightest degree of coercion" attached to them. This was collectivism both stripped of its socialist political scaffolding and consistent with a hierarchical organization of production. Gide pronounced cooperative association the highest form of solidarity among all the institutions for social economy. He envisioned "a

---

23. *RIP,* IV (1890), 153; V (1891), 603; Charles Lebrun, "Le Droit d'association," in Société d'économie politique et d'économie sociale de Lyon, *Compte-rendu analytique des séances* (1898–99), 296, 360–61; *RSS* (1906), 474; Alliance coopérative internationale, *Deuxième Congrès, 1896* (Paris, 1897), 62–63.

completely new form of collectivism. . . . . Not that revolutionary collectivism that prepares for the day when it possesses sufficient strength to expropriate the owners of capital, but that peaceful collectivism that seeks to enlarge capital resources." Paul Doumer, influential politician, associate of big businessmen, colonial proconsul, and future president of the Republic, put the case for cooperation in an even sharper political context. He predicted "an inevitable social revolution" that "will be violent if carried out as the result of a collision of interests." But the disaster could be averted. "The revolution," Doumer argued, "can be peaceful and fruitful if it is prepared carefully . . . if it follows from the evolution of morals and law." A relatively progressive politician, Doumer served as Léon Bourgeois' minister of finance in 1895–1896 and coauthored the ill-fated income tax bill. Perhaps that sobering experience led Doumer to place morals before law. In any event, once again the accent fell on moral reform, that "revolution in consciousness" of which bourgeois reformers of every ideological tendency made so much. Léopold Mabilleau, who doubted that cooperatives were the answer to the social question, at least conceded that they constituted "for the worker the best way to elevate his intellectual and moral situation" and that they represented "insurance for social peace." Likewise, Eugène Rostand, head of the Banque populaire of Marseille, enumerated four aspects of cooperation that contributed to the moral education of the working population: "participation in groups, the capitalization of honesty, a taste for independence, and manly sentiments."[24]

Cooperatives and associations held other, related attractions for bourgeois reformers. In the first place, they acquainted entrepreneurs and managers with workers' problems, especially their precarious existence, and forced them to confront the extremes of wealth and poverty that, as Fougerousse put it, separated society's

24. Duprat, *La Solidarité sociale*, 279; Charles Gide, "La Coopération," in Jules Siegfried *et al.* (eds.), *Les Applications sociales de la solidarité* (Paris, 1904), 47, 65; Michael Rust, "Business and Politics in the Third Republic: The Comité des forges and the French Steel Industry, 1896–1914" (Ph.D. dissertation, Princeton University, 1974), 340, 465; Léopold Mabilleau *et al.*, *Cours d'instruction civique* (Paris, 1902), 178–81; *Exposition 1900*, Classe 107, "Sociétés coopératives: rapport de Mabilleau," XVI, 6; Eugène Rostand, *A l'école de la coopération et à l'école du socialisme* (Paris, 1898), 11–14.

"head" and "tail." Every action taken by the rich to help the poor contributed equally to the moralization of each. This was particularly important because the rapid growth of enterprises increased the distance between employee and employer. As a practical matter, measures of solidarity were to be preferred over acts of charity because they involved "less cost and they make socially useful those who otherwise would become parasites or enemies." Associations such as profit sharing, mutual aid societies, and savings funds were a step toward resolving the social question, "the struggle between capital and labor having lost its justification once capital and labor become closely allied by their common interest."[25] Second, there was the factor of working-class self-help and respectability. Emile Cheysson, who counted the cooperative movement among the dozens of reform enterprises in which he took part, argued for a strategy that gave primary consideration to workers' ambitions for independence and self-improvement. Cooperatives filled the bill, for they incorporated elements that "accommodate the interests of workers without compromising those of other classes." Similarly, Gide singled out consumers' cooperatives as instruments for social education because their members applied the "practice and habits of solidarity" and acquired a sense of independence. The failure of a producers' cooperative in the Loire coal basin in 1899 was used to illustrate the point that without serious and respectable workers, cooperatives had little chance of success. In this case, problems stemming from insufficient funds and thin coal seams were compounded by the irresponsibility of the participants: "They were not drawn from the working-class elite . . . instead of select strongly disciplined men, used to obeying authority, one frequently encounters malcontents, strong-minded types who imagine themselves able to give orders and to send their foremen packing" on the slightest excuse.[26]

Finally, reformers active in the Ligue nationale de la prévoyance et de la mutualité and in the French section of the Alliance coopérative internationale (ACI) considered cooperatives an antidote to the

25. Auguste Fougerousse, *Patrons et ouvriers: Réformes introduites dans l'organisation du travail par divers chefs d'industries* (Paris, 1880), 229–57; Henry Buisson, *Le Rôle de la coopération et son application pratique* (Paris, 1897), 44; *RIP,* IV (1890), 153.

26. Emile Cheysson, *Les Ouvriers et les réformes nécessaires* (Paris, 1877), 7–8; Gide, *Les Institutions,* 217; *ACF,* 7th year (1899), 62–65.

harmful consequences of concentrated production. Control of production by capitalists rather than workers, which constituted the fundamental social innovation of the factory, had made a mockery of the solidarist principle that all enterprise should be based on an exchange among equal producers. The internal organization of industrial enterprise could not be substantially altered, but a network of cooperatives offered workers and small producers a realm of independence beyond the factory gates without impinging on established "economic, industrial, agricultural, and commercial interests."[27] Producers' cooperatives such as appeared in the late nineteenth century, although superficially resembling earlier workers' cooperatives, lacked a political dimension. Rather, they provided ambitious workers with an opportunity to act as collective capitalists and provided the bourgeoisie with "recruits from the working-class elite." One success story was that of Augustine Legrand, founder of a consumers' cooperative in Saint-Rémy s/ Avre (Eure). Legrand came from a working-class family and had been employed in the Waddington cotton mills, where his quick intelligence won him rapid advancement. In 1885 he left his job to organize the cooperative (perhaps with his employer's encouragement). The cooperative, which had a large warehouse, winery, cider press, and grocery outlet, won Legrand enough fame to earn him a silver medal at the 1889 Exposition. He capped his career as a member of the organizing committee of the social economy group for the 1900 Exposition. Mobility such as Legrand demonstrated led Henry Buisson, the secretary-general of the ACI at the turn of the century, a frequent contributor to the *Revue de la Solidarité Sociale* and the leader of a painting contractors' cooperative called Le Travail, to claim that properly constituted cooperatives exposed the "political fiction" of classes. They facilitated the "equitable distribution of the product of labor among the various factors of production": labor, intelligence (management), and capital.[28]

27. Lebrun, "Le Droit d'association," 360; *RIP*, V (1891), 106. For an interesting statement about the social purpose of the factory, see Stephen Marglin, "What Do Bosses Do? The Origins and Functions of Hierarchy in Capitalist Production," *Review of Radical Political Economics*, VI·(1974), 60–112.

28. Gide, *Les Institutions*, 517; *Exposition 1889*, I, 86–87; Mabilleau *et al.*, *Cours*, 180; *ACF*, 7th year (1899), 77–86; Buisson, *Le Rôle de la coopération*, 20, 31.

The reduction of classes to factors of production was itself a political fiction, but nonetheless useful. It enabled bourgeois reformers to make cooperatives attractive to capitalists. Although labor stood to gain protection against unemployment and "increasing misery," capital stood to gain an economic safety valve: "big industry, 'machine production,' could develop unhindered without the slightest threat of overproduction" as long as "consumers' and producers' cooperatives combined to maintain markets." Cooperatives had the added advantage of introducing order into ruinously competitive small enterprises and facilitating capitalist control of the market. Cooperatives, on a small scale, simply mirrored the socialization of production in the leading sectors of the economy.[29]

Bourgeois-supported associations for working-class independence produced a similar result in other ways. Charles Gide recorded the work of the Société pour le développement du tissage mécanique in Lyon. Financed by the city's bankers, industrialists, chamber of commerce, and the departmental general council, the Société initially made available small electric motors to run the looms of the independent weavers remaining in Lyon's Croix Rousse district, once the center of the silk industry. The weavers had fallen on hard times as a direct result of the silk entrepreneurs' decision to shift production into mechanized factories and to distribute some tasks to rural workers who "made do with lower wages." This move had as much to do with politics as with economies of scale and cost-cutting. It was, quite simply, a way to break the back of the exceptionally militant Lyonese workers' movement. The number of looms in Lyon fell from fifty to sixty thousand in 1848 to eighty-six hundred by 1900, whereas thirty-six thousand were installed in factories by the latter date. To arrest this "massacre" of small producers, the Société was organized in 1886 to subsidize new looms equipped with motors, thereby enabling the silk weavers to double their output and earn a living wage. Otherwise, they would suffer chronic unemployment because they could not be absorbed into the factories. That prospect alone impelled the Lyonese bourgeoisie to undertake their project. Gide recognized the Société's contribution to peace and order in Lyon and to the fortunes of the silk industry but considered

29. Duprat, *La Solidarité sociale*, 279.

it a "paternalist enterprise" rather than a true cooperative because the initiative came from the bourgeoisie and not from the workers.[30]

Gide's comments on the Société pour le développement du tissage mécanique illustrate the attitude of bourgeois reformers active in the cooperative movement. They were less interested in how associations worked or if they paid off than in association itself as an enterprise in solidarity. But among them, differences and contradictions appeared, reproducing the diverse perspectives of social liberals and their more conservative collaborators. The former stressed working-class independence, the latter paternalist intervention and hierarchy. Those differences were later played out in Gide's politics, those of his associate Edouard de Boyve of Nîmes, and in the French section of the ACI itself. Yet collaborators they all remained. Not accidentally, for example, did one such as Léopold Mabilleau occupy a place of honor in the portrait gallery of social liberal heroes.[31] The house of solidarist ideology accommodated diverse but compatible occupants.

Edouard de Boyve organized a consumers' cooperative in Nîmes during the early 1880s and edited its newspaper, *L'Emancipation*. The cooperative, known as the Abeille nîmoise (the bee of Nîmes), although remaining strictly a local institution, attracted considerable attention among bourgeois reformers nationwide thanks largely to de Boyve's efforts. He also headed the Société d'économie populaire of Nîmes, founded in 1884 by local businessmen and dedicated to the "union of all classes" through the propagation of "economic and social education, the only way to neutralize the partisans of violence."[32] The Société's work in popular education will be dealt with later; for the moment what interests us is its action on the cooperative front and especially de Boyve's contribution to an ideology of cooperative association.

De Boyve's Abeille functioned in close association with another cooperative, organzied about the same time, called Solidarité, originally an exclusively working-class operation started by individuals who had chosen the path of reform over that of revolution. They

30. *Exposition 1900*, V, 303–305.

31. *RSS* (1904), frontispiece; Edouard de Boyve, *Histoire de la coopération à Nîmes* (Paris, 1889), 34; Jean Gaumont, *Histoire générale de la coopération en France* (2 vols.; Paris, 1923), II, 99–120; *RIP*, V (1891), 322–23.

32. Gaumont, *Histoire générale*, II, 97.

created a form of "collective property" and ultimately expected to amass some capital. Together the Abeille and Solidarité became known as the Ecole de Nîmes, a label originally pinned on them by a hostile observer.[33] The local bourgeoisie, impressed by these efforts, gave moral and material support. De Boyve was instrumental in mobilizing that support. He pointed out that the workers' stake in property had rendered them sober and respectable, "steady and hardworking," and had kept them away from "unhealthy pursuits." De Boyve held up the Abeille as a model for class collaboration: cooperatives "bring together the best elements of all classes in society. . . . One can disregard egoists among the bourgeoisie as well as the drunks and the loafers among the working class. . . . The streetsweeper and the solid citizen are equals and should greet each other as brothers. . . . Among us, the class struggle does not exist; in our association classes have disappeared." The disappearance of classes really meant the disappearance of the apprehension of irreconcilable class antagonism. Cooperation's chief enemy was not a particular individual but a conception and political statement: "class struggle." De Boyve characterized socialism as a "nihilistic, hatred-ridden, destructive force." Cooperation, "intelligent practical socialism," strengthened national solidarity by effecting the "*harmony of capital and labor.*" It advanced "the union of workers . . . without weakening the creative power of capital." Associated labor, as de Boyve went to great lengths to point out, threatened neither private property, capital, nor national production. Those involved in the cooperative movement "understand that any system that aims to abolish property would provoke the flight of capital to other countries and stifle investment and accumulation." In a world in which an increasingly larger share of production was carried on through the association of capital, cooperators "only seek easier access to wealth."[34]

Despite its popular character, the Ecole de Nîmes came under attack by "political socialists" who considered it a diversionary tactic. Conversely, the Abeille's supporters denounced socialist-sponsored cooperatives for fostering "revolution." Charles Guieysse, an admirer

33. *Ibid.*, II, 98.
34. De Boyve, *Histoire,* 6–12, 15–16; *ACF,* 8th year (1900), 29, 31; *RIP,* V (1891), 598.

of the Ecole, a dabbler in nationalist syndicalism, and secretary-general of the Société des universités populaires, found both attitudes curious and contradictory: "The Ecole de Nîmes, in its ambition to transform society as a whole through cooperation, has a truly revolutionary mission, whereas the so-called socialist cooperatives seek only to promote the unity of the working class—a program, whatever its revolutionary pretensions, is fundamentally conservative." Guieysse's semantic somersault only illustrated the principle that how one dealt with cooperation on the political level depended on whose ox was being gored. Socialists stuck to class struggle, whereas solidarists pursued an "economic and social revolution through association and consent."[35] No one expressed the latter sentiments or addressed their contradictions better than did Charles Gide.

During his tenure as professor of political economy at Montpellier in the late 1880s and early 1890s, Gide had ample opportunity to observe the activities of the Société d'économie populaire of Nîmes and to become acquainted with de Boyve's work. This experience reinforced his conviction that cooperative association held the key to social peace. Like Bourgeois, Gide sought solutions external to the terrain on which production took place. Gide's conception of cooperation was enormously ambitious and far-reaching, placing him in a relatively radical position within the constellation of bourgeois reform. As much as the others, he operated within an ideological framework that accommodated concentration and the hierarchical social relations it entailed, but that did not prevent him from raising the alarm about the concentration of production and the growing power of cartels, price-fixing and marketing combines, and employers' *syndicats*, which were hardly unknown in France. They had appeared as a response to cutthroat competition and represented capital's efforts to organize a chaotic marketplace in the wake of the Great Depression and heightened international competition. Unattached by sentiment or ideology to laissez-faire, Gide shed no tears over the progressive disappearance of free competition. But he feared the socially explosive potential of big business's grip on the

35. Charles Guieysse, "Les Universités populaires et le mouvement ouvrier," *Cahiers de la Quinzaine*, 3rd ser. (1901), 21n; Léon Bourgeois, "Préface," in Buisson, *Le Rôle de la coopération*, 10–11.

market. "Formidable capitalist coalitions" rendered the consumer defenseless. Gide's use of "consumers," not producers, is a curious formulation to which I will return shortly. Gide believed that because all consumers, regardless of class, suffered the consequences of the concentration, all classes had an interest in cooperative solidarity. Their "common concern suffices to show us the road we must travel and allows us to outline a program, a vast program to tell the truth . . . for it aims at nothing less than the top-to-bottom reversal of the existing order—peacefully, of course."[36]

That program, reduced to its essentials, provided for the reproduction of capitalist associations for production (cartels, *syndicats*, and the like) in the sphere of consumption—the Abeille writ large: "In the presence of these gigantic producers' associations that have sprung up everywhere and that . . . threaten to become the standard form of economic organization, there is only one thing to do and that is to set up associations of consumers even more powerful and prepared to defend the general and permanent interests of society against the encroachments of monopoly." Gide's plan did not stop there. Consumers' cooperatives had the potential of becoming instruments of production, thereby replacing the individual capitalist. But capital remained: "The essential characteristic of the cooperative society, its original character, revolution if you please, is that capital is neither eliminated nor scorned—members of cooperatives are too practical-minded to imagine that they can absorb capital without paying the price—but reduced to its proper role, that is, as a factor of production in the service of labor and remunerated as such." The result was a world apparently turned upside down: "While under the current system it is capital which, monopolizing ownership, pockets the profits and labor earns a wage—under the cooperative system, by a reversal of the situation, it is the worker or the consumer who, as the owner, will pocket the profits and *capital will be reduced to the position of the simple wage earner.*" Thus the formation of popular associations for production did not spell the doom of capital but only placed it in its proper sphere, as a factor of production. As Henry Buisson had done, Gide attempted to excise politics from the

36. Charles Gide, "De la coopération et des transformations qu'elle est appelée à réaliser dans l'ordre économique," *REP*, III (1889), 476, 481; "L'Idée de la solidarité," 394.

social question by abstracting social relations from the human struggle that occurred in the world of production.[37]

The internal consistency of Gide's system rested on a crucial assumption that itself held political content: profit, "the motor of all social activity," derived exclusively from the price of commodities in the market and not from surplus value or unpaid labor. Capitalists sold at the highest prices; consumers purchased at those prices. The former sustained their advantage through monopolies and the ability to seize on special situations. They therefore exploited consumers, not producers. With the disappearance of these advantages prices would fall and consumers reap the benefits. But Gide did not consider the possibility that cheaper commodities lowered capital's labor costs and did not, therefore, necessarily diminish profits. This posed no problem for him because he located the relations of labor and capital in the realm of exchange, not production. By turning workers into associated producers and consumers—owners of individual property unconnected to capitalist enterprise—Gide proposed to eliminate the "authority" of capitalists without eliminating capital itself. Henceforth, capital would receive its "right to livelihood" consisting of that part of the surplus necessary for amortization and interest, "that part necessary for capital to keep going and reproduce itself." All that changed, then, was the relative distribution of profit—hardly a revolutionary transformation at all.[38]

Gide wound up with a model of a dual economy composed of unequal and barely articulated parts. Cooperatives existed in the interstices of capitalist production, their members neither totally independent nor totally dependent. This was a far cry from the national system of cooperative production laid out sixty years earlier by Charles Fourier, from whom Gide claimed intellectual descent and

37. Gide, "De la coopération," 482, 488; *RSS* (1906), 289.

38. Charles Gide, *La Coopération: Conférences de propagande* (Paris, 1906), 302–25; *RSS* (1905), 273, (1906), 289; Gide, "Le Néocollectivisme," 426–37. Gide's view of the source of profit bears some resemblance to that of the Ricardian socialists, especially Thomas Hodgskin, who located the source of profit in "unequal exchange," whereby the capitalist set the terms of the market in labor power. See Karl Marx, *Theories of Surplus Value*, trans. Jack Cohen and S. W. Ryazanskaya (Moscow, 1971), Pt. 3, pp. 263–319; Marx, *Grundrisse*, 240–41; and Maurice Dobb, "Marx's Critique of Political Economy," in Eric J. Hobsbawm (ed.), *Marxism in Marx's Day* (Bloomington, Ind., 1982), 80–81, Vol. I of Hobsbawm *et al.* (eds.), *The History of Marxism* (4 vols. projected; Bloomington, Ind., 1982–).

inspiration. Calling Fourier a "true prophet," Gide insisted that he held the true resolution of the social question in his hands. Unfortunately, according to Gide, the time had not been ripe for the reception of Fourier's ideas. Two generations of social upheaval had prepared the ground for the reception of Gide's version of the Fourierist tradition. Gide's version, however, was a bowdlerized and sanitized reading of the original. It excluded Fourier's utopia of personal liberation, and it emptied Fourier's vision of its radical-anarchist implications. Rather, Gide chose to emphasize (or, perhaps, to invent) Fourier's legacy as a "healthy socialism," a socialism not of "class struggle and expropriation," but of social harmony.[39]

Gide's attacks on socialism surpassed in vehemence his complaints about concentratèd capital. In his schema of four historically progressive "schools" of political economy—from primitive to advanced—Gide placed the *école d'égalité* (socialism) antecedent to the *école de solidarité*. The lines were clearly drawn. Solidarists sought harmony through cooperation and association; socialists offered only class struggle. Solidarists aimed at the transformation of the proletariat through cooperation; socialists envisioned the abolition of the wage system through expropriation. For solidarists, capital and labor followed parallel paths to a common destiny; for socialists, they stood as irreconcilable antagonists headed for an inevitable showdown. Finally, whereas socialists reached for equality, solidarists recognized "the diversity and inequality of individuals" and "vigorously condemned . . . any social system that tended toward uniformity and would reduce society to the state of inferior organisms—to animal colonies."[40]

Gide drew this caricature of socialism deliberately, not merely to score polemical points. Like other social liberals, he attempted to meet socialism on its own ground the better to defeat it. His language and historical references were bound to raise suspicions in respectable bourgeois circles. His use of slogans such as "the emancipation of the proletariat" risked exposing him to charges of drawing

39. *ACF*, 8th year (1900), 35–41, 9th year (1901), 42–43; Eric J. Hobsbawm, "Marx, Engels and Pre-Marxian Socialism," in Hobsbawm (ed.), *Marxism*, 12–13.

40. Charles Gide, *L'Ecole nouvelle* (Paris, 1890), 154; Gide, "L'Idée de solidarité," 390, 395–400; Gide, "De la coopération," 486; Gide, *Les Institutions*, 217.

from the socialist well. He professed admiration for Benoît Malon's "integral socialism," but—significantly—because of its "nationalist" character. Even Fourier was still regarded as a *partageux* (expropriator) in proper society. Thus the more "radical" Gide's formulations, the more he had to distance himself from anything that smelled of Marxist socialism.[41] Otherwise, he could not expect to get across his message that the political struggle against socialism entailed reforms in capitalist production. Gide was no trimmer; but neither could he afford any misapprehension about his motives, for his potentially serious antagonists stood to his right, not to his left, and he collaborated with some of them in the ACI.

By the mid-1890s the ACI had become a highly visible component in the network of parapolitical organizations for bourgeois reform. Its central committee reproduced that improbable but by now common coalition of social liberals and social economists, progressives and conservatives. A number of familiar names appeared on the committee's roster: de Boyve, Gide, Fougerousse, Charles Robert, Henry Buisson, Eugène Rostand, Charles Rayneri, Georges Picot; the industrialists Auguste Lalance, Félix Piat, and Baille-Lemaire; Albert Trombert, Cheysson, Mabilleau, Robert Pinot, Paul de Rousiers, Léon de Seilhac, and René Waldeck-Rousseau. The committee's honorary president was the Comte de Chambrun; its president, Jules Siegfried. Among the Alliance's foreign corresponding members, four Americans bear mentioning. They were Richard Ely, founder of the American Economic Association, sworn enemy of laissez-faire doctrines and an admirer of the German historical school of economics; Nicholas P. Gilman, also an economist and a publicist for profit sharing; Francis A. Walker, yet another economist critical of laissez-faire, well-known in France for his views, and the son of the social scientist and reformer Amassa Walker; and Charles Pillsbury, the flour magnate who experimented with paternalism—including profit sharing—in his mills, was an outspoken advocate of enlightened capitalism, and sponsored a coopers' production cooperative in Minneapolis.[42]

---

41. *Revue Socialiste*, No. 91 (1892), 90; Gaumont, *Histoire générale*, II, 124, 128.

42. Alliance coopérative internationale, *Deuxième Congrès*, x–xviii; Robert Church, "Economists as Experts: The Rise of an Academic Profession in America, 1870–1917," in

Social liberals were in the minority in the ACI, which came to be dominated by the right wing of the conservative coalition—those more in tune with the perspectives of big business and less estranged from political economy. Cheysson, Mabilleau, Robert, Pinot, Rousiers, Fougerousse, and Rostand all were involved in industry, banking, commerce, or insurance. They also played prominent roles in the Comité de défense, the Musée social, and the Société d'économie sociale. Men such as Gide, Buisson, and Bourgeois, though not hostile to business interests, tended to view cooperation in terms less narrowly circumscribed by the immediate concerns of capital. The combination made for occasional political infighting at meetings of the Alliance, which has been described in detail by Jean Gaumont. Gide and Fougerousse in particular engaged in several acrimonious exchanges.[43] Sporadic conflicts within the ACI, however, did not signify deep ideological divisions among its members. Disputes centered on questions of tactics rather than strategy. Social liberals tended to emphasize working-class independence, whereas their more conservative counterparts held to the principles of bourgeois leadership and control. For instance, the Alliance's 1895 congress voted down a proposal to provide a subsidy to a workers' glass-producing cooperative in Albi. Opponents argued that because the cooperative had been formed by glassworkers fresh from a bitter strike against management in the Verrerie of Carmaux, the proposal was essentially for political purposes and unduly influenced by syndicalist doctrines. Yet a few years later, the pages of the *Revue de la Solidarité Sociale* carried a favorable report on the cooperative, making the point that it posed "no menace to public peace." For the most part, however, factional lines were blurred. Gide occasionally connected the cooperative movement to the construction of what he called a "true socialist regime." But, as we have seen, his socialism was limited essentially to a community of consumers;[44] beyond that,

---

Lawrence Stone (ed.), *The University in Society* (2 vols.; Princeton, 1975), II, 586–87; William Leach, *True Love and Perfect Union* (New York, 1980), 312–13; Allen Johnson and Dumas Malone (eds.), *Dictionary of American Biography* (27 vols.; New York, 1928–81), Vol. X, Pt. 1, pp. 342–44, Vol. VII, Pt. 2, pp. 604–605.

43. Gaumont, *Histoire générale*, II, 509–617.

44. Alliance coopérative internationale, *Deuxième Congrès*, 138–39; *RSS* (1906), 474; *Revue Socialiste*, No. 91 (1892), 91.

it was basically a rhetorical flourish employed to underline the importance of framing collective solutions to the problems engendered by collective (social) production. It pointed away from the dictatorship of the bourgeoisie but not toward the dictatorship of the proletariat. At the center of his system stood the constructive collaboration of labor and capital and the repudiation of the politics of class struggle. None of his colleagues in the ACI could take issue with that position although even such relative progressives as Siegfried and Waldeck-Rousseau tended to place heavier emphasis on reform from above.

Auguste Fougerousse emerged as one of the chief spokesmen for the Alliance's conservative wing. Raised among the Catholic bourgeoisie of Lyon, he retained his early admiration for Le Play throughout his career. Fougerousse made his money in the construction business in Paris, specializing in state contracts. His experience in business and as a witness to the Commune convinced him of the importance of paternalism to further the cause of social peace, a subject on which he wrote several volumes and numerous articles for *La Réforme Sociale*. At the same time, during the mid-1880s, Fougerousse became involved in the Parisian cooperative movement, set up a small consumers' cooperative in his home neighborhood in the sixth arrondissement, and assisted de Boyve (who had traveled from Nîmes) in organizing a cooperative federation. Subsequently, Fougerousse got himself appointed secretary-general of the federation—much to the dismay of the local socialists. His nomination of two workers to the federation's advisory committee on economics only reinforced their suspicions that Fougerousse meant the appointments as a cosmetic device to conceal a takeover of Paris' cooperatives by the "bourgeois Protestant de Boyve and especially the bourgeois Catholic Fougerousse." His exercise of tight control over the federation confirmed their suspicions.[45]

Fougerousse's maneuver may have won him no friends among the Parisian workers, but it placed him in the mainstream of the bourgeois paternalist current that was evident in the ACI as elsewhere. Like his colleagues in the Alliance, Cheysson, Robert, Siegfried, and Rostand, he never conceded the leading role in reform to anyone

45. Gaumont, *Histoire générale*, II, 108–109.

other than the "upper classes," who, by virtue of their "fortune," deserved to exercise the "highest social functions." From this observation Fougerousse proceeded to what he considered a logical conclusion: "THEREIN LIES THE REASON, THE EXPLANATION, AND THE
LEGITIMIZATION FOR SOCIAL INEQUALITIES." Fougerousse leavened this mixture of arrogance and *bourgeois oblige* with a reminder
to industrialists of "the natural harmony that exists between the employer's pecuniary interest and his social duties." Although the obligation "to keep workers on the job during hard times demands
heavy sacrifices, it is, in the long run . . . good business." Given this
perspective, it is no surprise that Fougerousse constructed the role of
cooperatives on a very narrow basis. He had no patience with what
he called "cooperative collectivism" on the level of production. Such
a system led to "state socialism" and "the destruction of our industry
by foreigners." He dismissed as a dangerous pipedream the notion
that consumers' cooperatives could become instruments of production—one of Gide's favorite ideas. And, perhaps inadvertently,
Fougerousse hit on a glaring flaw in Gide's system, pointing out that
consumers had no necessary common interests as producers; that is,
they had no common class identity.[46]

The secretary-general of the ACI during most of the 1890s was
Charles Robert. Gaumont's account and the proceedings of the various congresses indicate that Robert spent most of his energies defending the prerogatives of capital and lining up support for a limited construction of cooperation. "We understand," he said, "that
there is no question of despoiling capital for the profit of labor, but
only of assigning to the one and to the other that portion legiti-
mately due each according to services rendered and risks run." Predictably, considering his role in the promotion of profit sharing,
Robert took an aggressively probusiness position. He resisted any
attempt to frame the Alliance's program along the lines set down by
his friend Charles Gide and the Ecole de Nîmes, whose timid efforts
at economic transformation he considered dangerously radical.[47]
That the Protestant Robert felt more at home ideologically with the

46. Fougerousse, *Patrons et ouvriers,* 240, 265; Fougerousse, "La Crise industrielle,"
293; Fougerousse, "Les Alchimistes sociaux," *RIP,* IV (1890), 78–82, 137–41.
47. Alliance coopérative internationale, *Deuxième Congrès,* 77; Buisson, *Le Rôle de la
coopération,* 102; Gaumont, *Histoire générale,* II, 651–53.

Catholic Fougerousse than with his own coreligionists (he and Gide were both active in the Association protestante pour l'étude des questions sociales) raises doubts about the utility of "social Christianity" as a frame of reference for an interpretation of bourgeois reform politics.

In any event, Robert required no spiritual inspiration for his war on socialism and socialist influence in the cooperative movement. If the cooperative machinery were to function effectively as an instrument of solidarity and social peace it could not be allowed to fall into the hands of "revolutionary socialists," who would make of it a "combat weapon." Under Robert's prodding the Alliance ruled out any politics that aimed at "organizing or taking over consumers' associations for the purpose of using their excess funds as a war chest to finance collectivism and revolution." Robert insisted that no political factors intrude on the Alliance's deliberations and its sponsorship of cooperatives. He meant, of course, politics of which he disapproved, for he was nothing if not political, and he made it abundantly clear that he considered cooperatives political instruments: "If the Alliance resolves to continue on the path marked out by its founders, it must use only peaceful, normal, and legal means to further the material and moral improvement of the laboring people" and it must "adhere to three fundamental principles: individual property, freedom of labor, and the spirit of association."[48]

Consumers' cooperatives and those organized by farmers generally exhibited no political coloration. The nearly 1,500 consumers' cooperatives operating by the end of the century were practical organizations. It is doubtful that their members had any sense of participating in an ambitious enterprise for social reconstruction. Producers' cooperatives, which numbered only 110 in 1899, were another matter. Anarchosyndicalist factions within the Bourses du travail operated several, and from them came the red tide that Robert and his associates hoped to stem. That was why René Waldeck-Rousseau, president of the Council of Ministers, introduced a bill in the Chamber of Deputies in 1899 legalizing the establishment of producers' cooperatives by labor unions. As explained by Paul Pic of Lyon, a political economist and collaborator with the Lyonese bour-

---

48. Alliance coopérative internationale, *Deuxième Congrès,* 52, 83.

geoisie in several paternalist projects, Waldeck's bill had three purposes: first, to pull the rug out from under left-wing syndicalists who made the cooperatives "revolutionary propaganda"; second, to encourage labor formations to take the path of "sensible social conservation"; and third, to enable organized workers to join with bourgeois reformers in the work of transforming wage laborers into cooperating producers, what Pic called a new middle class. Waldeck's plan went further than most of his friends in the Alliance would have felt comfortable with. They preferred tight control. Nevertheless, the plan was totally consistent with Waldeck's overall political outlook on the social question. Firmly committed to solidarism, brought up to value paternalism, and ideologically attuned to social liberalism, he expected that associated labor, independent and respectable, would contribute to "the harmony of social forces." Perhaps ingenuously—at least in the estimate of his biographer, Pierre Sorlin—but sincerely, Waldeck's social program turned on "indoctrinating workers with bourgeois virtues." He seriously wanted to "transform proletarians into capitalists." Moreover, Waldeck had become much less of a hard-liner on labor since he sent police and troops to the Anzin coal fields in 1884. During the strikes of 1899–1900 he repeatedly intervened, but more often than not to pressure employers into meeting their workers halfway and abandoning their union-busting tactics. Waldeck argued that the strikes reflected economic distress rather than political calculation and resulted "directly from the intensity of production and industrial advances." He considered it only just that workers share in the prosperity of the Belle Epoque.[49]

Nothing in Waldeck's project departed from the basic political principles that animated bourgeois patronage of cooperation: struggle against socialism; solidarity of capital and labor; working-class respectability and independence; and the cultural integration of workers into the world of capitalist production. If conflicts persisted within the ACI and other similar organizations—and they should not be minimized—the ideological consensus remained unbroken.

49. *ACF,* 7th year (1899), 116–17; *RSS* (1907), 148–52, 172; *Questions pratiques de législation ouvrière et d'économie sociale* (Paris, 1902), 96; Pierre Sorlin, *Waldeck-Rousseau* (Paris, 1966), 270, 473, 493.

Cooperative association simultaneously served the purposes of social reform and social defense, progressive improvement and counter-revolution.

Getting Together: Mutualism and Solidarist Ideology

In the 1890s a strong interest developed among bourgeois reformers, politicians, and social scientists in various forms of mutualism: *so-ciétés de secours mutuels* (mutual aid societies), popular savings banks, cooperative credit organizations, and *cercles populaires* (working-class clubs). This interest proceeded directly from the overall perspective governing bourgeois involvement in the social mechanisms of coop-eration. Mutualism, as Theodore Zeldin noted, has not been studied adequately, despite the abundance of available documentation.[50] It is a complete subject in itself and I do not pretend to give it anything resembling full justice. What follows is limited to two issues: how specific forms of mutual savings, credit, and social associations fit into the solidarist ideological framework; and why these institutions received the attention they did when they did.

We know from a number of recent studies that mutualism oc-cupied an important place in the political and economic organiza-tion of workers since the early years of the nineteenth century.[51] As industry absorbed an increasingly larger proportion of the labor force, workers carried the tradition into the factory and regarded au-tonomous mutualist organizations as their right against employers' claims to run them. Several pitched battles were fought during the latter years of the Second Empire between workers and employers over control of *caisses de secours mutuels* (disability insurance). Con-flicts over such issues receded in importance during the 1880s and 1890s, superseded by confrontations over the more decisive eco-nomic and political issues of wage rates, conditions of work, and control over the processes of production. Moreover, mutual associa-tion that encouraged working-class independence came to be viewed

50. Theodore Zeldin, *France, 1848–1945* (2 vols.; Oxford, 1973–77), I, 661–62.
51. Moss, *Origins;* Sewell, *Work and Revolution;* Ronald Aminzade, *Class, Politics, and Early Industrial Capitalism* (Albany, N.Y., 1981).

by politicians and businessmen as a positive force for social peace and solidarity. This did not signify a change in attitude so much as a recognition of the superiority of indirect over direct instruments of control, a recognition based on a realistic assessment of the hegemonic forces contained within concentrated production. Direct control, perhaps deemed necessary under certain conditions (strikebreaking, intimidation, and other applications of force), did not pretend to further the cultural integration of the working class. Mutualism, however, could be represented as a form of associated labor parallel to and interacting with associated capital. According to good marketplace calculations, it made sense to promote the organization of labor, the better to do business with capital without disrupting the smooth operations of production. Thus it was appropriately symbolic for the Société industrielle of Nantes to host the 1908 *fête mutuelliste* in celebration of its seventy-fifth anniversary. Presiding was the chairman of the Fédération nationale de la mutualité, Léopold Mabilleau.[52]

Léon Say, whose mastery of marketplace calculations at least equaled that of any of his contemporaries, believed mutualism to be full of promise. It had not developed its potential, he alleged, because state intervention—particularly legislation dictating the terms and financing of mutual aid societies—reinforced paternalism from above and stifled private initiative. This was, of course, the special pleading of a notorious fiscal conservative and bitter enemy of state intervention in social relations. In that respect Say stood closer to the position occupied by conservative reformers than that occupied by social liberals. Yet his views related to a conception of paternalism held by conservative reformers and social liberals alike as a system of indirect control combining working-class independence and bourgeois leadership. Between laissez-faire and state authority lay a middle road that led to the transformation of "paternal industrial institutions by concealing the employer's intervention while encouraging working-class initiative." In other words, Say was describing a mode of paternalism that had progressed from the level of patriarchy to that of social management. The principal organ of solidarist social

52. Fernand L'Huillier, *La Lutte ouvrière à la fin du second empire* (Paris, 1957), 37–55; *RIP*, IV (1890), 369, V (1891), 513; *RSS* (1908), 106.

liberalism took a similar position against direction from above, although for somewhat different reasons. The *Revue de la Solidarité Sociale* attacked the creation in 1898 of the Conseil supérieur de la mutualité as unnecessary and dangerous. It risked smothering mutualism under an administrative blanket and politicizing institutions that would be torn apart by political factionalism. That the Conseil was headed by the minister of the interior—implying police surveillance—did not help matters: "Mutualism is a movement depending on voluntary initiative which exceeds the narrow limits imposed by state guidance." Lacking that voluntarist component, mutualism could not function as a "mechanism for the social education" of workers.[53]

Noteworthy among the several forms of mutualism whose character bore the imprint of bourgeois intervention were popular credit associations and people's savings banks. As with cooperatives, to which these institutions bore a close relationship, popular credit and savings associations attracted the attention of bourgeois reformers less for their practical advantages than for their ideological and political utility. They came to be regarded as instruments of acculturation. Access to credit and the opportunity to save generated a spirit of enterprise, "respect for the value of labor, practical experience," and an attachment to property—all solid bourgeois values. Charles Rayneri, a member of the ACI's central committee and founder in 1883 of the Banque populaire de Menton (Alpes-Maritimes), drew attention to the political dimension. In the presence of the "incessant and formidable progress of socialism, we must turn our attention urgently to the association of individual forces." Despite his insistence that the principle of "*self-help*" constituted the basis of popular credit, Rayneri assigned the leading role in its formation to the "social authorities" (he made specific reference to Le Play), those "men of goodwill, solicitous of the interests and destiny of workers. *Banques populaires* contribute to the worker's education" under bourgeois leadership. Independence implied dependence and vice versa.[54]

---

53. Lewis, *Growth and Fluctuations*, 48–50; RSS (1907), 150, (1908), 164.

54. Eugène Rostand, in *Premier congrès*, 283; *Exposition 1900*, V, 311; Charles Rayneri, *Manuel des banques populaires* (Paris, 1896), 13–20; "self-help" rendered in the original English.

As early as the 1860s, leading figures in the big bourgeoisie sponsored the organization of cooperative credit associations for workers and farmers. The largest, the Société du crédit au travail, was capitalized at nearly 150,000 francs subscribed to by 898 investors. It financed small enterprises initially started up by groups of workers or petty producers. If successful, those enterprises were to return a minimum of 5 percent to the original shareholders. The Société's board of directors included Benoist d'Azy of the Western Railway Company and the coal mines of the Grand' Combe; the duc de Decazes of Decazeville mines; Henri Germain, a founder of the Crédit lyonnais; Louis Haphen of the Compagnie des Chemins de fer du Nord; Jules Simon; and Léon Say. Taking due note of this group, Jules Duval's *Economiste Français* pronounced it ideal for reconciling "the interests of labor and of capital." Despite its distinguished patronage, the Société du crédit au travail did not produce substantial results. Certainly the close police surveillance routinely exercised during the Second Empire had something to do with that. Moreover, by the time it received legal sanction in 1867, France was heading into a two-year period of multiple strikes that intensified police repression and scared off the bourgeoisie.[55]

It does not appear likely that any of the aforementioned gentlemen heard of the German Democrat and 1848 veteran Hermann Schultze-Delitzsch. But his pioneering work in the promotion of popular credit associations and consumer cooperatives received considerable attention among French solidarists at the end of the century. Schultze (he added the "Delitzsch"—his home town—to his name so as not to be misplaced among all the Schultzes in German assemblies), in common with many bourgeois Forty-eighters, had no use for working-class political struggle against capital. Yet his way, helping workers to help themselves, was equally political. Advertising himself a disciple of Proudhon and brandishing the "principle of solidarity," Schultze in 1865 laid the foundation for what became the Allegemeinen Verband der Deutschen Erwerbs- und Wirtschaftsgenossenschaften (General Union of German Credit and Economic Associations), which embraced more than nine hundred credit cooperatives by 1900. Schultze appealed to small entrepre-

55. *EF,* August 24, September 14, 1865; *Exposition 1900,* V, 312n.

neurs as well as workers, stood for economic freedom, but nevertheless called himself a socialist. For that reason, and because of his
anticollectivist politics, Ferdinand Lassalle considered Schultze a serious threat to his fledgling Workers Association. Lassalle may have
overreacted, as Marx told him, but it is easy to understand why
French solidarists admired Schultze's enterprise. Gide, Rayneri,
Fougerousse, and Rostand all referred to him with the greatest
respect.[56]

Eugène Rostand, a grand bourgeois from Marseille and active in
the local Société des habitations à bon marché, took on *banques populaires* as his special project. He organized a credit association in Marseille and went on to become president of the Centre fédératif du
crédit populaire en France, which had its offices in the Musée social.
Auguste Fougerousse was vice-president. Rostand made it clear that
the chief advantages of cooperative savings and credit lay in the
political, not the economic, dimension. He constructed a simple
mechanism. Workers, shopkeepers, clerks, and others accumulated
cash savings that went to finance enterprises, large and small. Capital
investment thus "ceased to be the exclusive preserve of the leisure
classes" while capital "fulfilled its proper role" of releasing "democratic energies." Something resembling a trickle-down effect occurred as "part of the enormous reserves held in savings banks
and those of major financial institutions converged in nourishing
streams" that reached as far as working people. But Rostand thought
it preferable for working people to give than to receive. The act of
saving itself rather than the subsequent payoff was of first importance. It encouraged hard work and respect for the "economic value
of labor" and reinforced "the mechanisms of solidarity." And, he
added with one eye on the bottom line, it made for good business.[57]

Mutual credit associations—as distinct from mutual aid societies—
functioned to a similar purpose, although not deliberately designed
to do so. As Gide pointed out, French efforts in that area lagged
behind those of other countries such as Germany, Britain, and Den-
mark. The bulk of those that existed were in the countryside, where

56. Rudolph Schlesinger, *Central European Democracy and Its Background* (London,
1953), 12–13; *Exposition 1900*, V, 307; Rayneri, *Manuel*, 15; Rostand, *A l'école*, 9.

57. *Exposition 1900*, V, 312; Classe 103, Associations coopératives de production, 457;
Rostand, in *Premier congrès*, 288; Rostand, *A l'école*, 3–8.

farmers formed marketing cooperatives. Aside from their practical benefits in the "preservation of small property," agricultural cooperatives performed a socially useful function. In the main hall of the Musée social a wall panel inscribed with uplifting aphorisms carried a statement from one of the leaders of the Société des agriculteurs de France (the big commercial farmers' organization): agricultural associations "reinforce devotion to that vocation which has provided the principal source of wealth of the country over the centuries [and] has bound countryfolk to their homes and to the soil they till." Marketing associations included both large and small proprietors and generally fell under the influence of the former, "who exercised a kind of patronage."[58]

Fewer credit associations existed. Those that did usually operated in conjunction with producers' cooperatives or provided low-cost or interest-free loans to worthy and enterprising workers. Rayneri's Banque populaire and the Banque cooperative des associations de production de France, founded in 1893 with a 500,000-franc gift from a businessman and self-professed disciple of Fourier and Victor Considérant, were examples of the first type; the credit association of Montceau-les-Mines known as Prudence an example of the second. In each case bourgeois and/or small businessmen collaborated with workers and artisans in financing various enterprises. The Société lyonnaise de crédit du travail, begun in the 1860s and still functioning in the late 1880s, was effectively dominated by leading figures of the Lyonese big bourgeoisie, including Henri Germain, Eugène Flotard, Jules Cambefort, and Henri Bonnardel. But the organization turned into another "capitalist" operation, performing banking services on a local scale similar to those performed on a national and international scale by the Crédit lyonnais.[59]

Clearly, this was not what Rostand, Rayneri, Gide, and others had in mind when they promoted cooperative credit as a model of solidarity-inspired reform. It hardly could be expected to generate within any working-class community what Rostand called a "gener-

58. *Exposition 1900*, V, 317.
59. *Ibid.*, 330; Gide, *Les Institutions*, 509; *Exposition 1900*, Classe 103, 456, 470–72, 486–87, 505–506; Gaumont, *Histoire générale*, II, 575; Jean Bouvier, *Naissance d'une banque: Le Crédit lyonnais* (Paris, 1968), Chap. 8.

ous and joyful spirit" of cooperation. Cooperative credit, a business like any other, was inflated by its advocates into a symbol of solidarity that bore little relationship to its operations. For it to become an effective instrument of solidarity two developments were necessary: channeling the bulk of available credit directly to producers' associations and convincing capitalists to reroute a portion of their idle capital into credit cooperatives. Neither seemed likely to occur. In the first instance, those associations that did exist—and the number tripled between 1899 and 1907—were relatively small affairs concentrated in the artisanal trades. Workers associated in these enterprises could not be expected to risk their control for an uncertain future in which they might find themselves hostage to banks. In the second, self-interest would be the only reason for capitalists to contribute generously to credit funds, either to enlarge their field of investment or to forestall workers' appropriation of capital without invitation. Given the distribution of political power, the latter eventuality appeared remote at best.[60] Thus cooperation in this sphere remained not much more than a gleam in the solidarists' eyes. Not so, however, in the case of *cercles populaires*, which enjoyed considerable currency by the end of the century.

The *cercles populaires* and *cercles ouvriers* at which bourgeois reformers aimed their attention should not be confused with the exclusively working-class or popular centers of sociability such as those described by Maurice Agulhon and Tony Judt for Provence.[61] The former, unlike the latter, received their initial impulses from a local bourgeoisie and generally operated under its aegis, if not its direct control. The Cercle Franklin of Le Havre, in which Jules Siegfried played a leading role, represented an early form of association that took shape later in the century. On the occasion of its founding in 1875, Siegfried outlined the perspective from which he and other bourgeois reformers approached their task: "We have founded the Cercle in the spirit of true liberty. It will have neither a political nor a religious character; for our ambition is not to serve a party or a

60. Rostand, in *Premier congrès,* 284; *RSS* (1907), 172; Marx, *Grundrisse,* 115–23, on mutual credit associations.

61. Maurice Agulhon, *La République au village* (Paris, 1970), Pt. 1, Chap. 4; Tony Judt, *Socialism in Provence, 1871–1914* (Cambridge, England, 1979), Chap. 6.

sect, but to develop the moral sentiments and independence that make the true citizen, one who, in keeping with his personal convictions, answers only to his conscience and obeys only the rule of duty. We are all bound up together; the leisure classes cannot be truly content if the working classes are not. Our work is genuinely one of fraternity and solidarity." No mere exercise in philanthropy, *cercles populaires*, notwithstanding Siegfried's disclaimer, exhibited a clear political dimension, namely, to replace the tensions of class antagonism with the bonds of class collaboration. That those tensions existed French industrialists conceded, judging from the vehemence with which they attempted to smother the fact in clouds of words. Typically, Charles Marteau, president of the Société industrielle of Reims, proclaimed in a speech to local workers in 1909 that "there is no class struggle; there is no confrontation between the exploiter on the one hand and the exploited on the other."[62]

Plus ça change, we might observe, recalling that such pronouncements had been the stock-in-trade of politicians and businessmen for decades. Gambetta's declaration that "there is no social question, only social questions" is only the most celebrated of countless similar statements. His vision, however, went no further than one of solidarity through common citizenship. Thirty years later, not even Léon Bourgeois considered that sufficient. The social and material context had changed, and with it ideological and political perspectives. Vague notions of community gave way to precise programs for association between classes, much as organized paternalism replaced patriarchy. There being no question of erasing class distinctions, reformers looked to mutual association to bring together workers and bourgeois on neutral ground. This had the paradoxical effect of validating social divisions within the Republic because the principle of association itself presumed the separate identity of classes. The purpose of association was to provide points of convergence between these divisions rather than to dissolve them.

62. *Exposition 1889*, II, 283; Charles Marteau, "Distribution des recompenses aux employés, ouvrières et ouvriers de l'industrie," *Bulletin de la Société industrielle de Reims*, No. 93 (1909), 289, quoted in Alberto Melucci, "Idéologies et pratiques patronales pendant l'industrialisation capitaliste: Le Cas de la France" (Thèse du troisième cycle, Ecole Pratique des Hautes Etudes, 1974), 285. I thank Melucci for kindly supplying me with a copy of his thesis.

Association between distinct and even antagonistic classes constituted the central theme of a political and ideological brief for *cercles populaires* written by Charles François, a lawyer from Lyon closely tied to the city's big bourgeoisie. Significantly, his article, "Apaisement social" (Social reconciliation), appeared in neither of the major propaganda journals of the social liberals or the social economists— the *Revue de la Solidarité Sociale* or the *Réforme Sociale*—but in a journal of sociological research and commentary, the *Revue Internationale de Sociologie*. Nowhere in his discussion did François draw an explicit connection between his concerns and those of social science. Apparently, the relationship was taken for granted. Characterizing the social question as more a matter of politics than economics, François viewed *cercles populaires* as mechanisms "to integrate the discontented worker into modern society."[63] This purpose was to be accomplished through the establishment of regular contacts between bourgeois students and workers, such as already had been taking place for several years in a group called the Cercle de Vaise in Lyon, in which students supported by members of the local business community organized informal gatherings with workers.

François took the Cercle de Vaise as a model for his ideal type of a *cercle populaire*. Unlike other similar organizations in Lyon and in Nîmes—the latter sponsored by the Société d'économie populaire—it had no religious foundation: Catholics, Protestants, and Jews participated. Confessional neutrality made good tactical sense because, François claimed, socialists had scored considerable successes in portraying priests and pastors as accomplices in the manipulation and exploitation of labor. Albert de Mun's *cercles catholiques* were criticized on those grounds in the report of the Congrès des cercles populaires in 1889: "The militantly political nature of that association excludes it from consideration as one committed to the proper social purpose of the *cercles populaires*." To avoid any hint of similar political manipulation, the students went out of their way to convince the inhabitants of the Vaise quarter (who had a long history of militancy) that they "had no intention of using them as a political springboard once again." Workers were justifiably distrustful, as they recalled their "collaboration in two revolutions (1789

63. Charles François, "Apaisement social: Les Cercles populaires," *RIS*, V (1897), 1–33.

and 1848) led by the middle class and subsequently appropriated by it." Meanwhile, other revolutions and other revolutionaries beckoned "these impoverished people who allow themselves to be duped by socialist promises. And yet, where is the man who, having everything to gain and nothing to lose, would not let himself be seduced by those who guarantee the improvement of his conditions—even at the cost of bloody struggle!" Material reform, despite its undeniable achievements, did not impinge on the level of consciousness, the terrain on which the primary struggle—the struggle for the working-class mind—was engaged.[64]

Bourgeois students were considered ideally suited for the struggle because of their youth, their energy, and their relative lack of identification with narrow class interests. They formed a potential elite that François and others believed necessary to combat socialism and to forge interclass ties. Emile Cheysson quoted with approval a graduate of the Ecole libre des sciences politiques and high state official, Max Leclère, who in 1892 urged students "to occasionally abandon their libraries and their theoretical pursuits to take an interest in, and become involved with the life of the people; to get down into the streets, not, as they had done in 1848, to fight alongside the worker, but to teach and calm him." Barely concealed elements of condescension and manipulation infiltrated other comments as well. In his guide to *cercles populaires*, François at times appeared to regard workers as little more than children in adult frames. He suggested speaking of "simple ideas," perhaps "a few words about the nation and the family. But touch upon these important subjects only in language [that] stirs by its very simplicity." Style mattered at least as much as content. The "good-natured remark, the not-too-subtle joke" always succeeded: "Amuse your workers and they are yours."[65]

These casual conversations and the crude psychologizing behind them accompanied deliberate attempts to extend bourgeois influence into the working-class family. It followed that women should be cultivated and involved in *cercles populaires*, for common wisdom among bourgeois reformers held that the key to unlocking the male

64. *Ibid.*, 4–5, 11–12; *Exposition 1889*, II, 245.
65. François, "Apaisement social," 1–2, 13–15, 32; Emile Cheysson, *Les Questions ouvrières* (Paris, 1892), 19.

worker's mind lay in his wife's hands. The wife, in her capacity as organizer of the household and principal child-rearer, was a potential source of "details about the home" and the channel through which one established among adolescents as well as adults "an ascendancy based upon forbearance and firmness." Similarly, the contacts developed in the *cercles populaires* provided access to information about health and safety conditions in the factory from the worker's rather than the employer's perspective. François, like many other bourgeois reformers, distrusted industrialists to operate their plants with the welfare of their work force uppermost among their priorities. Hence it was important to remain at arm's length from the *patronat*. Missionaries to the working class "will gain easy reception if the worker clearly understands that one has no connection to the employer." Likewise, workers themselves, with student auxiliaries if needed, handled security in the *cercle*. The local constable was nowhere visible. "From the worker's point of view he represents the muscle of the pitiless bourgeoisie, authoritarian and brutal," of which "the people must not be reminded."[66]

Cercles populaires and *cercles ouvriers* (the two terms generally were used interchangeably) could serve to remind the people of another, benevolent aspect of the bourgeois countenance. As centers for recreation and education, they provided settings—sometimes elaborate—in which workers engaged in a variety of associated activities. Games, gymnastics, outings, choral groups, amateur theater, lectures, and readings all were designed to produce maximum sociability and a spirit of mutualism among workers as well as between them and their bourgeois associates. By the time the German government closed down the Cercle mulhousien in 1887, it had become a flourishing social institution of two thousand members in which a host of recreational activities and practical forays into discussions of the social question had achieved a "rare success." Unlike François' portrait of class relations in Lyon, workers and employers in Mulhouse reportedly maintained "excellent relations" through the mediation of the Cercle. Nevertheless, it remained—deliberately—an association of distinct social groups. *Cercles philanthropiques*, in such

---

66. François, "Apaisement social," 14, 16.

places as Rouen, the Croix-Rousse district of Lyon, the capital, and numerous other towns, organized similar operations on more modest scales.[67]

Whatever its size and the range of its program, each *cercle* emphasized "healthy amusements," socialization, working-class independence, and sobriety. Although they offered relief from the monotonous daily toil of the mill, the shop, or the factory, *cercles* nevertheless reinforced the discipline of industrial labor by requiring the regular attendance and participation of their members. No apparent contradiction existed between this regimen, which reproduced patterns of indirect control characteristic of late nineteenth-century paternalism, and the encouragement of working-class independence.[68] Despite the ubiquitous presence of bourgeois patronage, workers frequently took a direct hand in the *cercles'* daily operations and in the management of their finances. Sobriety was not pursued exclusively for the benefits of salubrity. François insisted that the *cercle populaire* could displace the tavern as a center of working-class sociability. He noted the testimony of a journalist who became a pubkeeper so he could study workers' drinking habits at first hand. The journalist concluded—not surprisingly—that workers visited the tavern more for a spate of relaxation and conviviality after a hard day's work than simply to drink. Hence François optimistically expected the *cercle* to provide all the benefits of the tavern without an alcoholic atmosphere.[69]

Finally, the report on *cercles ouvriers* for the social economy group of the 1889 Exposition noted a related dimension to their political and ideological potential. Much as they might promote solidarity among workers and bourgeois, the *cercles* generated self-discipline and responsible political habits from within the community of

67. Edouard Petit, "L'Education sociale dans l'enseignement," *Deuxième congrès d'éducation sociale* (Bordeaux, 1907), 3; *Exposition 1889*, II, 236, 247; François, "Apaisement social," 21; *Bulletin des cercles populaires* for 1899 and 1900.

68. For a comparison with Britain, see Patrick Joyce, *Work, Society and Politics: The Culture of the Factory in Later Victorian England* (New Brunswick, N.J., 1980), Chaps. 3, 8; F. M. L. Thompson, "Social Control in Victorian Britain," *Economic History Review*, XXXIV (1981), 195.

69. François, "Apaisement social," 19.

workers. Here a kind of aristocracy played a key role. Judging from frequent

> contacts with enlightened workers, one is struck by their quick intelligence and their sensible judgment. Those who have not been blinded by political passions examine with a tight dialectic and indisputable competence the serious concerns of the laboring class; it is by no means too farfetched to expect that, in encouraging these talents, one may guide these intelligent workers to make of themselves the teachers of their less advanced comrades, to inspire among the latter a proper appreciation of social relations in combating the false notions that their worst enemies have such a great interest in peddling.

In Nancy, the Cercle du travail attached to the local *cercle ouvrier* produced mutual ideological reinforcement among workers and employers. It had been founded in 1876 "to bring together all workers in the spirit of mutual goodwill" and to further their "moral and material improvement through the development of a common outlook." Recreation and informal study encouraged moral improvement, and courses in industrial skills fostered material improvement: "Many young people, as a result of their good behavior and the technical training acquired at the Cercle, are much sought after by the region's industrial and commercial enterprises." Workers gained job security, employers a reliable labor force, and both the solidarity of mutual association.[70]

It was the third of these acquisitions that reformers and social scientists considered of the greatest importance. The economist and amateur psychologist Henri Marion prescribed "moral solidarity" for "all the disorders" afflicting the workplace. Drawing on the authority of J. S. Mill, Marion argued "the necessity, for a people that aspires to freedom, first to embrace order and become accustomed to obey." If ideological reproduction was to be more than a hit-or-miss business, however, solid institutional foundations were required. The solidarist philosopher Gabriel Séailles, echoing his like-minded contemporaries, found no more suitable mechanism for transmitting the habits of order and obedience than the school. In that setting the working class would learn respect for tradition and

---

70. *Exposition 1889,* II, 232, 242.

assimilate the national culture.[71] Whereas paternalism, with its welfare systems, cooperatives, and other modes of labor discipline, promoted the mechanical integration of workers into capitalist production, solidarist-inspired social education provided paternalism with its necessary complement on the level of cultural integration. Not even a bourgeois Republic could survive on the dispensation of bread alone.

71. Henri Marion, *De la solidarité morale: Essai de psychologie appliquée* (Paris, 1880), 242; Gabriel Séailles, *Patrie et patriotisme* (Troyes, 1910), 15.

VI
The Social Economy
of Popular Education

"Close the taverns, open the schools," demanded Emile Zola. More sedately, Léon Bourgeois announced, "The social problem is, in the last resort, a problem of education."[1] The novelist expressed a concern born of compassion; the politician recited a formula born of the reformer's practical calculation. Neither said anything new, but the context in which they spoke was new. Education's social function had been recognized at least a century earlier by the Marquis de Condorcet and several decades later by Auguste Comte. Condorcet advocated equality of educational opportunity to correct for disparities in wealth; Comte expected education to reinforce prevailing hierarchies of domination and subordination. Political economists, peddling their wares in the classroom as well as in the marketplace, engaged directly in educational reform or wrote readers on "civic and moral instruction" for use in primary schools.[2]

In the wake of the Industrial Revolution and the rise of the proletariat, educators took the gloves off. That happened first in England, where William Templar, the principal of the Manchester Model Secular School in the mid-nineteenth century, hammered at the precepts of "social economy" to his working-class students.

1. Quoted in *RSS* (1909), 146; *Education sociale*, 91.
2. Charles Secondat, Marquis de Condorcet, *Rapport sur l'organisation générale de l'instruction publique, fait à l'Assemblée législative, le 20 avril 1792* (N.p., n.d.), 290; Paul Arbusse-Bastid, *La Doctrine de l'éducation universelle dans la philosophie d'Auguste Comte* (2 vols.; Paris, 1957), II, 608. An example of a political economist as compiler of educational materials is Henri Baudrillart, whose *Manuel d'éducation morale et d'instruction civique* (Paris, 1885) went through seven editions between 1885 and 1895.

Templar "had an obsession with strikes." Charles Robert, no less obsessed with strikes, linked the "prosperity of industry" to the "moral and intellectual development of workers." This was not a view held exclusively by Frenchmen, as he pointed out. Victor Rice, superintendent of public education for the state of New York, considered "purely material interest" sufficient reason "not to allow the children of the common people to grow up in ignorance." Later on, when corporate organization stood poised to penetrate all the nooks and crannies of social life, Charles Steinmetz of General Electric argued that education "ought to prepare citizens for the modern industrial community." French political and social economists, facing a similar situation, took the same tack. Emile Levasseur began his survey of primary and popular education with the admonition that, in an age of universal suffrage, "it [becomes] necessary to enlighten the sovereign." Georges Picot drew attention to the new conditions of social production and to the dangers they posed for bourgeois hegemony if unaccompanied by comprehensive education reform: "We must organize instruments of social education. . . . The people must learn its duties. This problem exists at any time of crisis, but is particularly acute at this time when the people is master of its own destiny, when the people must be enlightened at whatever cost or risk perishing, when one must strive constantly and accept any sacrifice to liberate the nation from [social] fantasies that threaten its ruin, from utopias that possess it."[3]

The crisis to which Picot referred stemmed from the transformation of relatively backward industrial capitalism into advanced machine production. As early as 1865, Armand Audiganne, an exceptionally acute observer of the French industrial and social scene, noted that industrial concentration—then only in its infancy—

3. David Jones, "Socialization and Social Science: Manchester Model Secular School, 1854–1861," in Philip McCann (ed.), *Popular Education and Socialization in the Nineteenth Century* (London, 1977), 126–31; Charles Robert, *Discours prononcé à l'occasion de la distribution des prix de la Société d'enseignement professionnel du Rhône, le 12 juin 1870* (Lyon, 1870), 10; *De la nécessité de rendre l'instruction primaire obligatoire en France et des moyens pratiques à employer dans ce but* (Montbéliard, 1861), 7–9; Steinmetz quoted in James Gilbert, *Designing the Industrial State: The Intellectual Pursuit of Collectivism in America, 1880–1940* (Chicago, 1972), 194–97; Emile Levasseur, *Questions industrielles et ouvrières* (Paris, 1896), 299; Unions de la paix sociale, *Unions du Nord: Compte-rendu général* (Paris, 1893), 9–10.

"occupies more and more activities and embraces more and more interests." Working-class children must be enrolled in schools and equipped "to resist the distractions and the pressures of a life of labor." A reversal of the tendency toward concentration, as it picked up steam in the last decades of the century, was neither feasible nor desirable. Yet behind the political as well as economic benefits accruing to capital lay risks. Concentration produced its own contradictions. Sharper "antagonisms between capital and labor" followed directly from the transformation of production. As France emerged from the Great Depression at the end of the century, the price to be paid for ignoring the social consequences of that transformation weighed decisively in the calculations of reformers. What economic historians have discovered and contemporaries knew well was a veritable crisis in the wage system as the rate of price increases and profits outstripped that of wages.[4]

Class struggle took on a decidedly different aspect from that of the age of handicraft and competition. Previously, working-class militancy derived from artisanal social relations and powerful community forces. Industrial workers had no such traditions to draw upon. Thus, whereas they lacked the particular revolutionary spirit characteristic of earlier generations, they did not suffer the political limitations imposed by fractionalized units of production.[5] The new forces of production, erected on the ruins of the old, simultaneously provided the foundation for the bourgeois republican order and raised up a working class that potentially threatened that order. Small shops had engendered working-class solidarity and episodes of substantial revolutionary energy. Big business, organized according to a rationalized division of labor and operating in a fully integrated national market, undermined the productive base for such solidarity only to confront a working class mechanically integrated into, but culturally isolated from, the new system. If the future lay with the "rational and systematic association of capital, scientific

4. Arthur Fontaine, "La Solidarité dans les faits économiques," *Education sociale*, 54; *EF*, April 27, 1865; Sylvain Périssé, *Nouvelle forme de participation des travailleurs aux bénéfices industrielles* (Paris, 1910), 3; *RSS* (1908), 49; Jean Bouvier, *Histoire économique et histoire sociale* (Geneva, 1968), 25–34.

5. See the interesting discussion of this problem in Ronald Aminzade, *Class, Politics, and Early Industrial Capitalism* (Albany, N.Y., 1981), Chaps. 1, 9.

management, and manual labor," it would be beset by struggle and not blessed with social peace unless capital and labor marched forward in lock step. Education, a far more effective weapon than repression, held the key to social peace, once "the worker, formerly a simple instrument, becomes a devoted and intelligent collaborator" of capital. Far from diminishing the authority of the employer, education of selected workers expanded it: "The eye of the boss will become the eye of everyone."[6]

Social Education: A Question of Class

Working-class education involved more than merely routinized surveillance. It was intended to embrace "the instruction that the individual receives during his entire life." The term "social education" itself provides several clues as to what contemporaries had in mind and to the ideological baggage they brought to their enterprise: first, it underlines the corporate and associationist character of educational reform; second, it places working-class education within a comprehensive system of social management, which is why Charles Gide called social education "a vast and autonomous territory of social science" and why the historian Henri Hauser characterized it as a transmission belt for "social facts"; third, it assigns to education the task of explaining a world formed by "social technology" (advanced capitalist production) and regulated by "social economy" (labor's place in the relations of production); and, finally, it sets off the instrumental and ideological content of late nineteenth-century popular education from earlier forms.[7]

Social education encompassed the several spheres of paternalist reform—cooperatives, mutualism, profit sharing, and *banques populaires*—as well as the management of popular instruction. All of them qualified as instruments of social education in that they reinforced "social consciousness within individuals." All such associations that "tended to render more supportable the duties and the

---

6. François Husson, *La Seconde révolution française: Solution et dénouement pacifique de la question sociale ouvrière* (Paris, 1892), 110–11.

7. *RSS* (1908), 38; *Exposition 1900*, V, 181; Henri Hauser, *L'Enseignement des sciences sociales* (Paris, 1903), 327.

burdens of social life . . . tightened the bonds of mutual solidarity."[8] Therefore, although this chapter deals exclusively with the formation of young workers upon their exit from state institutions of primary learning, we should remember that contemporaries made no strategic distinctions between education and other modes of engineering corporate solidarity. Political considerations and political purposes remained identical.

Social education engaged the participation of a broad cross-section of businessmen, politicians, and reformers. Many familiar names will appear. Traditional ideological and political divisions dissolved in the presence of a general consensus on working-class education's social purpose. Emile Cheysson, who, as a loyal Catholic, ordinarily would not have been associated with the militantly anti-clerical Ligue française de l'enseignement, headed that organization's committee on antialcoholism in 1905. He sat at the same table as the widow of every clerical's archenemy, Jules Ferry. The same pattern held for the membership of the Congrès international de l'éducation sociale, held in conjunction with the 1900 Exposition, and its successor, the Société pour l'éducation sociale. Bourgeois presided over the congress. Joining him were Ferdinand Buisson, Siegfried, father and son, Mabilleau, Gide, and Arthur Fontaine, director of the labor office in the Ministry of Commerce. The Société counted among its members all of the above plus Octave Gréard, rector of the Académie de Paris; Eugène Rostand, president of the Cercle fédératif du crédit populaire; Charles Guieysse and Gabriel Séailles, both active in the *universités populaires* movement (see below); Emile Durkheim; Georges Benoît-Lévy; Henry Buisson, secretary-general of the French section of the Alliance coopérative internationale; the inspector-general of prisons; the managing director of the Société anonyme des forges et aciéres du nord et de l'est; dozens of provincial industrialists; and, in the spirit of bourgeois ecumenism, the chief rabbi of France.[9]

In his introduction to the proceedings of the congress, Buisson

8. Alliance coopérative internationale, *Deuxième congrès, 1896* (Paris, 1897), viii; *BSES*, I (1901), 20; *Exposition 1900*, V, 198; Léopold Mabilleau, *L'Instruction civique* (Paris, 1889), 16.

9. *Après l'Ecole* (1906–1907), 572–73, (1908), 237–52; *Exposition 1900*, "Enseignement et éducation," I, 474; *Education sociale*, viii; *BSES*, I (1901), 48–56.

defined social education as "that part of education which creates within us a consciousness of our social existence." Its purpose, he went on, was to establish the habits of "solidarity . . . in which each individual freely subordinates his activities to the interests of the collectivity." Beneath the solidarists' relentless denunciations of individualism, egoism, and the malevolent spirit of the marketplace ran a practical current: an apprehension of the danger that workers, through a process of ideological inversion, would take seriously the rights of the individual and even—in a flagrant violation of their "social duties"—abandon the road of peaceful collective association for the path of "the war of labor against capital." Arthur Fontaine, in a presentation at the Congrès d'éducation sociale, argued that each person "should learn to love work" and to accept "the sacrifices that each makes for the sake of the collectivity." He did not exempt capitalists, who had an obligation to share the profits of their good fortune and to contribute to the formation of young workers. On the same occasion, Léon Bourgeois spoke of the importance of workers and employers recognizing their common interests so as to contract with one another and thereby escape "disruption." Addressing the bourgeoisie as well as the working class, Bourgeois insisted that every "man is, in fact, born with a debt to society" because he benefits from the "accumulated labor of others." Profit sharing struck Bourgeois as an excellent way for capitalists to acquit that debt and to encourage association in production. A commentator on primary schools in the Vosges reported that children of all classes learned about the "benefits of mutuality, the marvels of association," and how the "division of labor" legitimized wage differentials.[10]

Despite all the talk of universal association and collaboration, the promoters of social education understood the advantages of extracting from the working masses a uniquely trained aristocracy of labor. At the Congrès d'enseignement des sciences sociales in 1900, Paul Crouzet criticized excessive patriotic indoctrination and vengeful

10. *Education sociale,* 114–15; Jean-Baptiste Graillet, "Le Travail et le capital," *Après l'Ecole* (1895), 110; Fontaine, "La Solidarité," 49–56; Léon Bourgeois, "Solidarité, Justice, Liberté," *Education sociale,* 87–94; G. Fluriel, "L'Education sociale par l'enseignement primaire," *ibid.,* 95–98.

hysterics in popular education. Such mind-numbing exercises "paralyzed" the engines of progress because they ignored instruction in the "necessities of the contemporary economic struggle." The worker, who "experiences material, intellectual, and moral degradation at the hands of the machine," received no "social instruction" to counteract the harsh realities of the "struggle for existence." But not everyone was equally receptive. Faced with the "impossibility of penetrating the compact masses," Crouzet concluded that "social education must be limited to the formation of a democratic elite."[11]

The three-year course in *enseignement primaire supérieur* (EPS) (advanced primary instruction), which took its final form in the 1890s, had been constructed for just such a purpose. Its graduates took jobs in skilled industrial occupations, whence they were targeted for foreman or low-level technical positions. According to plan, the knowledge received in the EPS qualified them to exert moral and political surveillance over their fellow workers. The sociologist François Simiand characterized the EPS curriculum as instruction in the "fundamental laws of social solidarity in the economic, scientific, and moral realms." In contrast to industrial schools and postprimary education, the EPS did not dwell heavily on vocational training but on such matters as the sociology of the family, civic responsibility, the duties of the "democratic elite," the "natural inequality of talent," the "diversity of social roles," and the nature and necessity of property. Instruction in political and social economy covered the division of labor, capital, the association of labor and capital, the legitimacy of interest, trade—foreign and domestic—cooperation, and the perils of alcoholism. However diverse the course of study, it reduced to the "facts" of "social science."[12]

In 1891, Alfred Fouillée, educator, politician, and social scientist, had broadcast the same message in somewhat exalted terms that nevertheless failed to conceal its political content. He located the "chief cause of [France's] current malaise," class conflict, in the "conflict of ideas and purposes both between different social classes and

11. Paul Crouzet, "Etat actuel de l'enseignement populaire social," *Premier congrès de l'enseignement des sciences sociales* (Paris, 1901), 237–38, 251–55.

12. François Simiand, "De l'enseignement des sciences sociales à l'école primaire," *ibid.*, 169–84.

between political parties; the solution lies in all forms of education that shape ideas according to a conception of absolute harmony. Yet another reason to instruct our youth in the social, economic and political sciences." Scientific study "will replace the intellectual and moral anarchy that threatens to split us up" with "national unity." History, for some the queen of the sciences, became, in Fouillée's hands, a whore. Those who study no history "fall prey to all sorts of fantastic and unrealizable utopias," but "only within the context of social science will history realize its mission and its educational value." Social science, he concluded, validated the "morality of history and politics."[13]

The Société pour l'éducation sociale devoted its energies to translating those sentiments into practice. Bourgeois and Gide collaborated on the accumulation of books and programs for primary social education, taking up such social facts as the meaning of money, human association, and the division of labor. One committee of the Société drew up a report on social engineering with specific reference to the work of Cheysson and Tolman. It identified the social engineer as one "knowledgeable in the social sciences" who belongs in "all important social groups: factories, cooperatives, and *syndicats*."[14]

Workers' *syndicats* came in for special attention as a natural extension of the Société's self-imposed mandate to focus chiefly on the labor question. Whereas the hard-liners among the social economists previously had considered *syndicats* weapons of class warfare, those involved in the politics of social education insisted on their positive contributions to the "social organization of labor," rendering them valuable instruments to combat the anomic forces latent in the productive process. Moreover, *syndicats*, as legitimate expressions of working-class interests, provided the necessary counterpart to *patron* organizations. Without the *syndicat*—and here was the bottom line—collective association between labor and capital would be all the more difficult to construct. This was not a radical position. Paul Passama, an expert on industrial organization not unfriendly to capital, believed that workers in a single enterprise or group of inte-

13. Alfred Fouillée, *L'Enseignement au point de vue national* (Paris, 1891), 255, 260, 289.
14. *BSES*, I (1901), 35–39, 83–84.

grated enterprises belonged in a single *syndicat*. Dangers existed, but also opportunities: "This concentration of working-class and *patronal* forces obviously creates the conditions for destructive strikes and lock-outs; but we can hope that the terrifying perspective of such conflicts will forestall any useless struggle and will constitute a guarantee for social peace."[15]

Preoccupations with the labor question stamped every project undertaken by the Société pour l'éducation sociale. Its section on primary education conducted a survey on discipline of schools around the country. More than twelve hundred responses were correlated by students of the Ecole normale supérieure of Saint-Cloud. Discipline, it turned out, had nothing to do with rapping the knuckles of hapless youngsters (although plenty of that went on in French schools). Rather, it was concerned with the "material order" in the classroom, and especially with the "organization of labor" according to the rules of "solidarity." One favorite mode of enforcing discipline was to divide a class into working groups—"little collectivities"—that engaged in manual labor such as gardening. Every form of association—gymnastic, shooting, choral, debate, anti-alcoholism—promoted discipline. The pursuit of these exercises fostered the internalization of acceptable social values, the progressive displacement of "*imposed* discipline by *consensual* discipline."[16]

Although chiefly designed for working-class children, the strictures of discipline held lessons for bourgeois children as well, who as adults entered into an inheritance of paternal responsibility. On their shoulders rested the burden of operating systems of class collaboration. They could teach by example and thereby present to workers the human face of capitalism: "The people, as it witnesses the bourgeoisie devoting part of its leisure to the instruction of the proletariat, will discover that those most favored by fortune accept the task of social education as a social duty."[17] "Those most favored by fortune" had, of course, more at stake than just the presentation of a benign countenance. As owners of the means of industrial produc-

15. Edouard Petit, *Rapport sur l'éducation populaire* (Paris, 1902–1903), 23; *BSES*, I (1901), 10–11, II (1902), 137–49, 242; Paul Passama, *L'Intégration du travail, formes nouvelles de concentration industrielle* (Paris, 1910), 339–40.

16. *BSES*, I (1901), 92–99.

17. *BSES*, II (1902), 165.

tion and as managers of the means of cultural reproduction, they and their counterparts in the bourgeois intelligentsia understood the relationship between the material interests of capital and ideological systems. Social education's utility lay in its effectiveness as a weapon directed against the social barriers to accumulation.

Revolutions in Consciousness: Universités populaires

"Between the time of leaving school and entering the barracks, during those dangerous years of adolescence when the passions are aroused, when the temptations of the cabaret and the street beckon, the youth, left to his own devices, runs the risk not only of forgetting what he has learned, but of losing any sense of morality." That call to alarm, sounded in 1904 by Gabriel Séailles, professor of philosophy in the Sorbonne, echoed throughout the French business, intellectual, and political establishment at the turn of the century. Ferdinand Buisson, "a simple worker in the field of education," as he modestly described himself, made the point three years earlier when he called attention to the empty years that separated the end of primary education from military service and full-time work. And Léon Bourgeois pointed out that working-class youths left primary school precisely at that "dangerous age" when the "adolescent crisis begins."[18]

Those Frenchmen self-appointed to defend the bourgeois republican order had good reason to be alarmed. In their view, young working-class men, cut loose from secure familial moorings and only partially integrated into the world of capitalist production, were easy pickings for socialists and syndicalists. In 1894, Georges Picot lamented the lack of instruction in social economy, which he considered the responsibility of businessmen and reformers: "We agree that any form of socialism will spell our ruin. . . . Yet, while we sit around wringing our hands, the enemies of the family, of property, of society itself sponsor *lectures and courses* . . . and young people pay attention to them!" The director of the Ecole normale

18. Gabriel Séailles, *Les Affirmations de la conscience moderne* (Paris, 1904), 81; *Annales de l'Université populaire lyonnaise*, No. 3 (1901), 21–23; Léon Bourgeois, *L'Education de la démocratie française* (Paris, 1897), 157.

of the Vosges urged workers in Mirecourt to "cultivate morality, strengthen their character, root out bad habits, and develop a fondness for work and a preference for order," but no one suggested that the development of those qualities be left to chance. That was the business of popular education. Séailles put the matter starkly in the subtitle to his pamphlet: "education or revolution."[19]

Popular education took many forms, and I will examine several. All of them shared three characteristics: first, as instruments of social education, they aimed to displace working-class consciousness, the product of "hate and prejudice," according to Léon Bourgeois, with "social consciousness"; second, despite lip service paid to cultural formation, they focused on the ideological integration of workers into the productive process to "arm them," as Waldeck-Rousseau put it, for the "combat" among industrial nations; finally, popular education organizations depended heavily for their viability on the direct involvement of the industrial bourgeoisie, its agents, or "anyone who may require a servant, a worker, an employee" for their ongoing operations as well as for financing.[20] Among the varieties of popular education, *universités populaires*, classes for workers, and centers of sociability expose social education's class function as the bourgeois hegemonic enterprise *par excellence*.

Universités populaires had only a brief existence, spanning the last few years of the nineteenth century and the first decade of the twentieth. They enjoyed a much less successful career than did the English "workingmen's colleges" with which they had some elements in common. If this were all, we should dismiss them without another word. But they provide a good example of how solidarist-corporatist ideology helped to shape popular education and make of it an experiment in class collaboration.[21] Moreover, *universités popu-*

---

19. Picot's speech at the 1894 congress of the Société d'économie sociale and the Unions de la paix sociale quoted in Jeanne Weill [Dick May], *L'Enseignement social à Paris* (Paris, 1896), 42–43; Graillet, "Le Travail et le capital," 45; Gabriel Séailles, *Coopération des idées: Universités populaires: Education ou révolution* (Paris, 1899), 1.

20. *Education sociale*, 476; BSES, I (1901), 17, II (1902), 163–65; Léopold Mabilleau, "Education sociale et coopération," *ACF*, 8th year (1900), 42–45; *Exposition 1889*, I, 276; Bourgeois, *L'Education*, 178.

21. Léon Dintzer, "Le Mouvement des Universités populaires," *Mouvement Social*, No. 35 (1962), 5–6; Charles Gide, "Travail intellectual et travail manuel," preface to Jacques Bardoux, *La Fondation universitaire de Belleville* (Paris, 1901), iii–xviii.

laires bore some striking resemblances to other forms of association located at the point of production.

The story of the *universités populaires* begins in Nîmes. In 1884, that city's bourgeoisie organized the Société d'économie populaire, which subsequently became a major force in the national cooperative movement. The founders of the Société had one overriding concern: "to hasten the fusion of classes through economic and social education, 'the only way to neutralize the agitations of those who preach violence.'" Edouard de Boyve, a leading figure in the Société, reported that its educational efforts were designed "to spread the message that only evolutionary and peaceful solutions can last and that revolutions produce only wholesale ruin." To that end the Société launched a program of evening meetings to which its members recruited workers to participate in discussions of current social and economic issues. These informal assemblages, from which all discussion of politics was rigidly excluded, prefigured other educational experiments, like the *universités populaires*, where bourgeois and workers rubbed elbows.[22]

The Société attracted the attention of Charles Gide, who taught in the University of Montpellier until 1894, when he moved to the Law Faculty in Paris. Gide conceived of social education and cooperation as twin engines to drive forward a "revolutionary" transformation of economic relations in which solidarity and harmony between entrepreneurs and workers would replace competition and struggle. Despite Gide's insistence that cooperatives would reduce the share of capital and increase that of labor, socialists considered them merely another bourgeois diversion. They argued, with some justice, that cooperative production remained embedded within a system of capitalist relations and tended to weaken working-class unity.[23] Without ascribing ulterior motives to Gide or anyone else, the fact remains that cooperation in education or in production did operate to reinforce the class harmony so eagerly sought by the proponents of social peace. That became apparent as the *universités populaires*

22. *Exposition 1889*, II, 243–44; Edouard de Boyve, *Histoire de la coopération à Nîmes* (Paris, 1889), 120; Charles Gide, *Economie sociale* (Paris, 1905), 252–58.

23. Charles Gide, "De la coopération et des transformations qu'elle est appelée à réaliser dans l'ordre économique," *REP*, III (1889), 486; Charles Guieysse, "Les Universités populaires et le mouvement ouvrier," *Cahiers de la Quinzaine*, 3rd ser., No. 2 (1901), 21n.

emerged briefly as a national movement in the late 1890s and early 1900s.

In Paris a self-educated printer and sometime anarchist named Georges Deherme set out to liberate his fellow workers from alcoholism, prostitution, and other assorted vices. Deherme had dabbled briefly in insurrectionary politics but had given that up for self-education and the education of others. In 1896, he started a journal, *La Coopération des Idées*, which was to serve as a vehicle to liberate a "proletarian elite, blinded and corrupted by a sentimental and gluttonous socialism." He denounced those socialists who "forget that social evils do not stem exclusively from economic sources. A reform of the laws . . . an alteration in the mode of the distribution of wealth, whether accomplished through legislation or by a revolution, would not eliminate evil." Instead, Deherme proposed to spread the word of "sociological science," by which he meant the study of "individuals grouped together socially," and the "collective social consciousness." Once workers were relieved of their worst material miseries, education would free them of the "grip of socialist utopias and revolutionary doctrines" and "deliver to the nation" individuals of "upright character and good sense." Deherme also included the bourgeoisie in his plan for a "moral revolution." He was quick to accuse that class of cynicism and complacency, hence his summons to "the rich as well as to the poor" to join in the great project to transform collective consciousness.[24]

Deherme labeled *La Coopération des Idées* a "sociological journal," signaling his conception of the *université populaire* as an instrument of socialization as well as liberation. Sociology had deep political meaning, which logically extended from academic social science. Its political dimension encompassed both understanding and strengthening the nature of the forces of social cohesion. True to sociological priciples, Deherme was concerned with establishing the reign of "justice and solidarity" without which, he believed, "democracy remained a dead letter."[25]

24. Jean Maitron, *Histoire du mouvement anarchiste en France, 1880–1914* (Paris, 1955), 242–43, 333; Séailles, *Les Affirmations*, 83–89; *La Coopération des Idées*, I (1896), 1, II (1897), 35–36, IV (1899), 20; Georges Deherme, *Auguste Comte et son oeuvre: Le Positivisme* (Paris, 1909), 118.

25. Max Turmann, *Au sortir de l'école: Les Patronages* (Paris, 1909), 35–37.

In an essay on Comte marked by embarrassingly excessive veneration, Deherme appropriated the spirit of corporate managerialism
embedded in Comte's work:

> A. Comte views individual appropriation and the concentration of capital as
> the ideal mode of conservation and production. But the capitalist is only a
> bureaucrat, an administrator of social wealth. He has debts to pay. Wealth is
> entrusted to him only so that it may bear fruit under his care. If he abuses it,
> if he uses it only for personal gain, then society will exercise its overriding
> right of confiscation and expropriation. The spiritual power, supported by a
> powerful public opinion, would excommunicate the squanderer of social
> capital. Corporations will boycott him. These sanctions constitute sufficient
> force to prevent the industrial and financial patriciate from becoming a para-
> sitic, corrupting, and tyrannical plutocracy.

Deherme coupled his appreciation of Comte with yet another blast
at socialism. He dismissed the "dogma of class struggle as gross non-
sense. Most of the time, socialism cannot maintain itself on even that
low level, as its pursuit of votes reduces to base demagogy. The *boulevardiers*, the lawyers without clients, the physicians without pa-
tients, and the starving journalists are as much socialists as they
were, twenty years ago, radicals."[26]

Like Comte, Deherme expected salvation to come from the working class—properly instructed. He addressed his appeals to the
"people," whose integration into society promised a "real civilization that does not exclude the majority, a civilization that does not
operate for the profit of a few, but one to which all are called and in
which all participate." Hence Deherme planned to "organize systematically syndicalist, cooperative, political, and social education."
Hence, also, Henri Hauser, historian and champion of social education and of the *universités populaires* queried: "Should we not speak
of sociology and political economy to those workers concerned with
changing the organization of labor and of society itself"?[27]

Of course, the summons to the rich held the hope that they would
appear with generous purses. This did not happen immediately. Con-

26. Deherme, *Auguste Comte,* 68, 118.

27. Turmann, *Au sortir de l'école,* 35; Georges Deherme, *Rapport sur l'enseignement social
en France* (Paris, 1900), 2; Hauser, *L'Enseignement des sciences sociales,* 372–73; John Laffey,
"Auguste Comte: Prophet of Reconciliation and Reaction," *Science and Society,* XIX (1965),
44–65.

sequently, Deherme joined with a cabinetmaker named Metreaux to organize a series of *soirées ouvrières* in Paris' eleventh arrondissement. Metreaux had been involved in a project in Montreuil, on the city's eastern outskirts, where workers engaged in a program of non-political cultural and scientific self-education. The inaugural *soirée* featured the social reformer and Protestant pastor Charles Wagner. Wagner followed in the footsteps of the Association protestante pour l'étude pratique des questions sociales, founded in 1887, "which had raised the banner of social solidarity" in large working-class cities such as Roubaix, Lille, and Rouen. The Association sponsored "a vigorous campaign against alcoholism, gambling, animal combat and all sorts of pornography." The first subsidy arrived soon after Wagner's *causérie*: 100 francs from the right-wing elitist, Maurice Barrès.[28]

At first glance it may seem odd that the archnationalist Maurice Barrès should have associated himself with an effort to elevate working-class culture. But we should remember that in their quest for the "soul" of France, right-wingers at the end of the century routinely glorified the laboring classes and sought to find ways to integrate them into the "national organism," despite caring little for their real interests. With their right hand they attacked socialism as a Marxist swindle and with their left they vilified liberalism as a vestige of alleged bourgeois moral bankruptcy. This attitude extended to the *universités populaires* movement. Charles Guieysse, who became secretary-general of the Société des Universités populaires and had vague syndicalist leanings, ridiculed bourgeois reformers for "constantly talking about the fusion of classes while in the same breath denying the existence of classes." But he also had nothing but contempt for socialists, those "doctors of Revolution who mouth phrases such as 'class struggle' and 'socialization of this and that.'" Guieysse's tendency to mimic the slogans of syndicalist militance, *épater la bourgeoisie*, and to denounce socialists as collectivist hotheads paralleled—not coincidentally—the ideological pronouncements of the Fédération des Jaunes. As in the case of Deherme, Guieysse claimed to champion working-class emancipation and the

28. *Exposition 1900*, V, 194; Jeanne Weill [Dick May], "Quelques réflexions sur les Universités populaires," *Revue Socialiste* (1901), 36–40.

abolition of the "proletarian condition." These ambitions, however, proved difficult to realize, given the conditions under which the *universités populaires* took shape, to say nothing of the ideological bent of their leaders.[29]

Revolutions in consciousness, sentiments, or ideals often disguise deeply conservative tendencies. Moreover, they may deflect attention away from other, more substantive, revolutions. Charles Gide placed great stock in the potential of cooperative production but appeared to be at least equally comfortable on the level of moral revolution. Thus he approvingly characterized the mission of the *universités populaires* as that of "realizing among all men the highest form of socialism, not the communism of goods, but the community of ideas and sentiments." Similarly, Léon Bourgeois called upon his associates in the Société pour l'éducation sociale "to make the revolution, not in the streets—violence achieves nothing—but in [workers'] consciousness."[30]

When the Société des Universités populaires was organized in 1899, Gabriel Séailles became its president. He headed its Comité de propagande that included Gide, Fontaine, Buisson, Auguste Keüfer, secretary-general of the conservative trade union, the Fédération du Livre, Ernest Lavisse, the nationalist historian, Anatole Leroy-Beaulieu, Léon de Seilhac, Edouard Petit, director-general of primary education in the Ministry of Education, and Dick May, secretary-general of the College libre des sciences sociales and former private secretary to the Comte de Chambrun.[31]

Séailles, a self-identified "radical solidarist," coupled a disdain for conventional politics with a commitment to aggressive social action on behalf of class collaboration and cooperation. He addressed himself to the bourgeoisie, at whose threshold lay the disappointments of the past and the hopes of the future. Cooperation, as in the *universités populaires*, provided, he said, a potent antidote to the poisonous doctrines of social Darwinists and "economic determinists" (socialists), for "the true law of society is not struggle, but unity, for

29. Guieysse, "Les Universités populaires," 13–14, 34–35. The phrase "national organism" comes from Zeev Sternhell, *La Droite révolutionnaire, 1885–1914* (Paris, 1978), 316.

30. *Exposition 1900*, V, 191; BSES, I (1901), 9.

31. Séailles, *Coopération des idées*, 1.

existence." Séailles summoned the bourgeoisie to its responsibilities, but insisted that it act contrary to its character by scuttling the ideology of the marketplace for that of the corporate community. In that sense he displayed a shrewd understanding of the direction toward which the market was heading: "We are not interested in imposing dogmas, in defending a tradition, in justifying a social hierarchy while masquerading as philanthropists. We recognize neither masters, leaders, nor bosses; our property is collective."[32]

Séailles, like Gide, offered a revolution of consciousness and ideas. He engaged in what appeared to be a radical critique of society, denouncing materialism and money-grubbing. But he ridiculed socialists and thereby exposed the fundamental conservative thrust of his message. Socialists had no answers. As for their revolutionary plans and programs, "nothing has changed except a few words and several individuals." Séailles reversed priorities: "Change individuals in order to change the social environment." Property "need not be considered sacred . . . but the social whole adds up to no more than the sum of individual virtues and energies."[33]

Universités populaires, according to Séailles, offered several advantages to the French bourgeoisie. The "social and moral education of the people" promised class unity and a "high level of harmony." More to the point, the "privileged classes" should understand that "under the new conditions created by our industrial and scientific civilization, social transformation will inevitably occur and that the process promises to be a good deal less violent and dangerous in the presence of enlightened men than among barbarians." Referring to the *universités populaires* as "cathedrals of democracy," Séailles expected them to form the foundation for "common labor" in "collective tasks"—"an apprenticeship in true solidarity." And when, in early 1900, the government accorded to the Société des Universités populaires the status of "*utilité publique*," Séailles took that as a demonstration that "the government of republican defense had remained faithful to its program."[34]

32. *Ibid.*, 2, 7.
33. *Ibid.*, 8–12.
34. Séailles, *Les Affirmations*, 82, 92–94, 96–108; Turmann, *Au sortir de l'école*, 357.

The extent to which Séailles' rhetoric added up to more than just pious hopes may be gauged in the brief career of Deherme's original foundation. That Deherme projected a huge role for the *université populaire* was reflected in his plans for its physical facilities in the artisan neighborhood of the Faubourg Saint-Antoine. In addition to lecture rooms and a library, the building included baths, showers, a gymnasium, a fencing area, laboratories, conversation areas, a pharmacy, space for "medical, legal, and economic consultations," dormitories, furnished rooms, a labor exchange, a school to train teachers in popular education, and an alcohol-free restaurant. The *université populaire*'s projected educational program ranged far and wide: physics, biology, astronomy, geography, anthropology, psychiatry, linguistics, logic, aesthetics, demography, law, political economy, criminology, and, of course, sociology.[35] Deherme had, in fact, framed a total leisure-time environment for those who took advantage of the *université populaire*'s facilities. He created the French equivalent of George Williams' YMCA, which appeared at about the same time in Britain and Canada and bore a similar design, complete with exercises in sobriety and physical training.

Deherme's ambitious plans never left the drawing board, nor did his program of courses, lectures, and recreation attract the throngs of workers that he expected. He claimed a total attendance of seven thousand in 1900, including forty-five hundred workers and day laborers, fifteen hundred clerks and employees, and a thousand assorted bourgeois and small tradesmen. These numbers cannot be corroborated so they must remain suspect. In his annual report on popular education in 1902, Edouard Petit did suggest that Deherme's clientele included a larger number of bourgeois than Deherme would have admitted. Petit also vigorously denied that the foundation was in financial trouble, thus leaving the impression that it was. The *université populaire* in Faubourg Saint-Antoine closed its doors in 1903,[36] but the story does not end there.

Several *universités populaires* sprang up in Paris at the same time. They were all a good deal more modest than Deherme's original

35. Weill, "Quelques réflexions," 42; Séailles, *Les Affirmations*, 90–91; Deherme, *Rapport*, 5.
36. Deherme, *Rapport*, 12; Petit, *Rapport* (1902–1903), 27–29.

project and tended to draw exclusively from their immediate neighborhoods. Members of the Société des Universités populaires actively supported them with small donations and with lectures in abundance. For instance, lecturers at the Solidarité in the thirteenth arrondissement included the historian Charles Seignobos, Henri Hauser, Ferdinand Buisson, and the ubiquitous Charles Gide. Curiously, or perhaps not so curiously, the working-class audience found least attractive Gide's lectures on political economy and sociology. They were far more interested in science and philosophy. Solidarité was an outgrowth of a consumers' cooperative, which, because it was frankly socialist-inspired rather than "scientific," did not benefit from the largesse of the Société des Universités populaires. Séailles and his collaborators obviously kept a tight rein. They made a virtue of political disengagement. As Dick May reported, the *universités populaires* "carry no flag. They are not socialist. They are not antisocialist. They are neither clerical nor anticlerical." But they did contribute to the formation of citizens, which was another kind of politics.[37]

Despite May's disclaimer, a survey of lectures offered during 1900 betrays the influence of established anticlerical bourgeois ideology. There were lectures on the religious congregations (by Léon Blum), clerical fortresses, the contradictions of religion, and Luther and free thought. But mostly the courses focused on more practical matters: public health, the family, the role of women in society, French colonies, the struggle against alcoholism, commercial geography, the organization of labor, and the practical applications of electricity.[38] However "value-free" these subjects might appear, they reflected the primary mission of social education to promote working-class acculturation.

Among the many *universités populaires* that appeared at the end of the century, the Fondation universitaire de Belleville stands out as an incarnation of social education's spirit of class collaboration. Established in 1899, the Fondation took its lead from the English "settlement schools," located mostly in London's East End, where young bourgeois students tutored workers. This arrangement supposedly

37. Weill, "Quelques réflexions," 169–83.
38. Turmann, *Au sortir de l'école*, 361–66.

encouraged solidarity. In Paris, several well-connected (and well-heeled) young intellectuals, impatient with Deherme's grandiose plans and meager results and less than enchanted with his bizarre politics, struck out on their own to organize a school, library, and conference center in Belleville—Paris' east end. There they planned to hold classes in "science, morals, literature, the arts, and social and economic questions."[39]

Startup funds for the Fondation, totaling nearly 5,000 francs, came from the Ligue de l'enseignement and from an assortment of businessmen and philanthropists. One of the founders, a student at the Ecole normale supérieure, Joseph Aynard, drew on the resources of his father, Edouard Aynard. At the end of the Second Empire and during the early years of the Third Republic, the elder Aynard, correctly determining the direction of the prevailing political winds, organized a conservative alliance for "social defense" between the Lyonese big bourgeoisie and the middle classes. "That orientation formed the basis of his subsequent political career" and constituted the main theme of his ideological tract, *Du rôle des classes moyennes*, published in 1907. Aynard had a special interest and long experience in social reform. He sponsored technical education in Lyon to provide a steady supply of competent workers for the silk industry. As a member of the Chamber of Deputies he focused on social questions: child labor, the conditions of work in coal mines, female labor, and workers' compensation. As a good paternalist, however, he opposed state intervention to reduce the number of hours in the working day. Aynard's support was reinforced by that of the widows of the bankers Isaac and Emile Pereire, the Bordeaux businessman Robert Johnston, Paul Leroy-Beaulieu, and Alphonse and Edmond de Rothschild. No evidence exists to suggest that such people controlled the Fondation, for many workers were involved from the beginning; indeed had they not been, the Fondation would have fallen flat from the start. But certainly, the presence of big bourgeois, even on the fringes, set limits to the degree to which the Fondation would act as an instrument of working-class self-emancipation.[40]

39. *Ibid.*, Pt. 3, Chap. 9; Weill, "Quelques réflexions," 46–49; Bardoux, *La Fondation, passim.*

40. M. Moissonnier and A. Boulmier, "La Bourgeoisie lyonnaise aux origines de l'union civique de 1920?" *Cahiers d'Histoire de l'Institut de Recherches Marxistes,* No. 4

Jacques Bardoux was the Fondation universitaire's chief organizer, and his account provides much of our information on the Fondation. His case bears comment, for it draws attention to the social consciousness of those involved in setting up the Fondation and to their social stations and their political orientation as well. In 1899, Bardoux had just completed his legal studies. His father, Agénor, an influential Orleanist turned republican politician in the 1870s, had capitalized on his political connections to gain a seat on the board of the Paris-Orléans railroad. Agénor Bardoux's firm position in France's banking-transportation establishment paid off in, among other things, an excellent match for his son. Jacques married the daughter of Georges Picot. Thus Jacques Bardoux had intimate ties to the worlds of high finance and big bourgeois paternalism.[41]

Bardoux displayed a keen appreciation of social education's role in reinforcing collective consciousness in the face of an increasing division of labor. In one report on the Fondation he quoted the social psychologist Gabriel Tarde: "Personal, direct contact among young people is especially lacking in our modern society, and it is by no means the least of the problems created by the growing urbanization of modern nations. To struggle against that tendency, to reknit the social fabric torn by mass culture, and to render it tighter and stronger . . . that is a noble aspiration." Unlike Deherme, Bardoux avoided the appearance of manipulation among his working-class collaborators. He recognized, as one contemporary commentator on the Fondation noted, that "if one wants to work toward pacification and social education, it is essential not to treat modest folk as chil-

(38), 109n; Bardoux, La Fondation, 15, 19, 29; "La Fondation universitaire," Musée social, Mémoires et documents (1902), 475, 477; Jean Jolly (ed.), Dictionnaire des parlementaires français (10 vols.; Paris, 1960–70), I, 428–29.

41. Levasseur, Questions, 328. Bardoux went on to carve out a brilliant career as a lawyer, journalist, chef de cabinet to Marshal Foch in 1918, high-level technocrat, and senator. His special interests included colonial reform, foreign affairs, and education. During the Vichy regime, Bardoux served as a national councillor on a commission to reform the constitution, a position entirely consistent with his long involvement in the technical administration of social matters. He ended public life as a member of the Chamber of Deputies of the Fourth Republic. In 1956 he did not stand for reelection and turned over his seat in the Puy-de-Dôme to his grandson, Valéry Giscard d'Estaing. See Emmanuel Beau de Loménie, Les Responsabilités des dynasties bourgeoises (4 vols.; Paris, 1943–63), I, 282–83, II, 26, 201, IV, 183, 192; Jolly (ed.), Dictionnaire, II, 458–59.

dren. Confidence ennobles, and confidence unites." To that end, Bardoux, Aynard, Pierre Leroy-Beaulieu, the son of the political economist, and others set themselves the task of "creating a spirit of camaraderie between those commonly called manual laborers and intellectual laborers."[42]

Bardoux and his collaborators' "modest efforts" to make a contribution to social peace bore fruit within a few months of the Fondation's installation at 151, rue de Belleville, on the southern slope of the Buttes Chaumont. Active membership at the end of 1899 stood at 112, of which 82 were students and 30 workers. This was not, however, the ratio that had been projected. Aggressive recruiting must have followed, for the membership lists one year later revealed a dramatic reversal of proportions: 353 workers and 134 students. During the next several years the Fondation's membership increased to nearly 1,000, of which 75 to 80 percent were workers. The occupational distribution of the workers reflected the predominance of skilled trades in that part of Paris. These were workers who had a tradition of self-education and, not incidentally, of political activism. Unskilled workers, demoralized by the "fatigues associated with monotonous and unpleasant labor," did not appear. Thus the effort to create a collective consciousness concentrated precisely on those workers who labored outside the huge enterprises of advanced capitalism and traditionally had provided the working class with its leadership cadres. This was the reason for the hostility exhibited toward the Fondation and other *universités populaires* by French syndicalist leaders.[43]

Formal courses and lectures played a secondary role at the Fondation universitaire. The heaviest emphasis lay on informal get-togethers between bourgeois students and workers—seminars in solidarity, as it were. Conversations tended toward subjects of light amusement—music, poetry, and popular tales—"designed to help the participants to forget their weariness after a hard day's work."

42. Bardoux, *La Fondation,* 14; Turmann, *Au sortir de l'école,* 134; *Cahiers de la Quinzaine,* 3rd ser., No. 10 (1900–1901).

43. Turmann, *Au sortir de l'école,* 352; Bardoux, "La Fondation universitaire," 474; Bardoux, *La Fondation,* 49–55; Bardoux, "L'Université populaire en France et en Angleterre," Musée social, *Mémoires et documents* (1907), 38.

These small groups had several advantages. "Each conversation that developed dissipated prejudices and reduced mutual mistrust." Moreover, small groups "reduced the chances of disorder, enlarged the opportunities for the expression of mutual goodwill, and multiplied the opportunities for personal contact." The relaxed atmosphere was reinforced by spacious quarters, by rooms for card games, and by a billiard parlor. Despite appearances, the Fondation, like Deherme's *université populaire*, was a carefully controlled leisure-time environment. Unlike Deherme, the organizers of the Fondation paid little attention to moral uplift. They believed that workers neither cared about moral questions nor aspired to "moral discipline"—a curious contradiction considering their professed respect for the working class.[44]

In their courses and public lectures, the Fondation's organizers drew on France's leading political and intellectual figures. Charles Gide played a key role. He defined the Fondation's mission in clearly political terms: to abolish the consciousness among manual laborers that their class interests separated them from intellectual laborers (managers and entrepreneurs). Denying that labor created value, he insisted that entrepreneurs, individually or collectively, calculated human needs and organized production to satisfy them. Hence exploitation was a myth and workers simply had to accommodate to that fact. The *universités populaires* existed to propagate the lessons of political and social economy, to promote social peace, and to combat the "Marxist program of class struggle."[45]

Economic, social, scientific, and philosophical subjects formed the core of lectures and courses. Joseph Chailley-Bert, the colonial publicist, spoke on the situation in South Africa; another colonialist, Félicien Michotte, lectured on the benefits of French colonies. In the same spirit, André Siegfried spoke on economic and social conditions in China and New Zealand. Germain Martin, an economic historian, discussed the development of big industry. André Lichtenberger, a historian of socialist movements, offered a course on socialism in the eighteenth century. In addition, audiences had the

44. Bardoux, "La Fondation universitaire," 479; "L'Université populaire," 57; Turmann, *Au sortir de l'école*, 347–49.
45. Gide, "Le Travail intellectuel," x–xi, xviii.

opportunity to hear about the miracles of science, the republican idea, and the rights of property.[46]

In addition to these individual lectures the Fondation offered a structured program of studies divided into five groups: philosophy, including psychology, will, habit, and instinct, and the psychology of crowds; literature, including the works of Mme de Staël, Rousseau, Hugo, Dumas *fils*, and Tolstoy; science, including instruction in the telegraph, the telephone, optics, acoustics, astronomy, and physics; art and aesthetics, in which painters and schools of paintings were analyzed; and economics—by far the most comprehensive group—which was run by André Siegfried, who focused on working-class questions and social laws, the social question in various countries, strikes, profit sharing, mutualism, British imperialism (Siegfried was an admirer of the British imperial propagandist Edward Gibbon Wakefield on whom he wrote a university thesis), and sociology. As Bardoux testified, these classes were modeled on the lycée curriculum. That, according to one post-mortem on the *universités populaires*, was precisely the problem: "Why did the *universités populaires* not provide the professional and technical education that promises benefits to both workers and capitalists? It seems that university graduates who tried to transform themselves suddenly into 'educators of the people' simply could not manage the job."[47]

The foregoing judgment gives Bardoux and his associates more credit for misplaced idealism than they deserve. Despite its big bourgeois connections, the Fondation never forged solid links to the Paris business community. As a result, the putative cooperation between labor and capital had no practical expression beyond the artificial environment of the Fondation itself. A more serious problem was that the Fondation, which survived Deherme's establishment by only two years despite its auspicious start, fell between two stools— or rather, could not make subject and object agree. The frankly political purpose—to combat socialism by joining together bourgeois and workers in good fellowship and serious study—had no concrete underpinnings. Bardoux admitted that it was difficult to recruit

---

46. Bardoux, *La Fondation*, 49–55.
47. Bardoux, "La Fondation universitaire," 485–93; Maurice Duhamel, *L'Education sociale du peuple et l'échec des Universités populaires* (Paris, 1904), 12–13.

bourgeois students to spend time at the Fondation or to take up residence in its quarters. That failure ruled out the possibility that the sons of the bourgeoisie could engage in what Emile Cheysson called "the practical work of social science, the scientific and neutral observation of the facts" of working-class social life.[48]

In the end, however, there was no way that the associationist message could have been broadcast without exposing the Fondation's political purpose. Only disguises remained, and the ingredients of high culture and ideology turned out to be a poor mixture. Workers, who were initially attracted by the Fondation's recreational amenities, displayed understandable skepticism of the motives of these high-minded young men whose professed altruism inadequately concealed their social and political concerns. Thus, in this case at least, one cannot take seriously Dick May's assertion that the *université populaire* "displayed no partisan banner." Bardoux himself had made no secret of the Fondation's fundamental political character. At a meeting of the Société d'économie sociale, of which his father-in-law, Picot, had been president in 1892, Bardoux announced—albeit prematurely—that the success of the Fondation universitaire had confounded those skeptics who argued that workers were "so completely taken up with the idea of class struggle peddled by Marxists" that they would refuse all collaboration.[49]

More practical and modest efforts, those carried on in the provinces, illustrate the character and goals of social education in a manner more concrete than the elaborate schemes of the Université populaire of the Faubourg Saint-Antoine and the Fondation universitaire de Belleville. A solid base had existed since the early 1890s, when a host of societies devoted to the social education of workers had sprung up. Organized by businessmen, lawyers, teachers, and doctors, these *sociétés d'instruction populaire*—as they were most commonly known—numbered more than a thousand by the end of the century. Significantly, the largest concentrations were in the industrial departments of the Nord, the Pas-de-Calais, and the Rhône. All of them engaged in one form or another of adult education, the or-

48. Bardoux, "La Fondation universitaire," 503–504; *Revue Populaire d'Economie Sociale*, III (1904), 54.
49. Turmann, *Au sortir de l'école*, 353.

ganization of libraries, and the dissemination of lectures. Many of these groups started *universités populaires*, which were a natural extension of their activities. By 1902, 75 had been established.[50]

More than just numbers and organizations, however, accounted for the difference between the Parisian and the provincial experiences. Each drew from the same ideological well, but in the provinces a clearer sense of priorities appeared to exist. There, as Edouard Petit noted, the *universités populaires* linked "the head and the hand [*la pensée et l'outil*]." Moreover, the practical businessmen who organized them understood that "one does not approach workers coming off a hard day's work in the same manner as one deals with young people obliged to attend school; one does not lecture an audience of workers as one lectures a group of *petits bourgeois* interested only in trivial and cheap amusements."[51]

Finally, organized labor and the bourgeois sponsors frequently collaborated closely in setting up the *universités populaires*. In Angoulême, for example, the local committee took great pains to complement—and not compete with—the educational projects of the Bourse du travail. (Many sections of the Fédération des Bourses du travail stood apart from revolutionary syndicalist politics without necessarily being agencies of class collaboration.) Frequently, *universités populaires* scheduled their events in the halls of the local Bourses, the better to facilitate "contact with the true working-class public" and to ensure the "collaboration of manual workers and intellectual workers." Those collaborative efforts were supposed to reinforce the Bourses' contribution to the "material, moral, and intellectual development of the working class" and, more important from the point of view of the provincial bourgeoisie, to demonstrate that social education was not merely another variation on the political manipulation of workers.[52]

In Tours the *université populaire* was the joint creation of a few

50. France, Ministère de l'Instruction publique et des Beaux-arts, *Rapport sur l'organisation et la situation de l'enseignement primaire public en France* (Paris, 1900), Pt. 3, Chap. 1; Petit, *Rapport* (1896–97), 47–49, (1901–1902), 42–43.

51. Petit, *Rapport* (1902–1903), 25–27; *Cahiers de la Quinzaine*, 3rd ser., No. 20 (1901), 5–6.

52. *Cahiers de la Quinzaine*, 3rd ser., No. 20 (1901), 11, 35; Petit, *Rapport* (1901–1902), 43; Crouzet, "Etat actuel," 250–51.

bourgeois—all Masons—and the officers of the local Bourse du travail. Each had something to offer the other. On the one hand, workers who had not associated themselves with the Bourse showed up for lectures and entertainment. On the other, the leaders of the Bourse provided their bourgeois collaborators with the opportunity to mix with workers and to demonstrate their goodwill. This was no small advantage. According to the Masonic brethren, workers in general "welcomed the project; however, there remained a residue of distrust stemming from their fear of being 'flim-flammed' [*roulés*], because they have been thoroughly worked over by the clerical organizations of the city, whose bourgeoisie is largely reactionary." Clericalism, in their view, demanded unceasing combat because of the social danger it presented. The social order did not benefit from the tendency of workers to identify a reactionary bourgeoisie with the Republic. Thus anticlericalism, couched in terms of "republican defense" (remember that this was the era of the Dreyfus affair), provided a meeting ground for bourgeois republicans and workers. Under these conditions, a discussion of social questions could be carried on within the limits of "the solidarity of citizens."[53]

Discussions of social questions rarely took on the aspect of freewheeling give and take. More commonly, lectures and seminars focused on social institutions and the so-called facts of social life. In Bar-le-Duc the organizers of the local *université populaire* ran conferences on cooperation, the relations between labor and capital, and definitions of property, all the while insisting that politics had absolutely no place in their program. Even newspapers were barred from the hall. Apparently they feared that partisan political brawls would poison the atmosphere of friendly class collaboration. Politics, after all, tended to derail the movement toward establishing a harmonious collective consciousness.[54]

Occasionally the bourgeois organizers of a *université populaire* confronted political questions head-on and made the most of them. In Montpellier they conducted their conferences in the Bourse du travail, which harbored some alleged "revolutionaries, even libertines." Furthermore, they began their courses at just the moment

53. *Cahiers de la Quinzaine*, 3rd ser., No. 20 (1901), 77–78.
54. *Ibid.*, 18–19.

when a dockers' strike in nearby Marseille had "overheated passions." Rather than evade the issue, they discussed the communalist movement of 1871 and encouraged the secretary of the Bourse to discuss workers' associations. All of this made the local police commissariat very nervous, and a police officer was dispatched to maintain order. He observed the scene, reported that "everything was calm," and left. By their own testimony, the *bourgeoisie montpéllerienne* harvested immense amounts of goodwill from the workers of that city.[55]

But the Montpellier experience was the exception that proved the rule. In Firminy, in the Loire textile, mining, and metallurgical zone, and in the northern mining town of Le Cateau, *universités populaires* for the most part restricted their activities to entertainment: choral societies, Sunday outings, poetry readings, and theater. Active worker participation in these industrial communities did not materialize, nor did the bourgeois sponsors seem to encourage such participation. Workers, especially in Firminy, pursued their interests through a series of strikes. Their revolution had nothing to do with ideas and sentiments.[56]

At about the same time that the Parisian *universités populaires* were being launched, a similar project took shape in Lyon. The Société lyonnaise d'instruction et d'éducation populaire, a foundation devoted to the "reconciliation of classes" and to social education, sponsored the formation of the Université populaire de Lyon, housed in a *maison du peuple* modeled after Deherme's installation in the Faubourg Saint-Antoine. As in the case of the Fondation universitaire de Belleville, students performed the organizational chores and the essential financing came from the city's big bourgeoisie, which previously had formed its own political front—the Société d'économie politique et d'économie sociale de Lyon.[57]

Founded in the early 1890s, the Société d'économie politique et d'économie sociale supported several paternalist reform projects: workers' savings banks, cheap cafeterias (*restaurants populaires*), and low-cost housing. Its leadership included the cream of Lyon's big bourgeoisie: Eugène Flotard, Auguste Isaac, the banker Jules Cambe-

---

55. *Ibid.*, 38–45.
56. *Ibid.*, 56–57.
57. *Annales de l'Université Populaire Lyonnaise*, No. 1 (1900), 3–4, No. 2 (1901), 15–16.

fort, the colonial propagandist and silk broker Ulysse Pila, a number of silk merchants and manufacturers, bankers, and Edouard Aynard. The Société took as its main business a propaganda program to interpret social facts to the working class. Among those facts, according to Aynard, were "economic laws [that] are inviolable and must be obeyed." Yet despite this fundamental ideological commitment to marketplace relations, the benefits of association in the workplace did not go unremarked. Association derived from the natural sociability of mankind. Politically, it provided a barrier to rampant individualism. Without it the nation was doomed to suffer an eternal cycle of despotism, a "Caesar or a Convention." Economically, association formed the foundation for "general improvement because it catalyzes the action of capital and releases the energies of individuals" so as to maximize their productivity. In the last analysis, all production, especially corporate forms, rested on association.[58]

The Université populaire de Lyon's original statutes indicate that it took the principle of association seriously on the practical level. Working-class adherents paid only 50 centimes per month; bourgeois members took up the slack through a substantial annual fee (the amount is not recorded). That in itself constituted a gesture of solidarity. The programs were designed to enable workers and their families to meet with "competent authorities" to discuss social questions, thereby producing the "union of intellectual and manual laborers." The director of the Université populaire, Madame Desparmet, a teacher in a lycée for young women, placed heavy emphasis on "enlightenment through science," especially social science, which she characterized as the principles underlying social solidarity. But routine invocations to solidarity would surely fall on deaf ears unless workers appreciated their essential contributions to industrial progress and the advantages derived therefrom. Perhaps anticipating the reaction of a working class that had undergone considerable verbal battering about progress without experiencing its tangible benefits (especially in Lyon), Madame Desparmet advised her bourgeois col-

58. Société d'économie politique et d'économie sociale de Lyon, *Compte-rendu analytique des séances* (1897), 425–40, (1898–99), 504–21; Hauser, *L'Enseignement des sciences sociales*, 218–19; Léon Say, *Exposition universelle de 1889, Groupe d'économie sociale: Rapport général*, 30–31, 40; Charles Lebrun, "Le Droit d'association," Société d'économie politique et d'économie sociale de Lyon, *Compte-rendu* (1898–99), 289–362.

laborators "to tell these workers . . . that we plan to undertake a genuine effort at social education and not allow it to be exploited for political advantage."[59]

Lyon's *université populaire* offered a standard mixture of courses and lectures: on the revolutions of 1789 and 1848, civic obligations, cooperative societies, literature, apprenticeship, elementary physics (but including an introduction to the X-ray), hygiene, profit sharing, and—appropriate to Lyon—colonial geography. Paul Pic, a vice-president of the Société d'économie politique et d'économie sociale and a professor of law, delivered a series of lectures on legislation to protect workers. He combined a deceptively radical critique of laissez-faire with a strong pitch for association and cooperation. The enlightened legislator, that is, the state, was guided by the principles of "social economy, as generous and democratic as classical political economy is selfish and aristocratic." Legislative relief from the ravages of competition and mechanization, initially conceived as instrumental reform, had a transcendent social mission to "enhance the rapprochement of capital and labor, the peaceful resolution of conflict, [and] the cooperation of investment and manual work in industrial production." Pic agreed with Charles Gide that cooperatives and *crédit populaire* were important forces in the radical yet peaceful process of working-class emancipation. But limits remained. The state had no business legislating a general cooperative system— that would constitute social revolution. Nor did the state have any business interfering with the economic laws that regulated wages. Some of Pic's collaborators, notably Edouard Aynard, would not have agreed with the social role he assigned to the state; but they could take comfort in his fidelity to economic laws and surely could appreciate the political advantages inherent in legislative social reform. And despite his ideological shadings toward social liberalism, Pic did not hesitate to be identified with more conservative reformers such as Léopold Mabilleau, Paul de Rousiers, Hippolyte Passy, and Jacques Bardoux.[60]

Although Madame Desparmet may have barred the doors of the

59. *Annales de l'Université Populaire Lyonnaise,* No. 1 (1900), 6–7, 11, No. 2 (1901), 4, 10–11, 24–29.

60. *Ibid.,* No. 2 (1901), 31–44, 54–55; *Revue Populaire d'Economie Sociale,* I (1902–1903).

Université populaire to politics, the politics of republican solidarity received a good deal of attention. Exhortations to republican defense remained a tried and tested weapon to mobilize class collaboration and provided the occasion for flights of demagoguery. At a session in March, 1901, Ferdinand Buisson denounced "political jesuitism, economic jesuitism, and [somewhat redundantly] religious jesuitism." He dismissed enemies of class solidarity and of the Republic as purveyors of "caesarist and clerical poisons." Not to be outdone, the secretary-general of the Université populaire, a fast-rising politician named Edouard Herriot, declared war on "tradition and reaction" in the name of "progress and the education of our democracy." But even such inflammatory rhetoric harbored a conservative message: "To those who accuse us of being revolutionaries we reply frankly that a revolution is the punishment visited on a nation that refuses to evolve."[61] *Ancien régime* cultural values, recalling a simpler world of corporate order and hierarchy, may have appeared attractive to an embattled ruling class. But those same values discounted the legitimacy, the propriety, and the necessity of free labor and mobile capital, in a word, the modern world of social production. Thus, the Lyonese bourgeoisie (Catholic to a man) that funded the Université populaire (and later Herriot himself) found no cause for alarm in such anticlerical polemics. Matters of fundamental class interest admitted of no confessional distractions. For capital as well as for labor, *Erst kommt das Essen, dann kommt die Moral.*

Evenings Well Spent: Cours d'adultes and conférences populaires

Universités populaires were not the only weapons in the French bourgeoisie's political arsenal. At the 1895 congress of the Sociétés d'instruction et d'éducation populaire hosted by Jules Siegfried in Le Havre, the assembled reformers, businessmen, and politicians resolved to accelerate the expansion of working-class education beyond the primary years across a broad front. At issue, they said, was not merely a "question of education" but a "national and social

61. *Annales de l'Université Populaire Lyonnaise*, No. 3 (1902), 26–27, 56–63.

question." Adult education had three purposes: to provide for moral and civic indoctrination; to instruct in general culture; and to provide vocational training (*enseignement technique et professionnel*). Although moralization and acculturation, or positive instruction in the work ethic, were closely linked to practical instruction, sometimes in the same program, I will consider them separately. That separation, however, is largely artificial. Political and productive considerations consistently overlapped.[62]

Although the adult education movement did not take off until the 1890s, its origins go back to the Second Empire. By the end of the 1860s more than 31,000 classes for workers existed, serving an estimated 780,000 students. They focused primarily on alphabetization and apparently achieved some success in reducing illiteracy at a time when state schools had not fully taken over the job. The entrepreneurs of upper Alsace, consistent pioneers in paternalism, organized evening schools for their workers in 1864. The Société d'instruction populaire de Mulhouse, backed by the local *société industrielle*, offered courses in reading, writing, elementary calculation, some language training, and industrial design. The students, who ranged in age from sixteen to twenty-five, followed courses in direct correlation to their position in the labor hierarchy. Unskilled and semiskilled workers in the metal, spinning, weaving, and dyeing industries learned reading and writing—but little else. Skilled artisans and white-collar workers studied somewhat more sophisticated subjects.[63]

The Alsatian bourgeoisie exercised tight control over its labor force and thus had few concerns about law and order. No attempt was made to enforce ideological discipline directly. J.-J. Bourcart, a textile manufacturer who financed a class for workers in his town of Guebwiller (and also financed Jean Macé), kept his eye on efficiency and productivity: "A well-trained worker is like a smooth-running machine." Both employers and employees stood to gain from diligent labor: "According to the law of industrial economy . . . the worker's wage is in direct proportion to the quality of his labor. . . .

62. *BMAP* (1895), 103–106.

63. Maurice Gontard, *Les Ecoles primaires de la France bourgeoise* (Paris, n.d.), 189–94; *Bulletin de la Société industrielle de Mulhouse*, XXXIV (1864), 289–300, XXXVI (1866), 353–59, XL (1870), 453–57.

By harnessing the laborer's intelligence we raise the standard and the value of his output; as a result, his wages will increase." Bourcart did not need to explain that profits would increase as well. He also expected a political payoff. Workers ran the school through a committee elected from a list he approved, thus encouraging "solidarity among all classes."[64]

Between 1878 and 1888 the number of nontechnical *cours d'adultes* and of students in attendance dropped precipitously throughout France. In some departments they disappeared altogether. Several government decrees in 1882, 1884, and 1887 encouraging their survival apparently had no effect. Commentaries on these statistics provide no clues about their demise. Two explanations are possible, the second more significant than the first. In the first place, the establishment of a national system of obligatory primary education shifted the burden of teaching basic skills entirely to state schools. Thus adult education as previously conceived lost its *raison d'être*.[65]

Second, social priorities had shifted along with the changing rhythm of the French economy. After an initial spurt during the Second Empire, France's second industrial revolution had begun to move into top gear by the end of the Third Republic's first decade. At the same time and during the subsequent decade the socialist movement, decapitated by the slaughter of the *communards* and then crippled by fratricidal warfare, did not display the sustained militancy that would characterize it in the 1890s. Taking advantage of the labor movement's relative weakness, businessmen and reformers concentrated their educational efforts on vocational training. Courses in technical and vocational instruction flourished and continued in importance through the 1890s while *cours d'adultes* languished, to reappear under the impact of adjusted social priorities. With the revival of the labor and socialist movements and the advent of concentration it was not enough to train workers in industrial skills. Serious efforts at working-class cultural integration required the for-

64. Eugène Véron, *Les Institutions ouvrières de Mulhouse et de ses environs* (Paris, 1866), 333–38; F[17] 12529, AN.

65. *Journal officiel de la République française,* April 7, 1882, July 22, 1884, January 20, 1887; "Situation scolaire des départements," in France, Ministère de l'Instruction publique et des Beaux-arts, *Recueil des monographies pédagogiques publiées à l'occasion de l'exposition universelle de 1889* (4 vols.; Paris, 1889), II, 1–260; BAIP, LIX (1896), 488.

mation of "worthy workers" whose "grasp of the relations of labor and capital [will] serve the cause of harmony."[66] Because those relations had undergone a qualitative change, the French bourgeoisie could not afford to take chances.

Glimpses of the recognition that labor did not live by skill alone, or that "skill" itself had taken on new meaning, appeared before the mid-1890s. The town of Pont-Salomon (Haute-Loire), a metallurgical center, organized adult courses in 1888 for young workers who had interrupted their regular studies to go into the factory. For the members of the Société industrielle of Amiens in 1880, extramural education held high priority: "One cannot emphasize enough the importance of acquainting the elite of our working class with a science that deals with the conditions of life and social progress, that limits the mind to the rational consideration of facts, and that guards against dangerous utopias and ill-considered actions." The "science" in question—political economy—contributed to the production of useful labor while fashioning the mind. The industrialists of Amiens also recognized a kindred spirit when they encountered one. At a session of the Société industrielle in 1885 they took note of one of Emile Cheysson's statistical surveys on wages for the Société d'économie sociale. They drew the proper political conclusions. Cheysson had provided powerful arguments against socialism: "It is to his honor that he works for social peace in exposing the prejudices exploited by the enemies of public order."[67]

The defenders of public order, according to Paul Crouzet, designed adult education to provide an "apprenticeship in social life." Workers, who initially learned moral lessons about solidarity and foresight in the primary school, could not be expected to sustain their concentration in the factory without positive reinforcement. Comments from provincial organizers of adult education consistently repeated that message: "Teachers are trying to develop a *social sense* among adolescents" (Ardèche). Include in civic instruction "notions of social morality" (Ariège). "We must turn workers' atten-

66. *Éducation sociale,* 398.
67. Memorandum from the rector of the Academy of Clermont-Ferrand, January 7, 1888, in F[17] 11850, AN; *Bulletin de la Société industrielle d'Amiens,* XVIII (1880), 73, 362–63, XXIII (1885), 291.

tion toward their social role" (Nièvre). More direct forms of positive reinforcement were available. The adult education organization in Saint-Calais (Sarthe) required students to pay a fee for each course attended. It did this for two reasons: to encourage regular attendance and to "get young people used to the idea of self-sufficiency and thrift by putting aside some of their earnings for a useful expense of the greatest importance." Bourgeois *patronages* played important roles, "more social than strictly educative," by surrounding "working-class adolescents with a moral milieu." A member of the Comité girondin de la Société pour l'éducation sociale in Bordeaux urged the formation of *patronages* for the twin purposes of "calming the worker's restlessness" and "securing social harmony." Associations of former students who banded together to provide moral leadership to their younger peers performed the same function. They constituted a "popular elite" at the head of "the army of labor."[68]

Action followed words in the second half of the nineteenth century's final decade. In 1894 there were roughly 8,000 courses available; by 1897 that number had tripled; and by 1903 nearly 45,000 programs existed. In a curious display of late Victorian morality, young men and women were segregated. Courses available to the latter grew spectacularly as a percentage of the total, perhaps reflecting the increased flow of women into the labor market. Only 11 percent of the courses in 1894 served women; nine years later that figure reached 36 percent. In the Basses-Pyrénées, only 2 of 122 courses offered in 1895 were available to women; by 1899 that number had increased to 182 of 666. Attendance varied tremendously from place to place and from season to season. Edouard Petit estimated that 57 percent of those registered attended regularly. Realities of working-class life sometimes confounded the best-laid bourgeois plans. In the heavily industrialized Pas-de-Calais several villages and towns reported no adult education or had dismantled existing programs. Workers either lived too far from town to travel the road regularly, worked in factories several kilometers from home, or were simply

68. Crouzet, "Etat actuel," 241; *BAIP,* LIX (1896), 490, LX (1896), 40, 51–52; Petit, *Rapport* (1902–1903), 5–6, 43; *Après l'école* (1896), 89; Godefroy Ratton, *Education populaire et sociale* (Bordeaux, 1905), 123; Crouzet, "Etat actuel," 246.

too tired after a day's work to drag themselves to lectures. Nevertheless, by the end of the century nearly all departments had some form of adult education in at least 80 percent of their communes.[69]

Financing for *cours d'adultes* and public lectures depended heavily on local and private subsidies. At no time did the state provide more than a fraction of the funds required for their operation (6 percent in 1903). Nonrenewable state subsidies generally amounted to 200 to 400 francs, except in the case of adult education associations in Paris and in Lyon (coincidentally, the only French cities with prefectures of police). Municipal councils, in most cases dominated by the local bourgeoisie, supplied the lion's share of funds, and it is at least arguable that such sources qualify as "public." *Sociétés industrielles* in Mulhouse, Amiens, Elbeuf, Lille, and Saint-Quentin, chambers of commerce, and the Société de géographie commerciale of Le Havre took up the slack. Industrial firms also lent a hand. In the Pas-de-Calais, for example, the Société houillère de Liéven (a coalmining company) donated 200 francs toward the establishment of evening courses for teenage mineworkers. In Corbeil (Seine-et-Oise), the Feray-Oberkampf textile company sponsored similar courses, mixing subjects of general and political education—history, geography, patriotism—with those of more immediate relevance such as the importance of the textile industry for the national economy.[70]

The best measure of private involvement in adult education is in the number of associations for popular education and associations for social education that appeared during the last decade of the century. These local societies with their businessmen, doctors, lawyers, and teachers exercised complete authority over the organization and content of adult education. I have referred to them above in connection with the foundation of *universités populaires*.[71] Some had been functioning for one or two decades, but the number of new societies grew dramatically in the late 1890s. To these must be added local societies affiliated with the Ligue de l'enseignement, whose *fin-de-siècle*

69. Petit, *Rapport* (1896–97), 11–16, (1902–1903), 54–57; *Exposition 1900*, V, 189; France, Ministère de l'Instruction publique et des Beaux-arts, *Rapport*, 552–64; A. Bançal, *L'Enseignement populaire dans le département des Basses-Pyrénées* (Paris, 1900), 40; F[17] 11919, AN; *Exposition 1900*, "Enseignement et éducation," I, 211.

70. *BMAP* (1895), 102; Petit, *Rapport* (1902–1903), 54–57; F[17] 12526, 11919, 11923, AN; *BAIP*, LIX (1896), 492, LX (1896), 57.

71. Petit, *Rapport* (1902–1903), 25–27.

congresses had been heavily dosed with discussions of social education; more than eight hundred of a total of two thousand had been
formed between 1889 and 1900. Only toward the latter date did these
organizations extend their networks into the towns and even the villages of France. Indeed, those active in the Ligue had publicized
rural adult education for several years previously with the intention
of "turning the youth of the countryside into intelligent workers,
and not place-seekers in towns already swollen with disturbingly
large numbers of *déclassés*."[72]

The content of *cours d'adultes* translated the ideological abstractions of social education into concrete terms. Moral exhortations
not only preached socially determined behavior; they also insisted
on the nobility of labor, the duty to work, and the ethical imperative
to collaborate in the productive process. Morality reduced to the responsibility of the working class to accept, respect, and defend prevailing social relations. Commercy, an industrial town in the Meuse,
had a typical program of studies. It was organized according to a
series of *dictées* (much like primary courses) subscribed under key
words or phrases: "*Labor*: All labor is honorable and useful; the
loafer loses his dignity and ends up as a burden on society. *Order*:
Disorder is a source of trouble and all kinds of misery. *Thrift and
Savings*: Savings assures one's well-being and one's independence; it
furnishes us with resources for times of sickness, unemployment,
and old age. *Respect for Property*: Property is the right of ownership
and of the free disposition of possessions; it is inviolate and sacred.
Solidarity: All men are united in solidarity; the interests of one are
linked to the interests of all . . . we have the duty to prepare the best
future for succeeding generations by labor and association."[73]

A little speech entitled "Labor and Capital" written for general
distribution among *cours d'adultes* took up directly the matter of
class relations. The author, J.-B. Graillet, insisted on the responsibility of workers to conduct themselves with discipline and diligence.
It was in their own interest to do so, given the symbiotic relationship between labor and capital and capital's provision of the means

---

72. Bançal, *L'Enseignement populaire*, 45–109; F¹⁷ 12526, AN; *Exposition 1900*, "Enseignement et éducation," I, 470; *BLFE*, V (1885), 56.

73. *Carnet de résumés de leçons se rapportant à l'éducation sociale avec maximes et plans par
un groupe d'instituteurs de la circonscription de Commercy* (Commercy, 1904), 29–53.

whereby the worker improved his condition, owned property, and accumulated savings. Thus doctrines of class struggle rested on false conceptions regarding social antagonisms and the exploitation of labor. Each person, Graillet insisted, received a wage commensurate with his contribution to the productive process. Hence wages and profits were qualitatively, if not quantitatively, identical. Labor had legitimate claims to the "right to work," whereas claims to the "rights of workers" led inevitably to insurrection, as in 1848. Modern forms of production, far from rendering the worker a slave to capital, had precisely the opposite consequences. The division of labor promoted efficiency, productivity, and cooperation. Rather than wiping out jobs, machinery produced lower prices, increased demand, and created new jobs. Moreover, capital built projects of immense utility and spectacular grandiosity, such as the Suez Canal, and made necessities, such as cotton underwear, less expensive. Finally, Graillet singled out profit-sharing as "one of the easiest and most effective ways to end the antagonism between capital and labor."[74]

Cours d'adultes in a town in the Haute-Saône treated topics such as the rewards of labor, workers' retirement plans, working-class housing, physical and moral hygiene, "our colonies," Madagascar, and the benefits of collaboration and association. Similar courses in the Somme heavily emphasized colonies, as did those in Villeneuve-le-Roi (Seine-et-Oise). In Angoulême, moral lessons were linked to subjects of practical application: hygiene, geography, taxes, railroads, and, once again, colonies. Perhaps the ubiquitous presence of lessons dealing with France's colonial possessions was coincidental; or perhaps it was related to the contemporary international struggle for imperial position. Surely the financial backing for popular lectures on empire supplied by two colonial lobbies, the Comité Dupleix and the Syndicat des explorateurs français, was not inspired by purely philanthropic sentiments. As Edouard Petit explained, "We must acquaint peasants with our foreign holdings." The principal organ for popular adult education, *Après l'école*, did just that. One of its issues featured Henri Hauser reporting on a colonial exposition in Marseille. Hauser waxed lyrical about the economic potential of

74. Graillet, "Le Travail et le capital," 43–48, 109–12.

France's empire. "The era of explorations has passed," he announced; "that of development is now upon us." He noted with particular satisfaction the installation for native workers of French systems of paternalist reform and association in Algeria.[75]

Samples of moral lessons designed for adult education collected for the instruction section of the 1900 Exposition show a consistent pattern. They harped (the only word) on good citizenship, acceptable social behavior, the abuses of alcohol and tobacco, order, and economy, the latter illustrated by a pamphlet titled the *Cahier de Franklin* (*Poor Richard's Almanac?*). "Duties toward the homeland" received a good deal of attention, leavened by the writings of Paul Déroulède—still a favored model despite his flagrantly antisocial political behavior. Although lip service was paid to developing habits of independent thought among young workers and to treating them like "serious and reasonable young adults and not like children," the mode of instruction was relentlessly didactic and insufferably condescending: "It is only by the repetition of the same ideas that an understanding of civic virtues will be slowly assimilated and will neutralize the dangerous influence of the street, the factory, and even the family." (The family, normally considered to be a fortress of order, is here portrayed as a potential source of disorder. This view may help to account for the increased intervention of public authorities in the management of families, as described by Jacques Donzelot.)[76] Moreover, although these lessons routinely celebrated individual initiative and various other nostrums of political economy, they focused most directly on the virtues and the necessity of working-class socialization, association, and collaboration.

Moral lessons such as these bore a striking resemblance to those that filled the pages of primary school readers, confirming the impression that they served chiefly to reinforce existing or forgotten habits. One such reader, reprinted seven times, extolled the nobility of labor and the satisfaction of work well done; described in exquisite detail the uses of industrial raw materials and the operation of factories; and counseled its readers to develop a taste for order,

75. *BAIP*, LVIII (1895), 964–65; F¹⁷ 11923, AN; *Après l'école* (1895), 126–27, (1906–1907), 47–50; Petit, *Rapport* (1896–97), 24.

76. *Exposition 1900*, "Enseignement et éducation," I, 41–43, 199–200; Jacques Donzelot, *La Police des familles* (Paris, 1977), Chap. 3.

thrift, punctuality, and regular work habits. A lesson on civic morality focused on the responsibility of citizens to pay taxes, the most equitable form of distributing civic burdens ("the poor pay the least, the rich the most"). The state used that money, so the explanation went, to "defend us against our enemies" and to build roads, canals, and railways. Therefore, "a tax is the money that we *loan* the government; it returns that money to us *in another form*. That is why each must pay the *exact* amount without *complaint*."[77]

Public lectures, somewhat less structured and less formal variations on the *cours d'adultes*, proliferated at an even more rapid rate than the courses. Edouard Petit estimated that the number of popular lectures grew from over 10,000 in 1895 to over 97,000 by 1897. As with the *cours d'adultes*, little action had occurred on that front before the 1890s. Again, social priorities appear to have been at work. The greatest concentration of public lectures was in the western, northern, and eastern industrial regions: Le Havre, Avesnes, Roubaix, Arras, Lunéville, Montmédy, to name just a few. Unique situations occasionally made for exceptions to this pattern. In the Basses-Pyrénées a landowner named Pierre Tourasse had funded a Société d'éducation et d'instruction populaire in 1885 and left it 100,000 francs at his death. Armed with this sizable sum, the Société spawned a number of rural local societies in the 1890s.[78]

Tourasse's largesse, although exceptional in its magnitude, was not exceptional as a mode of financing public lectures. The local associations for popular education served as conduits for the distribution of funds as did special-interest and parapolitical groups such as colonial and geographic societies. In Paris a series of public lectures on profit sharing and on employer and worker associations benefited from the support of Alfred Thuillier, building contractor and senator. These and other local initiatives did not exist in isolation. Both the Société nationale des conférences populaires and the Société Franklin played important organizing and coordinating roles.[79]

The Société nationale des conférences populaires originated during the Boulanger crisis, when both conservative republicans and so-

77. E. Devinat, *Livre de lecture et de morale* (Paris, 1895), 83–84, 115–18.

78. Petit, *Rapport* (1896–97), 22; *Après l'école* (1896), 570; Bançal, *L'Enseignement populaire*, 41–45.

79. *BLFE*, V (1885), 12–14.

cial liberals (somewhat overreacting) perceived a threat to democracy. Political demagoguery, they believed, fed easily on popular gullibility. An army reserve officer named Guérin-Catelain, a man of strong republican and conservative convictions, launched the Société with the help of a group of businessmen and bureaucrats from the Paris region. His roster of honorary members featured a distinguished complement of politicians, social scientists, reformers, and businessmen: Bourgeois, Buisson, Raymond Poincaré, Gréard, Ferry, Baudrillart, Levasseur, the industrialist Adolphe Bischoffsheim, the banker Edmond Goudchaux, and Jules Siegfried. The Société published and distributed readings for use in mostly rural settings. Subjects ranged from the technical—glassmaking, photography, coalmining—to the politically and morally uplifting—hygiene, La Fontaine's *Fables*, *Nos colonies*, *Sonnets héroïques*, and the Declaration of the Duties of the Citizen framed by the Thermidoreans in 1795. Many of these readings were accompanied by slides. If it accomplished nothing else, the Société introduced the magic lantern into the depths of provincial France.[80]

At the Société's annual meeting in 1893, the inspector-general of primary education sounded the keynote for his colleagues' contribution to social education: "As far as I am concerned, ignorance is a social danger, ignorance is the worst social danger, ignorance is the only social danger." Twelve years later, one commentator who followed the Société's work closely noted its progress in combating ignorance and providing for "the ordinary worker an agreeable diversion from his worries and his daily labor." Its programs were pitched at just the right level "to penetrate the popular consciousness and to lay out in the simplest terms general ideas without trying, by the use of rhetorical tricks or complex discussions, to descend into analytical details which the masses with their simple habits of thought can neither understand nor even follow."[81]

Despite the marvels of the magic lantern and the condescension that its use implied, books by the thousands stocked popular libraries across the country. The organization chiefly responsible for their dissemination was the Société Franklin, founded in 1864 during that

80. *Annuaire de la Société Nationale des Conférences Populaires* (1893), no pagination.
81. *Bulletin Mensuel de la Société Nationale des Conférences Populaires* (1890, 1893, 1906–1907), no pagination; Ratton, *Education populaire et sociale*, 22, 40–42.

first wave of industrialization. By the end of the century it had coordinated the distribution of more than one million volumes. Charles Robert became secretary-general of the Société Franklin at its inception and remained until his death in 1899. In the 1890s Adolphe d'Eichthal, Charles Thierry-Mieg, Bischoffsheim, Albert Gigot, and Jules Siegfried served on its board. Many of the Société Franklin's books found their way to rural or small-town public libraries, which served as social centers and as centers for public lectures as well as public libraries. One of them, the Bibliothèque Henri de Rothschild in the Oise, occupied a "large and luxurious" building donated by the banker. It contained reading rooms, game rooms (chess, *loto*, and dominoes), and a museum of natural history.[82]

The activities of public libraries—urban and rural—varied according to the interests of the local bourgeoisie. The wool manufacturers of Roubaix set up a Bibliothèque populaire d'économie sociale. Organized according to the practical and ideological perspectives of social education, the library contained five areas of documentation: science and morality, cooperation, mutualism, trade-union questions, and social economy. Similarly, a library and discussion groups sponsored by the Comité girondin of the Société pour l'éducation sociale concentrated on colonies, colonial administration, and geography. They were designed to encourage young workers to seek their fortunes in the "magnificent French colonial empire."[83]

Most of the public libraries had heterogeneous collections that mixed the sacred and the profane: books on patriotism, French history, and French classics stood side by side with those dealing with steam engines, the proper application of chemical fertilizers, and the general principles of agriculture.[84] Libraries in the one department for which we have extensive documentation, the Drôme, exhibited just such a mixture and some curiosities. Public libraries in several strictly rural communes carried an inordinate number of books on

82. *EF*, April 17, 1864, quoted in *Bulletin Mensuel de la Société Pour l'Amélioration et l'Encouragement des Publications Populaires,* in F^{1a} 632, AN; *Bulletin de la Société Franklin* (1894), viii, 76.

83. Ratton, *Education populaire et sociale,* 141–45, 257–58.

84. The Bibliothèque des écoles de fabriques in the Seine-et-Oise stocked volumes of technical popularization (*Les Merveilles de la chimie, Les Chemins de fer, La Vapeur, L'Hydraulique*), geography, colonial exploration, and moral uplift (*Histoire des quatre ouvriers anglais d'après Samuel Smiles*), in F^{12} 4766, AN.

colonies. But such curiosities may have been more apparent than real if "rural France, thanks to the work of social educators," was to understand "the principles of reason, equity, and solidarity." According to contemporary conventional wisdom, French colonial enterprise realized all those civic virtues. More predictably, the lignite-mining town of Nyons' Bibliothèque populaire de l'union ouvrière self-consciously stocked materials for the moral elevation of the "laboring classes," and the *patrons* of the library in Romans donated to the local Bourse du travail *La Solution française de la question du Maroc* and an edition of Gambetta's selected speeches. The "tribune of the people" was, as I have noted elsewhere, an early apostle of class collaboration.[85]

The tendency in *cours d'adultes* and public lectures to reduce the ideological principles of social education to their simplest terms was the deliberate choice of a bourgeoisie that simultaneously feared and disdained working-class political consciousness while requiring its collaboration in the international "economic warfare" of the *fin-de-siècle* and thus attempted to reproduce bourgeois cultural values. Alfred Foullié put it succinctly: "Political economy, aside from its applications to industry, commerce, and finance, alone is able to prevent the adolescent from falling prey to utopian fantasies; it explains the real relations between labor and capital. Everyone must study economic and social questions, because the only way to establish domestic peace will be to reduce misery and to increase, with the general wealth, the general welfare." The solution to the social question lay in the transformation of consciousness, in "the introduction and the development of the true principles of social economy," without which "wrongheaded fanaticism, revolutionary fantasies, and absolutely false conceptions about life, society, and the state" would remain embedded in "working-class philosophy."[86]

The campaign to turn working-class political consciousness onto the path of association and collaboration did not mark the limits of social education. Capital required steady, skilled, and disciplined hands as well as obedient heads. Efficiency and productivity in the workplace also had their political dimension.

---

85. Ratton, *Education populaire et sociale*, 99; Drôme: Bibliothèques populaires libres, in F¹⁷ 13050, AN.

86. *Après l'école* (1906–1907), 244; Fouillée, *L'Enseignement*, 294.

VII
Accumulating Mental Capital
Industrial Education

Emile Cheysson observed in a course on labor relations delivered to apprentice social managers at the Ecole libre des sciences politiques that "the growth of productivity is in itself a force for moral education."[1] Cheysson's point was simple: when the system delivers the goods, the chances that social peace will reign are greater than under conditions of adversity. Although not a profound observation—nor even necessarily accurate (good times for some could be bad times for others)—his message does reflect the importance assigned by reformers and managers to efficient and productive labor, without which the system could not be expected to deliver the goods. Businessmen, of course, had always known this and therefore had long been interested in the technical training of workers. In the late nineteenth century, however, a broader perspective on the purposes and goals of industrial education appeared.

Industrial education not only provided French business with the means to promote productivity and efficiency; it also was designed to link ideological reproduction to the mundane routines of daily labor. The workplace and its ancillary installations for vocational training became another setting for social education. The acquisition and application of industrial skills were to contribute to the worker's social consciousness as an indispensable partner with capital; he was to develop a spirit of association with capital instead of a

1. Emile Cheysson, "Cours d'économie politique," *Journal des Economistes,* 4th ser., XX (1882), 363.

fatalistic acquiescence in his prescribed destiny as simply a cog in a gear. Accordingly, a "moral" consideration in Charles Gide's opinion, industrial education included subjects beyond those required to sharpen specific skills, so as to provide an "antidote to the division of labor." This did not mean, Gide pointed out, that workers should be trained to comprehend the overall productive process. Just the opposite; the purpose of industrial education was to develop specific and generally unrelated skills. For political rather than practical reasons, it became all the more necessary for the worker "to reproduce in his imagination the complete process to which he contributes."[2]

Social priorities, as I suggested in the preceding chapter, partially dictated the timing of the installation of programs for industrial education. To these must be added economic considerations. During the 1880s French industry suffered from the effects of the Great Depression, manifested in a falling rate of both profit and prices. Yet investment in new capital goods continued, in France as elsewhere, spurred by exceptionally low interest rates, expectations of burgeoning demand, and the availability of new technologies. Despite these potentially favorable prospects we may still wonder why businessmen undertook capital expansion at a time when the rate of return on capital was depressed. There are two reasons. First, international competition forced them to take such a course. Second, rates of return on cheap new capital could offset low rates on the old if production became more efficient and thereby less costly. This second consideration brings us to labor. Cost-cutting on the labor front can take two forms: downward pressure on wages and/or increased productivity relative to fixed or even slightly rising wages. (During a cycle of declining prices real wages may go up without a commensurate increase in money wages.) Whereas the former entailed political risks, the latter promised abundant dividends should workers be properly trained and distributed along strategic points in the productive process. The development of up-to-date capital goods, geared primarily to sustaining French industry's competitive position in the world market, could not produce the desired benefits unless efficiently applied to holding down the unit labor cost of output.

2. *Exposition 1900*, V, 186–87.

Hence, in the words of one commentator, the development of technical education was "urgent."[3] Moreover, as an extra bonus to capital, the costs of such education—never very high—devolved upon society as a whole.

Political factors relating directly to association and collaboration also entered into the calculations behind the push for industrial education. From Saint-Quentin, a center of textile manufacturing and sugarbeet refining, came the word that technical education, among other things, "brings together in a community of reciprocal and inseparable interests the two instruments of well-being: the boss and the worker"—in other words, solidarity on the shop floor. For the patrons of the Société d'enseignement professionnel de Lyon, technical training not only encouraged habits of precise manual manipulations and instructed workers in the general application of machinery but functioned as an exercise in "discipline and civic education." The Société industrielle of Elbeuf launched a program in technical education for the city's workers with the stated purpose of furthering "progress in commerce and in industry," encouraging the sciences and technology, and developing "the moral interests of the nation." And the Association polytechnique of the Pyrénées-Orientales created apprentice courses for both sexes in the hope of preventing "young men and women freshly emerged from primary school from falling into dangerous habits of idleness."[4] With the introduction of manual training into the primary curriculum in the 1880s, the risk that French working-class youth would fall into such dangerous habits was considerably reduced. It may seem odd that such a modest exercise as manual training partially sprang from political and ideo-

3. Jean Bouvier, François Furet, and Marcel Gillet, *Le Mouvement du profit en France au xix siècle* (Paris, 1965), 44 and appendixes; David Landes, *The Unbound Prometheus* (Cambridge, 1969), Chap. 5; Société industrielle de Saint-Quentin et de l'Aisne, *Rapport sur l'enseignement professionnel* (Saint-Quentin, 1885), 8, in F¹⁷ 11706, AN; *Exposition 1900*, V, 184–85; *BSES*, III (1903), 27; Eugène Buhan, *De la création d'une école d'apprentissage à Bordeaux* (Bordeaux, 1885), 3–6; W. Arthur Lewis, *Growth and Fluctuations, 1870–1913* (London, 1978), 47.

4. Société industrielle de Saint-Quentin et de l'Aisne, *Procès-verbaux* (Saint-Quentin, 1882), 27, in F¹⁷ 11706, AN; *Après l'Ecole* (1896), 381; Paul Melon, *L'Enseignement supérieur et l'enseignement technique en France* (Paris, 1893), 320; *Exposition 1900*, "Enseignement et éducation," Vol. VI, Pt. 1, p. 283.

logical considerations. But, as in other areas of social reform, that was indeed the case.

Busy Hands: Gustave Salicis and the Ideology of Manual Training

At ceremonies marking the opening of the Ecole nationale d'enseignement professionnel in Vierzon (Isère) in 1883, the president of the council of ministers and minister of education, Jules Ferry, insisted that "the National School . . . must be above all the school of labor. . . . Today's primary school is fundamentally vocational, which defines its purpose to prepare the child to become a laborer, the prescribed future of the overwhelming majority of French citizens." Never inclined to mince words, Ferry expressed in characteristically blunt language the conventional wisdom of the French political classes and industrial bourgeoisie: those destined to labor in the service of national production must be trained in rudimentary manual skills at the earliest possible age. Such training, preparatory to more advanced technical instruction for some, belonged in the primary school, where the progeny of workers and farmers normally began and ended their formal education.[5]

Two legislative actions laid the foundations for manual training integral to and associated with the primary school. The first, a law of December, 1880, provided for the establishment of manual-training schools designed "to develop among young people destined for manual vocations the necessary dexterity" to equip them for productive labor. Execution of the bill's provisions, however, did not follow immediately upon promulgation. It seems that the largely privately financed apprentice schools and vocational schools (the subject of the following section) absorbed the functions for which those schools had been projected. A second law, in March, 1882, established the principle of obligatory manual training in all public primary schools. This legislation, according to Gustave Salicis—who inspired it—sig-

5. Speech delivered on May 3, 1883, quoted in Gabriel Compayré, *Etudes sur l'enseignement et sur l'éducation* (Paris, 1891), 148; Gustave Salicis, *Enseignement du travail manuel* . (Paris, 1889), 17.

nified the general consensus that labor was "at once the wellspring of morality and the foundation of national prosperity." Manual training's function was to inspire a "taste for manual labor" and develop eye-hand coordination—"those two fundamental tools for work in every sort of industry." It also facilitated a process of selection by defining and encouraging the "aptitudes of children" before channeling them into appropriate modes of technical instruction. By the end of the century, after some false starts because of the failure of the Ministry of Education to appropriate sufficient funds for specialized teachers, manual training for both sexes had been fully integrated into the primary program.[6]

Salicis, manual training's chief architect and advocate, had close connections to both the social economists and solidarist reformers. In the late 1890s, he was associated with the Musée social. Following implementation of the 1882 law, Salicis took on the task of organizing a teachers' college to train those teachers necessary to make the program work. His contributions earned him the ultimate recognition: a workshop attached to a primary school in Montluçon (Allier) named in his honor. That manual-training school had been founded with the moral and financial support of the republican senator Joseph Chantemille, a wealthy wholesaler from Montluçon.[7]

Salicis had firm opinions about manual training, to which he brought by now familiar ideological baggage. Because he played the central role in the planning and execution of manual training programs, his views bear quoting at length:

> We have in our midst four million children who, in the immediate future, will be forced by inexorable necessity to earn their sustenance by wage labor, who will be engaged in a harsh daily struggle to master the soil, stone, wood,

6. Ferdinand Buisson, *L'Enseignement primaire et supérieur en France* (Paris, 1887), 16; Félix Martel and Georges Ferrand, "Ecoles primaires supérieures, écoles d'apprentissage et écoles nationales professionnelles," in France, Ministère de l'Instruction publique et des Beaux-Arts, *Recueil des monographies pédagogiques publiées à l'occasion de l'Exposition universelle de 1889* (4 vols.; Paris, 1889), II, 279; *BLFE,* V (1885), 36–37, VI (1886), 64; Salicis, *Enseignement,* 14; *Congrès international de l'enseignement technique commercial et industriel, tenu à Bordeaux, 16–21 septembre 1895* (Bordeaux, 1895), 11; F[17] 11630, AN.

7. Gustave Salicis, "Enseignement du travail manuel," Musée Pédagogique, *Mémoires et documents scolaires,* 2nd ser., No. 33, 54; Buisson, *L'Enseignement primaire,* 15; *BLFE,* V (1885), 218; Gustave Vapereau, *Dictionnaire biographique des contemporains* (4 vols.; Paris, 1890), I, 315.

metals, all raw materials; who will have to shape, mold, and transform those materials with their own hands; and who for ten years, from age three to thirteen . . . will barely have become acquainted with their fathers' tools or their mother's needles! What can we expect of the best of them? The ability to read, more or less write, barely do sums, recite by rote. . . . Many will have learned a few phrases about Neustria and Austrasia, the consequences of the battle of Testry, and the capitulary of Kiersy s/ Oise. . . . But none will have the slightest notion of the labors to which they devote their entire life.[8]

Obviously, the habits ingrained by political economy died hard.

Salicis' iron law of vocational determinism derived from a conception of unalterable class relations that coincided with the conventional wisdom of educational and other social reformers. What was the primary school, after all, if not the training ground for future workers and soldiers? Forty years later that wisdom still prevailed. Alexis Léaud and Emile Glay, in their authoritative survey of primary education, pronounced manual labor training in primary schools "logical" and "natural" because "it constitutes the destiny of three-quarters of our students." Not content to make the purely practical case for manual training, Salicis and others raised political considerations. Good workers—which is to say reliable workers— had become, it was claimed, increasingly rare because of working-class illusions about the prospects for mobility. These illusions, reinforced by a generalized distaste for manual labor, produced a growing population of *déclassés*, parasitic on society and constituting a reservoir of "nuisances" and troublemakers. In contrast, the properly educated "manual laborer, having been cured of the contagious inclination to idleness, will be won over to morality and consequently to moderation."[9]

Moral values, however, always seemed to be traded in the form of utilitarian currency. Economic considerations, especially those related to the global position of French production, remained important. Salicis went so far as to insist that manual training was an essen-

8. Compayré, *Etudes,* 150–51.

9. Henri Bourgeois, *Etude sur l'enseignement technique professionnel dans les écoles primaires* (Chartres, 1891), 29; Alexis Léaud and Emile Glay, *L'Ecole primaire en France* (Paris, 1934), 178; "Le Travail manuel dans l'éducation des enfants," *RS,* XXXIV (1897), 839–40; Gustave Salicis, "L'Enseignement du travail manuel," France, Ministère de l'Instruction publique et des Beaux-Arts, *Recueil des monographies,* IV, 397.

tial "precondition for economic success in international markets." He claimed that if French industry reduced its labor costs in relation to productivity by five centimes per day, manual training would pay for itself. (How he arrived at that number is anyone's guess.) Foreigners, went another argument, prepared workers for technical training by introducing the habits of manual labor in the first years of primary education. French workers too often failed to take advantage of classes for apprentices and *cours d'adultes*. No one not predisposed to developing manual skills could be expected to learn anything after a hard day's work. French colonies also stood to gain from manual training. As the *Réforme Sociale* pointed out, young people sent to the colonies "are incapable of handling difficult tasks, because they do not know how to work. . . . Colonization requires skillful, intelligent workers of long standing, formed, at the earliest age, by manual labor."[10]

The plans for manual training programs drawn up by Salicis reveal something more than either a reformer's zeal for social improvement or a bureaucrat's mania for system and order. "Let us recall," he wrote in a report on manual training for the 1889 Exposition, "that experimental psychology has long since determined that *habits become second nature*." Thus manual training shaped not only skills and regular habits but also the inner life of those subject to its discipline. Mechanical integration produced cultural integration. Where Emile Cheysson invoked social science to buttress a system of social engineering, Salicis enlisted the psychological science of behavioral conditioning to the same purpose. Science, in both cases, served as handmaiden to class-determined social politics.[11]

Salicis, if anything, applied the principles of social engineering more rigorously than did Cheysson, Robert, the solidarists, and other architects of corporate reform. In a remarkable document, entitled "Organisation complète de l'enseignement national," he explained how education should replicate predetermined class positions, thereby reinforcing them. The plan divided the entire popu-

10. Salicis, "L'Enseignement," IV, 397; Salicis, *Enseignement,* 14; A. Delvaille, *Le Travail manuel à l'école* (Bayonne, 1884), 6; "Le Travail manuel dans l'éducation des enfants," 844.

11. Salicis, "L'Enseignement," IV, 395–96.

lation into the leisure class and the working class. At no point, beginning at age three, did the twain meet. The former's educational system was firmly in place and required little adjustment. Not so in the case of the latter, for which Salicis outlined a comprehensive program. According to his scheme, every working-class child between the ages of three and fifteen would receive routine elementary education laced with heavy doses of manual training. Upon leaving primary school, future workers would be obliged to attend four years of evening courses to sharpen their work habits. (Postprimary industrial education, as we will see in the following section, generally followed this pattern.) The only distinctions made at this level were between those directed toward unskilled and skilled labor; but in both instances the form of education itself became a central fact in the selection process. Education continued until the age of twenty-one for elite workers, who learned elements of social economy, hygiene, and geography in more evening schools. What gave Salicis' plan coherence was a relentless process of political conditioning: "*Morality*, that is to say the idea, the necessity, the regimen of *duty*, must be taught systematically, in graduated sequences, and uncluttered with fuzzy notions [*sans métaphysique*] from kindergarten forward." All of this, Salicis insisted, met the social demands imposed by what he called (perhaps in an unconscious parody of Comte) the "empirical period" in the universal history of labor, when the "anarchy" of free labor submitted to the discipline of social managers.[12] It is hard to imagine a more blatant—and brutal—example of the tyranny of determinist psychology in the service of a class-bound ideology.

In practice, manual training at the primary level involved the simple manipulation of objects, presumably in the conviction that by fine tuning eye-hand coordination one produced obedient and disciplined minds. Children who underwent this regimen—and few could escape—went through graded programs that began with simple exercises in paper cutouts and proceeded through modeling, woodworking, fancy iron work, metal grinding, and a variety of other simple skills. By 1889, Salicis' ambitions for a nationwide net-

12. *Ibid.*, IV, 387; *Enseignement primaire et apprentissage* (Paris, 1885), 162–63.

work of manual training *ateliers* attached to primary schools had not yet materialized, and those that did exist frequently were poorly equipped. Nevertheless, in several industrial regions such as the Loire, the Haute-Loire, the Nièvre, and the Nord combined public and private resources produced well-outfitted facilities. Elsewhere, students spent their days off from school in workshops and factories, where, "under controlled conditions and stimulated by a modest wage," they learned to work up materials and become habituated to disciplined labor.[13]

Manual training for both industrial and agricultural labor also began to appear at the level of the Ecole primaire supérieure (EPS). As noted in Chapter VI, the EPS had been designed to extend elementary education for that part of the working-class population that was expected to assume highly skilled or—less frequently—supervisory positions and whose social discipline required instruction in the "fundamental laws of solidarity." Although the original curriculum, formulated during the mid-1880s, did not include exercises in manual labor, by the end of the decade *ateliers* attached to the EPS had become relatively common throughout the French public school system.[14] They neither displaced nor superseded the largely privately funded apprentice schools and vocational schools. Rather, the EPS broadened the pool from which an aristocracy of labor was drawn. But with its combination of manual training and social conditioning, the EPS had no monopoly on practical instruction encased within an ideological carapace, as the case of Charles Somasco demonstrates.

Somasco, owner of a large machinery works in Creil (Oise), set up a school for manual labor on the grounds of his factory. It was frequently cited as a model of its kind. Although the school did not operate strictly as an apprentice school, it recruited from among working-class youngsters who had earned primary school certificates, signifying six years of satisfactory diligence. Thus it served as something of a halfway house between elementary education and

13. Salicis, "L'Enseignement," IV, 404–408, 419–52; *Education sociale,* 191.

14. François Simiand, "De l'enseignement des sciences sociales à l'école primaire," *Premier congrès de l'enseignement des sciences sociales* (Paris, 1901), 169; Salicis, "L'Enseignement," IV, 419–52.

full-time work in his plant or those of others in the immediate region. The Ecole Somasco, as educational reformers familiarly referred to it, provided a social education as well as one in the development of manual skills. Indeed, the former took clear precedence. Accordingly, Somasco concentrated the school's efforts on instilling in future workers respect for manual labor and enthusiasm for the factory. Through close surveillance of the students' progress, he could identify those whose moral development and social attitudes recommended them for responsible tasks on the shop floor. The school, in other words, aimed to shape elite workers whose exemplary behavior would provide a model for their comrades and, not incidentally, who would act as the eyes and ears of the boss. Above all, the Ecole Somasco taught solidarity, dedication to work, and social discipline; its atmosphere and design replicated that of a workshop; its students trained "to become accustomed to a life of labor, made to understand that because their future lay in the collective life of the factories where they will spend a part of their existence, they must view them as sanctuaries of labor and maintain among themselves relationships of mutual respect and brotherhood."[15]

Labor within the productive process—ordinarily simply a matter of routinized mechanical procedures—turned into an active collaboration engaging the head and heart as well as the hands. Manual training was the initial phase in the development of working-class moral and social consciousness. Industrial and technical education constituted the next and, for most, the final phase in instruction as to how their world worked.

Work and Study: Schools for Production

A government report on the state of technical education drawn up by Henri Tresca in 1885 offered for it the following justification: "In these times a nation's power is measured by its industry, as previously by its military establishment, and nations have recognized that technical education has become a necessity." Twenty years later, the principal organ of solidarism echoed Tresca's sentiments. It, too,

15. *Exposition 1900*, "Enseignement et éducation," Vol. VI, Pt. 1, pp. 229–34.

placed the "interests of national production" at the highest level of priority and argued that the working-class vocational school served the cause of solidarity by "releasing employers from their problems and sparing workers their ordeals." Despite their delphic rhetoric about "problems" and "ordeals" (strikes? exploitation?), the solidarists' point is clear: workers and employers shared a common, national interest in industrial education that superseded class differences. Education reformers expressed similar sentiments and concerns. The notables of the Ligue de l'enseignement were alarmed that "foreigners have launched a war of production against us. . . . Monsieur Jacques Siegfried has cited the statistics conveying that depressing news." Industry required fully formed workers, and for that purpose apprenticeship in the workplace no longer sufficed.[16]

Apprenticeship, in the form of on-the-job-training, originated in the small workshop. The system could not be transferred to large-scale industry for reasons of both efficiency and politics. Industrial concentration had destroyed the "entente" between workers and employers that had formed the basis for apprenticeship. Moreover, too many employers put selfish interests before those of their class, to say nothing of the nation, by exploiting their apprentices by forcing them to undertake all sorts of tasks without regard for their need to learn a productive skill. In the opinion of the president of the Comité de patronage des apprentis de la Gironde, speaking at the second Congrès d'éducation sociale, employers who substituted low-paid apprentices for qualified workers who would command higher wages stood guilty of "stupid stinginess."[17] Employers who closely measured short-term costs at the expense of long-term gains frequently were reluctant to allocate labor time and machinery for the purpose of instruction. Furthermore, trade unions allegedly resisted expanded apprenticeship for the very sensible reason that it escaped their control and undercut their bargaining position by flooding the labor market. There was, however, a more compelling reason to abandon apprenticeship and locate industrial education in a setting

16. Henri Tresca, *Rapport sur l'organisation de l'enseignement technique* (Paris, 1885), 5; *RSS* (1904–1905), 99; *BLFE*, VI (1886), 420–28.

17. Buhan, *De la création d'une école d'apprentissage*, 9–10; *Bulletin de la Société industrielle d'Amiens*, XXI (1883), 204; F. Pech, "L'Apprenti: Ce qu'il est trop souvent, ce qu'il devrait être," *Deuxième congrès de l'éducation sociale* (Bordeaux, 1908).

separate from the workplace. For impressionable and unprepared youths, the factory atmosphere held great dangers and unavoidable temptations, "offering the child unhealthy moral examples and habits of work . . . . deplorable consequences, not only for the moral level of the working classes, but also for their material condition and the economic position of the entire nation." [18]

Charles Gide agreed—in part. Technical instruction situated apart from the workplace insulated young men and women against "dangerous associations" and "coarse talk." Also, no factory school was equipped to offer training in specific skills and in more general technical subjects. Yet Gide raised another consideration about the rigid separation of work and study: "We know from experience that one does not learn a manual skill properly and especially one does not learn to enjoy it" unless one entered the labor force directly upon ending the period of instruction. Too many young workers disdained manual labor and expected to become foremen. Instead, they swelled the ranks of the *déclassés*. The problem divided into three components: first, to separate the place of study from the place of work while maintaining a steady flow of workers from one to the other; second, to provide for gradations within the working class, that is, to establish hierarchies of industrial education corresponding to the levels of skillful worker, foreman, and production boss; and third, on the ideological level, to link technical training to values and behavior appropriate to capitalist production. None of this directly involved, as we shall see, the appropriation of the worker's knowledge by the employer. Scientific management lay at least another decade ahead. Rather, industrial education formed skills among those who had none and introduced to those possessed of skills a more general knowledge of the productive process, so as to equip them to serve as noncommissioned officers in the army of labor. [19]

Entrepreneurs and the municipal governments of industrial towns, to some degree prompted by legislation, took the lead. More and more companies, and the *sociétés industrielles* and chambers of com-

18. *Bulletin de la Société industrielle du Nord* (1889), 81; Buhan, *De la création d'une école d'apprentissage*, 11.

19. *Exposition 1900*, V, 186–87; *Bulletin mensuel du commerce et de l'industrie* (1906), 7–8; Aimée Moutet, "Les Origines du système Taylor en France: Le point de vue patronal," *Mouvement Social*, No. 93 (1975), 15–50; Tresca, *Rapport*, 44.

merce that crystallized their interests, recognized that "for big business the well-equipped industrial school makes the most sense; because all the work can be directed toward the single purpose of developing vocational skills." A further advantage was "the positive moral environment inherent in a school." Legislation passed in late 1880, following a parliamentary report describing the woeful state of technical education, led to the establishment of several state-sponsored full-time vocational schools and apprentice schools. A typical installation was that of Armentières (Nord), which offered courses geared toward serving that city's linen-sheeting industry and its machine shops. Students in this *école mixte* (boys and girls together, which was unusual) also worked several hours daily in factories. Despite this state initiative and because of a bureaucratic logjam in the Ministry of Education (responsibility for industrial education was to be transferred to the Ministry of Commerce in 1892), few publicly supported schools of this type appeared. Two dozen schools and *cours publics* organized by municipalities and *sociétés industrielles* in Saint-Quentin, Lyon, Elbeuf, Roubaix, Nantes, Lille, and elsewhere did receive modest subsidies from the Ministry of Commerce. Nevertheless, initiatives and operations remained in private hands, a state of affairs validated by a law of November 2, 1892, requiring every department to set up a supervisory committee composed of businessmen to oversee apprentice education.[20] This arrangement made eminent sense if only because employers in France's industrial centers required workers armed with a variety of skills, whose training would be ill-served by rules imposed from above. Moreover, as I have argued throughout, the French bourgeoisie had a firm grasp of both the practical and the ideological functions of education.

Predictably, technical education received its most powerful impulse in areas of intense industrial and commercial activity. Nowhere did the rule hold truer than for Lyon, whose bourgeoisie organized the Société d'enseignement professionnel du Rhône in 1864. By the mid-1880s, the Société enrolled eight thousand students in dozens of evening courses devoted mostly to the various skills required by the

20. *Bulletin de la Société industrielle du Nord* (1889), 81; *Exposition 1889*, I, 295–96. Melon, *L'Enseignement supérieur*, 294; Jean-Baptiste Paquier, *L'Enseignement professionnel en France* (Paris, 1908), 68–74; Tresca, *Rapport*, 5–19, 47–50; Pech, "L'Apprenti," 8.

silk industry, recently emerged from its artisanal to its industrial stage, and its ancillary machine shops. Many instructors were former students who had risen to the level of foreman or plant supervisor. They considered themselves to be engaged in a mission of social education, which "popularized the principles of solidarity by the example and the practical application of technical knowledge." This approach reinforced the Société's stated commitment to the primacy of private initiative in the educational enterprise by providing "a terrain on which the well-off and those who aspire to becoming well-off could meet."[21]

In keeping with the spirit of private initiative, the Société drew 50 percent of its capital from individual contributions, 33 percent from the city and the chamber of commerce, and 17 percent from the state. A registration fee of 3 francs per semester was required of all students. The imposition of a fee had less to do with fiscal exigencies than with moral considerations: "Those who have paid generally apply themselves diligently and work at their courses. Moreover, the modest fee encourages their commitment to the entire project and preserves their dignity, as it rules out any suggestion of charity." The message, appropriate to a bourgeois enterprise, was clear: there is no free lunch, or at least none worth consuming. And bourgeois enterprise it was. Founded by the silk merchant and banker François Arlès-Dufour, the Société's officers and biggest backers included several presidents of the Lyon chamber of commerce; numerous local industrialists; one of the founders of the Crédit lyonnais, Henri Germain; the managing director of the Compagnie du gaz de Lyon, Joseph Ançel; Auguste Isaac; and Edouard Aynard. The Société's statutes listed four honorary members: Jules Simon, Charles Robert, Victor Duruy, and Emile Levasseur.[22]

During the second half of the 1880s 30 percent fewer students were enrolled in the Société's programs than a few years earlier. According to its own testimony and that of the *rapporteur* on industrial

21. *Exposition 1889,* "Enseignement et éducation," I, 677; Léon Say, *Exposition universelle de 1889, Groupe d'Economie sociale: Rapport général* (Paris, 1891), 43–45; *Exposition 1889,* I, 228; *Annuaire de la Société d'enseignement professionnel du Rhône* (Roanne, 1879), 29, in F[17] 12541, AN.

22. F[17] 11706, AN; *Exposition 1889,* "Enseignement et éducation," I, 678–79; *Annuaire,* 7–22, in F[17] 12541, AN.

education for the 1889 Exposition, this decline reflected the Société's strength, not its weakness. The reasons confirm my speculations in the preceding chapter, for it turns out that the number of elementary courses in grammar and arithmetic declined but those in technical subjects increased. The establishment of universal primary education and a consequent sharp drop in illiteracy accounted for this change. Once the generation of inadequately schooled older workers passed from the scene, the Société could shift more of its resources to the technical education of young workers. According to the same accounts, the Société's efforts paid abundant practical and political dividends. Workers became more mobile, and a labor aristocracy was forming. A "multitude of workers became supervisors or foremen," a true "elite" that boosted the city's economy and its industry's ambitions to maximize productivity. Moreover, simply bringing together "thousands of young people" in the evening proved to be "a useful enterprise" because it encouraged them "to work, instead of doing nothing or getting into trouble," to seek to "improve themselves through education" rather than embracing "dangerous utopias as a means of improving their condition." Finally, and most important from a "moral" perspective, the Lyonese working class learned "habits of order and discipline." Even, or perhaps especially, men of skill—the cadres from which working-class militants traditionally came—required strong doses of "order and discipline."[23]

The textile factory owners of Saint-Quentin pursued industrial education for the city's and the region's workers with equal energy. External pressures, in the form of lower tariffs on cotton goods and competition from Lille and the Vosges, forced them to develop new products and to retool. Their efforts bore fruit. By the end of the 1880s Saint-Quentin had become the center of a flourishing muslin-sheeting industry and beet-sugar refining, which would not have happened without the infusion of cadres of skilled workers, foremen, and commercial employees. The region's Société industrielle played the key role in the formation of those cadres during the 1880s.[24]

23. *Annuaire*, 64, in F^{17} 12541, AN; *Exposition 1889*, "Enseignement et éducation," I, 678, 680; *Après l'Ecole* (1896), 312.

24. Michael Smith, *Tariff Reform in France, 1860–1900* (Ithaca, N.Y., 1980), 226; Société industrielle de Saint-Quentin et de l'Aisne, *Rapport sur l'enseignement professionnel* (Saint-Quentin, 1885), 26–36, in F^{17} 11706, AN.

The obsolescence of apprenticeship in the workplace provided the initial motivation for the Société industrielle's efforts. Labor, unshackled from the restraints of preindustrial corporations, floated aimlessly from industry to industry in a state of demoralization. Both employers and workers paid a heavy price: the former in their inability to count on a stable and productive work force, the latter in their lack of discipline and material security. The challenge of industrial education, as the members of the Société industrielle saw it, was to transform the worker from a rootless factory hand into one who "rises above his daily task" as he "learns to love his work." Taking as its motto "self-help" (rendered in the original English), the Société's programs for industrial education combined "serious practical training" in the various productive processes with the "moral improvement" of workers, carried out through studies of political economy, the wage system, and strikes. Saint-Quentin's vocational school received students when they left primary school at age thirteen. It provided three years of free education and ran on a substantial annual budget of 150,000 francs, 60 percent of which came from the Société industrielle and other private sources. Thus handsomely endowed, Saint-Quentin's industrial school was situated in a large building that housed not only classrooms and model *ateliers* but a library and conference hall. Courses, aside from those designed for "moral improvement," included instruction in the operation of textile machinery, boilermaking, furniture construction (another of the city's industries), machinery mounting and construction, and industrial design. Each course was supplemented by long hours (as much as six per day) devoted to manual labor. The Société industrielle also established an apprentice school to train workers from the city's rural hinterland into which its industries had spread. Also a three-year program drawing from the same age cohort, that school incorporated into its routine six hours of daily labor in factories and workshops.[25]

Graduates of these schools did not lack for work nor did they fail to live up to expectations, at least according to the testimony of the

25. Société industrielle de Saint-Quentin et de l'Aisne, *Rapport*, 14; *Self-Help* (Saint-Quentin, 1882); Ecole professionnelle de Saint-Quentin, in F^{17} 11706, AN; *Exposition 1889*, "Enseignement et éducation," Vol. VI, Pt. 1, pp. 274–77, I, 672; Melon, *L'Enseignement supérieur*, 325.

Société industrielle. Trained in specific productive skills, these workers "were placed in various industries according to their capabilities" and reportedly "gave their employers complete satisfaction," both in their dedication to productive labor and in their personal comportment. Efficiency, measured in political as well as in productive terms, remained an important consideration. These apprentices "certainly will turn into elite workers and then excellent foremen . . . acquainted with the latest productive techniques" and able to transmit the "employer's orders in the most favorable manner." Even broader horizons opened up. Once tested on the job, the foreman "may then stand in for the boss himself in supervising certain aspects of the overall operations of the plant. The worker's position will improve proportionally; and the boss will lose nothing, neither with regard to the quality and the speed with which the work is accomplished, nor with regard to that certain peace of mind indispensable for anyone running a large establishment." [26]

The several dozen active members of the Société industrielle of Amiens (Somme) harbored practical and political preoccupations similar to those of their counterparts in Saint-Quentin. Founded in 1861, the Société took as its main task the promotion of the interests of the region's textile industries through a comprehensive program of workers' education. Its statutes proclaimed its intention to "strengthen the working class's respect for labor, thrift, and education." To that end the Société financed a series of free technical courses inaugurated in the mid-1860s. By the 1880s they were housed in a specially constructed building containing workshops, a library, a smoking room, and an industrial and commercial museum. The courses, taught during the evening, ranged over a wide variety of subjects, not all of them technical but clearly targeted to the region's business interests. In addition to textiles (wool, linen, and cotton), which employed 36,000 workers mostly in Amiens and Abbeville, those interests included metallurgy, centered in Amiens and occupying 6,400 workers, and chemicals—chiefly in dye workers in Amiens—to service the production of printed cloth. [27]

26. Société industrielle de Saint-Quentin et de l'Aisne, *Statutes,* in F¹⁷ 11706, AN.

27. *Exposition 1889,* "Enseignement et éducation," I, 719–20; Edouard Petit, *Rapport sur l'éducation populaire* (Paris, 1896–97), 47; Adolphe Joanne, *Géographie de la Somme* (Paris, 1879), 32–34. Joanne's figures on the number of workers probably approximate closely the numbers employed a decade later.

These courses recruited from among elements of the working-class population that the Société industrielle expected to occupy supervisory positions in Amiens' factories or take white-collar jobs in commercial houses. Hence, for future white-collar workers, instruction was provided in foreign languages (German, English, and Italian), accounting, and commercial geography. Political factors also entered into the Société's calculations: "One cannot hope for more than that the elite of our working class become acquainted with the science that reveals the foundations of, and the conditions for society's progress . . . such training equips the mind to take a rational course and blocks the temptations of dangerous utopias or insupportable *revendications*." Amiens' apprentice school, organized in 1888, limited itself to training ordinary workers for the city's industries. Its program relegated "theoretical instruction" to a secondary role; the bulk of the eight-hour day was taken up by manual labor in the school's machine shops and iron foundry. Instruction concentrated on the mastery of specific tasks designed to make of the worker a "capable handler of tools." Finally, the Société industrielle employed that favorite device of entrepreneurs to keep workers on their toes—the prize competition. One such exercise involved rural workers engaged in the preparation of velvets, which demanded "extraordinary concentration and manual dexterity." The competition produced a "healthy rivalry among the workers, who attach great value to the prizes offered: medals, diplomas, and cash premiums." Competitions not only rewarded efficiency and productivity but also "long and loyal service."[28]

As in the case of Saint-Quentin and Amiens, the Société industrielle of Elbeuf (Seine-Inférieure) focused its educational attention on servicing the region's varied textile industries. By 1889, the Société ran fifteen public courses, for which it charged no fees, in industrial design, mechanized weaving, machine construction (especially electrical apparatuses), and the application of chemistry to dyeing. A total of 735 students were enrolled, of which 153 were women. A curious sexual division of enrollment prevailed, however. Young men attended courses during the day, but young women attended only in the evening. Presumably this arrangement reflected

28. *Exposition 1889*, "Enseignement et éducation," I, 721–23; *Bulletin de la Société industrielle d'Amiens*, XVIII (1880), 363, XXI (1883), 198.

the future prospects that each could expect: men, combining work with study and thus developing a social as well as a technical consciousness, could aspire to higher positions within the labor force open exclusively to them; women, who remained unskilled laborers, realistically could harbor no such ambitions.[29]

The Ecole professionnelle of Saint-Etienne (Loire), begun in 1882, operated a program that enrolled the sons of workers, foremen, plant supervisors, and shopkeepers. They entered at ages twelve or thirteen and were propelled through a four-year course of work and study that occupied their daylight hours. Most of their study time was spent learning practical skills applicable to the dominant industries of the region—metallurgy and textiles. During the second year the routine was broken by occasional lectures in political economy, apparently the school's only concession to the principles of moral improvement. Of greater significance, time spent in actual manual labor increased fourfold between the first and the fourth year, giving the apprentice workers a running start toward their full-time occupation as industrial workers. Variations on this model appeared elsewhere: in Reims, Epinal, Lille, Grenoble, and indeed in almost every industrial center throughout France.[30]

Industrial schools associated with a single industry or situated in a town dominated by a single industry channeled their students as much as possible directly toward predetermined jobs. At Creusot, the Ecole Schneider, begun in 1882 (and to be distinguished from the grammar school that the company subsidized), enrolled 372 students in 1898. It prepared skilled workers for the company's machine shops, foremen, and clerks. Only a small percentage did not remain to take up the assignments for which they had been trained. In the late 1870s, the Compagnie des Chemins de fer du Nord installed an *atelier d'apprentissage* on the grounds of one of its large depots and repair shops in Tergnier (Aisne). This workshop-as-school was well stocked with machinery, a model forge, and facilities for industrial design. Restricted to the sons of white-collar employees and workers over the age of twelve (who were expected to follow in their fathers'

29. *Exposition 1889*, "Enseignement et éducation," I, 715–16; *Exposition 1900*, Vol. VI, Pt. 1, p. 301.

30. Tresca, *Rapport*, 5–19, 77–78; *Exposition 1889*, I, 293, 320–21; Say, *Exposition universelle*, 124–25; F[17] 11706, AN.

footsteps), the school ran ten hours per day, during which time students not only learned the skills appropriate to the railroad industry but produced a marketable commodity—iron bindings for railway carriages. In return, the company paid the apprentices daily wages ranging from 1 to 2 francs (low by contemporary standards). Sixty percent earned no more than 1 franc 25. Average annual profits on sales of the bindings came to a spectacular 30 percent on the company's initial investment. As Tresca remarked, what began as a "paternalist enterprise" turned into "good business." These results demonstrated that "properly supervised apprentices who earn only a modest wage, backed up by a suitable contingent of experienced workers, can produce at nearly the same rate as more accomplished workers." Moreover, the company reaped the further advantage of adapting its future workers to routine and habits of discipline. Le Havre's Ecole d'apprentissage organized its youngsters into work teams that had to keep strict accounts of productivity, costs, and prices. For their labor making simple machine parts they were paid 1 to 3 francs per day. The city's employers, who had financed the school through the Société industrielle, shunted large orders to the school's workshops, thereby turning their original philanthropy into a neat profit.[31] In neither the case of the Nord railway company nor of the bourgeoisie havraise could the patrons of industrial schools be accused of "stupid stinginess."

Several textile firms in Saint-Chamond (Loire) joined forces in the mid-1880s to set up an Ecole pratique d'industrie. Its program, graded to conform to the local industry's labor requirements, turned out ordinary workers, "well-trained skilled workers," and "efficient draftsmen" from whose ranks companies recruited foremen. All of the nearly one hundred students who passed through the school annually went directly to work in local mills, where they had no difficulty finding jobs; employers welcomed them, confident of their productivity and efficiency. The same pattern of graded industrial education with a heavy accent on the formation of elite cadres of workers was repeated elsewhere. In 1888, the chamber of commerce and the municipal government of Saint-Nazaire financed a Société d'instruction populaire that concentrated on teaching skills associ-

31. *Exposition 1900*, Vol. VI, Pt. 1, pp. 379–80; Tresca, *Rapport*, 68–75.

ated with shipbuilding (Saint-Nazaire had France's largest shipbuilding industry). The workers who were trained went on to become foremen and shop bosses. The Ecole des ouvriers mineurs in Alais (Gard), a few kilometers down the road from the Grand' Combe coal mines, enrolled selected workers eighteen years of age and older, taught them arithmetic, chemistry, minerology, geology and mining, and sent them back down into the pits as crew chiefs to direct squads of ordinary mineworkers. The school had been established and expanded as a direct result of the burgeoning demand for coal generated by the second and third railway networks. It reinforced the often repressive and manipulative efforts of employers to wrench their quasi-peasant workers from their rural moorings and turn them into productive workers. Professionally trained pit bosses acted essentially as the companies' agents of regimentation in the mines and received privileges and benefits accordingly.[32]

Industrial training frequently took place during nonworking hours, much like the system characteristic of the classes for workers. The Ecole industrielle pour apprentis organized by the Société industrielle de Nantes enrolled, in 1885, 105 students who attended classes from 5:30 A.M. to 8:00 A.M. during the summer and from 6:00 A.M. to 8:00 A.M. in the winter. They trained for jobs as machinists, metal-grinders, coppersmiths, founders, steamfitters, and cabinetmakers. Their studies included courses in French, mathematics, physics, chemistry, machinery operation, and industrial design. Previously, such training, on a much cruder level, would have been delivered at the workplace. But that setting was deemed inappropriate by the school's managers, who feared that the combination of work and study in the factory would sacrifice the benefits of the latter in favor of the former. In other words, they made a distinction between short-term pecuniary interests and long-term class interest. So as to encourage parents to make the sacrifice of enrolling their children in a serious apprentice program rather than simply throwing them onto the unskilled labor market, "condemning them to

32. *Exposition 1900,* Vol. VI, Pt. 1, pp. 111–13; Melon, *Enseignement supérieur,* 307, 309, 326; Arthur Morin, *De l'organisation de l'enseignement industriel et professionnel* (Paris, 1862), 9; Rolande Trempé, *Les Mineurs de Carmaux* (2 vols.; Paris, 1971), Vol. I, Chaps. 2–3.

perpetual ignorance," the Société industrielle donated three kilos of bread per week to needy families. It also supplied modest amounts of cash, part of which was deposited in a local savings bank, "to teach the habits of thrift." The school measured its success in the nearly 100 percent of its graduates, equipped with a "natural disposition" to work under strict discipline, who entered the work force. In contrast to "so many others who disdain manual labor," they willingly "enlisted in the ranks of the industrial army." This was not the only instance in which a military metaphor found its way into the language of social politics. A French representative to a conference on vocational education in Brussels called for industrial education "to shape itself so as to serve usefully and intelligently the needs of the common soldier, that is, the worker, in the great army of labor." One historian recently suggested that "the image of the army, of workers as soldiers and bosses as field commanders, substituted a conception of solidarity and interdependence based on shared values for the neutrality of marketplace relations of exchange."[33]

Although the overwhelming number of industrial schools enrolled only workers or workers-to-be, a few set up programs for the sons (never daughters) of the local *patronat*. They differed from the workers' program in quality, sophistication, and intensity. For instance, the Ecole industrielle of the northern textile town of Tourcoing, founded in 1889 and funded exclusively from private sources and from the chamber of commerce, was designed to train foremen, master mechanics, production bosses, and clerks. Its working-class clientele attended classes in the evening. Sons of manufacturers attended the same school, but during the day, and they studied not discrete skills but the entire productive process carried on in the factories that they someday would run. Similarly, in Saint-Etienne the local apprentice schools provided special training for the sons of factory owners who subsequently entered family businesses, as did the Ecole industrielle in Epinal (Vosges). And Roubaix, whose bour-

---

33. *Exposition 1889,* I, 321; Tresca, *Rapport,* 10, 75–77; Société industrielle de Nantes to the minister of education, February 15, 1878, in F[17] 12540, AN; *Bulletin de la Société industrielle d'Amiens,* XXI (1883), 195, 204; Alberto Melucci, "Idéologies et pratiques patronales pendant l'industrialisation capitaliste: Le Cas de la France" (Thèse du troisième cycle, Ecole Pratique des Hautes Etudes, 1974), 192.

geoisie ran a handsomely equipped *école de tissage* in which workers learned the manipulation of mechanized looms after hours, also had a school for dyeing in which the sons of manufacturers studied specialized subjects such as chemistry to prepare them for their future roles as industrialists.[34] If these courses for the scions of the bourgeoisie accomplished nothing else but the adoption of efficient business practices and the assimilation of proper paternal values, they were well worth the modest investment.

The daughters of the working class, as the above-mentioned case of Elbeuf suggests, received special treatment. In words echoing those of Emile Cheysson, the republican senator Henri Tolain connected women's work to the reproduction of family life. A secure family "assured the stability of the nation's social state" in direct proportion to its contribution to the "moral and material well-being of the working class." Hence the purpose of female education was twofold: first, to provide women with the tools to manage their households carefully and efficiently; and second, "to live from their labor and, if married, to add their wages to the frequently insufficient and unreliable resources of their husbands."[35]

Vocational training for young working-class women did correspond closely to their work and domestic cycle. This meant a heavy concentration on such modest skills as those required to measure and cut patterns in cloth and to assemble the pieces into garments for the ubiquitous *confection* (ready-to-wear) industry. In addition, since women were expected to marry and raise a family, they learned the basics of domestic economy. For the most part, foundations devoted to women's vocational training grew out of private initiatives leavened by subsidies from municipal governments. The Ecole municipale des filles in Nancy, for instance, set up in 1881 to compete with the Catholic Ecole libre professionnelle des jeunes filles, specialized in the teaching of sewing and embroidering.[36]

Similar establishments appeared throughout France at about the

---

34. *Exposition 1900*, Vol. VI, Pt. 1, p. 253; *Exposition 1889*, I, 321; Société industrielle de Saint-Quentin et de l'Aisne, *Rapport*, 23–24, in F[17] 11706, AN; Tresca, *Rapport*, 78–79.

35. *Exposition 1889*, I, 303.

36. Simiand, "De l'enseignement des sciences sociales," 173; Tresca, *Rapport*, 12; F[17] 11706, AN; *Exposition 1900*, "Enseignement et éducation," I, 362–65.

same time. One of them, the Société nantaise pour l'enseignement professionnel des jeunes filles, founded by Ange Guépin in 1869 and continued by his widow through the 1880s, enrolled young women from "poor but upright families." They received instruction in the rudiments of *confection*, household management, and moral lessons to prepare them for "respectable and decently paid work" and for child-rearing. Most of these women took jobs as ordinary laborers. Of the several hundred who passed through the school, only a few managed to secure white-collar employment. In Montluçon (Allier), the municipality, with help from the central government, set up an Ecole primaire supérieure for young women where they practiced manual training exercises and learned sewing and basic design. The school enrolled mostly daughters of workers in the local glass and metallurgical industries. The Société industrielle of Reims organized an Ecole professionnelle et ménagère des jeunes filles in which teen-age girls learned "manual skills appropriate to household work" and took courses enabling them to find work as laundresses and seamstresses.[37]

Paris had had an Ecole professionnelle des jeunes filles operating since the mid-1860s, supported by an impressive array of banking and industrial luminaries. The school, still flourishing in 1889, provided the standard instruction in arithmetic, French, hygiene, design, *confection*, and sewing. It also arranged contracts with industrial firms to place its students. The young women (really girls aged twelve and up) were subjected to a considerable ideological barrage. One of the *dames patronnesses*, displaying an unusually clear bourgeois consciousness for a woman of that class, enthusiastically lectured her charges on "labor, the great benefactor of the world. . . . The new Prometheus, it masters light, condenses steam, and transports thoughts by controlled electricity from one end of the world to the other. . . . Father of all virtue, it inspires personal dignity and respect for the dignity of others."[38]

37. Société nantaise pour l'enseignement professionnel des jeunes filles, *Compte-rendu, 1884–85;* Madame Guépin to the minister of education, April 18, 1884, Mayor of Nantes to the prefect of the Loire-Inférieure, August 25, 1887, F¹⁷ 12540, AN; F¹⁷ 11706, AN; Say, *Exposition universelle,* 125.

38. *Exposition 1889,* I, 295; *EF,* September 1, 1864.

Supervised workshops for women, known as *ouvroirs*, frequently substituted for formal schools. There women, under the "friendly surveillance" of bourgeois men and women, learned appropriate work and moral habits. In the heavily industrialized town of Le Puy (Haute-Loire), a society of *dames protectrices* organized instruction in tailoring, hygiene, economy, and *morale*. These philanthropic women were determined to combat the immorality endemic to the workplace. In Lille, where Catholic bourgeois women controlled the moral molding of their working-class counterparts, a competing Société du denier des écoles laïques created *ouvroirs* to equip young girls to take their place in the city's labor force. The *ouvroirs* also equipped them to cope with a modern world dominated by "unceasing struggle and economic upheaval." In contrast to Catholic *ouvroirs*, which, it was alleged, only trained servants, those of the secular variety formed "women capable of sustaining intelligent and free labor."[39] (In this case and in that of the Ecole municipale des filles in Nancy, anticlerical sentiments reinforced, or went hand in hand with, efforts to integrate young women into the world of bourgeois relations—a world whose amorality the church had repudiated.)

But Catholics were getting the idea—at least with regard to young men. By the 1890s, Catholic industrial institutes, although not as ubiquitous as their secular counterparts, exhibited the same qualities and purposes—a response we should expect in the decade of the *ralliement*, when class questions overrode other political considerations. *Ecoles catholiques d'apprentissage* served to "protect the child during his critical adolescent years, detach him from unhealthy workshops which are centers of impiety, socialism, and dissipation." These "apprentice schools are nurseries for elite workers." The Institute of the Brothers of Christian Schools in Saint-Etienne won a grand prize at the 1900 Paris Exposition for its four-year vocational school. The first year was spent in the study of subjects only partially absorbed in primary school. In the second year, students trooped to

39. *Après l'Ecole* (1896), 530–32; Jean Merley, *L'Industrie en Haute-Loire de la fin de la monarchie de juillet aux débuts de la troisième république* (Lyon, 1978), 274; BLFE, V (1885), 92–94. For the activities of Catholic women in one part of France, see Bonnie G. Smith, *Ladies of the Leisure Class: The Bourgeoises of Northern France in the Nineteenth Century* (Princeton, 1981).

factories where they chose (or were directed to) specific vocations. Three half-days were spent in actual work during the third year with the remainder of the week devoted to technical training. Factory work occupied all the daylight hours during the fourth year; study took place during the evening. As in other cases, this highly structured system produced a pool of workers from which factory owners could draw foremen and supervisors, skilled in their work and imbued with praiseworthy moral values.[40]

The propagation of moral values consistent with the process of working-class cultural integration also animated the work of the Association polytechnique and the Association philotechnique. The Association polytechnique, founded in 1830, had what may be called a primordial solidarist inspiration; it appeared immediately following the battlefield collaboration of students of the Ecole polytechnique and workers during the *trois glorieuses* of July.[41] Perhaps some of those young engineers had developed a social conscience under the influence of an eccentric mathematics teacher at Polytechnique named Auguste Comte. Or they may have been inspired by the martyrdom of one of their comrades, Evariste Gallois, whose death on the barricades abruptly terminated what promised to become a spectacular career in mathematics.

In any event, the association's organizers recognized the futility of insurrection and set out to lead their erstwhile working-class allies of the barricades down another road. They embarked on a "crusade against ignorance" to disseminate "the basic element of the positive sciences in the laboring populations." By such means workers would become instructed in the fundamentals of "modern society," not the least of which was the contribution of their own labor.[42]

During its formative years the Association polytechnique concentrated on supplementing inadequate public primary education with "literary and scientific" courses conducted in the evenings and on Sundays. Once public education became comprehensive and more or less universal in the 1880s, the Association's attention turned to technical training for manual workers and white-collar employees,

40. *RS,* XXX (1895), 79; *Exposition 1900,* V, 188.
41. *Exposition 1889,* "Enseignement et éducation," I, 709; F[17] 12529, AN; *BMAP* (1895), 155.
42. *BMAP* (1895), 3–8; *Exposition 1900,* Vol. VI, Pt. 1, p. 462.

whose numbers were growing enormously in the last two decades of the century. By 1900 it offered seven hundred courses that attracted fourteen to fifteen thousand students annually in Paris alone. Provincial spinoffs were established in the 1890s in Aix-en-Provence, Perpignan, Bordeaux, Nice, and Auxerre and suburban installations in the working-class towns of Ivry, Charenton, Pantin, Argenteuil, and Levellois-Perret. As a demonstration of its solidarist commitment, one of the Association's sections in Paris operated in the headquarters of the Bourse du travail; its staff there, as elsewhere, included current and former students of the Ecole polytechnique. In that respect it bore a close resemblance to the Foundation universitaire de Belleville. Most of the Association's courses had immediate practical application: machinery construction, industrial design, tailoring, and carriage-making for manual laborers; accounting, foreign languages, stenography, and typing for white-collar workers. Its public lectures, however, included heavy doses of political propaganda, especially on the colonial front: "Nos colonies, leur utilité, leur avenir"; "L'Empire coloniale de la France"; "De l'esprit colonial français." But whether technical or political, the Association's efforts, according to its own testimony, succeeded in forming large numbers of skilled workers whose acquired talents enabled them to command high wages in the labor market, "the preferred route to social emancipation" and to the fulfillment of social peace. However inflated its claims, the Association polytechnique had the right idea and thus attracted powerful political and financial backing: Léon Bourgeois, Paul Cambon, Félix Faure, Charles de Freycinet, René Goblet, and Raymond Poincaré among the former; the Belle Jardinière department store, the plumbing contractors syndicate, the Compagnie financière de Suez, the Banque Franco-Egyptienne, the Compagnie des Chemins de fer du Nord, the Compagnie Fives-Lille, and the Compagnie des assurances Le Soleil among the latter.[43]

In 1848 the Association philotechnique split off from the Association polytechnique. No record of the reasons for the schism exists; probably the organizers of the Association philotechnique had a

43. *Exposition 1889*, I, 315, "Enseignement et éducation," I, 710; *BMAP* (1895), 8, 38–40, 125–27, 141, 156–57, (1897), 172–73; Petit, *Rapport*, 44–47; *Exposition 1900*, Vol. VI, Pt. 1, p. 464.

more pragmatic and less theoretical bent than those involved in the work of the Association polytechnique. Both enjoyed big business support, already visible in the 1860s: the bankers Louis Bischoffsheim and Achille Fould, the textile magnate Ernest Feray, the publisher Henri Hachette, the chocolate tycoon Emile Menier, and the iron-master Louis Wendel. The Association philotechnique had a nar-rower focus than its parent, limiting itself to providing technical instruction for young working-class adults "appropriate to their vo-cation" and to their standing in the social hierarchy. This approach, which fitted education to a predetermined class position, had been common for some time: "Industrial education ought to begin and end with facts, and not dwell on theories from which are derived real applications. Instead of systematic deductive reasoning, which inevitably enlarges the intelligence, it should limit itself to the devel-opment of a practical sense."[44] The Association set up six categories of courses according to corresponding trades: electricians and elec-trical workers, mechanics, bookbinders, shoemakers and leather-cutters, garment workers, and insurance clerks. By the early 1890s there were 401 such courses attended by 7,000 workers annually. In 1899 the number of registrants had risen to 8,240. Although it made no effort to perform exercises in solidarity as did the Association polytechnique, the Association philotechnique did not conceal its political mission. A letter to the minister of public instruction from the Association's president (obviously written to request a subsidy) emphasized its purpose to train "skilled workers and good citi-zens. . . . From the political view," he continued, "the augmentation of popular education has equal importance. Previously relegated to the humblest social stations . . . workers today occupy their rightful place in this era of political equality; but the rights with which they are armed can pose a formidable challenge if the state . . . does not anticipate that peril with appropriate measures."[45] When one seeks to dip into the public purse, no plausible argument should be ruled

44. *Exposition 1889*, "Enseignement et éducation," I, 710, "Groupe d'économie sociale," I, 316–17; F[17] 12532, AN; Morin, *De l'organisation de l'enseignement*, 26.

45. Melon, *Enseignement supérieur*, 323; Félix Martel, "Les Sociétés d'enseignement primaire," France, Ministère de l'Instruction publique et des Beaux-Arts, *Recueil des Monographies*, VI, 508–509; *Exposition 1889*, VI, 288–89; President of the Association philotechnique to the minister of education, February 10, 1879, in F[17] 12532, AN.

out. Yet the appeal to public order and social peace presumably was expected to carry particular force.

Yet, as I have noted, relatively few industrial schools benefited from state subsidies. Only with the formation of the Conseil supérieur de l'enseignement technique in the early 1890s and the assumption by the Ministry of Commerce and Industry of the coordination of industrial education did state intervention galvanize increased activity. Heightened concern about international economic competition apparently contributed to the state's deeper involvement. The educational reformer Paul Crouzet observed that the sudden spurt of interest in industrial education resulted from a "patriotic obsession to challenge Germany's supremacy" in European markets. In a tract published by the rabid imperialist and fellow traveler of the social economists, Hachette, Gabriel Compayré—himself a persistent promoter of industrial education—characterized such education as a "social necessity," especially under the prevailing conditions of sharpened foreign competition. Charles Gide agreed; more sophisticated machines demanded fine skills, for "victory in the industrial struggle belongs to those possessed of the best workers and foremen." Nevertheless, the arguments for industrial education repeatedly returned to the social and political dividends anticipated. In whatever form they took, installations for industrial education "associate pedagogy and economy, the university and labor, the vast world of employers and employees." For the sponsors of the Ecole manuelle d'apprentissage in Boulogne s/Mer the preparation of "skillful and honest workers" promised a "great social improvement."[46] Exactly what form the bourgeoisie of Boulogne expected "social improvement" to take we do not know. But it seems safe to assume that considerations involving the solidarity of labor and capital and those involving social peace had not escaped them.

46. F[17*] 3209, AN; Paul Crouzet, "Etat actuel de l'enseignement populaire social," *Premier congrès de l'enseignement des sciences sociales,* 247; Compayré, *Etudes,* 145; *Exposition 1900,* V, 182; Léaud and Glay, *L'Ecole primaire,* 248; F[17] 11706, AN.

Conclusion

During the first fifteen years of the Third French Republic's existence, the great political issues of the day only marginally touched on the relations of labor and capital and the social organization of production. Politicians did not totally ignore social questions. Léon Gambetta frequently denied the social question's existence (which suggests that it preyed on his mind), and Jules Ferry, in defense of his aggressive colonial policy, insisted that "social peace, in this industrial age, is tied to the expansion of markets." Nevertheless, the social question remained as a kind of background noise during those years. Intraclass conflict on economic questions, rather than struggle between rulers and ruled, dominated the headlines in the 1870s and early 1880s. This was, after all, the age of laissez-faire and competition in politics as well as in economics. Besides, as Eric Hobsbawm has pointed out, it cannot be argued with much confidence that a monolithic bourgeois ruling class had captured state power in France or anywhere else.[1]

Changes began to occur in the latter 1880s, and during the next two decades new political constellations appeared. Driven by powerful forces, including transformations in production, depression, and the growth of the labor movement, leading ruling-class elements carrying a variety of political baggage formed a consensus to defend order at home and to stake out imperial positions abroad. In France, as elsewhere, such new political combinations did not always en-

1. Jules Ferry, *Le Tonkin et la mère-patrie: Témoignages et documents* (Paris, 1890), 38; Eric J. Hobsbawm, *The Age of Capital* (New York, 1975), 249–50.

289

dure, but at least they indicated current trends.[2] These tendencies toward the crystallization of a ruling-class bloc in France did not show up initially in the theater of high politics. But offstage, in the precincts of bourgeois parapolitical associations, where industrialists, managers, politicians, and politicized intellectuals gathered and drew up plans for France's "social machinery," the foundations of a national conservative consensus took form. Those associations provided the programmatic framework and the ideological resources for what became a ruling-class bloc, hammered into shape on the anvil of the social question.

Consensus on the primacy of labor/capital relations generated political alliances that transcended divisive economic issues, cultural values, and religious allegiances. As the clouds of disorder gathered, "republican defense"—a venerable and frequently empty slogan—took on precise ideological and political content as class divisions came to define the contours of French society. Industrial labor, as never before, had become a major presence on the social landscape. There also could be no turning back from the progressive march of capital accumulation, which inevitably would enlarge that presence. Thus republican defense came to mean social defense. The new conditions rendered meaningless such labels as "opportunist," "radical," "liberal," Progressiste, "clerical," and "anticlerical." However useful they may be for keeping track of shifting ministerial lineups, they tell us little about what happened on the level of social politics. Substantial redefinitions are in order, even extending to a reconsideration of who belonged on the "left" and who on the "right." I have tried to indicate these redefinitions in the telling of the story, where we find such disparate figures as Charles Gide and Georges Picot or Léon Bourgeois and Albert Gigot joining forces with other businessmen, managers, and social scientists on the major questions involving the relations of capital and labor.

The same pattern extended to the political arena, where the professional politicians, formally divided by parties, acted in concert when high stakes appeared on the table. As Jean Estèbe observed of

2. Compare, for instance, *Sammlungspolitik* in Germany, Francesco Crispi's right-wing coalition in Italy, Joseph Chamberlain's imperial preference party in Britain, and the industrial-agrarian alliances of the McKinley-Roosevelt-Taft years in the United States.

the generation that occupied cabinets after 1889, they "fulfilled their essential task, which was to consolidate the sociopolitical system and to ensure its viability." Equally important and directly related, they bent all efforts "to maintain the stability of the nation and to prevent antagonistic classes and groups from chewing up one another." No doubt existed, however, as to which way they tilted. One of them, Paul Doumer, Léon Bourgeois' minister of finance in 1895 and the only cabinet minister between 1871 and 1914 who could claim genuine working-class origins, sat on several boards of directors and in 1900 became vice-president of the Union des industries minières et métallurgiques, a lobby organized by Robert Pinot, who had become secretary-general of the Comité des forges after a brief stint running the Musée social.[3]

Such close relations were, to be sure, nothing new in France. The universal regard for capital's social interests—often expressed in terms of "national solidarity" or "national production"—however, produced more than opportunistic alliances and brought together those who appear at first glance to have had little in common. They turned out to have had much in common. Thus Gabriel Séailles, a "radical solidarist" according to John Hayward, easily collaborated with the patrician Jules Siegfried, the archconservative Léopold Mabilleau, and the people's banker Eugène Rostand in the Société d'éducation sociale. Mabilleau had been the original choice of Bourgeois and Ferdinand Buisson to serve as the Société's secretary-general.[4] All of them, as Séailles put it forcefully, worried about revolution. All of them were conservatives on the labor question.

Previously unthinkable political alignments became commonplace. Neither Siegfried nor Paul Delombre, both Dreyfusards and Protestants, had any difficulty getting along with the mostly Catholic members of the Société d'économic sociale in the operation of the Musée social or on the board of the Société française des habitations à bon marché. Nor should we forget Delombre's praise for Emile Cheysson as the consummate "social engineer," Delombre's interest

3. Jean Estèbe, *Les Ministres de la République, 1871-1914* (Paris, 1982), 181, 226.

4. John Hayward, "The Cooperative Origins, Rise and Collapse of the 'Universités populaires,'" *Archives Internationales de Sociologie de la Coopération*, No. 9 (1961), 14; *Revue Populaire d'Economie Sociale*, I (1902-1903), 74-75.

in profit sharing, or Léon Bourgeois' salute to the Comte de Chambrun.[5] (It is no accident that hardly a whisper of the Dreyfus Affair, supposedly tearing France apart in the late 1890s, can be heard in the annals of conservative or solidarist reform.) Similarly, Edouard Aynard and Siegfried, being free-traders, fought the Méline Tariff. Yet Aynard shared Jules Méline's social outlook, if not his tactics, and Siegfried served as minister of commerce in 1893 after the tariff had become law. Moreover, both the Catholic banker and industrial tycoon from Lyon and the professional paternalist and veteran republican from Le Havre spoke in complementary ideological accents: Aynard about economic laws that "determine the movement of human labor"; Siegfried about erecting "fortresses of order."[6] Charles Jonnart, a deputy representing the coal interests of the Pas-de-Calais, strikebreaker *manqué*, and Aynard's son-in-law, summed up the prevailing view: "[I] joyfully welcome the new political climate because it contributes enormously to social peace." Certain issues, not the least of them the social question, clearly took precedence over others. Indeed, Buisson claimed that the Congrès d'éducation sociale's "greatest achievement" was in providing a forum for those with "different economic interests" to discuss common social concerns.[7]

Buisson only registered what already had happened. Conflict in many spheres did not preclude collaboration on the level of class interest, where the consensus on the social question reigned. We can see further how this worked by glancing at several locations along the political continuum. In 1899, an alliance of businessmen and farmers formed the Comité républicain du commerce et de l'industrie. The Comité, headed by Alfred Mascuraud, president of the Paris jewelers' association, was organized to engage in "republican

5. *Temps*, February 9, 1910.

6. Eugene Golob, *The Méline Tariff: French Agriculture and Nationalist Economic Policy* (New York, 1944), 168n, 187–89; Michael Rust, "Business and Politics in the Third Republic: The Comité des forges and the French Steel Industry, 1896–1914" (Ph.D. dissertation, Princeton University, 1973), 53; Léon Say, *Exposition universelle de 1889, Groupe d'économie sociale: Rapport général* (Paris, 1891), 40.

7. Jonnart quoted in Jean-Marie Mayeur, *Les Débuts de la troisième république, 1871–1898* (Paris, 1973), 208. As minister of public works in early 1894, Jonnart refused to recognize the right of public employees to strike (Jean Jolly [ed.], *Dictionnaire des parlementaires français* [10 vols.; Paris, 1960–70], VI, 2030); *Education sociale*, 476.

defense" against the "reactionary army" (presumably clericals, royalists, and Boulangist veterans). Reflecting the old politics, the Comité was a throwback to the 1870s, yet with an interesting twist that shows the intrusion of the labor question. Reactionaries, according to Mascuraud, were everywhere, but nowhere more dangerous than in their agitation behind the outbreak of strikes in the northern coalfields and the "terrorism" of May Day demonstrations. One blinks in disbelief: reactionaries responsible for strikes and workers' demonstrations? Was this a case of mistaken identity or did Mascuraud and his colleagues regard as an enemy anyone—syndicalist or protofascist—who challenged republican order? The latter explanation seems the more plausible, for the Comité constantly harped on the importance of establishing "domestic order" and "social peace" and on the "heavy responsibilities" of "managers of businesses and capital" to support a "sensible politics" of social reform.[8] All were sentiments perfectly compatible with a conservative social perspective and worthy of the Société d'économie sociale, whose members normally would not have found much to recommend in the Comité républicain.

Yet another example of the many faces of conservative social politics appeared in 1901 with the formation of the Alliance républicaine démocratique. Unlike the Comité républicain, the Alliance had a distinctly big bourgeois and exclusive flavor reminiscent of several parapolitical associations. Its membership included Siegfried, Maurice Rouvier, Eugène Etienne, Joseph Caillaux, Joseph Magnin (former governor of the Bank of France and one-time Gambettist radical), and two relative newcomers whose names would become synonomous with the politics of order: Louis Barthou and Raymond Poincaré. The Alliance was not a party or a faction in any ordinary sense, but rather a general staff "closely tied to the business world" formed to make certain that the politics of republican defense neither departed from the path of orderly progress nor made any concessions to "collectivist" pressures. The latter was a reference to Waldeck-Rousseau's allegedly soft line on the labor question, demonstrated in

8. Madeleine Rebérioux, *La République radicale?* (Pais, 1975), 51; *Bulletin Mensuel du Commerce et de l'Industrie* (January, 1906), 5–6, (February, 1906), 15–17, (June, 1906), 5, 11–13.

his support for a further liberalization of the laws on association.[9] The members of the Alliance had nothing against reform, as long as it remained orderly, carefully controlled, and securely in the grip of those whose social status validated their leadership.

Even though the Alliance was formed to provide conservative ballast against the allegedly "radical" list of Waldeck's cabinet, several individuals otherwise associated with the Alliance's organizers could not stomach the move. Thus two years later, in response, Georges Picot, Auguste Isaac, Edouard Aynard, Jules Méline, Alexandre Ribot, and others formed the Fédération républicaine. The Fédération was formed from Méline's parliamentary group, the Alliance des républicains progressistes, and two other associations, the Union libérale républicaine and the Association nationale républicaine. The Association nationale numbered among its founders Jules Ferry and Gambetta's former sidekick, Eugène Spuller, who by the early 1890s had become one of the most vocal republican spokesmen in support of the *ralliement*—a neat trick for a formerly rabid anticlerical. The formation of the Fédération républicaine suggests less a new departure than a manifestation of the chronic tensions within the conservative coalition, though these tensions never reached the point of crisis.[10]

Further along the political continuum stood the Unions des amis de la paix sociale, whose evolution I discussed in Chapter I. Hardly distinguished for their militant republicanism in the 1870s and 1880s, the Unions' perspective on the labor question and their dedication to the "science of social peace" qualified them for admission into the great coalition for republican defense in the 1890s. Furthermore, their evolution paralleled and may have reinforced the emergence of France's version of the "iron and rye" alliance and the *ralliement*. It is at least clear that the conservative consensus solidified in Méline's government (1896–1898), in Waldeck-Rousseau's (1899–1902)—despite the cavils of the big bourgeoisie—and in those that followed (especially Georges Clemenceau's and Aristide Briand's, 1906–1909

9. Rebérioux, *La République radicale?* 54.

10. Eugène Spuller, *L'Evolution politique et sociale de l'église* (Paris, 1893), Chap. 15. For details on the Fédération républicaine, see William Irvine, *French Conservatism in Crisis: The Republican Federation of France in the 1930s* (Baton Rouge, 1979), Chap. 1.

and 1909–1911) reaped the harvest already prepared in the network of parapolitical associations since the late 1880s.

Other political mutations—deeper and more enduring—occurred in the context of building a conservative consensus. The phrase, quoted in the Introduction, "neither enemies to the left nor to the right," should not be taken as a literal expression of bourgeois reform's political perspective, for surely the "left" did not embrace socialists and militant syndicalists and the "right" did not embrace superpatriots and aspiring putschists. Leaving aside the socialists on the left and the lunatics on the right, plenty of room remained for potential major political conflict. Yet that did not happen. Instead, progressive social liberals, social engineers, managers, and conservative reformers along with leading politicians associated with them came together—not as a "third force" between right and left, but as a single, unified ruling-class bloc open to all respectable political tendencies, one that stood above factions, as Waldeck put it in 1902, and perhaps even above parties.[11]

The implicit repudiation of the liberal-democratic tradition of brokerage politics required the abandonment of the marketplace model of social relations from which such politics derived. Once the market model was abandoned, and with it the myth that workers and employers stood as equals in the sight of the Hidden Hand, no further barrier existed to authoritarian politics. Collective production demanded an analogous politics of social management, one that knew no parties and for which there was no progress without order, no social peace without class collaboration. Once again, this new departure found its original articulation and justification within the ranks of the corporate paternalists and the solidarists. Certainly, significant differences existed within those ranks. For conservative reformers closely tied to big business such as Picot, Cheysson, and Robert, social defense could not be entrusted to politicians but should be conducted by businessmen under the tutelage of social managers—that is, themselves. Ultimately, they were less concerned with efficiency, rationalization, or even national unity than with the entrepreneurs'

11. *Bulletin Mensuel* (January, 1906), 21. For a discussion of the "third force," see Leonard Minnich and Edward W. Fox in Edward M. Earle (ed.), *Modern France* (New York, 1951), Chaps. 7–8.

authority. Yet they understood that that authority could not be separated from broader political considerations, as Cheysson's politicized social science and Picot's "struggle against revolutionary socialism" made clear. They, and not the superpatriots and the aspiring putschists, constituted the true right in French politics. That judgment, however, does leave at least one nagging loose end: Where should we place a man like Jules Siegfried, the very role model of the enlightened *grand bourgeois*? Perhaps he bridged the two reformist tendencies, or he symbolized the conservative coalition's elasticity.

Solidarists and social liberals displayed a similar distrust of politics as usual, denounced the "quarrels among parties," and summoned politicians to remold themselves into "efficient social architects." Unlike their more obviously conservative associates, they did not worship at the altar of capital, nor did they flirt with repression, union-busting, or yellow unionism. Men such as Bourgeois and Gide insisted that the bourgeoisie as well as the working class submit to their system. Bourgeois did not trust the bourgeoisie to root out capital's "abuses"; Gide expected cooperation to rescue capitalism from itself. Yet, acting as political engineers working to rationalize social relations, the solidarists reinforced the social economists' drive to install order and discipline in the workplace. Both shared similar assumptions: that no tolerable alternative to the capitalist order existed; that corporate forms of association, usually incarnated in reform from above, spelled the best hope of containing class struggle; and that working-class movements infected with socialism posed a grave threat to the Republic's integrity. On the last point social liberals took an especially hard line. They did so not only because socialism represented disorder and struggle, but because its existence threatened to undermine their reformist plans through guilt by association. Their brand of social management, with its emphasis on cooperative association, on opposition to the principles of competition, and on making workers junior partners in the reconstitution of national solidarity looked like socialism in the eyes of the timid and the nervous in France's business community. Of course, it was not, but that did not matter. What did matter was that social liberals had to distance themselves as far as possible from the socialist left, which had the effect of pushing them to the right and locking them into the conservative consensus. There they played the role for which they were best suited as a function of their accurate perception of the social implications of collective production: that of turning an often narrow system of corporate paternalism into an ideology of solidarist reform and making of it an instrument appropriate to a regime of "national capitalism." [12]

Neither solidarist reform nor corporate paternalism could guarantee the unchallenged reign of social peace. The escalation of labor/capital confrontations between 1906 and 1914 appeared to discredit the reformers' best laid plans. Yet despite the conservative thrust of that period, no openly authoritarian, antiparliamentary, or antidemocratic tendencies attracted serious attention. Why? Some might argue that the political classes were too closely wedded to liberal institutions to contemplate abandoning them. Perhaps. It may be that whatever the limitations of reform to contain actual or potential working-class militance, the organized forces of the labor movement were relatively weak (compared with, say, the SPD in Germany). If so, then the goal of preserving and extending bourgeois hegemony did not require scuttling democratic political forms and even allowed occasional if fitful bouts of "radicalism" (Emile Combes and to a lesser extent Clemenceau and Briand).

Finally, I must return briefly to the theme of "counterrevolution" introduced in the first chapter. Purists will object that logically one cannot have a counterrevolution without a prior revolution, and the historians among them will point out that nothing resembling revolution loomed on the horizon of *fin-de-siècle* France. To the first objection I only can respond that historical forces, especially those driven by class struggle, do not obey the rules of logic; to the second that, from the perspective of those directly or indirectly associated with control over the means of production, the escalation of labor militancy looked like an assault on the socioeconomic foundations of the Republic. In other words, a challenge to bourgeois political power appeared to be imminent. We know better, but those who regarded as potentially revolutionary every working-class challenge to the capitalist way of doing business were not simply whistling up a storm. They took them seriously, as well they should have without

12. *RSS* (1906), 290–91. The phrase "national capitalism" comes from Victor Kiernan, *Marxism and Imperialism* (London, 1974), 34.

the benefit of hindsight. Hence I insist on the fundamentally counter-revolutionary thrust of bourgeois social politics.

Even—or perhaps especially—the solidarists, whose preoccupation with the reform and improvement of working-class life and labor cannot be dismissed simply as opportunism, took up positions as guardians of the established order against "revolution in the streets." They claimed to know what was good for the people because they were armed with the principles of social science. Those principles taught that families, communities, and nations operated in a state of equilibrium regulated by some internal mechanism which it was the business of the social scientist to understand. Should a society spin out of the state of equilibrium and succumb to conflict, that constituted a "pathological" condition to be cured by fixing the mechanism. From the point of view of social science neither economics nor ideology had anything to do with the functioning or malfunctioning of the mechanism, so that it could be fixed without reference to outside forces. Not that social science was politically neutral, as I have taken some pains to point out. It became a powerful instrument for the politics of order, of counterrevolution.

The republican mayor of Amiens put the matter in practical terms in 1880. He called for the "popularization of science . . . not only to develop the mind, but to produce the maximum quantity of useful labor." The last word, however, should be granted to a dissenting voice, that of Octave Pierre, of the radical Bourse du travail of Montpellier. Pierre made an appearance and gave a brief speech at the Congrès d'éducation sociale in 1900. He reminded his audience that "science always has served capital, and that it was with the aid of science that the bourgeoisie in 1789 made the Revolution; this is why workers distrust science. As for the remedies proposed, they are palliatives, sedatives, of which we have had quite enough; now the worker himself must reclaim what rightfully belongs to him."[13] Thus did a modest worker expose what his bourgeois contemporaries attempted to conceal and what historians, following them, largely have ignored.

13. *Bulletin de la Société industrielle d'Amiens* (1880), 73; *Education sociale*, 325.

Index